The M.A.K. Halliday Library Functional Linguistics Series

This series focuses on studies concerning the theory and application of Systemic Functional Linguistics. It bears the name of Professor M.A.K. Halliday, as he is generally regarded as the founder of this school of linguistic thought. The series covers studies on language and context, functional grammar, semantic variation, discourse analysis, multimodality, register and genre analysis, educational linguistics and other areas. Systemic Functional Linguistics is a functional model of language inspired by the work of linguists such as Saussure, Hjelmslev, Whorf, and Firth. The theory was initially developed by Professor M.A.K. Halliday and his colleagues in London during the 1960s, and since 1974 it has held an international congress every year at various continents around the world. It is well-known for its application in a variety of fields, including education, translation, computational linguistics, multimodal studies, and healthcare, and scholars are always exploring new areas of application.

Qingxin Xu

Appraisal Approach to Conflict Styles

Computational Mapping of Disputant's Attitudinal Disposition Patterns in Family Mediations

Springer

Qingxin Xu
Xiamen University
Xiamen, China

ISSN 2198-9869 ISSN 2198-9877 (electronic)
The M.A.K. Halliday Library Functional Linguistics Series
ISBN 978-981-95-6255-8 ISBN 978-981-95-6256-5 (eBook)
https://doi.org/10.1007/978-981-95-6256-5

This Springer imprint is published by the registered company Springer Nature Singapore Pte Ltd.
The registered company address is: 152 Beach Road, #21-01/04 Gateway East, Singapore 189721, Singapore

Dedicated to the memory of my grandfather,
Jikun Xu,
who gave me the world to explore
and the confidence to navigate it as an
independent woman.
I carry his pride with me.

Foreword

When Qingxin Xu arrived at the University of New South Wales to commence her PhD candidature, I was intrigued by the data she planned to analyse: the often heated exchanges between spouses engaged in attempts at conflict resolution on mainland Chinese television. This was not "reality TV" in the Western sense, where participants desperately seek fame, celebrity status, and an enhanced following on social media. Rather, these were programs aimed at genuinely assisting troubled marriages, with participants given the opportunity to air their grievances with a view to resolving them and with feedback and advice by experienced counsellors. This was linguistically rich material indeed.

Qingxin's purpose was to explore, in this performative setting, the linguistic means by which these participants negotiated their relationship differences and constructed for themselves and their partners the social roles of "wife" and "husband". More particularly, her interest was in the language choices by which they constructed themselves as either the "aggrieved" party in the relationship or their partner as a "wayward spouse".

This book is a testament to the ground-breaking success of her project. It provides unique insights into the language of intimate family relationships, not just in Chinese settings, but probably into the language of intimate family relationships in many other cultural settings. More specifically, it provides truly novel insights into how the participants deploy the options for evaluative meaning making available in Chinese for "performing" a range of "identities" or "personae", and into how these "personae" may be fluid, even in the short timeframe of these recorded-for-television interactions. Noteworthy is the book's development of the concept of "attitudinal disposition" (recurrent patterns of evaluative language that reflect a speaker's self-presentational style) and its demonstration of how these patterns both reflect and reshape the dynamics of linguistically performed conflict and dispute.

I would also draw potential readers to the impressive achievements on display in the book in demonstrating a subtle and sophisticated application of the Systemic Functional Linguistics grounded Appraisal model and in extending this model to deal with evaluative meaning making possibilities not previously attended to in the model. I was, and remain in awe of, Qingxin's ability to marshal the resources of high-level computational linguistic tools (for example, the data mining and pattern identification available through the *R* language) to discover patterns in the use of evaluative language, which are only identifiable when the totality of a speaker's contribution to an ongoing exchange can be taken into account—a possibility associated with these tools. In this, the book contributes in a very meaningful way to the relatively infrequent scholarship in which novel findings are achieved through the co-applications of human linguistic and computational linguistic analysis.

I am honoured to have been invited to offer this foreword. I commend the book to anyone interested in how socio-semiotic analyses of this type can reveal how who we are is determined by what we say.

School of the Arts and Media
University of New South Wales
Sydney, NSW, Australia
September 2025

Peter R. R. White

Acknowledgements

It is with profound appreciation that I express my deepest thanks to those whose contributions have significantly influenced the final outcome of this book.

This project originated as a PhD dissertation submitted to the University of New South Wales in 2021, under the supervision of Dr. Peter R.R. White, whose erudite guidance, unwavering support, and insightful comments played a pivotal role in completing this research. Dr. White's meticulous written feedback on every version of my analysis was invaluable, encouraging me to sharpen my thinking and elevate my work to new heights. I literally feel like I am a different person after finishing my PhD.

I am deeply grateful to the academic community, particularly within the Systemic Functional Linguistics circle in Sydney and China, for providing opportunities to engage with distinguished colleagues who are driving advancements in linguistic theory while also applying their expertise in discourse analysis.

Research scholarships from UNSW and Xiamen University enabled me to pursue my PhD studies financially and present my research at various conferences domestically and internationally, which proved invaluable for the development of this book.

I extend my sincerest thanks to Series Editors Prof. Chenguang Chang and Prof. Guowen Huang, as well as Springer's Senior Editor Ms. Rebecca Zhu and Production Editor Mr. Prasanth Anandan, for their support in publishing this work within the prestigious M.A.K. Halliday Library Functional Linguistics Series.

Furthermore, I acknowledge the following published articles that have been adapted into chapters of this book:

- Xu, Q. (2024). Identifying disputants' attitudinal variations in family mediations: A data mining approach. *Discourse Studies*, *26*(5), 693–719. https://doi.org/10.1177/14614456241237378
- Xu, Q., & White, P. R. R. (2021). 'My husband always crosses the line': Textual identity and presentation of 'the self' in family conflict communication. *Journal of Research in Applied Linguistics*, *12*(2), 52–73. https://doi.org/10.22055/RALS.2021.17009

Lastly, I express my deepest gratitude to my family—past and present—for their unconditional support, love, and encouragement throughout this journey.

Any remaining errors or inaccuracies in the manuscript are solely attributed to the author's responsibility.

Qingxin Xu

Competing Interests The author has no competing interests to declare that are relevant to the content of this manuscript.

Contents

Chapter 1
Conflict Styles Decoded: Appraisal Foundations and Research Genesis

Contents

1 The Genesis of the Research

This book reports a linguistic investigation of how disputing spouses argue in family dispute resolution exchanges, a research trajectory deeply rooted in my personal experiences. Growing up in a typical three-generational Chinese household, I was an intimate witness to the complex dynamics of familial verbal interactions. Beyond the expected love and warmth, verbal confrontations constituted a significant emotional landscape of my childhood. The vivid memories of arguments between my mother and grandmother—where my grandmother's linguistic prowess seemed to overwhelm my mother's more subdued communicative style—would later become a foundational inspiration for this scholarly exploration.

These childhood observations found resonance years later in an emerging media phenomenon: televised family dispute resolution programmes in mainland China.

Q. Xu, *Appraisal Approach to Conflict Styles*, The M.A.K. Halliday Library Functional Linguistics Series, https://doi.org/10.1007/978-981-95-6256-5_1

Table 1.1 Online viewers' comments on the disputing spouses' verbal behaviours

Viewer's comments	English translation of the comments
先生很不錯了啦!女人好強勢	The husband is quite nice! The wife is so pushy
一眼看出這個女很強勢	Obviously, this woman is very pushy
男人唯唯诺诺、窝窝囊囊，女人伶牙俐齿、咄咄逼人	The man is obsequious and is such a wimp. The woman is good at arguing and is aggressive

These primetime reality TV shows invite everyday couples entangled in long-term family disputes—often on the brink of divorce—to publicly negotiate their conflicts. Guided by a 'host' and scrutinised by family relationship experts, the participants engage in complex discursive performances of accusation and self-defence. The purported objective of the programme is to assist the disputing spouses in resolving their differences as they receive feedback and counselling from the relationship experts there in the studio. Crucially, the 'reality', if there is a reality at all, is construed entirely by the disputants' discursive performance: their narratives of past events, their evaluation of the self and others, and sometimes their explicit articulation of values and beliefs. Consequently, the discursive self-presentation in such dispute resolution settings becomes paramount, significantly influencing both the experts' perceptions and the potential mediation outcomes.

My initial intuition about communicative diversity was further validated through extensive social media discourse surrounding these programmes. Viewers didn't just passively consume these interactions; they actively analysed and categorised the communicative styles of the participants. For instance, in one particularly memorable episode,[1] online commenters quickly characterised a couple's interaction through nuanced linguistic descriptors: the husband was perceived as 'obsequious', the wife as 'pushy' (as illustrated in Table 1.1)—demonstrating how quickly and intuitively audiences decode communicative performances.

A similar taxonomic impulse to characterise and classify conflict behaviour emerges within the academic domain of interpersonal conflict communication studies. Scholars in this field have predominantly relied on surveys and interviews where disputants self-report their own and their antagonists' behaviours,[2] developing the influential concept of 'conflict style' (Blake & Mouton, 1964; Guerrero, 2020; Rahim, 1983, 2023; Thomas, 1976, 1992; Thomas & Kilmann, 2008). The 'conflict

[1] This episode was broadcast by *Gold Medal Mediation* (China Jiangxi Radio and Television Network) on 21 August 2020. The video and online comments are available on YouTube: https://www.youtube.com/watch?v=iqa3aJxQocw

[2] Take the Thomas-Kilmann instrument (Thomas & Kilmann, 1978), one of the most influential conflict-style studies, as an illustration. The instrument measures subjects' responses to conflict situations by means of a survey questionnaire. In the survey, subjects are asked to choose the statement that best describes their behaviour in a conflictful situation. There are 30 pairs of statements corresponding to five interpersonal conflict-handling modes. A conflict-handling profile will be mapped based on the subject's scores in each mode. The method shows that in such studies, the conflict style of the subjects is identified based on their self-perceived behaviours, rather than on their actual behaviours in a real conflict setting.

style' is defined as 'patterned responses, or clusters of behaviour, that people use in conflict' (Hocker & Wilmot, 2018, p. 152). In several studies, five types of 'conflict style' are identified, with a disputant's behaviour assigned to a given category according to their behaviour being assessed along a specific dimension: integrating, obliging, dominating, avoiding, and compromising (Folger et al., 2017; Rahim, 1983, 2023). While methodologically distinct from my linguistic approach, these studies were conceptually generative. Their proposal for taxonomised 'conflict styles' demonstrated two critical insights: first, that individuals involved in conflictual communication tend to exhibit observable behavioural variations, and second, that these variations can be meaningfully sub-classified into a limited set of recognisable patterns. This taxonomic approach suggested a possible research trajectory: could a comparable classificatory taxonomy emerge from a systematic exploration of disputants' language use? My study would thus pivot from 'conflict styles' to 'conflictual language styles'—a nuanced examination of disputants' discursive self-presentation.

To explore disputants' discursive self-presentation, I sourced data from the Chinese family dispute resolution programmes, the reality TV genre mentioned above. The reasons are twofold. One is that naturally occurring conflictual interaction data are notoriously difficult to obtain due to the emergent nature of the conflict, as well as for privacy and ethical reasons (Grimshaw, 1990; Jackson & Jacobs, 1980; Leung, 2002). Researchers have consequently advocated for reality TV as a viable alternative to private conversational data (Boberg, 2021; García-Gómez, 2018; Harbin, 2023; Lorenzo-Dus & Blitvich, 2013). The other reason is that these programmes feature unique quasi-authentic dispute resolution interactions, produced to resolve genuine family disputes. While acknowledging potential performative elements, the dispute resolution interactions are legally sanctioned mediation services embedded within the Chinese legal system (Hawes & Kong, 2013; Kong & Hawes, 2015). Rooted in China's deep cultural tradition of grassroots dispute resolution (Barnes, 2007; Diamant, 2000; Read & Michelson, 2018), these programmes serve as a contemporary mass media adaptation of traditional conflict mediation practices. The Chinese central government's regulation and censorship, to a certain degree, guarantee the authenticity of the dispute resolution interactions (Hawes, 2024; Hawes & Kong, 2013; Shei, 2013). Thus, my interest became how the disputants (particularly disputing spouses) in the Chinese reality TV mediation programmes presented themselves through the language options they favoured (or disfavoured) and how these discursive self-presentations vary across the different speakers.

By 'discursive self-presentation', I mean the tendencies in the linguistic options a disputant employs in a given communicative situation, which collectively constitute their distinctive 'discursive conflictual style'. My research was fundamentally driven by an exploratory question: Could recurrent patterns in language use emerge that would allow meaningful clustering of disputants into discrete groups, characterised by internal linguistic similarities and inter-group differences?

It does need to be recognised that, in investigating possible variations in theses disputants' discursive presentation of self, my work owed a debt to the highly influential tradition of what is termed 'sociolinguistics' or 'variationist' linguistics (Coupland, 2007b; Eckert, 2012; Eckert, 2018; Eckert & Rickford, 2002; Labov, 1963, 1972; Pratt, 2023; Tagliamonte, 2012). This scholarly approach has historically investigated how linguistic features might correlate with, and hence be indexical of, socio-demographic markers such as class, gender, age, place of origin, and education level. Traditionally, the linguistic indicators most typically attended to have been phonological or lexical variables, for example, vowel change, consonant cluster reduction, the final and preconsonantal, nominal suffixes, to name just a few (Boberg, 2021; Chambers et al., 2013; Labov, 1972; Labov et al., 2006; Pratt, 2023; Sandow, 2022; Stratton, 2022; Wolfram, 2017). In some cases, the variation was more obviously semantic, for example, variation in how mothers questioned, informed or commanded their children (e.g., Hasan, 1989, 2009).

This research tradition was related to my project in that it considered how linguistic features might be related to, or indicative of, the 'self' being discursively presented. However, it was not directly relevant because unlike traditional sociolinguistic studies tracking demographic indexicality, I followed Goffman's (1959, 1981) performative conceptualisation of self—understanding the discursive 'self' as performative and contingent, arising from situated social interactions (more details in Chap. 2). Although preliminary studies revealed intriguing gender-related linguistic variations,[3] my primary analytical focus remained on interactional identity performance rather than demographic categorisation.

Another substantial body of linguistic scholarship was directly relevant to my project: the research concerning the textual performance of identity and persona. The scholarship elucidates how the various ways people speak may relate to who they are, the roles they are playing, the relationships into which they are entering as they speak, and how they want to come across to those they are addressing. The scholarship includes the longstanding interest of Systemic Functional Linguistic (hereafter SFL) in investigating how speakers variably present themselves as they negotiate status and familiarity (Firth, 1950; Halliday, 1978; Halliday & Hasan, 1985; Hasan, 1973; Hasan, 2020; Martin, 1992, 2009a; Poynton, 1989, 1990).

More particularly, the scholarship also includes more recent work by SFL-based scholars, which references the Appraisal framework (Iedema et al., 1994; White, 1998, 2002, 2016; Martin, 2000; Martin & White, 2005). Appraisal conceptualises evaluative meaning-making as one of the interpersonal functionalities of language. It also provides a systematic account of evaluative meaning-making resources by taxonomising them into three systems: ATTITUDE,[4] ENGAGEMENT and GRADUATION, addressing different aspects of the linguistic configuration of evaluation. ATTITUDE encompasses both positive and negative assessments that are explicitly mentioned (inscribed) or implied (invoked). It broadly distinguishes three types of assessments—Affect, Judgement, and Appreciation, which concern the evaluation of

---

[3] The research project took me in a different direction and accordingly these findings were not dealt with in this book.

[4] Following the SFL conventions, system names are written in small capital letters.

emotion, human behaviour, and artefact, respectively. ENGAGEMENT addresses the issue of dialogic positioning and the negotiation of heteroglossic diversity (e.g., 'monogloss' or 'heterogloss'). Finally, GRADUATION handles the resources for scaling the ATTITUDE or ENGAGEMENT options in terms of intensity or prototypicality. In Appraisal-based identity studies, discursive self-presentation and variation in self-presentation are analysed by exploring tendencies in a speaker/writer's use of evaluative meaning-making resources, for instance, the speaker/writer's attitudes towards the self and the others. The Appraisal-based identity scholarship was strongly influential on the formulation of my research and, accordingly, will be discussed in more detail below and in later chapters.

In what follows, I will outline how my initially ambitious aim was narrowed down to a workable research project by concentrating on a specific subset of linguistic resources—attitude-associated resources—and how this personal observation evolved into a scholarly investigation that offers novel insights into the broader understanding of discursive identity construction. Thus, what follows in this chapter is a description and explanation of this pinning-down process. Specifically, I will articulate the rationale behind adopting multiple lines of inquiry into the patterns of evaluative language use among disputing spouses, accompanied by a comprehensive analytical and methodological overview of each line of inquiry. In pinning down this process, I drew upon key theoretical aspects of SFL/Appraisal-based identity studies, while also incorporating methodological perspectives from Conversation Analysis, sociolinguistics, and pragmatics. Details of this pinning-down process will be found in Sect. 2. Following this foundational exposition, Sect. 3 will introduce the research's original contribution, and Sect. 4 will preview the key findings. This chapter will conclude with a book outline in Sect. 5.

2 The Pinning-Down Process

2.1 Attitudinal Disposition: An Appraisal Approach to Discursive Style

The pinning-down process was fundamentally shaped by the Appraisal framework literature, particularly studies exploring textually performed identity. The Appraisal framework provides a taxonomy for systematically tracking speakers' use of evaluative language (detailed in Chap. 2). Researchers have had extensive discussions about the construction of affiliation and communal identity through shared values (Inwood & Zappavigna, 2021, 2023; Knight, 2013; Martin, 2008b, 2010; Tann, 2010, 2012; Zappavigna, 2019, 2021, 2025; Zappavigna & Martin, 2018a).

Of particular relevance to the current research is the Appraisal scholarship concerning textual identity construction. This body of work analyses discursive self-presentation and variations in the self-presentation by tracking tendencies in speakers' deployment of evaluative meaning-making resources, with a specific emphasis on attitudinal resources. Previous research has explored textually performed identity across diverse text types, including movie reviews, youth justice conferencing, casual conversation, online chats, and academic writing (Carrió-Pastor, 2025; Cunningham & Link, 2021; Eggins & Slade, 1997; Hommerberg & Lindgren, 2023; Hood, 2010; Inwood & Zappavigna, 2023; Jing & Xu, 2023; Lei, 2025; White, 2025; Xu & Jing, 2024; Zappavigna & Martin, 2018b; Zheng & Stewart, 2024).

I mention here just some examples by way of illustration. Martin's work (Martin, 2008a, 2009b, 2010) illustrated how speakers are associated with distinct 'identity' groupings through patterns of attitudinal meanings that signal alignments with particular communities of shared values. Zappavigna's work on social media (2011a, 2012, 2018, 2022, 2023) revealed how users construct 'ambient affiliations' through attitudinal expressions, thereby creating specific online 'identities'. White's analysis of journalistic discourse (1998) developed an account of the different 'voices' of English-language journalism, with the account attending to authorial preferences for different attitude categories and their more delicate choices within these categories in the Appraisal system. His work demonstrates that systematic variation in journalistic discourse can be understood as different self-presentations, at least when 'self' is conceptualised through certain established institutional roles related to particular patterns in the journalists' use of evaluative language. Additionally, Martin and White (2005) introduced the concept of 'evaluative key', arguing that different 'evaluative keys' are associated with the distinct journalistic roles (or 'selves')—'reporter', 'correspondent', and 'commentator'. Similarly, Coffin (1997, 2006) identifies a three-way system of patterned linguistic choices in secondary school historical discourse. Don's studies (2007a, 2016) also show the possibility of associating email discussion list participants with different 'attitudinal dispositions' based on systematic variations in their preferences for particular types of attitudinal meanings. Finally, Xu and Jing's (2024) data mining of 25,000 anonymous *danmu* comments characterises two broad identities of online video viewers—'spectator' and 'player', with each identity category consisting of several subtypes. In summary, these studies collectively demonstrate that patterns of the speakers/writers' use of Appraisal resources, particularly attitudinal meaning-making resources, 'can be related to particular rhetorical effects and construct particular authorial identities or personas' (Martin & White, 2005, p. 161). Notably, however, none of the prior work has investigated discursive identity construction across multiple speakers in immediately interactive, adversarial, and multiparty spoken discourse.

The inquiry into recurrent attitudinal meaning-making patterns offers critical insights into disputants' self-presentation within family dispute resolution exchanges. White (2008) argues that attitudinal assessments transcend mere personal viewpoint expression, instead serving complex communicative and interpersonal functions that strategically position audiences and negotiate solidarity. In family dispute resolution exchanges, where all disputants competitively seek to validate their narrative interpretations before a mediation panel (as set out in Chap. 3), their attitudinal arrangements reveal their positioning of the self and others, perception of the disputes, and discursive identity construction in front of the mediators. The systematic exploration of attitudinal dispositions can thus unveil variations in disputants' discursive behaviours. Specifically, this analysis probes several critical dimensions: Do disputants exhibit similar or divergent attitudinal patterns? Are there discernible recurring configurations in attitude-related resource deployment? During intense conflict, one might anticipate shared negativity towards an antagonist, potentially constructing a collective antagonistic 'self'. However, intriguing questions emerge: Do all disputants express equivalent degrees of negativity? What self-oriented attitudes do they advance when discussing disputes? Are there instances of attitudinal complexity—such as simultaneously antagonistic and conciliatory stances? Apart from the antagonist and the self, do disputants attitudinally discuss any other issues, for example, the children, the in-laws, or the relationship per se? Moreover, can we identify distinctive attitudinal arrangement clusters analogous to the three-way 'voices' observed in journalistic, history, and academic discourses? The potential to characterise unique attitudinal disposition typologies in family dispute interactions represents a compelling scholarly endeavour.

All this pointed me towards adopting what I term 'attitudinal disposition' as the main focus of my inquiry. The term denotes the discursive style or textual persona construed via speakers' deployment of attitudinal meaning-making resources. Conceptually, the term draws inspiration from Don's (2007b) and White's (2008) notion of 'evaluative disposition', which was used to address the patterns of Appraisal resource co-occurrence that constitute particular evaluative stances. 'Attitudinal disposition' also resonates with related terms that explore linguistic identity construction via patterns in the use of Appraisal resources, including 'evaluative style' (Martin & White, 2005), 'voice' (Coffin, 2006; Hood, 2012; White, 1998, 2012), 'textual persona' (Don, 2007a, 2017), 'persona' (Inwood & Zappavigna, 2023; Zappavigna & Martin, 2018b), and 'character' (Bartley & Trevisan, 2024). In addition, 'disposition' aligns with the 'style as individual disposition approach' (Blake & Mouton, 1964; Rahim, 2023; Thomas, 1976) in most conflict style studies, which treat conflict style as relatively 'stable over time and across situations' (Friedman et al., 2000, p. 33).

By 'attitudinal disposition', I foreground the 'attitude' aspect in the disputants' use of evaluative language. Hence, a disputant predominantly condemning an antagonist would be understood as exhibiting a distinctly different attitudinal disposition from one engaging in self-praise or demonstrating more complex evaluative positioning.

2.2 *Two Perspectives on Attitudinal Disposition*

As noted, attitudinal disposition is broadly concerned with the tendencies in disputants' use of evaluative meaning-making resources, with particular emphasis on attitudinal resources (resources for conveying or activating positive or negative assessments). In disputants in family dispute resolution exchanges, this exploration focuses on participants' attitudes towards the self, antagonist, and others, analysing both the polarity (positive or negative) and the explicitness of expression (explicit or implicit).

Drawing on Appraisal-based textual identity scholarship, the analysis explored the similarities and differences in disputants' attitudinal preferences, revealing critical insights into the universality or variability of discursive performance within family dispute resolution contexts. The research investigated three potential analytical scenarios. First, did all disputants convey broadly similar attitudes, suggesting a consistent and uniform attitudinal approach? Second, did some disputants share attitudinal similarities while others diverged, indicating distinct attitudinal subtypes? Third, did disputants advance entirely individualised attitudes, resisting systematic categorisation or meaningful grouping? These questions oriented the research towards a comprehensive analysis of attitudinal variability as one line of analysis for exploring the construction of disputants' attitudinal disposition. By systematically identifying, classifying, and quantifying attitudinal expressions—both explicitly and implicitly conveyed—the study aimed to map the nuanced landscape of disputants' attitude variations in family dispute interactions.

While the disputants' attitudes apparently constitute a pivotal aspect of their attitudinal disposition, I resolved that additional useful insights might be provided if, as well as tracking the disputants' use of values of attitude, I also tracked how those expressions of attitude were framed. Consider a wife's condemnation of her husband: 'My husband crosses the line'. This single attitudinal proposition could, of course, be presented in many other ways, such as

1. 'My husband *always* crosses the line',
2. 'My husband *occasionally* crosses the line',
3. '*I have the feeling that* my husband has crossed the line',
4. '*It's beyond doubt that* my husband has crossed the line', or
5. 'My husband goes *way beyond* crossing the line'.

Although these propositions advance the same fundamental attitude—a condemnation of the husband—they differ in their degrees of authorial involvement in advancing the attitude and openness to negotiating the attitude being advanced. The Appraisal literature has outlined two critical domains of resources for framing attitudes: resources for scaling (e.g., upscaling or downscaling—the system of GRADUATION) and resources for dialogic framing (e.g., monoglossing or heteroglossing—the system of ENGAGEMENT). These resources reveal how speakers modulate their stance and personal investment in attitudinal assessments. Scholars like White (2003, 2012, 2025) have demonstrated that dialogistic formulations allow authors to indicate nuanced stances and degrees of personal commitment. Similarly, Hood and Zhang (2020) have observed how explicit positive attitudes, when coupled with upscaling devices, can construe a particular field of academic knowledge and configurate bonds with putative readership.

In the context of family dispute resolution, the disputants' preferences in framing attitudes are also an essential part of their discursive self-presentation. The disputants who mainly present the antagonist-oriented condemnations as bare, intensified assertions would be reasonably considered as enacting a different attitudinal disposition from those who mostly frame such condemnations as more negotiable and with a lot of 'hedging' (Crompton, 1997; Hyland, 2004, 2019; White, 2000, 2003, 2025) devices. Consequently, these thoughts directed me to extend my exploration of the disputants' attitudinal disposition to encompass not only the attitudes deployed by disputants but also their preference in framing these attitudes.

While existing SFL and Appraisal literature has extensively explored how scaling and dialogistic engagement formulations can invoke attitudinal assessments (Don, 2016; Hood, 2010, 2012; Hood & Martin, 2007; Hood & Zhang, 2020; White, 1998, 2003, 2012, 2016, 2025), scholarly attention has been limited in examining the precise mechanisms of how these formulations grade or dialogistically frame attitudes. To the best of my knowledge, no previous work has systematically associated recurrent patterns in speakers' framing choices with their discursive identity construction. By attending to the variability in disputants' framing of the attitudes, this research offers a broader perspective on existing SFL/Appraisal-based textual identity studies, particularly regarding the scope of attitudinal disposition. The study also extends our understanding of the complex, multi-dimensional nature of attitudinal meaning-making by exploring the intricate co-occurrence of multiple axes or systems within the Appraisal framework. This approach recognises that linguistic identity is not a monolithic construct but a nuanced interplay of linguistic choices.

Thus far, my description of the pinning-down process has crystalised how I came to identify two complementary lines of inquiry into attitudinal disposition construction: (1) the disputants' construal of attitudinal disposition vis-à-vis the attitudes they favoured and (2) the disputants' construal of attitudinal disposition vis-à-vis how these attitudes were linguistically framed. Both lines of inquiry share a common focus: the disputants' deployment of attitude-associated resources. This book thus reports the findings regarding the variability in the disputants' construal of attitudinal disposition in family dispute resolution exchanges: the tendencies in their attitudes and their framing of the attitudes.

2.3 *Synoptic and Dynamic Views*

The exploration of attitudinal disposition raises methodological questions about the appropriate textual scope for tracking and characterising patterns. The highly interactive nature of dispute resolution discourse introduces challenges in determining the optimal analytical approach. For example, should the exploration of attitudinal disposition focus on a disputant's deployment of attitudinal meaning within a single turn or across multiple turns? If multiple turns are considered, should these turns be consecutive or situated within a specific phase of the dispute resolution interaction? Furthermore, if multiple turns are selected for analysis, what constitutes an appropriate number of turns to adequately characterise the disputant's attitudinal disposition? The inherent dynamism of conversational discourse means that disputants might favour one set of attitudes in some turns but a different set in another chunk of text. There is no doubt that the scope of the text determines the patterns by which the disputants' discursive self-presentation would be characterised. These methodological questions underscore the complexity of tracking attitudinal meaning-making in interactive discourse.

Existing SFL/Appraisal-based identity scholarship predominantly adopt a 'synoptic' view of evaluative meaning-making resources. This approach is particularly well-suited to institutional discourse types, such as journalistic writing in White's (e.g., 1998, 2003, 2008, 2020, 2021, 2025) work or academic texts in Coffin's (1997, 2006) work, where authors typically maintain a consistent attitudinal positioning throughout their communication. Studies examining written institutional texts often reveal relatively stable deployment of attitude-associated resources across the entire text. Similarly, research on short-form digital communication, like email list posts in Don's (2007a, 2007b, 2016) work and tweets in Zappavigna's (e.g., 2011a, 2014a, 2014b, 2018, 2019, 2022, 2023) work, has found that the brevity of these texts naturally constrains attitudinal variation. In such contexts, the synoptic approach proves effective, as the limited textual space provides little opportunity for significant attitudinal shifts. Consequently, previous identity studies have typically sought to characterise discursive identity by examining tendencies observable across entire conversations, complete texts, or distinct stages.

However, family dispute resolution exchange represents a complicated text type characterised by three distinctive aspects. First and foremost, it is a text type of immediately interactive multiparty spoken discourse. The immediately interactive nature of the data gives rise to the emergence of dispute or conflict (Oetzel & Ting-Toomey, 2013; Stewart & Maxwell, 2010) and the contingency of dispute resolution and conflict style formation (Garcia, 2019; Greatbatch & Dingwall, 1997; Keck & Samp, 2007; Meier et al., 2021; Speakman & Ryals, 2010). The family dispute resolution data sourced from reality TV programmes adds another layer of complexity to private dispute resolution exchanges regarding the composition of the immediate communicative participants. While the mediations typically addressed in conflict communication literature usually involve three parties (two disputants and one mediator), this data involves ten participants interacting directly in the communicative event—with different participants at different points in the episode. These participants include two disputing family members (in this case, the disputing spouses), one host/ess, and seven mediators. Each communicative participant's input can potentially change the direction of the interaction and influence the discursive performance of the other participants. Hence, the disputants' evaluative meaning-making arrangements in family dispute resolution exchanges are emergent and contingent. (While strictly speaking, the disputants can plan what to say before coming to the mediation. Nevertheless, their discursive performance in the actual mediation is not and cannot be pre-prepared and is subject to change as the interaction progresses.)

Secondly, dispute resolution inherently involves multiple stages (Bush, 2013; Garcia, 2019). In this family dispute resolution data, each reality TV episode, spanning 38–40 min, comprises five stages: Pre-mediation, Problem Discussion, Group mediation, Private Mediation, and Post-mediation (with detailed exploration provided in Chap. 3). The complexity of these interactions is evident in the shifting of addressees across different stages. During the Problem Discussion stage, disputants engage with each other and the hostess, allowing them to strategically choose their addressee—either their antagonistic spouse or the hostess. The Private Mediation stage introduces a different dynamic, with disputants communicating individually with mediators. Other stages permit more flexible addressing, enabling interactions with the antagonist, hostess, or mediators. These stage transitions inherently modify contextual variables, potentially influencing the disputants' attitudinal orientations. Existing sociolinguistic scholarship has documented linguistic 'style shifting' (Becker et al., 2022; Chambers et al., 2013; Hernández-Campoy, 2016; Rickford & Mcnair-Knox, 1994) as a result of 'audience design' (Androutsopoulos, 2014; Bell, 1984, 2002; Bucholtz, 2009; Metz, 2021; Pizer, 2021) or 'speaker design' (Coupland, 2001; Sandow, 2022; Schilling-Estes, 2002; Soukup, 2013). These studies have demonstrated how language users strategically deploy stylistic resources in response to situational changes, genre variations, audience composition, and interlocutor characteristics (Auer, 2007; Coupland, 2007a; Johnstone, 2009; Lin, 2023; Morikawa, 2019). Moreover, within conflict management research, approaches to conflict can also be conceptualised as strategies or intentions, suggesting that these orientations may vary based on relationship dynamics (Friedman et al., 2000). For example, individuals might choose different conflict management approaches when dealing conflict with subordinates, peers, or bosses (Rahim, 2023; Rahim & Magner, 1995). While linguistic adaptability across different situational settings is well-documented, the stability of attitudinal orientation within a single dispute resolution episode remains underexplored. Zappavigna and Martin's (2018a) study of young offenders' identity construction in youth justice conferences, which observed persona shifts across different stages, inspired a critical investigation into the consistency of disputants' self-presentation. Accordingly, one fundamental research question emerges: Do disputants maintain a consistent attitudinal 'self' when addressing different participants (e.g., antagonist, host/ess, and mediators) and across various mediation stages? This inquiry promises to unveil nuanced insights into the dynamic nature of discursive identity construction in interactive dispute resolution contexts.

Moreover, the Problem Discussion stage in my data, an extended mediation phase lasting 20–30 min, provides a unique opportunity to explore the stability of disputants' discursive self-presentation. During this stage, all contextual factors remain stable, with disputing spouses directly confronting each other over the same family dispute issue in front of the same mediation panel in an unchanged physical setting. While one might anticipate consistent evaluative arrangements of a disputant under stable contextual factors, the potential for observable shift patterns would suggest a more complex identity construction process. Such shifts would indicate that disputants potentially construct multiple attitudinal 'selves' or diverse aspects of a singular attitudinal self within the same communicative context. These findings could enhance our understanding of dispute resolution exchanges and discursive identity construction. If there are any such shift patterns, it would be worth probing the potential motivations behind the attitudinal disposition shifts. What might trigger these shifts? For example, do disputants tend to modify their attitudinal dispositions in response to the antagonist's input, the host's elicitation, or other contextual factors? These questions invite a nuanced exploration of the dynamic nature of attitudinal disposition construction.

Subsequently, the complicated nature of family dispute resolution data afforded me another line of inquiry into the disputants' discursive self-presentation, moving beyond the static 'synoptic' view prevalent in SFL/Appraisal-based identity studies. This approach situates identity construction within the unfolding text, investigating recurrent patterns of attitudinal disposition shifts as the interaction progresses. Theoretically grounded in SFL's concept of 'logogenesis' (Halliday & Matthiessen, 1999), this approach builds on previous text analysis studies by Halliday and others (Halliday, 2002, 2004; Hao & Humphrey, 2012; Iedema & Degeling, 2001; Kellogg & Kalkhoran, 2021; Klein & Unsworth, 2014; Martin, 1999; Zappavigna, 2011b). It contributes to the scholarship by tracking the gradual development of discursive self-presentation in a multiparty adversarial interaction, examining both the construction and stability of attitudinal dispositions.

In summary, under the influence of the aforementioned SFL/Appraisal literature and the complexity of my family dispute resolution data, I adopted two lines of inquiry when investigating the disputants' construal of attitudinal disposition. One line of inquiry was to adopt a 'synoptic' view of attitudinal disposition construction. The investigation focused on the disputants' overall attitudinal arrangements in the Problem Discussion stage, the longest and most prominent stage in the whole mediation. It sought to identify and characterise recurrent patterns in how the disputants conveyed and negotiated attitudinal meanings within this 20–30-min interaction. This line of inquiry was 'synoptic' because it treated the disputants' language use as a collection of choices in the whole text. It explored the types of 'self' the disputants presented in family dispute resolution.

The other line of inquiry was to adopt a 'dynamic' view of attitudinal disposition construction. It focused on the stability/fluidity of the disputants' language use as the text unfolded. In other words, did the disputants present the same attitudinal 'self' throughout the dispute resolution interaction? Considering the complexity of my data, I adopted two sub-lines of inquiry in the dynamic exploration.

One sub-line of inquiry was to track the disputants' attitudinal arrangements across different mediation stages. The purpose was to examine whether the disputants enacted the same attitudinal disposition when the communicative setting changed (e.g., change from discussing the dispute issues in the main mediation studio to talking to the mediators individually in private mediation rooms), and whether they constructed the same attitudinal disposition when interacting with different people (i.e., antagonist, hostess, and mediators). Based on the Speech Accommodation Theory (Giles, 1973; Giles & Ogay, 2007)—which assumes that 'individuals possess a speech repertoire from which they can select speech forms depending on the nature of situational constraints' (Giles, 1973, p. 89)—one might expect a disputant to use and shift linguistic choices to accommodate change in the communication context. Exploring the stability of attitudinal disposition across multiple mediation stages tested this hypothesis.

The other sub-line of inquiry was to track the disputants' attitudinal arrangements within the Problem Discussion stage. The focus was on the stability/fluidity of the disputants' attitudinal disposition when all contextual variables remained stable. While it might be expected that disputants enact different discursive dispositions at different mediation stages or when interacting with different people, it was novel to explore whether they changed their disposition within one mediation stage. If they did so, was the change an idiosyncratic choice or a more common phenomenon with a recurrent pattern observable among multiple disputants? Additionally, if they did so, what were the contextual factors motivating such changes? Hence, the sub-line of inquiry (attitudinal disposition stability within one stage) went beyond the existing scholarship on style-shifting, or textual personae change. Previous scholarship had only examined style shifts where linguist choices were made in different contexts. My family dispute resolution data provided an opportunity to explore the stability of disputants' discursive self-presentation over a relatively extended time span (20–30 min) in the same communicative setting. Any findings regarding patterns in the disputants' deployment of attitude-associated resources, whether with shifts or without, would provide valuable new insights. The fluidity of the disputants' linguistic choice, within and across stages, is undoubtedly an essential aspect of the disputants' discursive self-presentation.

The synoptic view and the dynamic view offered complementary perspectives into the disputants' discursive self-presentation in family dispute resolution exchanges. Based on the two aspects of attitudinal disposition (i.e., attitudes and the framing of the attitudes) and the two views (synoptic versus dynamic), I arrived at three major lines of inquiry to explore the disputants' discursive self-presentation vis-à-vis their use of attitude-associated resources. As will be discussed in detail in the following chapters, this exploration revealed the multifacetedness of discursive self-presentation.

2.4 *Three Lines of Inquiry*

By way of rounding off the discussion just provided, I offer the following. The three lines of inquiry were (1) a synoptic view focusing on attitudes, (2) a synoptic view focusing on the framing of the attitudes, and (3) a dynamic view of attitudinal disposition construction. Each line of inquiry explored a specific aspect of the disputants' use of attitude-associated resources and had its own research questions.

The first line of inquiry—a synoptic view focusing on attitudes—examined tendencies in the disputants' attitudinal expressions in the Problem Discussion stage. It treated the disputants' talk within this stage as a complete text and tracked recurrent patterns in the disputants' attitudinal positioning of the self, the antagonist, and the others. The broad research question guiding the analysis concerned the disputants' attitudinal positioning: What similarities or differences could be found among the disputants regarding their attitudes towards themselves and others? This analysis was directed at discovering tendencies in the disputants' preferences for attitude-associated resources: whether their preferences were broadly similar across the dataset (suggesting a uniform attitudinal disposition being verbally enacted by the disputants), whether some disputants had similar preferences while differing from others (suggesting sub-types of attitudinal disposition), or whether all the disputants used the resources in idiosyncratic ways (suggesting no observable basis for grouping the disputants into sub-types of attitudinal disposition).

The second line of inquiry—a synoptic view focusing on framing the attitudes—explored tendencies in how the disputants framed the attitudinal expressions in the Problem Discussion stage. The analysis recorded whether the attitudinal expressions were intensified, mitigated, or left unscaled, and also tracked how these attitudinal expressions were framed dialogistically. The analysis also explored whether the disputants deployed both the scaling and the dialogistic framing devices simultaneously when advancing a particular attitude. The broad research question guiding the analysis was similar to that of the first line of inquiry: what might be the similarities and differences across the disputants in the dataset regarding their choices in the framing of the attitudes and the relationship between these tendencies and their textually performed identity?

The third line of inquiry—a dynamic view of attitudinal disposition—explored the development of the disputants' attitudinal disposition as the interaction progressed. It placed the disputants' use of attitude-associated resources into an unfolding timeframe and examined the stability/fluidity of their attitudinal positionings. The broad research question guiding the analysis concerned the progression of the disputants' attitudinal positioning: How did the disputants develop their attitudinal disposition as the interaction unfolded? There were three sub-lines of inquiry in this part of the project. One was to explore attitudinal disposition stability/fluidity across different mediation stages in the whole dispute resolution episode. This sub-line of inquiry examined whether the disputants presented the same 'self' or the same aspect of the 'self' as the dispute resolution unfolded. The second sub-line of inquiry was concerned with attitudinal disposition shifts vis-à-vis addressee change across different mediation stages. This line of analysis focused on whether the disputants presented the same or the same aspect of the 'self' when interacting with different people. The last sub-line of inquiry investigated the stability/fluidity of the disputants' attitudinal disposition within the Problem Discussion stage. This sub-line of inquiry examined if the disputants deployed the same self or the same aspects of the 'self' across this single communicative context. In short, the dynamic view of attitudinal disposition offered fresh insights into the stability/fluidity of disputants' discursive self-presentation vis-à-vis their deployments of the attitude-associated meanings.

Table 1.2 summarises the three lines of inquiry by which I explored the disputants' enactment of attitudinal disposition. Each line of inquiry offered a unique insight into the disputants' self-presentation via their use of attitude-associated

Table 1.2 Three lines of inquiry

Synoptic	A synoptic view of attitudes • What attitudes do disputants prefer?
	A synoptic view of the framing of the attitudes • How do disputants frame these attitudes?
Dynamic	A dynamic view of attitudinal disposition • How stable are the disputants' attitudinal preferences as the interaction unfolded (across different stages/ when interacting with different addressees) • How stable are the disputants' attitudinal preferences within the Problem Discussion stage (when the context of situation remained stable)?

resources. The multiple lines of inquiry afforded a multidimensional investigation of the disputants' discursive identity construction.

It is worth noting that the attitudinal dispositions characterised in this book were only concerned with one particular aspect of the disputants' discursive self-presentation: the discursively construed identity regarding the speakers' preference in attitude-associated resources. Undoubtedly, other semiotic resources also contribute to the disputants' discursive performance in family dispute resolution. Considering the adversarial and interactive nature of family dispute resolution, another pivotal aspect of the disputants' discursive self-presentation would be their negotiation of disagreements, which I also explored during my PhD candidature and labelled it as the disputants' 'argumentative disposition'. Given the space limitations of this book, I have not been able to address this substantial body of work in this book. Nevertheless, the 'attitudinal' aspect of the disputants' self-presentation (reported in this book) reveals the multifacetedness of textual identity construction. It is beyond the scope of this research to argue for a comprehensive and exhaustive exploration of the disputants' discursive self-presentation covering all relevant semiotic resources. The purpose of the research was to explore how insights into the functionality of evaluative language offered by the SFL/Appraisal scholarship could enhance our understanding of discursive identity construction in conflictual interactions.

2.5 *Identify Tendencies with Computational Tools*

Through the aforementioned pinning-down process, I developed research questions and methodologies to address them. My decision to investigate similarities and differences across multiple disputants using numerous variation parameters posed a challenge. Most existing SFL/Appraisal-based identity studies focused on small datasets with two or three speakers/writers or fewer than a dozen short texts, conducted through nuanced manual annotations and interpretative discussions. In contrast, my dataset was substantially larger: 12 disputants talking continuously for 230 minutes across 1147 turns and 5282 moves (detailed in Chap. 3). Moreover, my research focus involved a wide range of variation parameters in attitudinal disposition enactment, specifically the co-articulation of multiple features from Appraisal systems (i.e., ATTITUDE, ENGAGEMENT, and GRADUATION) and subsystems (e.g., attitude type/ polarity/ target/ explicitness, upscaling/ downscaling, and monoglossing/ heteroglossing). Performing analyses on such a dataset with numerous variables from both synoptic and dynamic perspectives was beyond the capabilities of manual labour alone. These factors motivated me to deploy computational tools for multivariate analysis.

While software tools (e.g., the UAM Corpus Tool (O'Donnell, 2008)) and corpus linguistics methods have been quite widely used to support Appraisal-framework studies (Almutairi, 2021; Aloy Mayo & Taboada, 2017; Bednarek, 2008, 2009; Hunston, 2011; O'Donnell, 2014; Su & Hunston, 2019a, 2019b; Tupala, 2019), to my knowledge, no previous studies have employed computational tools in the manner I did. Specifically, I first conducted a nuanced manual Appraisal annotation of the disputants' talk, then processed the annotation data in the *R* (R Core Team, 2025) programming environment. I utilised multiple *R* data mining packages, particularly clustering (or cluster analysis) methods, to assist pattern recognition and systematically track variations among the disputants (details in Chap. 3). It is crucial to note that I did not treat the patterns extracted by computational tools as definitive answers. Instead, I contextualised these patterns with the disputants' deployment of attitude-associated resources and explored the insights they might reveal. The subsequent chapters will demonstrate that many computer-recognised patterns offer fresh insights into subtle or unexpected data patterns that might have remained undetectable through human intuition or traditional manual methods.

Supplemental materials for this volume, including datasets (containing full transcriptions and Appraisal annotations) and reproducible *R* codebase for data processing and analytical workflows, are hosted in an open-access GitHub repository[5] accompanying the publication to facilitate replication studies and methodological transparency.

3 Research Highlights

The pinning-down process outlined in the preceding sections has progressively revealed a series of original contributions to SFL/Appraisal-based discursive identity scholarship. As my research approach took shape, multiple innovative dimensions emerged, each addressing critical gaps in existing linguistic identity research.

Some highlights have already been implicitly established through the previous discussions. For instance, (1) from a theoretical standpoint, the research challenges conventional, static models of identity by conceptualising discursive self-presentation as a dynamic, context-responsive semiotic practice. By integrating Goffman's dramaturgical theory with SFL semiotic approach to evaluative

[5] https://github.com/xu-qingxin/Appraisal-Approach-to-Conflict-Styles.git

meaning-making, this research provides a nuanced analysis of large-scale conversational data while preserving linguistic and sociological insights. (2) This research explores discursive self-presentation in a previously under-investigated text type: immediately interactive, multiparty, adversarial interactions. By focusing on family dispute resolution exchanges, the study addresses a gap in the current literature. (3) The research adopts a comprehensive approach to characterising disputants' discursive self-presentation. Rather than examining attitudes in isolation, the study simultaneously investigates both the attitudes conveyed by speakers and their linguistic framing of these attitudes. This dual focus provides a more nuanced understanding of attitudinal disposition. (4) The research provides a multifaceted exploration of discursive identity construction by examining language use from both synoptic and dynamic perspectives. This approach reveals the complex, multidimensional nature of identity performance, a theme that will be elaborated in subsequent chapters. Moreover, (5) the study extends existing scholarship by exploring the stability or fluidity of attitudinal disposition within an extended exchange where the contextual situation remains relatively consistent. This approach offers insights into the unfolding of speakers' discursive performance over time.

In addition to all these previously established contributions, this research makes another two original contributions. (6) One is to conduct multivariate analyses with a holistic view towards attitudinal positioning. (7) The other is to identify patterns in a computing environment with data mining methods. Details of these two contributions are elaborated below.

This research conducted multivariate analyses on a dataset of multiple speakers, a contribution to the existing SFL/Appraisal-based discursive identity analysis. Existing SFL and Appraisal-based studies typically examined attitudinal positioning along single 'attitudinal axis' (White, 2008), including attitudinal target, polarity, attitude types, and attitude explicitness. In contrast, this research adopts a holistic approach to attitudinal positioning. By introducing the notion of 'attitudinal complex' (more details in Chap. 4), the study simultaneously tracks four attitudinal axes across multiple speakers. Additionally, this research also tracked the framing of the attitudes: whether the attitudes were framed via additional dialogistic engagement or scaling devices. This multivariate approach represents a methodological innovation. Unlike previous studies that compared two speakers or focused on isolated linguistic parameters, this research identifies recurrent patterns across multiple disputants via multiple parameter combinations. The multivariate analyses enabled a comprehensive examination of attitudinal identity construction, revealing intricate patterns of linguistic variation that would remain invisible through traditional qualitative methods.

The final major contribution lies in the deployment of data mining methods to semantics-oriented analysis. Recognising the limitations of manual processing when dealing with multiple variation parameters, the research leveraged computational tools—specifically multivariate and cluster analysis techniques in the *R* environment. This methodological approach enhanced the efficiency and depth of data analysis. By utilising computational algorithms, the study could identify highly complex, multi-factorial patterns of similarity and difference in disputants' deployment of attitude-associated resources. Beyond providing insights into attitudinal disposition, the research demonstrates the potential of computational tools in linguistic identity research.

In short, these contributions collectively advance our understanding of discursive identity as a dynamic, context-responsive semiotic practice. By integrating theoretical innovation, methodological rigor, and computational analysis, the research offers a comprehensive framework for exploring linguistic identity construction. Subsequent chapters will provide detailed elaboration of these contributions, systematically unpacking the theoretical, methodological, and analytical innovations introduced in this study.

4 Key Findings

This book reports findings from three interconnected lines of inquiry that collectively illuminate the complex landscape of disputants' discursive self-presentation through their deployment of attitude-associated resources. The research reveals a multidimensional heterogeneity of disputant's attitudinal disposition, exploring both the attitudes the disputants preferred and how they framed these attitudes, and from both a synoptic view and a dynamic view.

By way of a preview, under the first line of inquiry, I focused on the similarities and differences in the disputants' preference for resources which were specifically attitudinal—tendencies in the type of attitudes they favoured. Key findings highlighted both commonalities and variations. Consistent patterns emerged, such as disputants' uniform negativity towards antagonists and positive self-assessment. However, substantial variations were observed in three critical aspects: (1) the disputants' attitudinal orientation towards the self, the antagonist, and associated individuals; (2) range of attitudes deployed during the interaction; and (3) expressiveness in advancing the attitudinal expressions that were of their central communication concerns.

The second line of inquiry examined how disputants framed attitudinal expressions, particularly the attitudes of their central communication concern in the family dispute resolutions—attitudes directed at the self and antagonist. Findings also revealed both similarities and diversities. For instance, disputants consistently articulated explicit spousal condemnation through bare assertions and intensifications. Meanwhile, a wide range of variations emerge across the disputants. Findings of computational clustering analysis suggest a 'cline of attitudinality', capturing the nuanced quality of speakers' attitudinal presence.

The above two lines of inquiry explored the disputants' attitudinal disposition construction from a synoptic perspective, taking the disputants' language choice in the Problem Discussion stage as a complete text. The final line of inquiry concerned the stability of the disputants' attitudinal arrangements in an unfolding family dispute resolution exchange. The exploration identified multiple shifts and unshift patterns concerning their preference of the attitudes and the framing of the attitudes.

Findings suggested a universal tendency among disputants to present different aspects of 'self' as contextual situations evolved. Subsequently, a cline of the 'radicality of shifts' is proposed to characterise whether the disputants' attitudinal disposition shifts were relatively more radical or less radical. In short, the final line of inquiry reveals a certain degree of fluidity in the disputants' attitudinal disposition construction.

Nevertheless, determining whether the research yielded a definitive conclusion about the disputants' attitudinal disposition or provided a foundation for taxonomising attitudinal disposition subtypes remains a complex endeavour. The inherent complexity stems from the multifaceted nature of attitudinal disposition construction, which involves numerous meaning-making resources and prompted a multidimensional exploration. The research findings ultimately illuminated the intricate and nuanced character of attitudinal disposition and discursive self-presentation.

Notably, there was no singular, unequivocal answer to the question of 'who the disputants were' in these family dispute resolution exchanges. Instead, the disputants revealed different facets of self, with their evaluative language presenting varied identities when examined through different analytical lenses. The disputants' attitudinal dispositions emerged as dynamic and contextually responsive, resisting simplistic categorisation.

The subsequent chapters will delve deeper into these nuanced findings, unpacking the intricate mechanisms of attitudinal disposition construction in family dispute resolution exchanges.

5 Book Outline

This book is organised into eight chapters. The current chapter introduces the origin and scope of the research, outlining three lines of inquiry for examining disputants' discursive self-presentation, with a particular focus on their construal of attitudinal disposition.

Chapter 2 establishes the theoretical foundations that underpin the study's conceptualisation of the discursive self-presentation. By synthesising insights from Goffman's dramaturgical view of self and SFL, the chapter proposes a nuanced theoretical perspective for understanding how individuals craft identity through evaluative language.

Chapter 3 presents the methodological framework for investigating disputants' discursive self-presentation through the Appraisal framework. It first introduces the dataset from the reality TV mediation genre, detailing its composition and registerial features. The chapter then presents the analytical methods including the data transcription conventions, principles for annotating Appraisal resources, and methods for measuring evaluative preference. Finally, the chapter introduces the data processing method, a novel approach that employs data mining techniques in a computational environment to conduct multivariate Appraisal analysis.

The empirical investigation unfolds across Chaps. 4–7, systematically reporting findings along three investigative lines. Chapter 4 offers a synoptic exploration, examining the attitudes preferred by disputants and providing a static perspective on attitudinal choices. Building upon this, Chap. 5 expands the synoptic exploration by focusing on disputants' preferences in framing attitudinal expressions, offering deeper insights into their communicative strategies. Chapter 6 takes a dynamic perspective, investigating the stability and fluidity of disputants' attitudinal dispositions in the whole mediation episode. It examines whether disputants prefer the same set of attitudinal meaning-making resources across different mediation stages and when interacting with different addressees. Chapter 7 continues with the dynamic exploration by focusing on any potential disputants' attitudinal preference change during the 20–30-min-long Problem Discussion stage, when the context of situation remained unchanged. These two dynamic chapters reveals the evolving nature of discursive self-presentation, demonstrating how identity is not fixed but constantly negotiated through linguistic interactions.

The concluding Chap. 8 synthesises the key research findings, offering a broader interpretative perspective. It argues for the multifacetedness of attitudinal disposition and discursive identity construction, situating the research within wider scholarly conversations. By drawing together the threads of investigation, this chapter provides a comprehensive understanding of how individuals construct and present themselves through language in adversarial communicative contexts.

References

Almutairi, B. A. A. (2021). Towards estimating global probabilities of evaluation in English based on automatic extraction of least delicate Appraisal in large corpora. *Language Sciences, 88*, 101432. https://doi.org/10.1016/j.langsci.2021.101432

Aloy Mayo, M., & Taboada, M. (2017). Evaluation in political discourse addressed to women: Appraisal analysis of Cosmopolitan's online coverage of the 2014 US midterm elections. *Discourse, Context & Media, 18*, 40–48. https://doi.org/10.1016/j.dcm.2017.06.003

Androutsopoulos, J. (2014). Languaging when contexts collapse: Audience design in social networking. *Discourse, Context & Media, 4–5*, 62–73. https://doi.org/10.1016/j.dcm.2014.08.006

Auer, P. (Ed.). (2007). *Style and social identities, alternative approaches to linguistic heterogeneity*. De Gruyter Mouton. https://doi.org/10.1515/9783110198508

Barnes, B. E. (2007). *Culture, conflict, and mediation in the Asian Pacific*. University Press of America.

Bartley, L., & Trevisan, P. (2024). "We can fix this. Let's get you out of trouble, son": An analysis of the transitivity and appraisal patterns in the Netflix TV show When They See Us. *Applied Linguistics, 0*(0), 1–16.

Becker, K., Khan, S. D., & Zimman, L. (2022). Beyond binary gender: creaky voice, gender, and the variationist enterprise. *Language Variation and Change, 34*(2), 215–238. https://doi.org/10.1017/S0954394522000138

Bednarek, M. (2008). *Emotion talk across corpora*. Palgrave Macmillan. https://doi.org/10.1057/9780230285712

Bednarek, M. (2009). Language patterns and ATTITUDE. *Functions of Language, 16*(2), 165–192. https://doi.org/10.1075/fol.16.2.01bed

Bell, A. (1984). Language style as audience design. *Language in Society, 13*(2), 145–204.
Bell, A. (2002). Back in style: Reworking audience design. In P. Eckert & J. R. Rickford (Eds.), *Style and sociolinguistic variation* (pp. 139–169). Cambridge University Press. https://doi.org/10.1017/CBO9780511613258.010
Blake, R. R., & Mouton, J. S. (1964). *The managerial grid.* Gulf Publishing.
Boberg, C. (2021). *Accent in North American film and television: A sociophonetic analysis.* Cambridge University Press. https://doi.org/10.1017/9781316579817
Bucholtz, M. (2009). From stance to style: Gender, interaction, and indexicality in Mexican immigrant youth slang. In A. Jaffe (Ed.), *Stance: Sociolinguistic perspectives* (pp. 146–170). Oxford University Press. https://oxford.universitypressscholarship.com/view/10.1093/acprof:oso/9780195331646.001.0001/acprof-9780195331646-chapter-7. Accessed 5 August 2020
Bush, R. (2013). Mediation skills and client-centered lawyering: A new view of the partnership. *Clinical Law Review, 19*, 429.
Carrió-Pastor, M. L. (2025). A functional classification of aggressive digital replies to Pedro Sánchez' posts on X. *Journal of Pragmatics, 245*, 19–34. https://doi.org/10.1016/j.pragma.2025.06.003
Chambers, J. K., Trudgill, P., & Schilling, N. (Eds.). (2013). *The handbook of language variation and change* (2nd ed.). Wiley-Blackwell.
Coffin, C. (1997). Constructing and giving value to the past: An investigation into secondary school education. In F. Christie & J. R. Martin (Eds.), *Genres and institutions: Social processes in the workplace and school* (pp. 196–230). Cassell. http://www.goodreads.com/book/show/3398705.Genre_And_Institutions_Social_Processes_in_the_Workplace_and_School. Accessed 8 May 2018
Coffin, C. (2006). *Historical discourse: The language of time, cause and evaluation* (Continuum discourse series). Continuum.
Coupland, N. J. R. (2001). Language, situation and the relational self: Theorizing dialect-style in sociolinguistics. In P. Eckert & J. R. Rickford (Eds.), *Style and sociolinguistic variation* (pp. 185–210). Cambridge University Press. http://le.alma.exlibrisgroup.com/view/action/uresolver.do?operation=resolveService&package_service_id=5665578030002746&institutionId=2746&customerId=2745. Accessed 26 November 2019
Coupland, N. J. R. (2007a). Aneurin Bevan, class wars and the styling of political antagonism. In A. Peter (Ed.), *Style and social identities: Alternative approaches to linguistic heterogeneity* (pp. 213–245). De Gruyter Mouton. http://orca.cf.ac.uk/3699/. Accessed 30 June 2018
Coupland, N. J. R. (2007b). *Style: Language variation and identity*. Cambridge University Press.
Crompton, P. (1997). Hedging in academic writing: Some theoretical problems. *English for Specific Purposes, 16*(4), 271–287. https://doi.org/10.1016/S0889-4906(97)00007-0
Cunningham, K. J., & Link, S. (2021). Video and text feedback on ESL writing: Understanding attitude and negotiating relationships. *Journal of Second Language Writing, 52*, 100797. https://doi.org/10.1016/j.jslw.2021.100797
Diamant, N. J. (2000). Conflict and conflict resolution in China: Beyond mediation-centered approaches. *Journal of Conflict Resolution, 44*(4), 523–546. https://doi.org/10.1177/0022002700044004006
Don, A. (2007a). *A framework for the investigation of interactive norms and the construction of textual identity in written discourse communities: The case of an email list.* Unpublished Ph.D Thesis, University of Birmingham.
Don, A. (2007b). An approach to the analysis of textual identity through profiles of evaluative disposition. In *ASFLA 2007 proceedings*.
Don, A. (2016). "It is hard to mesh all this": Invoking attitude, persona and argument organisation. *Functional Linguistics, 3*, 9. https://doi.org/10.1186/s40554-016-0033-1
Don, A. (2017). Stance-taking and the construal of textual persona in written contexts: Social contact revisited. *Linguistics and the Human Sciences, 13*(1–2), 70–95. https://doi.org/10.1558/lhs.30713

Eckert, P. (2012). Three waves of variation study: The emergence of meaning in the study of sociolinguistic variation. *Annual Review of Anthropology, 41*(1), 87–100. https://doi.org/10.1146/annurev-anthro-092611-145828
Eckert, P. (2018). *Meaning and linguistic variation: The third wave in sociolinguistics*. Cambridge University Press.
Eckert, P., & Rickford, J. R. (Eds.). (2002). *Style and sociolinguistic variation*. Cambridge University Press. https://doi.org/10.1017/CBO9780511613258
Eggins, S., & Slade, D. (1997). *Analysing casual conversation*. Cassell.
Firth, J. R. (1950). Personality and language in society. *The Sociological Review*, 37–52.
Folger, J., Poole, M. S., & Stutman, R. K. (2017). *Working through conflict: Strategies for relationships, groups, and organizations* (8th ed.). Routledge. https://doi.org/10.4324/9781315296296
Friedman, R. A., et al. (2000). What goes around comes around: The impact of personal conflict style on work conflict and stress. *International Journal of Conflict Management, 11*(1), 32–55. https://doi.org/10.1108/eb022834
Garcia, A. C. (2019). *How mediation works: Resolving conflict through talk* (Studies in interactional sociolinguistics). Cambridge University Press.
García-Gómez, A. (2018). Dragons' Den: Enacting persuasion in reality television. *Discourse, Context & Media, 21*, 1–9. https://doi.org/10.1016/j.dcm.2017.09.014
Giles, H. (1973). Accent mobility: A model and some data. *Anthropological Linguistics, 15*(2), 87–109.
Giles, H., & Ogay, T. (2007). Communication accommodation theory. In N. J. Mahwah (Ed.), *Explaining communication: Contemporary theories and exemplars* (pp. 293–310). Lawrence Erlbaum.
Goffman, E. (1959). *The presentation of self in everyday life*. Doubleday Anchor Books.
Goffman, E. (1981). *Forms of talk*. University of Pennsylvania Press.
Greatbatch, D., & Dingwall, R. (1997). Argumentative talk in divorce mediation sessions. *American Sociological Review, 62*(1), 151–170. https://doi.org/10.2307/2657457
Grimshaw, A. D. (1990). *Conflict talk: Sociolinguistic investigations of arguments in conversations*. Cambridge University Press.
Guerrero, L. K. (2020). Conflict style associations with cooperativeness, directness, and relational satisfaction: A case for a six-style typology. *Negotiation and Conflict Management Research, 13*(1), 24–43. https://doi.org/10.1111/ncmr.12156
Halliday, M. A. K. (1978). *Language as a social semiotic: The social interpretation of language and meaning*. University Park Press.
Halliday, M. A. K. (2002). So you say "pass"…thank you three muchly. In J. J. Webster (Ed.), *Linguistic studies of text and discourse. Collected works of M.A.K. Halliday* (Vol. 2, pp. 228–254). Continuum.
Halliday, M. A. K. (2004). Things and relations: Regrammaticizing experience as 49 technical knowledge. In J. J. Webster (Ed.), *The language of science. Collected works of M.A.K. Halliday* (Vol. 5). Continuum.
Halliday, M. A. K., & Hasan, R. (1985). *Language, context, and text: Aspects of language in a social-semiotic perspective*. Deakin University.
Halliday, M. A. K., & Matthiessen, C. M. I. M. (1999). *Construing experience through language: A language-based approach to cognition*. Cassell.
Hao, J., & Humphrey, S. (2012). The role of "coupling" in biological experimental reports. *Linguistics and the Human Sciences, 5*(2), 169–194.
Harbin, M. B. (2023). Don't make my entertainment political! Social media responses to narratives of racial duty on competitive reality television series. *Political Communication, 40*(4), 464–483.
Hasan, R. (1973). Code, register and social dialect. In B. Bernstein (Ed.), *Class, codes and control* (pp. 160–193). Routledge. https://journals.equinoxpub.com/books/article/view/25629
Hasan, R. (1989). Semantic variation and sociolinguistics. *Australian Journal of Linguistics, 9*(2), 221–275. https://doi.org/10.1080/07268608908599422

Hasan, R. (2009). In J. J. Webster (Ed.), *Semantic variation; meaning in society and in sociolinguistics* (The collected works of Ruqaiya Hasan). Equinox.

Hasan, R. (2020). Tenor: Rethinking interactant relations. *Language, Context and Text, 2*(2), 213–333.

Hawes, C. (2024). Moral transformation in the Chinese legal system: Contradiction or complementary relationship? In Y. Guo (Ed.), *Jiaohua: Chinese ideas and practices of moral transformation* (pp. 85–101). Springer Nature. https://doi.org/10.1007/978-981-97-9487-4_5

Hawes, C., & Kong, S. (2013). Primetime dispute resolution: Reality TV mediation shows in China's "harmonious society". *Law & Society Review, 47*(4), 739–770. https://doi.org/10.1111/lasr.12046

Hernández-Campoy, J. M. (2016). *Sociolinguistic styles*. John Wiley & Sons, Ltd. https://doi.org/10.1002/9781118737606.fmatter

Hocker, J., & Wilmot, W. (2018). *Interpersonal conflict* (10th ed.). McGraw-Hill Education.

Hommerberg, C., & Lindgren, M. (2023). *Depicting the consumer of experiential luxury: Identities, values and consumption goals in online reviewer discourse on wine, perfume and chocolate*. Palgrave Macmillan. https://doi.org/10.1057/978-1-137-60080-6

Hood, S. (2010). *Appraising research: Evaluation in academic writing*. Palgrave Macmillan.

Hood, S. (2012). Voice and stance as APPRAISAL: Persuading and positioning in research writing across intellectual fields. In K. Hyland, C. S. Guinda, & C. Sancho Guinda (Eds.), *Stance and voice in written academic genres* (pp. 51–68). Palgrave Macmillan Limited.

Hood, S., & Martin, J. R. (2007). Invoking attitude: The play of graduation in appraising discourse. In R. Hasan, C. M. I. M. Matthiessen, & J. J. Webster (Eds.), *Continuing discourse on Language: A functional perspective* (pp. 739–764). Equinox Publishing Ltd. https://journals.equinoxpub.com/books/article/view/25351

Hood, S., & Zhang, D. (2020). GRADUATION in play with other systems of meaning in the enactment of interpersonal relations. *Journal of Foreign Languages, 43*(6), 21–41.

Hunston, S. (2011). *Corpus approaches to evaluation: Phraseology and evaluative language* (1st ed.). Routledge.

Hyland, K. (2004). *Disciplinary discourses: Social interactions in academic writing*. University of Michigan Press.

Hyland, K. (2019). *Metadiscourse: Exploring interaction in writing* (Bloomsbury classics in linguistics) (2nd ed.). Bloomsbury Academic.

Iedema, R., & Degeling, P. (2001). From difference to divergence: The logogenesis of interactive tension. *Functions of Language, 8*(1), 41–78. https://doi.org/10.1075/fol.8.1.03ied

Iedema, R., Feez, S., & White, P. R. R. (1994). *Media literacy: Disadvantaged Schools Program*. NSW Department of School Education.

Inwood, O., & Zappavigna, M. (2021). Ambient affiliation, misinformation and moral panic: Negotiating social bonds in a YouTube internet hoax. *Discourse & Communication, 15*(3), 281–307. https://doi.org/10.1177/1750481321989838

Inwood, O., & Zappavigna, M. (2023). Conspiracy theories and white supremacy on YouTube: Exploring affiliation and legitimation strategies in YouTube comments. *Social Media + Society, 0*(0), 1–16. https://doi.org/10.1177/20563051221150410

Jackson, S., & Jacobs, S. (1980). Structure of conversational argument: Pragmatic bases for the enthymeme. *Quarterly Journal of Speech, 66*(3), 251–265. https://doi.org/10.1080/00335638009383524

Jing, Y., & Xu, Q. (2023). Danmu video as the resemiotised: An attitudinal analysis of home visit. *Media, Culture & Society, 45*(4), 753–768. https://doi.org/10.1177/01634437231158514

Johnstone, B. (2009). Stance, style, and the linguistic individual. In A. Jaffe (Ed.), *Stance: Sociolinguistic perspectives* (pp. 29–52). Oxford University Press.

Keck, K. L., & Samp, J. A. (2007). The dynamic nature of goals and message production as revealed in a sequential analysis of conflict interactions. *Human Communication Research, 33*(1), 27–47.

Kellogg, D., & Kalkhoran, S. A. (2021). "And that": Halliday's logogenesis, sociogenesis, and phylogenesis in Darwin's tangled bank. *Language and Literature: International Journal of Stylistics, 30*(3), 213–228.
Klein, P. D., & Unsworth, L. (2014). The logogenesis of writing to learn: A systemic functional perspective. *Linguistics and Education, 26*, 1–17. https://doi.org/10.1016/j.linged.2013.12.003
Knight, N. K. (2013). Evaluating experience in funny ways: How friends bond through conversational hum. *Text & Talk, 33*(4–5), 553–574. https://doi.org/10.1515/text-2013-0025
Kong, S., & Hawes, C. (2015). The new family mediator: TV mediation programs in China's "harmonious society". In R. Bai & G. Song (Eds.), *Chinese television in the twenty-first century: Entertaining the nation* (pp. 33–50). Routledge. https://opus.lib.uts.edu.au/handle/10453/33904. Accessed 26 May 2018
Labov, W. (1963). The social motivation of a sound change. *Word, 19*(3), 273–309. https://doi.org/10.1080/00437956.1963.11659799
Labov, W. (1972). *Sociolinguistic patterns*. University of Pennsylvania Press.
Labov, W., et al. (2006). *The atlas of North American English: Phonetics, phonology, and sound change: A multimedia reference tool*. Mouton de Gruyter.
Lei, L. (2025). Appraisal as a weapon of killing: An ecocritical discourse analysis of animal depiction in nature documentary series *The Blue Planet*. *Language Sciences, 110*, 101725. https://doi.org/10.1016/j.langsci.2025.101725
Leung, S. (2002). Conflict talk: A discourse analytical perspective. *Studies in Applied Linguistics and TESOL, 2*(3), 1–19. https://doi.org/10.7916/D8FB52F2
Lin, Y. (2023). Towards a comprehensive model of style-shifting: Evidence from sibilant variation in Mandarin. *Language & Communication, 89*, 23–41. https://doi.org/10.1016/j.langcom.2022.12.004
Lorenzo-Dus, N., & Blitvich, P. G.-C. (Eds.). (2013). *Real talk: Reality television and discourse analysis in action*. Palgrave Macmillan. https://link.springer.com/book/10.1057/9781137313461. Accessed 10 October 2018
Martin, J. R. (1992). *English text: System and structure*. John Benjamins Publishing Company.
Martin, J. R. (1999). Grace: The logogenesis of freedom. *Discourse Studies, 1*(1), 29–56. https://doi.org/10.1177/1461445699001001003
Martin, J. R. (2000). Beyond exchange: APPRAISAL systems in English. In S. Hunston & G. Thompson (Eds.), *Evaluation in text: Authorial stance and the construction of discourse* (pp. 142–175). Oxford University Press.
Martin, J. R. (2008a). Innocence: Realisation, instantiation and individuation in a Botswanan town. In A. Mahboob & N. K. Knight (Eds.), *Questioning linguistics* (pp. 32–76). Cambridge Scholars Publishing.
Martin, J. R. (2008b). Tenderness: Realisation and Instantiation in a Botswanan Town. In N. Nørgaard (Ed.), *Systemic functional linguistics in use* (Odense working papers in language and communication) (pp. 30–62).
Martin, J. R. (2009a). Language, register and genre. In C. Coffin, T. Lillis, & K. O'Halloran (Eds.), *Applied linguistics methods: A reader* (1st ed., pp. 1–27). Routledge. https://www.routledge.com/Applied-Linguistics-Methods-A-Reader-1st-Edition/Coffin-Lillis-OHalloran/p/book/9780415545457. Accessed 4 June 2019
Martin, J. R. (2009b). Realisation, instantiation and individuation: Some thoughts on identity in youth justice conferencing. *DELTA: Documentação de Estudos em Lingüística Teórica e Aplicada, 25*(SPE), 549–583. https://doi.org/10.1590/S0102-44502009000300002
Martin, J. R. (2010). Semantic variation: Modelling realisation, instantiation and individuation in social semiosis. In M. Bednarek & J. R. Martin (Eds.), *New discourse on language: Functional perspectives on multimodality, identity, and affiliation* (pp. 1–34). Bloomsbury Publishing.
Martin, J. R., & White, P. R. R. (2005). *The language of evaluation: Appraisal in English*. Palgrave Macmillan.

Meier, T., et al. (2021). I blame you, I hear you: Couples' pronoun use in conflict and dyadic coping. *Journal of Social and Personal Relationships*, 02654075211029721. https://doi.org/10.1177/02654075211029721
Metz, M. (2021). Ideology, identity, and pedagogy in English language arts teachers' linguistic styling in U.S. classrooms. *Linguistics and Education, 64*, 100942. https://doi.org/10.1016/j.linged.2021.100942
Morikawa, N. (2019). #YesAllWomen's language: Women's style shifting in feminist discourse on Twitter. *Discourse, Context & Media, 28*, 112–120. https://doi.org/10.1016/j.dcm.2018.11.001
O'Donnell, M. (2008). Demonstration of the UAM CorpusTool for text and image annotation. In *Proceedings of the ACL-08: HLT demo session. ACL-HLT 2008* (pp. 13–16). Association for Computational Linguistics. https://www.aclweb.org/anthology/P08-4004. Accessed: 23 June 2021
O'Donnell, M. (2014). Exploring identity through appraisal analysis: A corpus annotation methodology. *Linguistics and the Human Sciences, 9*(1), 95–116. https://doi.org/10.1558/lhs.v9i1.95
Oetzel, J. G., & Ting-Toomey, S. (Eds.). (2013). *The SAGE handbook of conflict communication: Integrating theory, research, and practice* (2nd ed.). SAGE Publications.
Pizer, G. (2021). To be seen and/or heard: audience design in bimodal bilingual families. *International Journal of Bilingual Education and Bilingualism* [Preprint]. https://www.tandfonline.com/doi/abs/10.1080/13670050.2018.1517723. Accessed 11 September 2025.
Poynton, C. M. (1989). *Language and gender: Making the difference*. Oxford University Press.
Poynton, C. M. (1990). *Address and the semiotics of social relations*. PhD Thesis, University of Sydney. https://ses.library.usyd.edu.au/handle/2123/2297. Accessed 6 January 2020
Pratt, T. (2023). Affect in sociolinguistic style. *Language in Society, 52*(1), 1–26. https://doi.org/10.1017/S0047404521000774
R Core Team. (2025). *R: A language and environment for statistical computing*. R Foundation for Statistical Computing. http://www.r-project.org/
Rahim, M. A. (1983). A measure of styles of handling interpersonal conflict. *Academy of Management Journal, 26*(2), 368–376. https://doi.org/10.5465/255985
Rahim, M. A. (2023). *Managing conflict in organizations* (5th ed.). Routledge. https://doi.org/10.4324/9781003285861
Rahim, M. A., & Magner, N. R. (1995). Confirmatory factor analysis of the styles of handling interpersonal conflict: First-order factor model and its invariance across groups. *Journal of Applied Psychology, 80*(1), 122–132. https://doi.org/10.1037/0021-9010.80.1.122
Read, B. L., & Michelson, E. (2018). Village dispute mediation in China, 2002–10: An enduring institution amid rural change. *Asian Journal of Law and Society, 5*(2), 433–452. https://doi.org/10.1017/als.2018.6
Rickford, J. R., & Mcnair-Knox, F. (1994). Addressee-and topic-influenced style shift: A quantitative sociolinguistic study. In D. Biber & E. Finegan (Eds.), *Sociolinguistic perspectives on register* (p. 0). Oxford University Press. https://doi.org/10.1093/oso/9780195083644.003.0011
Sandow, R. J. (2022). Attention, identity and linguistic capital: Inverted style-shifting in Anglo-Cornish dialect lexis. *English Language & Linguistics, 26*(4), 677–695. https://doi.org/10.1017/S136067432100040X
Schilling-Estes, N. (2002). Investigating stylistic variation. In J. K. Chambers, P. Trudgill, & N. Schilling-Estes (Eds.), *The handbook of language variation and change* (1st ed., pp. 375–401). Blackwell Publishing Ltd.. https://doi.org/10.1002/9780470756591.ch15
Shei, C. (2013). How "real" is reality television in China? On the success of a Chinese dating programme. In N. Lorenzo-Dus & P. G.-C. Blitvich (Eds.), *Real talk: Reality television and discourse analysis in action* (pp. 43–65). Palgrave Macmillan. https://doi.org/10.1057/9781137313461_4
Soukup, B. (2013). Austrian dialect as a metonymic device: A cognitive sociolinguistic investigation of Speaker Design and its perceptual implications. *Journal of Pragmatics, 52*, 72–82. https://doi.org/10.1016/j.pragma.2012.12.018

Speakman, J., & Ryals, L. (2010). A re-evaluation of conflict theory for the management of multiple, simultaneous conflict episodes. *International Journal of Conflict Management, 21*(2), 186–201. https://doi.org/10.1108/10444061011037404

Stewart, K. A., & Maxwell, M. M. (2010). *Storied conflict talk: Narrative construction in mediation*. John Benjamins Publishing.

Stratton, J. M. (2022). Tapping into German adjective variation: A variationist sociolinguistic approach. *Journal of Germanic Linguistics, 34*(1), 63–102. https://doi.org/10.1017/S1470542721000088

Su, H., & Hunston, S. (2019a). Adjective complementation patterns and judgement: Aligning lexical-grammatical and discourse-semantic approaches in appraisal research. *Text & Talk, 39*(3), 415–439. https://doi.org/10.1515/text-2019-2031

Su, H., & Hunston, S. (2019b). Language patterns and attitude revisited: Adjective patterns, attitude and appraisal. *Functions of Language, 26*(3), 343–371. https://doi.org/10.1075/fol.16030.su

Tagliamonte, S. A. (2012). *Variationist sociolinguistics: Change, observation, interpretation*. Wiley-Blackwell. https://www.wiley.com/en-us/Variationist+Sociolinguistics%3A+Change%2C+Observation%2C+Interpretation-p-9781405135900. Accessed 9 February 2025

Tann, K. (2010). Imagining communities: A multifunctional approach to identity management in texts. In M. Bednarek & J. R. Martin (Eds.), *New discourse on language: Functional perspectives on multimodality, identity and affiliation* (pp. 163–194). Bloomsbury Publishing.

Tann, K. (2012). The language of identity discourse: Introducing a systemic functional framework for iconography. *Linguistics and the Human Sciences, 8*(3), 10071. https://journals.equinoxpub.com/OLDLHS/article/view/10071. Accessed 8 April 2021

Thomas, K. W. (1976). Conflict and conflict management. In M. D. Dunnett (Ed.), *Handbook of industrial and organizational psychology* (pp. 889–935). Rand McNally.

Thomas, K. W. (1992). Conflict and conflict management: Reflections and update. *Journal of Organizational Behavior, 13*(3), 265–274. https://doi.org/10.1002/job.4030130307

Thomas, K. W., & Kilmann, R. H. (1978). Comparisons of four instruments measuring conflict behavior. *Psychological Reports, 42*(3), 1139–1145.

Thomas, K. W., & Kilmann, R. H. (2008). Thomas-Kilmann conflict mode. *TKI Profile and Interpretive Report, 1*, 1–11.

Tupala, M. (2019). Applying quantitative appraisal analysis to the study of institutional discourse: The case of EU migration documents. *Functional Linguistics, 6*(1), 2. https://doi.org/10.1186/s40554-018-0067-7

White, P. R. R. (1998). *Telling Media Tales: The news story as rhetoric*. Doctoral Thesis, University of Sydney.

White, P. R. R. (2000). Dialogue and inter-subjectivity: Reinterpreting the semantics of modality and hedging. In M. Coulthard, J. Cotterill, & F. E. Rock (Eds.), *Working with dialog* (pp. 67–80). Max Niemeyer Verlag.

White, P. R. R. (2002). Appraisal - The language of evaluation and stance. In J. Verschueren et al. (Eds.), *The handbook of pragmatics* (pp. 1–23). Amsterdam.

White, P. R. R. (2003). Beyond modality and hedging: A dialogic view of the language of intersubjective stance. *Text, 23*(2), 259–284. https://doi.org/10.1515/text.2003.011

White, P. R. R. (2008). Praising and blaming, applauding and disparaging - Solidarity, audience positioning and the linguistic of evaluative disposition. In G. Antos, E. Ventola, & T. Weber (Eds.), *Handbook of interpersonal communication* (Handbooks of applied linguistics) (pp. 567–594). Mouton de Gruyter.

White, P. R. R. (2012). Exploring the axiological workings of "reporter voice" news stories—Attribution and attitudinal positioning. *Discourse, Context & Media, 1*(2–3), 57–67. https://doi.org/10.1016/j.dcm.2012.10.004

White, P. R. R. (2016). Evaluative contents in verbal communication. In *Verbal communication*. De Gruyter Mouton. https://doi.org/10.1515/9783110255478-006

White, P. R. R. (2020). The putative reader in mass media persuasion – Stance, argumentation and ideology. *Discourse & Communication, 14*(4), 404–423. https://doi.org/10.1177/1750481320910512

White, P. R. R. (2021). Textual anticipation and the putative reader in persuasive discourse. *Journal of Foreign Languages, 44*(1), 2–20.

White, P. R. R. (2025). Appraisal theory and the analysis of point of view in news and views journalism – Unpacking journalistic "persuasiveness". *Language & Communication, 100*, 95–107. https://doi.org/10.1016/j.langcom.2024.11.005

Wolfram, W. (2017). Dialect in society. In F. Coulmas (Ed.), *The handbook of sociolinguistics* (pp. 107–126). Blackwell Publishing. https://doi.org/10.1002/9781405166256.ch7

Xu, Q., & Jing, Y. (2024). Ambient identity construction via massive anonymous danmu comments. *Language Sciences, 104*, 101631. https://doi.org/10.1016/j.langsci.2024.101631

Zappavigna, M. (2011a). Ambient affiliation: A linguistic perspective on Twitter. *New Media & Society, 13*(5), 788–806. https://doi.org/10.1177/1461444810385097

Zappavigna, M. (2011b). Visualizing logogenesis: Preserving the dynamics of meaning. In S. Dreyfus, S. Hood, & M. Stenglin (Eds.), *Semiotic margins: Meaning in multimodalites* (pp. 211–228). Continuum. http://sro.library.usyd.edu.au:80/handle/10765/108502. Accessed 11 July 2018

Zappavigna, M. (2012). *Discourse of Twitter and social media: How to use language to create affiliation on the web.* Continuum. https://www.bloomsbury.com/us/discourse-of-twitter-and-social-media-9781441141866/. Accessed 1 August 2020

Zappavigna, M. (2014a). Ambient affiliation in microblogging: Bonding around the quotidian. *Media International Australia, 151*(1), 97–103. https://doi.org/10.1177/1329878X1415100113

Zappavigna, M. (2014b). Enacting identity in microblogging through ambient affiliation. *Discourse & Communication, 8*(2), 209–228. https://doi.org/10.1177/1750481313510816

Zappavigna, M. (2018). *Searchable talk: Hashtags and social media metadiscourse*. Bloomsbury.

Zappavigna, M. (2019). Ambient affiliation and #Brexit. In V. Koller, S. Kopf, & M. Miglbauer (Eds.), *Discourses of Brexit* (pp. 48–68). Routledge. https://doi.org/10.4324/9781351041867-4

Zappavigna, M. (2021). Ambient affiliation in comments on YouTube videos: Communing around values about ASMR. *Journal of Foreign Languages, 44*(1), 21–40.

Zappavigna, M. (2022). Social media quotation practices and ambient affiliation: Weaponising ironic quotation for humorous ridicule in political discourse. *Journal of Pragmatics, 191*, 98–112. https://doi.org/10.1016/j.pragma.2021.12.003

Zappavigna, M. (2023). Digital intimacy and ambient embodied copresence in YouTube videos: Construing visual and aural perspective in ASMR role play videos. *Visual Communication, 22*(2), 297–321. https://doi.org/10.1177/1470357220928102

Zappavigna, M. (2025). "I'm sorry Dave, I'm afraid I can't do that": Moral regulation in refusals by LLM chatbots. *New Media & Society* [Preprint]. https://journals.sagepub.com/doi/full/10.1177/14614448251356686. Accessed 11 September 2025.

Zappavigna, M., & Martin, J. R. (2018a). #Communing affiliation: Social tagging as a resource for aligning around values in social media. *Discourse, Context & Media, 22*, 4–12. https://doi.org/10.1016/j.dcm.2017.08.001

Zappavigna, M., & Martin, J. R. (2018b). *Discourse and diversionary justice*. Palgrave Macmillan.

Zheng, Y. D., & Stewart, N. (2024). Improving EFL students' cultural awareness: Reframing moral dilemmatic stories with ChatGPT. *Computers and Education: Artificial Intelligence, 6*, 100223. https://doi.org/10.1016/j.caeai.2024.100223

Chapter 2
Semiotic Selves: Goffman Meets Systemic Functional Linguistics

Contents

1 Introduction

As outlined in the previous chapter, the overarching theme of this study is the discursive self-presentation by the disputants in my dataset of marital conflict resolution exchanges—and, specifically, those aspects of self-presentation associated with what I have termed attitudinal disposition. This theme entails two main topic areas: (1) discursive self-presentation and (2) tendencies in the use of the evaluative meaning-making resources which I am proposing to be crucial in shaping certain aspects of this self-presentation. This chapter is concerned with the prior scholarly literature which has laid the theoretical foundations for my conceptualisation of the discursive self-presentation and for the treatments of the resources of evaluative meaning-making by which I investigated presentations of the self in my dataset.

The chapter is divided into two sections, each addressing a key area of inquiry. Firstly, Sect. 2 explores the concept of discursive self-presentation within Goffman's dramaturgical framework, offering insight into *what* constitutes discursive

Q. Xu, *Appraisal Approach to Conflict Styles*, The M.A.K. Halliday Library Functional Linguistics Series, https://doi.org/10.1007/978-981-95-6256-5_2

self-presentation under my research design. The chapter then attends the second topic area, that is, evaluative language. Section 3 delves into the theoretical foundations of SFL that guided my analysis of evaluative language in the context of interpersonal communication. This section examines *how* SFL conceptualises the interpersonal functionality of language, particularly with regards to the role of evaluative meaning making in constructing social relationships.

2 What Is Discursive Self-Presentation

2.1 Dramaturgical View of 'Self' and 'Self-Presentation'

An ideal investigation of the 'discursive self-presentation' should start with a definition of the word 'self' because different conceptualisations of the 'self' will lead to entirely different research designs and conclusions. As noted, among the various approaches to 'self' in circulation, this study's conceptualisation of the 'self' is grounded in Erving Goffman's (1959, 1967) dramaturgical view of human social interaction. By quoting Robert Ezra Park, Goffman explicitly states that the 'self' is defined by the role an individual plays in a particular situation.

> [...] the word person, in its first meaning, is a mask. It is rather a recognition of the fact that everyone is always and everywhere, more or less consciously, playing a role... It is in these roles that we know each other; it is in these roles that we know ourselves. [...] this mask is our truer self, the self we would like to be. [...] We come into the world as individuals, achieve character, and become persons.
> (Park, 1950, pp. 249–250, as cited in Goffman, 1959, pp. 19–20)

In simple words, Goffman's dramaturgy conceptualises the 'self' as a stage performance in social interaction. The 'self' is not an individual and private concept but a shared and public reality with its primary existence in social interaction (Torpey & Johnson, 2013). An individual, as an actor in social interactions, performs different roles in different situations. To sustain their performance, the individual presents particular aspects of the self in each situation, by which the individual guides and controls the impression the others form of the individual. The 'self' is in the performance. The 'self-presentation' is the performance. Accordingly, disputing in family dispute resolutions is a performative act, and disputants' utterances as such are modes of self-presentation.

The dramaturgical view on 'self' and 'self-presentation' offers useful guidance for my project by providing theoretical foundation in the following four aspects. Firstly, it provided a theoretical rationale for exploring one's publicly presented personhood via pure linguistic analysis. According to Benwell and Stokoe (2006), Goffman's work has its roots in the American Pragmatism, including Mead's (1934) endeavour 'to show that mind and the self are without residue social emergents; and that language, in the form of the vocal gesture, provides the mechanism for their emergence' (Mead, 1934, p. xiv). Given that interactions primarily take place through discourse, actual instances of language use provide linguistic specifics and empirical evidence for 'the discursive production of selves' (Davies & Harré, 1990; Harré, 1991). A person's identity is 'produced in and through the clusters of discursive practices of self-presentation' (Harré, 1991, p. 53). For this study, understanding the personhood of the dispute resolution participants required focusing solely on their language use within he discourse. The disputants' selves were constructed within the discursive practice—that is, the dispute interactions, per se. In other words, the disputants' discursive self-presentation in family dispute resolution interactions—or at least key aspects of that discursive self-presentation—could be practically examined by identifying and characterising repeated patterns in the disputants' use of evaluative language during those interactions. There was no need to look outside of the text in search for some pre-established identity labels.

The second aspect of the guidance provided by this dramaturgical view was that it pointed me to towards an awareness of the multiplicity of selfhood. Goffman's dramaturgy permits recognising the possibility of multiple selves in three senses. One sense is that the one unified and continuous self can be presented differently in different situations, as noted by Davies and Harré: 'the very same person experiences and displays that aspect of self that is involved in the continuity of a multiplicity of selves' (1990, pp. 46–47). Secondly, it recognised the possibility of multiple interpretations arising from the same self-presentation practice due to the unique cultural resources held by each interaction participant and observer. This understanding highlighted how different individuals can perceive the same utterance in distinct ways, leading to potentially multiple 'selves'. The third sense of multiplicity involves change in 'footing', which arises when 'participant's alignment, or set, or stance, or posture, or projected self is somehow at issue' (Goffman, 1981, p. 128). Given this understanding, it was likely that disputants would present different aspects of themselves or modify their regular presentation as the dispute resolution interaction progressed. In summary, the multiplicity of selfhood afforded by the dramaturgical view of 'self' encompasses a more constant 'self', more emergent and temporary 'selves', different interpretations of these 'selves', and changes in 'selves' within interactions. This perspective guided me to consider all these aspects of 'self' when analysing the disputants' self-presentation in my dataset of family dispute interactions.

The third insight from the dramaturgical perspective is derived from Goffman's distinction between 'performance' and 'front'. He defines 'performance' as 'all the activity of an individual which occurs during a period marked by his continuous presence before a particular set of observers and which has some influence on the observers' (Goffman, 1959, p. 22). Goffman uses the term 'front' to refer to a specific 'part of the individual's performance which regularly functions in a general and fixed fashion to define the situation for those who observe the performance' (Goffman, 1959, p. 22). While some scholars argue that the limitation of dramaturgy is to construe people 'as actors with lines already written and their roles determined by the particular play they find themselves in' (Davies & Harré, 1990, p. 52), I view the 'limitation' differently. I considered the distinction between 'performance' and 'front' as affording a possibility of identifying both general tendencies of disputants' self-presentation as a conventionalised way of behaving in the given situation and the specific choices made by each disputant or groups of disputants as their individualised and unique discursive styles. Any recurring patterns among all disputants, if there were any, could be interpreted as the 'collective representation' (Goffman, 1959, p. 27) of how disputants typically behave. In contrast, tendencies in the disputants' evaluative meaning-making arrangements could be interpreted as the patterned variations in the disputants' discursive self-presentation.

The last key insight from Goffman's dramaturgical view of 'self' lies in its emphasis on the co-constructedness of 'self-presentation'. For Goffman, self-presentation is a duet. On one hand, individuals perform by 'giving' or 'giving off' (Goffman, 1959, p. 2) expressions which make an impression on the observers. On the other hand, observers perceive and 'take seriously the impression that is fostered before them' (Goffman, 1959, p. 17). Consequently, the meaning of self-presentation does not lie in an individual's conscious awareness or self-perception of the performance. Rather, it lies in the observer's impression or interpretation of the performance. This notion of co-constructionism informed my reading position as a researcher in the exploration of the disputants' self-presentation. Although I was not in the immediate presence of the disputant resolution interaction, I was beyond doubt an observer of both the disputants' presentation and of those immediately involved in the interaction. Therefore, my role as an observer, framed by this dramaturgical view of 'self,' was to seriously consider the impressions the disputants' self-presentation might leave me with. The 'seriousness' of this process was reflected in the principled and systematic linguistic analysis I adopted when analysing the disputants' speech. My role as an observer did not, therefore, involve trying to decipher or decode what the disputants 'really meant' by their self-presentation, but rather aimed at identifying the linguistic cues they used for impression management. Moreover, Goffman notes that it is commonplace when the observers 'may misunderstand the meaning that a cue was designed to convey, or may read an embarrassing meaning into gestures or events that were accidental, inadvertent, or incidental and not meant by the performer to carry any meaning whatsoever' (1959, p. 51). To successfully stage a character, the performer is responsible for employing specific techniques of 'impression management'. The performers 'mobilise his activity so that it will convey an impression to others which it is in his interests to convey' (Goffman, 1959, p. 4), which means that I, as an observer and discourse analyst, was responsible for identifying the linguistic cues used by disputants for their 'impression management' and fostering impressions accordingly. Therefore, the disputants' discursive self-presentation was co-constructed not only between them but also with those immediately involved in the interaction and with myself as an outside observer.

2.2 *Defining the 'Self' and 'Self-Presentation'*

Drawing on this notion of dramaturgy (in contrast to the classical approach to selfhood, which views 'self' as a unified, coherent, and immaterial subject of consciousness (Anderson et al., 2020; Olson, 2020)), I understand the 'self' as contingent and temporary, arising from social interactions. I perceived 'self' to be constructed, defined, and perceived through the individual's engagement in performing particular social actions (not necessarily pre-established social roles). Accordingly, I understood 'self-presentation' to be the product and the process of the individual's engagement in social interaction.

In this sense, 'self' and social interaction are in a dialectical relationship. Family dispute resolutions are occasions whereby issues of self-presentation have to be managed by disputants primarily through discourse processes. What disputants *are* is partly constituted by how they discursively present themselves in the dispute resolution interactions. According to the SFL-/Appraisal-based textual identity studies (see Chap. 1 for details), one prominent aspect of their self-presentation lies in how the disputants evaluatively positioned themselves and how they were evaluatively positioned: what types of attitudes they used or favoured and how they framed these attitudes.

This conceptualisation of the 'self' sets the current study apart from much existing discourse-based identity research, which generally assumes a 'transcendental self' or 'true self' external to the discourse (see Benwell & Stokoe, 2006 for an overview). Such research explores certain distinct linguistic features which are culturally recognised as indexical of speaker attributes entailed by the external 'self', such as conventionalised social membership categories of ethnicity, gender, class, or regionality (e.g., the 'sociolinguistics' or 'variationist' linguistics studies discussed in the previous chapter). These linguistic features can also project stereotypical character attributes such as 'nerdiness' (Bednarek, 2012), 'otherness' (Günthner, 2007), 'men-ness' (Georgakopoulou, 2007), and 'sexual suggestiveness' (Starr et al., 2020). Typical examples include an Australian 'self' signalled by the use of the address term of 'mate' (Rendle-Short, 2009) versus an American young masculine 'self' indexed by the use of the address term of 'dude' (Kiesling, 2004), or a Beijing cosmopolitan 'self' constructed by the frequent deployment of rhotacisation (Zhang, 2008) versus a cosmopolitan Taiwanese or Hongkonger 'self' identified by de-rhotacisation (Zhang, 2018). In contrast, my study was not concerned with aspects of 'self' that may be associated with such indexicality. Likewise, it did not take for granted that there was a 'self' necessarily associated with these speakers being disputants in these family conflict resolution exchanges. I did not assume a category of selfhood associated with my speakers being spouses involved in marital conflict. My analysis neither aimed to identify the indexicality between certain linguistic features and some assumed 'disputant-ness'. For this study, the disputants' 'selves' were constructed by their discursive practices in actually situated interactions, with the properties of the disputants being analysed as emergent from the family dispute interaction as such. The disputants' identity began 'to develop when individuals interact with others and play roles' (Aboulafia, 2020). The disputants' self-presentation was discourse-sensitive and discursively constructed.

So far, this section has dealt with the theoretical foundations concerning the question of *what*—what is disputants' discursive self-presentation? The following section addresses the question of *how*—the ways in which relevant prior literature influenced *how* I went about relating tendencies in the disputants' deployment of the resources of evaluative meaning to the discursive self-presentations thereby being enacted.

3 How to Unpack Discursive Self-Presentation

This section focuses on how, by reference to patterns of deployment of evaluative meaning, I went about unpacking the disputants' discursive self-presentation, as conceptualised in the previous section. It is concerned with the theoretical foundations I relied on when undertaking this process, which involved carrying out a principled linguistic analysis of actual situated language use in terms of the communicative participants' self-presentation.

3.1 General Semiotic Resources for Discursive Self-Presentation

First and foremost, this study viewed self-presentation as a semiotic practice: a meaning-making practice in social interaction. This view principally aligns with Goffman's dramaturgy, as well as Goffman's influencers: Peirce's and Mead's views on 'self' and self-presentation (Colapietro, 1988; Wiley, 1994). Under this view, self-presentation is a semiotic object 'always subject to interpretation by the person engaged in symbolic interaction and exchange' (Bakker, 2011, p. 187). Viewing self-presentation as a semiotic practice also aligns with SFL's view about the relationship between language users' identity and their language use. According to Halliday, the language users 'are not only **creators** of the text; we are also **created by** it. "You" and "me" are brought into being by language' (Halliday, 2002, p. 228, emphasis in original). SFL conceptualises language user's identity as a continuum extending between collective and individual along a cline of individuation (Halliday, 1978; Martin, 2009; Martin & Rose, 2007). Accordingly, my exploration of the disputants' discursive self-presentation investigated the disputants' deployment of semiotic resources available in the given culture, sub-culture, and speech community. The exploration focused on what semiotic resources were available for the disputants to mobilise in the family dispute resolution settings; and what repeated patterns could be found among multiple disputants concerning their deployment of the available semiotic resources, by which they were able to enact various discursive personae.

Multiple semiotic resources may be functional in terms of unpacking an individual's self-presentation. The semiotic resources include both linguistic and extra-linguistic meaning-making options. For example, Goffman (1959) proposes that information about the individual's self-presentation is accessible by examining the 'carriers' (or 'sign-vehicles'), including the resources for 'giving' and 'giving off' expressions. Similarly, Firth (1950) suggests that an examination of language users should cover both 'the verbal action' and 'the non-verbal action' of the interaction participants. The discursive construction of the 'self', as a semiotic event, is an event on many levels (Halliday, 2002). Generally speaking, linguistic resources refer to the linguistic choices an individual makes and the meanings realised by these linguistic choices. In contrast, the extra-linguistic resources include a list of multimodal semiotic resources, such as paralinguistic features, gestures, and body movements (Bednarek, 2010; Martin & Zappavigna, 2019; Zappavigna & Logi, 2024; Zappavigna & Martin, 2018).

That being said, it is beyond this study's scope to attend to all the semiotic resources deployed by the disputants in their self-presentation. This study focused on a narrow range of meaning-making options, which were linguistic and were associated with evaluative meaning-making.

3.2 *Evaluative Meaning-Making and Evaluative Disposition*

Briefly speaking, evaluative meaning-making is concerned with how language is used to convey and source attitudes and values and how interactants are aligned in relation to those attitudes and values (White, 2015). Among various approaches to the evaluative, such as stance and stance-taking (Du Bois, 2007; Jaffe, 2009; Kiesling, 2022) and modality (Aijmer, 2016; Giannakidou & Mari, 2021; Nuyts, 2016; Palmer, 2001; Van Der Auwera & Aguilar, 2016), I followed the theoretical account of evaluative meaning-making within the SFL paradigm, whose substantial body of Appraisal-based textual identity studies was strongly influential on the formulation of my research (see Chap. 1 for details).

SFL conceptualises evaluative meaning-making as one of the interpersonal functionalities of language. Evaluative meaning-making is concerned with issues including language user's subjectivity in the texts and intersubjectivity with voices inside and outside of the texts, language user's feelings and values and the linguistic mechanisms for sharing the feelings and values, language user's construal of textually performed identities, and their dialogical positioning of a putative audience. Notably, SFL provided my study with a systematic account of evaluative meaning-making resources—the Appraisal framework. In the Appraisal framework, the evaluative meaning-making resources are taxonomised into three systems: ATTITUDE, ENGAGEMENT, and GRADUATION, addressing different aspects of the linguistic configuration of evaluation. ATTITUDE is concerned with positive or negative assessments conveyed (i.e., via inscription) or activated (i.e., via invocation). It broadly distinguishes three types of assessments: emotional response (termed 'Affect'), evaluation of behaviour and character (termed 'Judgement'), and evaluation of things, processes and situations (termed 'Appreciation'). These higher-level categories of ATTITUDE are further divided into the more delicate subsystems. ENGAGEMENT addresses the issue of dialogic positioning and the negotiation of heteroglossic diversity. It offers several levels of distinction by reference to the degree of heteroglossic diversity allowed in the text (e.g., 'monogloss' or 'heterogloss'). The last mode of meaning, the subsystem of GRADUATION, deals with the resources for scaling the attitude or engagement options in terms of intensity (termed as 'force') or prototypicality (termed as 'focus').

There are two reasons why I chose SFL's conceptualisation of evaluative meaning-making to unpack the disputants' discursive self-presentation. The first reason is that the evaluative meaning-making resources have a well-defined position in the SFL's stratified model of language (Halliday, 1978; Halliday & Hasan, 1985; Halliday & Matthiessen, 2014), making the linguistic analysis of disputants' evaluative meaning-making manageable. As noted, discursive self-presentation can be realised and unpacked by an arguably non-exhaustive list of semiotic resources. An analysis without a strategic choice of the resources will be random and time-consuming. Under SFL's stratified model of language as social semiosis, the evaluative meaning-making resources situate on the stratum of what Halliday has termed the stratum of 'semantics' (e.g., Halliday, 1994) and Martin has termed the stratum of 'discourse semantics' (e.g., Martin, 1992; Martin & Rose, 2007). Situated between the stratum of lexicogrammar and the context plane, this stratum in SFL is broadly termed the stratum of 'meanings'. Accordingly, an analysis about the disputants' deployment of evaluative meaning-making resources orients towards the resources for meaning instead of the resources for wording. From above, the meaning on the discourse semantics stratum is '"the way into language" from context – the set of strategies for construing, enacting and presenting non-language as meaning' (Matthiessen et al., 2010, p. 189). From below, the meaning on the discourse semantic stratum is the abstraction of 'patterns of lexicogrammatical patterns and lexicogrammar in turn addresses patterns of phonological ones' (Martin, 1992, p. 12). Therefore, by adopting the SFL's conceptualisation of evaluative meaning-making, I narrowed down my focus to exploring the patterns in the disputants' use of evaluative meanings, rather than on scrutinising the phonological and lexicogrammatical patterns in the disputants' speech.

The second reason why I chose SFL's conceptualisation of evaluative meaning-making is that analysing patterns of the speaker/writer's use of evaluative resources, particularly the attitude-associated resources, has been demonstrated as a valuable and valid perspective into the construal of authorial identity. Martin and White make it explicit that the patterns in the use of Appraisal resources within texts 'can be related to particular rhetorical effects and construct particular authorial identities or personas' (2005, p. 161). White (2008) proposes the notion of 'evaluative disposition' to address the co-occurrence patterns of Appraisal resources that constitute particular evaluative stances of the language user. Previous studies (Eggins & Slade,

1997; Don, 2007, 2017; White, 2008, 2020a; O'Donnell, 2014; Zappavigna & Martin, 2018) have attended to the construal of textual personae by reference to the speaker/writer's use of Appraisal resources in several text types, for example, movie review, youth justice conference, casual conversation, and online chats. These studies indicate that identifying and characterising the recurrent patterns in the disputants' evaluative meaning-making arrangements is a reliable approach to describe and characterise their discursive self-presentation. To be more specific, the disputants' evaluative meaning-making patterns offer three layers of analysis into their self-presentation. One layer is that by identifying clusters of evaluative meanings favoured or avoided by individual disputants and recurrent patterns among multiple disputants, I could distinguish and characterise different ways of disputants' self-presentation in functionally comparable texts. The recurrent patterns shared by multiple disputants could be interpreted as discursively construed attitudinal disposition types available in the given text type. The second layer is that analysis of the disputants' evaluative working offers an insight into their subjective positions being advanced and negotiated in the text. The subjective positions reveal their authorial stances towards the immediate communicative participants—the disputants' self, the others, and the self in relation to others. The third layer of analysis is to unpack the disputants' negotiation of dialogical positioning and their construal of a putative audience (White, 2020b, 2021). The disputants' evaluative arrangements indicate their positioning of the self and the others in the communication. The evaluative arrangements also reveal the disputants' presumptions about the intended or assumed audience regarding the degree of solidarity and their interactive engagement with the putative audience. In short, all these three layers of analysis offer pivotal and nuanced insights into what is clearly a key aspect of the disputants' discursive self-presentation.

It needs to be noted, as outlined in the previous chapter, that I went beyond the existing SFL/Appraisal literature by conducting a multivariate analysis how the speaker/writer's use of evaluative language and their enactment of an evaluative textual identity. As discussed in Chap. 1 and the previous paragraph, the existing SFL/Appraisal literature has mostly used evaluative meaning-making resources to investigate the speaker/writer's construction of textual identity vis-à-vis the speaker/writer's preference for specific attitudes. Following this tradition, I investigated the disputants' self-presentation concerning the attitudinal assessments—their feelings or institutionalised feelings—what types of attitudes they conveyed and at what frequencies. However, I went beyond the prior research by attending to not only the similarities and differences across the disputants regarding their preference for any given attitude or attitudinal features but also the disputants' preference for combinations or subset of attitudes—whether some disputants deployed the same subset of attitudinal expressions in a similar fashion. Additionally, I also did not limit the exploration on 'what types of attitudes the disputants favoured', but rather extended the scope of the analysis to 'how the disputants framed their attitudes'. The analysis about the framing of the attitudes involved features from multiple systems and subsystems in the existing Appraisal framework. In Appraisal terms, it explored the tendencies in the disputants' co-articulation of key options in the ATTITUDE,

ENGAGEMENT, and GRADUATION systems. Therefore, the multivariate Appraisal analyses conducted in this research offered us a comprehensive exploration in the co-occurrence of the evaluative meaning-making options and the multidimensional relationship between the disputants' evaluative meaning-making and their enactment of a discursive persona.

Moreover, my research also contributes to the existing SFL/Appraisal literature by taking both a synoptic view and a dynamic view of the speaker/writer's use of evaluative language. As noted in Chap. 1 and the previous sections, most existing SFL/Appraisal-based identity studies examined the speaker/writer's use of evaluative language when their speech was considered as a complete text. In my study, I also investigated 'how the disputants conveyed the attitudes in an unfolding interaction'. The latter perspective added a dynamic element to the disputants' evaluative meaning-making practice. The disputants were treated as immediate interactants, whose deployment of evaluative meaning-making resources were restrained by the changing of the context of situation and the evaluative meaning-making practice of the other interactants. My analysis particularly focused on the stability/fluidity of the disputants' use of evaluative language, that is, the tendencies in their deployment of attitude-associated resources in an unfolding text. What attitudes did the disputants favour at different mediation stages and when they were interacting with different people? Did the disputants deploy the same attitude-associated resources throughout the extended Problem Discussion stage when the context of situation remained unchanged? If they had different attitudinal preferences as the dispute resolution unfolded, were there any patterns in the disputants' shift of preference, what might motivate the shifts? Accordingly, based on the data features, I conducted a comprehensive exploration on the stability/fluidity of the disputants' attitudinal arrangements from a dynamic perspective. The findings of this perspective revealed patterns of consistent shifts in the disputants' use of the evaluative language across different mediation stages and when they were interacting with different addressee. The findings also suggested a certain degree of fluidity in the disputants' attitudinal preference even when the context of situation arguably remained the same. In other words, the disputants were found to present different 'selves' or different aspects of the 'self' when their language use was considered against an unfolding timeframe. Therefore, my study developed the SFL/Appraisal scholarship by exploring the connections between patterns in the stability of a speaker's attitudinal preference and their discursive identity: how tendencies in the way a speaker shifts their attitudinal arrangements can be related to their presentation of the self.

4 Chapter Summary

This chapter has established the theoretical foundations for this book. Drawing on Goffman's notion of dramaturgy, I have defined 'self' as contingent and constructed through an individual's engagement in particular social actions. Accordingly, 'self-presentation' was seen as semiotic practice, which can be investigated by looking into the individual's deployment of semiotic resources in actual situated interactions. After reviewing the theoretical concepts for unpacking the disputants' discursive self-presentation, the chapter has specified the semiotic resources focused on in the analyses being reported here: the evaluative meaning-making resources. These theoretical and methodological considerations were pivotal to my attempts at systematically tracing the disputants' discursive self-presentation in adversarial interactions.

It was intended that this chapter would serve as the theoretical basis for the approach I adopted to explore the disputants' discursive self-presentation. Chapter 1 provided a preliminary overview of the nature of the project's data and its analytical methodology. The next chapter offers a more comprehensive discussion of these.

References

Aboulafia, M. (2020, Spring). George Herbert Mead. In E.N. Zalta (ed.) *The Stanford encyclopedia of philosophy*. Metaphysics Research Lab, Stanford University. https://plato.stanford.edu/archives/spr2020/entries/mead/. Accessed 13 January 2021.

Aijmer, K. (2016). Modality and mood in functional linguistic approaches. In J. Nuyts & J. Van Der Auwera (Eds.), *The Oxford handbook of modality and mood* (pp. 496–514). Oxford University Press. https://doi.org/10.1093/oxfordhb/9780199591435.013.37

Anderson, E., Willett, C., & Meyers, D. (2020, Spring) Feminist perspectives on the self. In E.N. Zalta (ed.) *The Stanford encyclopedia of philosophy*. Metaphysics Research Lab, Stanford University. https://plato.stanford.edu/archives/spr2020/entries/feminism-self/. Accessed 12 January 2021.

Bakker, J. I. H. (2011). The "semiotic self": From Peirce and Mead to Wiley and Singer. *The American Sociologist, 42*(2), 187–206. https://doi.org/10.1007/s12108-011-9140-3

Bednarek, M. (2010). *The language of fictional television: Drama and identity*. Continuum.

Bednarek, M. (2012). Constructing "nerdiness": Characterisation in "the big bang theory". *Multilingua: Journal of Cross-Cultural and Interlanguage Communication, 31*(2), 199–229. https://doi.org/10.1515/multi-2012-0010

Benwell, B., & Stokoe, E. H. (2006). *Discourse and identity*. Edinburgh University Press.

Colapietro, V. M. (1988). *Peirce's approach to the self: A semiotic perspective on human subjectivity*. SUNY Press.

Davies, B., & Harré, R. (1990). Positioning: The discursive production of selves. *Journal for the Theory of Social Behaviour, 20*(1), 43–63.

Don, A. (2007). An approach to the analysis of textual identity through profiles of evaluative disposition. In *ASFLA 2007 proceedings*.

Don, A. (2017). Stance-taking and the construal of textual persona in written contexts: Social contact revisited. *Linguistics and the Human Sciences, 13*(1–2), 70–95. https://doi.org/10.1558/lhs.30713

Du Bois, J. W. (2007). The stance triangle. In R. Englebretson (Ed.), *Stancetaking in discourse: Subjectivity, evaluation, interaction* (pp. 139–182). John Benjamins Publishing.

Eggins, S., & Slade, D. (1997). *Analysing casual conversation*. Cassell.

Firth, J. R. (1950). Personality and language in society. *The Sociological Review*, 37–52.

Georgakopoulou, A. (2007). Positioning in style: Men in women's jointly produced stories. In P. Auer (Ed.), *Style and social identities: Alternative approaches to linguistic heterogeneity* (pp. 393–418). De Gruyter Mouton.

Giannakidou, A., & Mari, A. (2021). *Truth and veridicality in grammar and thought: Mood, modality, and propositional attitudes*. University of Chicago Press. https://doi.org/10.7208/chicago/9780226763484.001.0001
Goffman, E. (1959). *The presentation of self in everyday life*. Doubleday Anchor Books.
Goffman, E. (1967). *Interaction ritual: Essays in face to face behavior*. Patheon Books.
Goffman, E. (1981). *Forms of talk*. University of Pennsylvania Press.
Günthner, S. (2007). The construction of otherness in reported dialogues as a resource for identity work. In P. Auer (Ed.), *Style and social identities: Alternative approaches to linguistic heterogeneity* (pp. 419–444). De Gruyter Mouton.
Halliday, M. A. K. (1978). *Language as a social semiotic: The social interpretation of language and meaning*. University Park Press.
Halliday, M. A. K. (1994). *An introduction to functional grammar* (2nd ed.). E. Arnold.
Halliday, M. A. K. (2002). So you say "pass"...thank you three muchly. In J. J. Webster (Ed.), *Linguistic studies of text and discourse. Collected works of M.A.K. Halliday* (Vol. 2, pp. 228–254). Continuum.
Halliday, M. A. K., & Hasan, R. (1985). *Language, context, and text: Aspects of language in a social-semiotic perspective*. Deakin University.
Halliday, M. A. K., & Matthiessen, C. M. I. M. (2014). *Halliday's introduction to functional grammar* (4th ed.). Routledge.
Harré, R. (1991). The discursive production of selves. *Theory & Psychology, 1*(1), 51–63. https://doi.org/10.1177/0959354391011004
Jaffe, A. (Ed.). (2009). *Stance: Sociolinguistic perspectives*. Oxford University Press.
Kiesling, S. F. (2004). DUDE. *American Speech, 79*(3), 281–305. https://doi.org/10.1215/00031283-79-3-281
Kiesling, S. F. (2022). Stance and stancetaking. *Annual Review of Linguistics, 8*, 409–426. https://doi.org/10.1146/annurev-linguistics-031120-121256
Martin, J. R. (1992). *English text: System and structure*. John Benjamins Publishing Company.
Martin, J. R. (2009). Realisation, instantiation and individuation: Some thoughts on identity in youth justice conferencing. *DELTA: Documentação de Estudos em Lingüística Teórica e Aplicada, 25*(SPE), 549–583. https://doi.org/10.1590/S0102-44502009000300002
Martin, J. R., & Rose, D. (2007). *Working with discourse* (2nd ed.). Continuum.
Martin, J. R., & White, P. R. R. (2005). *The language of evaluation: Appraisal in English*. Palgrave Macmillan.
Martin, J. R., & Zappavigna, M. (2019). Embodied meaning: A systemic functional perspective on paralanguage. *Functional Linguistics, 6*(1), 1–33. https://doi.org/10.1186/s40554-018-0065-9
Matthiessen, C. M. I. M., Teruya, K., & Lam, M. (2010). *Key terms in systemic functional linguistics*. Continuum. https://www.bloomsbury.com/us/key-terms-in-systemic-functional-linguistics-9781847064400/. Accessed 20 December 2019
Mead, G. H. (1934). In C. W. Morris (Ed.), *Mind, self, and society: From the standpoint of a social behaviorist*. The University of Chicago Press.
Nuyts, J. (2016). Surveying modality and mood: An introduction. In J. Nuyts & J. Van Der Auwera (Eds.), *The Oxford handbook of modality and mood* (pp. 1–9). Oxford University Press. https://doi.org/10.1093/oxfordhb/9780199591435.013.37
O'Donnell, M. (2014). Exploring identity through appraisal analysis: A corpus annotation methodology. *Linguistics and the Human Sciences, 9*(1), 95–116. https://doi.org/10.1558/lhs.v9i1.95
Olson, E.T. (2020, Winter) Personal identity. In E.N. Zalta (ed.) *The Stanford encyclopedia of philosophy*. Metaphysics Research Lab, Stanford University. https://plato.stanford.edu/archives/win2020/entries/identity-personal/. Accessed 12 January 2021.
Palmer, F. R. (2001). *Mood and modality* (Cambridge textbooks in linguistics) (2nd ed.). Cambridge University Press.
Park, R. E. (1950). *Race and culture*. Free Press.
Rendle-Short, J. (2009). The address term mate in Australian English: Is it still a masculine term? *Australian Journal of Linguistics, 29*(2), 245–268. https://doi.org/10.1080/07268600902823110

Starr, R. L., Wang, T., & Go, C. (2020). Sexuality vs. sensuality: The multimodal construction of affective stance in Chinese ASMR performances*. *Journal of SocioLinguistics, 24*(4), 492–513. https://doi.org/10.1111/josl.12410

Torpey, M. J., & Johnson, N. H. (2013). Goffman's theory of self and the social order: Trust and conflict in an intercultural education workplace. In C. N. Candlin & J. Crichton (Eds.), *Discourses of trust* (Palgrave studies in professional and organizational discourse) (pp. 133–148). Palgrave Macmillan. https://doi.org/10.1007/978-1-137-29556-9_9

Van Der Auwera, J., & Aguilar, A. Z. (2016). The history of modality and mood. In J. Nuyts & J. Van Der Auwera (Eds.), *The Oxford handbook of modality and mood* (pp. 10–29). Oxford University Press. https://doi.org/10.1093/oxfordhb/9780199591435.013.37

White, P. R. R. (2008). Praising and blaming, applauding and disparaging - Solidarity, audience positioning and the linguistic of evaluative disposition. In G. Antos, E. Ventola, & T. Weber (Eds.), *Handbook of interpersonal communication* (Handbooks of applied linguistics) (pp. 567–594). Mouton de Gruyter.

White, P. R. R. (2015). Appraisal theory. In K. Tracy, C. Ilie, & T. Sandel (Eds.), *The international encyclopedia of language and social interaction* (pp. 1–7). John Wiley & Sons, Inc.

White, P. R. R. (2020a). Attitudinal alignments in journalistic commentary and social-media argumentation: The construction of values-based group identities in the online comments of newspaper readers. In M. Zappavigna & S. Dreyfus (Eds.), *Discourses of hope and reconciliation: J. R. Martin's contribution to systemic functional linguistics* (pp. 21–38). Bloomsbury Academic. https://doi.org/10.5040/9781350116092.ch-002

White, P. R. R. (2020b). The putative reader in mass media persuasion – Stance, argumentation and ideology. *Discourse & Communication, 14*(4), 404–423. https://doi.org/10.1177/1750481320910512

White, P. R. R. (2021). Textual anticipation and the putative reader in persuasive discourse. *Journal of Foreign Languages, 44*(1), 2–20.

Wiley, N. (1994). *The semiotic self.* University of Chicago Press.

Zappavigna, M., & Logi, L. (2024). *Emoji and social media paralanguage.* Cambridge University Press. https://doi.org/10.1017/9781009179829

Zappavigna, M., & Martin, J. R. (2018). *Discourse and diversionary justice.* Palgrave Macmillan.

Zhang, Q. (2008). Rhotacization and the "Beijing smooth operator": The social meaning of a linguistic variable1. *Journal of SocioLinguistics, 12*(2), 201–222. https://doi.org/10.1111/j.1467-9841.2008.00362.x

Zhang, Q. (2018). *Language and social change in China: Undoing commonness through cosmopolitan mandarin* (1st ed.). Routledge.

Chapter 3
Computational Appraisal in Action: Data, Methods, and Analytical Principles

Contents

1 Introduction

This chapter outlines the data and methods by which the linguistic investigation of the disputants' discursive self-presentation was performed. It first introduces the dataset, including the reality TV mediation genre from which this project sourced its data, the dataset composition, and the data's registerial features. The chapter then presents the analytical methods used for the investigation. It describes the data transcription conventions, principles for annotating Appraisal resources, and methods for measuring the disputants' 'preference' for a particular type of attitude-associated resources. Finally, the chapter introduces the data processing method, a novel approach to conducting a multivariate linguistic analysis in a computing environment using data mining methods.

Q. Xu, *Appraisal Approach to Conflict Styles*, The M.A.K. Halliday Library Functional Linguistics Series, https://doi.org/10.1007/978-981-95-6256-5_3

2 Data

2.1 Sourcing Data from Gold Medal Mediation

This research sourced its data from one Chinese reality TV mediation programme: *Gold Medal Mediation* (金牌调解), produced by Jiangxi Satellite TV Network. First aired in March 2011 and remaining popular since then, new episodes are released daily. Broadly speaking, *Gold Medal Mediation* transforms a traditional reality TV programme from an entertaining talk show into a semi-formal platform for alternative dispute resolution. It purports to assist everyday people resolve family disputes through grassroots mediation rather than relying on judicial processes. The programme has received several national awards for its faithful presentation of family ethics and social code of conduct in Chinese society, including the 'TV Landmark Top Ten Best Television Shows' awarded by the Chinese media watchdog (National Radio and Television Administration[1] and 'Top Ten Best Legal Television Shows' by China Radio and Television Association[2]). Notably, one hostess and two mediators were acknowledged as recipients of the 'National Award for Excellent People's Mediator' presented by China's Ministry of Justice.[3]

Each episode of *Gold Medal Mediation* features a hostess, two or three disputants, and a mediation panel consisting of seven members: one master mediator and six observers. The disputants are ordinary couples aiming to resolve domestic chaos and relationship turmoil, including disputes over family property, tensions between in-laws, and challenges related to filial piety. The master mediator and the observers are family relationship experts, legal advisors, psychiatrists, and social workers. In this monograph, 'mediator' is used as an umbrella term to refer to the entire mediation panel. There is no audience present on set at the TV studio (Fig. 3.1).

Gold Medal Mediation episodes follow a structured format: during the first half of the programme, the disputants are invited to discuss their conflict issues by outlining their concerns and grievances directly to the mediators. Following this discussion phase, in the second half of the episode, the mediators provide guidance and advice based on the information shared. Most episodes end up with what appear to be voluntary agreements reached among the disputants. Therefore, *Gold Medal Mediation* offers a rich source of spoken language data consisting, for example, of individual complaints, accounts of events, confrontations where individuals level accusations or defend their past actions against criticism, and feedback and advice provided by the mediators.

I chose to source my data from episodes of this one programme rather than from multiple programmes (there are currently more than ten similar conflict resolution programmes being broadcast on mainland Chinese television) because of several considerations. Firstly, focusing on one programme allows for greater consistency

[1] http://jxntv.cn/jm/pages/20121203/48681.shtml

[2] https://yule.sohu.com/20131018/n388452082.shtml

[3] http://www.jxntv.cn/jm/pages/20121109/47697.shtml

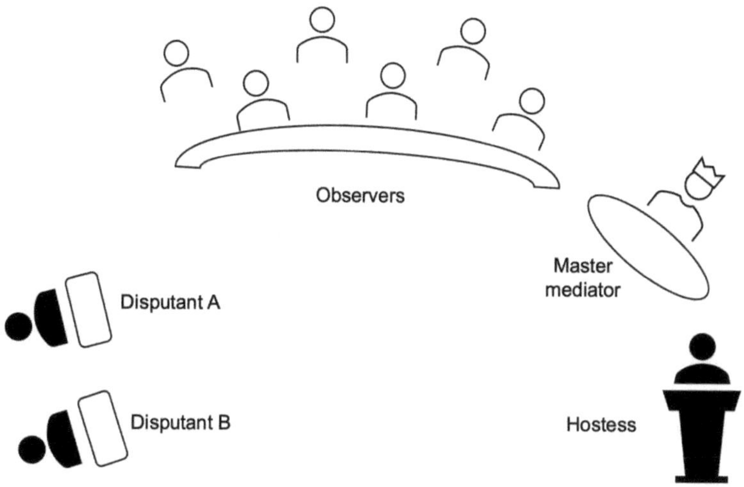

Fig. 3.1 Layout depiction of the *Gold Medal Mediation* TV studio

in production style elements that might influence the way disputants present themselves discursively. This includes factors such as episode length, time allocated to individual speakers, and physical setting of the interaction, which could all impact how individuals construct their attitudes within these settings. Furthermore, by concentrating my analysis on a single reality TV mediation programme, I can explore in detail how participants discursively present themselves in the same communicative setting and how participants articulate their values and beliefs within this specific context and examine how different analytical perspectives can shed light on various aspects of adversarial communication.

Nevertheless, my research is not about *Gold Medal Mediation* as such. This monograph is not complementary to existing discussions of the programme from a legal studies perspective (Hawes, 2024; Hawes & Kong, 2013) or content analysis from a media studies perspective (Zhang & Chen, 2017). Rather, my project used the conversational data from *Gold Medal Mediation* primarily for linguistic purposes. The core interest lies in examining how disputants construct their discursive self-presentation through the use of evaluative language in these interactions.

2.2 *Description of the Dataset*

2.2.1 Composition of the Dataset

The dataset comprises six *Gold Medal Mediation* episodes, approximately 230 min in total. All six episodes involve heterosexual couples on the verge of divorce due to alleged infidelity by one spouse. The focus of this study is exclusively on the conversational content contributed by the disputing spouses. In the discussions that follow, it will be helpful to refer to the party accused of marital wrongdoing as the 'wayward' spouse and the accuser as the 'aggrieved'. This distinction is crucial in understanding the dynamics of marital conflict interactions. The dataset includes three episodes where a wayward husband faces an aggrieved wife, and another three episodes where a wayward wife confronts an aggrieved husband (see Table 3.1 for a detailed breakdown of the episodes and their participants).

In the dataset, each disputant is assigned a disputant ID (e.g., 'Wife_H01_AW'), which consists of three components (from left to right): their marital role (wife or husband), the episode number (H01), and a two-digit code representing their waywardness status (AW). The first digit of the code tracks whether the speaker is accused of being unfaithful or is accusing their partner of infidelity This is denoted by 'W' for 'wayward' or 'A' for 'aggrieved'. The second digit indicates the speaker's marital status: 'H' for 'husband' and 'W' for 'wife'. Therefore, a disputant ID such as 'Wife_H01_AW' represents the wife in episode H01, specifically an aggrieved wife. Similarly, 'Husband_H03_WH' would indicate the husband in episode H03, specifically a wayward husband. Notably, if two participants have the same episode ID (such as both being in episode H01), they are part of the same disputing couple.

All disputants in the dataset are characterised by three common aspects that provide a comparable foundation for analysis. Firstly, all disputants are couples in heterosexual marriage with lengths of 16–30 years, indicating similar relationship dynamics as opposed to those in newlywed couples. Secondly, most speakers engage in private business, particularly family-owned businesses rather than holding positions in institutional settings such as government agencies, hospitals, or state-owned enterprises. This commonality in profession suggests that the disputants share a similar socio-cultural background, which could shape the frames of their beliefs, values, and potentially, behaviours. Finally, due to the identical marriage lengths of 16–30 years across all couples, along with having adolescent or adult children, the speakers are likely to belong to the same age range of 40–55. Based on these similarities, this monograph focuses on investigating any recurring patterns in the disputants' use of evaluative language and how these might be related to their discursive self-presentation. Variations in deployment of evaluative meaning-making resources based on social or demographic factors such as age, gender, or socio-economic status are not examined.

2.2.2 Stages of Each Episode

The episodes within the dataset typically last approximately 38–40 min. Each episode is divided into five mediation stages: Pre-mediation, Problem Discussion, Group mediation, Private Mediation, and Post-mediation. For illustration purposes, Table 3.2 uses Episode H03 as an example to outline the activities that occur in each of these stages.

This study focused on the disputants' talk in three stages: (1) Problem Discussion, (2) Private Mediation, and (3) Post-mediation. These are the stages when the

Table 3.1 Snapshot of the episodes and their disputants

Episode ID	First show date	Marriage length	Residence	Mediation outcome	Disputant ID	Profession	Waywardness
H01[a]	22 December 2017	20+ years	Chongqing	Resolved	Wife_H01_AW	Unknown	Aggrieved wife
					Husband_H01_WH	Commercial driver	Wayward husband
H02[b]	25 December 2017	20+ years	Hebei	Resolved	Wife_H02_AW	Vendor	Aggrieved wife
					Husband_H02_WH	Vendor	Wayward husband
H03[c]	15 April 2018	31 years	Hubei	Resolved	Wife_H03_AW	Housewife	Aggrieved wife
					Husband_H03_WH	Car dealer	Wayward husband
W01[d]	10 June 2018	20+ years	Jiangxi	Resolved	Wife_W01_WW	Family business	Wayward wife
					Husband_W01_AH	Family business	Aggrieved husband
W02[e]	07 October 2018	24 yers	Henan	Trial reconciliation for 6 months	Wife_W02_WW	Family business	Wayward wife
					Husband_W02_AH	Family business	Aggrieved husband
W03[f]	14 April 2019	16 years	Hunan	Divorced	Wife_W03_WW	Shop owner	Wayward wife
					Husband_W03_AH	Unknown	Aggrieved husband

[a]Data source URL: https://www.youtube.com/watch?v=tlOP0MJ6bJw&list=PLWyKG_HBHHZkVpIyGVM2qWunWdkF4mWpf&index=618&t=0s
[b]Data source URL: https://www.youtube.com/watch?v=r941Hrd2H2c&list=PLWyKG_HBHHZkVpIyGVM2qWunWdkF4mWpf&index=615&t=0s
[c]Data source URL: https://www.youtube.com/watch?v=m7ZTUArAZ1g&list=PLWyKG_HBHHZkVpIyGVM2qWunWdkF4mWpf&index=513&t=0s
[d]Data source URL: https://www.youtube.com/watch?v=S8wAA5Upevs&list=PLWyKG_HBHHZkVpIyGVM2qWunWdkF4mWpf&index=457&t=0s
[e]Data source URL: https://www.youtube.com/watch?v=qAaF7cejsYo&list=PLWyKG_HBHHZkVpIyGVM2qWunWdkF4mWpf&index=339&t=0s
[f]Data source URL: https://www.youtube.com/watch?v=nmje-ootRw0&list=PLWyKG_HBHHZkVpIyGVM2qWunWdkF4mWpf&index=162&t=0s

Table 3.2 Stages of each episode (exemplified by Episode H03)

Mediation stage	Turn	Venue	Persons present	Speaker(s)
Pre-mediation	0	Interview room	Wife	Wife
Problem Discussion	1–148	TV studio	Hostess, Husband, Wife, and seven mediators	Hostess, Husband and Wife
Group Mediation	149–159			Seven mediators
Private Mediation	160–177	Private mediation room A	Mediator A and Husband	Mediator A and Husband
	178–189	Private mediation room B	Mediator B and Wife	Mediator B and Wife
Post-mediation	190–221	TV studio	Hostess, Husband, Wife, and seven mediators	Hostess, Husband, Wife, and Master mediator

disputing spouses directly interact with each other and with the hostess/mediators. Specifically, the Problem Discussion stage usually lasts from 20 to 30 min, which represents a significant portion of the dispute resolution process. In this stage, the disputing spouses directly confront each other in front of the mediators, with minimal engagement with the hostess but without any direct involvement from the mediators. From a dramaturgical view of 'self-presentation', it becomes apparent that the spouses are not simply discussing the problem at hand; rather, they aim to present specific aspects of the 'self' through their discursive performance in front of the mediators, who will later comment on the dispute and the disputants themselves. In this research, the disputants' talk in the Problem Discussion stage was analysed both synoptically (looking at the overall picture) and dynamically (examining the change dynamics over time) regarding the disputants' construal of attitudinal disposition. The other two stages—Private mediation and Post-mediation—involve direct interaction between spouses and mediators. These stages usually last around 10–15 min. Given that these stages are crucial for the development of a dispute resolution, the talk in these stages is used to explore the stability and fluidity of the disputants' attitudinal disposition from a dynamic perspective.

2.3 *Describing the Register*

In order to better understand the disputants' use of evaluative language, it is necessary to describe the data vis-à-vis the three contextual variables (Halliday, 1978; Halliday & Hasan, 1985): Field, Tenor, and Mode.

2.3.1 Field and Mode

The Field of the data is relationship breakdown mediation. It involves: (1) the disputants' outlining of their concerns, grievances, complaints, and their versions of events relating to these; (2) confrontations between the disputants where they level accusations or defend their past actions; (3) elicitation and facilitation from the hostess; and (4) comments and advice provided by the mediators.

The Mode of the data is multiparty, immediately interactive, face-to-face unscripted conversation.

2.3.2 Tenor

Tenor, or the 'interactant relations' in the situation (Hasan, 2020), is of particular relevance to this study's interpersonal focus. Multiple parameters have been proposed in the existing SFL literature to systematically describe the Tenor of texts (Berry, 2016; Bowcher, 1999; Hasan, 2014, 2020; Lukin et al., 2011; Poynton, 1989, 1990). This study follows Martin's (1991, 1992, 2009) modelling of Tenor and describes the interactant relations in the data along two dimensions: status and contact. Status refers to 'the relative position of interlocutors in a culture's social hierarchy' (Martin, 1992, p. 525). It is related to 'social role' in Hasan's model (2014, 2020) and 'power' in Poynton's model (1990). The status between the interactants can be equal or unequal. Contact is concerned with 'the degree of involvement among interlocutors' (Martin, 1992, p. 528). It is about the speaker/writer's alignment and affinity with others and is related to 'social distance' in Hasan's model and 'distance' in Poynton's model. The contact between the interactants can be close or distant.

As multiparty interactions, family dispute resolution exchanges involve two sets of interactant relations. One is the relation between the two disputing spouses, the other being the relation between the disputants and the mediators (including the hostess). To unpack the power dynamics in the dataset, I describe the Tenor of family dispute resolution exchange from two aspects: (1) the Tenor relations between the disputing spouses and (2) the Tenor relations between the disputants and the mediators/hostess.

2.3.2.1 Tenor Between the Two Disputing Spouses

Broadly speaking, the disputing spouses exhibit equal status and have close social contact. The equal status is partly determined by the two speakers' relatively stable social roles outside of the mediation context: as husband and wife. Additionally, within the mediation setting itself, the equal status is further reinformed by the two speakers' contingent roles in the interaction: dispute participants. Preliminary analysis of the conversational features in their talk suggests that both spouses have similar opportunities to express themselves (turn duration, overlap with each other's speech, and patterns of turn-taking) and are equally attended to through comments from the hostess or mediators. This equality is particularly notable given the intense nature of the dispute context. Meanwhile, concerning the contact between the two disputing spouses, they have close social contact for being married for over 15 years and share a significant amount of common knowledge due to this long-term relationship.

However, besides having equal status and close social contact, the disputing spouses are attitudinally disaligned regarding their perceptions of themselves, their spouse's behaviour, and their marriage. Their attitudinal disalignment is evident through their frequent advancement of negativity directed towards each other. As will be detailed later, all participants in this study consistently chose to construe a negative stance against their spouse, although they might vary regarding their degree of negativity towards each other and their preferred evaluative meaning-making mechanism to advance the negativity. Temporally, the disputing spouses first discuss their problems in the Problem Discussion stage. Then their talk is commented on by the mediators in the later stages. Under Goffman's dramaturgical view of 'self-presentation', the spouses attempt to present specific aspects of the 'self' to guide and control the impression left on the mediators. They engage in competitive performances to convince the mediators with their versions of events from the marriage (events which they typically frame as casting their spouses in a negative light and/or casting themselves in a favourable light) and their attitudinal positioning of the self and the antagonist. In summary, despite having equal status and close social contact, the disputing spouses find themselves in a competitive situation where they are attitudinally detached from each other.

2.3.2.2 Tenor Between the Disputants and the Mediators

In contrast to their relatively equal status with each other, the disputing spouses and the mediators (including the hostess) exhibit unequal and deferential status. Although the mediators are not allowed to speak during the Problem Discussion stage, they offer comments later in the Group/Private Mediation and Post-mediation stages. These comments are often evaluative and advisory, reflecting their authoritative position as 'experts' invited to facilitate the mediation process. As such, it can be expected that the disputants will tend to treat the mediators' comments and advice with deference—a dynamic frequently observed in the disputants' language. For instance, the address terms used by both sides underscore this status inequality: whereas the hostess and mediators address the disputants as 'Mr.' and 'Mrs.' rather than calling their first names, the disputants refer to the mediators as 'teacher', an honorific title showing respect or deference in their culture.

Regarding the contact between the disputants and the mediators, it is distant because these individuals are strangers until they participate in the reality TV mediation process together. However, as further explored in subsequent chapters, each disputant actively seeks to establish alignment with the mediators throughout the exchange. They attempt to do so by projecting their personal value positions and cultural norms onto the mediators, assuming the mediators as 'likeminded' audiences (White, 2020b, 2025). That is to say, the disputants work towards having the

Table 3.3 The contextual characterisation of the data

Contextual variable		Description
Field		Relationship breakdown mediation
Tenor	Between the two disputing spouses	Equal status; close social contact; but attitudinally disaligned
	Between the disputants and the mediators/hostess	Unequal and deferential status; distant social contact; but each disputant seeks attitudinal alignment with the mediators
Mode		Multiparty, immediately interactive, face-to-face unscripted conversation

mediators align with them attitudinally over evaluations of their own behaviour and that of their spouse (but they might fail in this, of course). Furthermore, the disputants also aim to influence the mediators in adopting a similar evaluative stance towards both parties (the self and the antagonist) in the same way as they do.

It's worth noting that the data's Tenor is complicated by the discourse's macro-genre: a reality TV programme. Overall, the adversarial exchange in the dataset is a highly complex communication mode, different from that in private settings. Though all exchanges are unscripted, unstructured, and un-institutionalised, the immediate presence of the mediation panel, cameras, also awareness of potential TV viewers, add an unavoidable performative element to the language choices made by interactants. Each time a spouse speaks, they simultaneously address both the interactants who are immediately and physically present in the studio and an imagined 'virtual' audience, or a 'hearer', in Goffman's terms (1974). This means that the communicative acts are not simply a matter of contesting meanings between spouses, but also involve potentially seeking to position these virtual audience to view them positively, consider their assessments as valid or well-founded, or find their version of events plausible. Thus, the act of speaking simultaneously involves arguing with each other and attempting to present themselves in a positive light before the virtual addressee. Additionally, they might present their partner unfavourable. The tenor relations between spouses and the virtual addressee mirror those between the spouses and the mediators.

The contextual features of the family dispute resolution register discussed so far are summarised in Table 3.3.

3 Research Methods

3.1 Transcription

Video recordings of the episodes were transcribed into Chinese using ELAN ('ELAN', 2020), an open-source software allowing me to add text notes (transcriptions and/or annotations) to video or audio recordings. I followed Halliday's

Table 3.4 Transcription key

Symbol	Meaning
..	Pause, short (< 150 milliseconds)
...	Pause, untimed (> 150 milliseconds)
... (1.2)	Pause, timed
()	Paralinguistic features, such as sob, cry, or laughter
==	overlap of speech (occurs in sets of two turns)

proposal that only features that were 'important for the purpose in hand' should be transcribed (Halliday, 1989, p. 48). I made the following transcription decisions by incorporating existing transcription conventions in both SFL and Conversation Analysis—Halliday (1989), Eggins and Slade (1997), Zappavigna and Martin (2018), and Du Bois (2006).

The transcription included the speaker or turn holder, the immediate addressee (as inferred from the speaker's language and body direction while making the utterance), and each turn's duration. These conversational features were used in analysing the frequency of the speaker's use of evaluative language. Meanwhile, all the false starts, repetitions, fillers, hesitations, and overlaps were transcribed as is. These features were helpful when identifying instances of oppositional stances or disagreements. As well, because the analysis was concerned with resources on the discourse semantics stratum (see Chap. 2), the texts were segmented into moves (Martin, 1992; Sinclair & Coulthard, 1975a) (Sect. 3.2.6 in this chapter explains why I took the move as the unit of analysis). The transcription recorded the speaker's pauses to make the written transcription readable but without adding any punctuations. The last decision proved significant because it turned out that the disputants' pauses did not converge with the utterance's grammatical units. The disputants tended to pause before making an explicit attitudinal assessment or providing an ostension signalling an attitudinal assessment. The transcription key of this monograph is summarised in Table 3.4.

The transcription, that is, the Chinese texts, was annotated for the disputants' use of evaluative language. Annotation principles are introduced in the following sections. In this monograph, English translation is provided of the Chinese texts. Excerpt 3.1 illustrates a transcription example.

3.2 *Annotating Attitudinal Meaning-Making Resources: Appraisal*

As indicated previously, the focus of the analyses being reported here was on what I chose to term the 'attitudinal disposition' of the disputants, as revealed through tendencies in their deployment of resources associated with attitudinal

Excerpt 3.1 Transcription example

Turn	Speaker	Move	Utterance (Chinese)	Utterance (English translation)
69	Hostess_W01	1	为什么呢	Why
		2	你不觉得奇怪吗	Don't you find it weird
70	Wife_W01_WW	1	那我怎么知道	Well how can I know
		2	因为..因为我们如果有真的..有什么我们就没有必要回来	Because.. because if we had real.. had any issues we didn't need to come back
		3	我也没有必要跟我老公讲我..我是在那里	There was no need for me to tell my husband about that I.. that I was there
		4	我们三个人在那里多玩了一天	The three of us played there for one more day
		5	我也没有必要跟他坦白这个东西	I didn't need to confess this to him
		6	我完全可以把这个东西隐瞒	I could have wholly hidden this thing
		7	==因为我们是坦白的啊==	==Because we were honest==
71	Husband_W01_AH	1	==他跟你...他已==经隐瞒不了了嘛	==He and you... he already== can't hide it any more
		2	因为那个人已经找到厂里	Because that person has come to our factory
		3	要跟她吵架了	Came to quarrel with her
72	Wife_W01_WW	1	是==他老婆==也到过我公司	Yes ==his wife== has also been to our company
73	Husband_W01_AH	1	==要==	==Want to==
74	Hostess_W01	1	为什么	Why

meaning-making—meanings by which positive or negative assessments are conveyed, either explicitly or implicitly. I tracked the disputants' attitudinal arrangements by annotating the data based on the Appraisal framework (see Chap. 2 for details). Figure 3.2 illustrates the Appraisal annotation taxonomy used in this research. The following strategies were taken when annotating the Appraisal resources.

3.2.1 Delicacy and Variable Control

The first strategy to be addressed in connection with such Appraisal framework annotations is around issues of the delicacy of the analysis. I did not seek to take the analyses to the deepest levels of delicacy provided by the Appraisal framework literature. For the ATTITUDE system, attitudinal instances were classified only at the level of the three broad categories: Affect, Judgement, or Appreciation. The subcategories of Judgement and Appreciation were not further distinguished (for reasons outlined below). For the GRADUATION system, a general distinction was made

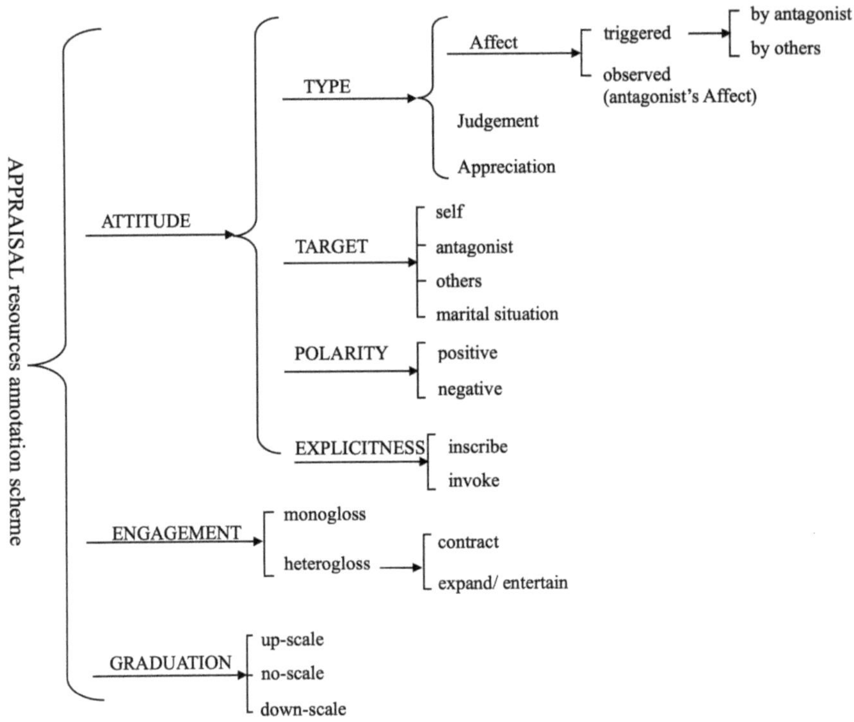

Fig. 3.2 Appraisal resources annotation scheme

concerning the tendency of the scaling, either to upscale or to downscale, or without any additional scaling devices. The nature of the meaning being scaled—either about intensity or prototypicality—was not tracked.

The reasons for these treatments are twofold. For one thing, because this research aims to identify patterns and tendencies vis-à-vis disputants' deployment of evaluative meaning-making resources, moving down one delicacy level in the Appraisal system means adding more variables to the pattern recognition. Methodologically, being specific with many variables may make it possible to identify idiosyncratic differences among the individual disputants, but at the same time, it makes the data overly complex. Hence, the annotation taxonomy I deployed operated at the delicacy levels that could best capture the recurrent patterns among multiple speakers in the dataset.

Additionally, the annotation taxonomy I chose to deploy kept the variables that could best describe the dataset. This reason has relevance to the treatment of Appreciation and Judgement in the ATTITUDE TYPE subsystem. The annotation did not track details of Appreciation because such instances were infrequent in the data. As well, the annotation did not classify Judgement into subcategories because in family dispute resolution data, the attitudinal orientation of a Judgement, or whether there is a Judgement at all, is highly audience-specific. Specifically, the particular subcategory of Judgement is determined by the value position a person brings into the reading. For example, if a husband reports the wife's behaviour of blocklisting him (an instance in Episode W01), it can be inferred that the husband aims to position the audience to Judge the wife negatively. However, which specific subcategory the Judgement falls into is subject to the audience's interpretation. For an audience who holds that 'It is not normal for a spouse to blocklist the other', the wife's behaviour can be criticised for breaching normality. For the audience holding that 'It is immoral for a spouse to blocklist the other', the wife will be condemned for violating propriety. The different standards held by people when making a Judgement give rise to multiple interpretations of a single behaviour. Very likely such standards are not codified in written documents or surveilled by religious or legal institutions. Accordingly, the analysis did not classify the Judgemental instances into more delicate categories because of the highly audience-specific nature of behaviour assessment in dispute resolution exchanges.

3.2.2 Tracking Attitudinal Targets

The second annotation strategy was concerned with the systematic tracking of the attitudinal target. In the existing literature, the attitudinal target is conceptualised as the 'Appraised' (Martin & White, 2005) or the ideational aspect of a 'coupling' (Almutairi, 2021a; Hao & Humphrey, 2012; Zappavigna, 2019; Zappavigna et al., 2008). What is being evaluated in the family dispute resolution register is highly centralised around the people involved in the dispute or the relationship. All the attitudinal objects can be condensed into three targets: the self, the antagonist, and a third party (e.g., an intruder into the relationships, an in-law, or a child, who is one of the triggers for the relationship breakdown). Accordingly, the annotation tracked the disputants' evaluation of three attitudinal targets: the self, the antagonist, and the others. The disputants' attitudinal positioning of these three targets revealed their construal of the 'self', the 'other', and the 'self' in relation to the 'other'.

3.2.3 Tracking Triggers of Affect

The third annotation strategy focused on the ATTITUDE TYPE of Affect. Specifically, rather than classifying the emotional responses regarding the psychological type of the emotion (e.g., dis/satisfaction, un/happiness, and in/security), my annotation tracked the nature of the Affectual instance construed either as an authorial emotion triggered by an external source or as a reported emotion observed by the speaker. If the emotion was construed as an emotional reaction, it was tagged as triggered Affect. The annotation recorded if the trigger was the antagonist (or the antagonist's behaviour) or others. This strategy was helpful to distinguish the disputants' evaluative meaning-making strategy in family dispute resolution in that the annotation identified two types of Affectual assessments, which have different evaluative meaning-making mechanisms in the dispute resolution exchange.

The first type of Affectual assessment is the 'negative Affectual response triggered by the antagonist or the antagonist's behaviour'. Such assessments construe an authorial feeling as a negative emotional reaction to the antagonist or the antagonist's behaviour. From the evaluative meaning-making perspective, negative Affectual responses of this type function as a token to ultimately invoke a negative Judgement directed at the antagonist, that is, for having caused the disputant to feel bad. The Husband_W01_AH's utterances in Excerpt 3.2 illustrate this type of Affectual assessment (The linguistic formulations realising Affect are highlighted in bold). The husband reports what the wife said to him. Then he reports the negative feelings he had after hearing his wife's words. The husband's negative feelings, which are construed as extreme unhappiness, function as attitude tokens inviting the addressee to evaluate the trigger of the feelings—the wife—negatively.

The other type of Affectual assessment tracked in my annotations was 'observed other people's Affectual response'. Such assessments report an observed feeling of another person, other than the speaker themselves. The observed feeling has the potential to invoke an attitudinal evaluation directed at the emoter or the trigger (Martin & White, 2005, pp. 46–47) of the feeling, according to whether the observed Affect is viewed as socially appropriate or inappropriate. For example, reporting that someone was angry potentially invokes a negative Judgement towards the emoter, on the basis that being angry is often socially deprecated. This potential for observed Affect to act as a token of Judgement in this way is, obviously, very much dependent on the context. Husband_H03_WH's utterances in Excerpt 3.3 are examples of observed Affects functioning as tokens for evaluating the emoter, in this excerpt, the antagonist. He reports the wife's extreme anger to position the audience to evaluate her emotional outburst as an inappropriate overreaction. Because the trigger of the wife's emotions was the husband himself, these observed Affectual

Excerpt 3.2 Negative Affectual response triggered by the antagonist

Turn	Speaker	Move #	Utterance (Chinese)	Utterance (English translation)	Affect
58	Husband_ W01_AH	1	嗯...跟我亲口说啊	Hmm... she said this to me herself	
		2	她说她喜欢他	She said she liked him	
		3	他在她心里很重要啊	(she said) He was important in her heart	
		4	他会照顾她好她啦	(she said) He would take care of her and take good care of her	
		5	我就..看到她	I just.. saw her	
		6	她在我..心口..在我心里就是..跟一把刀一样的	She **in my.. heart.. in my heart she was.. like a knife**	-ve Affect; triggered; trigger: antagonist's words
		7	刺得我好痛啊	(she) **Stabbed me so badly**	-ve Affect; triggered; trigger: antagonist's words

Excerpt 3.3 Observed Affect functioning as a token of evaluating the emoter

Turn	Speaker	Move #	Utterance (Chinese)	Utterance (English translation)	Affect
47	Husband_ H03_WH	1	有	Yes	
		2	以前我是车行上班的	I used to work in a car dealer	
		3	我那店里老板呢组织我们一伙人去那个庐山旅游吧	My boss in the store organised a group of us to go to that Mt. Lu to travel	
		4	就是几个女的站在那里	It was just a few women standing there	
		5	她几个人拍像	A few women took photos	
		6	我也拍了一下	I also took a picture of them	
		7	她就气得不得了	She became very **angry**	-ve Affect; observed; emoter: antagonist; trigger: self
		8	跳..跳到岩下去..说	Jump.. jump off the rock.. she said	
48	Wife_H03_ AW	1	那是什么原因你说	You tell what the reason was	
49	Husband_ H03_WH	1	好多人阻止她	Many people tried to stop her	
		2	她气得哭得哭得很难受	She was so **angry** that she **cried** and **cried** very **miserably**	-ve Affect; observed; emoter: antagonist; trigger: self
		3	那个拍个像有什么关系呢..天哪	What's the problem with simply taking a picture.. God	

instances have the potential to invoke a negative Judgement of the wife based on her negative Affect towards him.

Besides functioning as a token of evaluating the emoter, instances of observed Affects also have the potential to invoke evaluation directed at the trigger of the feeling. Wife_W03_WW's utterances in Excerpt 3.4 offer an example. The wife reported the unhappiness of her daughter, whom the husband wronged. The observed negative Affectual reactions of the daughter were triggered by the husband's interrogation and search. By reporting the observed Affects, the wife invited the audience to judge the trigger of the Affects—the husband—negatively.

The analysis revealed wide variation, across the dataset, in terms of the disputants' deployment of Affectual assessments. Not all disputants had instances of Affectual evaluation, and the disputants differed in their preference for authorial triggered Affects or observed Affects (to be discussed in detail in later chapters).

Excerpt 3.4 Observed Affect functioning as a token of evaluating the trigger of the feeling

Turn	Speaker	Move #	Utterance (Chinese)	Utterance (English translation)	Affect
180	Husband_ W03_AH	1	我就是说你如果拿了..你就拿出来	I just said if you stole the money.. you just take it out	
		2	==不拿出来==	==If you don't take it out==	
181	Wife_W03_ WW	1	==你就讲了==这些吗	==Did you say== this only	
		2	你搜她书包了没有	Didn't you search her school bag	
182	Husband_ W03_AH	1	我没搜她书包	I didn't search her school bag	
		2	我拿==书包==	I took ==her school bag==	
183	Wife_W03_ WW	1	==那她==为什么每天都是那样委屈	==Then== why did she **feel** she **had been** seriously **wronged** every day	-ve Affect; observed; emoter: daughter; trigger: antagonist
		2	那样眼泪汪汪的	(she had been) So **teary**	-ve Affect; observed; emoter: daughter; trigger: antagonist
		3	是干什么呢	Why was that	
		4	早上也不吃..还要我妈给她送到学校里面去呢	She didn't eat in the morning.. I had to ask my mum to accompany her to the school	

The annotation method on Affectual assessments captured the speakers' construal of feelings and the patterned variations in the disputants' attitudinal positioning strategy.

3.2.4 Annotating Explicitness

The final strategy for annotating the Appraisal resources was in the treatment of ATTITUDE EXPLICITNESS. In this, I brought together the proposals made by the existing scholarship around the cline of explicitness (Don, 2016; Macken-Horarik & Isaac, 2014) and the meaning-making mechanisms of invocations (Don, 2016; Hood & Martin, 2007; Hood & Zhang, 2020; Macken-Horarik & Isaac, 2014; Thompson, 2014; White, 1998, 2012). The research's annotation procedure for ATTITUDE EXPLICITNESS was mainly informed by White's (1998) distinction of different 'modes of Judgement': inscribe and invoke (provoke and evoke). According to White, an inscription is realised by explicitly evaluative terminology. Invocations of provocation and evocation involve either other Appraisal values (e.g., intensifications, assessments of counter expectation in the case of provocation) or purely experiential tokens in the case of evocation. Accordingly, the explicitness annotation was done in three steps. I first made a primary distinction between inscription and invocation. Then I identified the ostensions signalling an attitude. In utterances when there were no obvious attitudinal ostensions, the co-text and context were considered to see if there were any potential attitudinal meaning-making at play. Any linguistic formulation that signalled an attitude, including explicitly evaluative terminology, attitudinal ostensions, and co-textual cues, was annotated under the umbrella term of 'attitude signal'. Instances containing explicitly evaluative terminology were treated as inscribed attitudes or inscriptions. Other instances were treated as invoked attitudes or invocations. Details of each step are introduced below.

3.2.4.1 Annotating Inscription

Inscriptions were identified by checking corpora for a linguistic item's stability in realising an evaluative meaning. The two contemporary Chinese corpora used were the BCC developed by Beijing Language and Cultures University (http://bcc.blcu.edu.cn) and Media Language Corpus developed by China's National Language Resources Monitoring and Research Centre (http://ling.cuc.edu.cn/RawPub/). Strictly speaking, no linguistic formulation can be absolutely evaluative or non-evaluative, or positive or negative, in all contexts. A linguistic item with relatively stable evaluative meanings in the relationship communication context was annotated as an attitude signal of inscription. Table 3.5 presents some inscription examples. The linguistic formulations realising the inscriptions are highlighted in bold.

3.2.4.2 Tracking Attitudinal Ostensions

Attitudinal ostensions refer to instances of other Appraisal values (e.g., instances of GRADUATION or ENGAGEMENT) which have the potential to invoke an attitudinal assessment. Attitudinal ostension is related to the 'Russian doll' phenomenon (Thompson, 2014) where an expression of one category of evaluation may function as a token (i.e., an indirect expression) of a different category. For example, an instance of GRADUATION or ENGAGEMENT can potentially invoke an attitudinal assessment. As well, an instance of Affect or Appreciation can activate an assessment of Judgement. This phenomenon is very well investigated in the existing literature (Don, 2016; Hood & Martin, 2007; White, 2003, 2012). Such attitudinal ostensions alert the audience that subjectivity is at play and that potential attitudinal assessments are at risk. Table 3.6 lists some attitudinal ostension examples chosen from Episode_W02. The linguistic formulations realising the attitudinal ostensions are highlighted in bold. The attitude signals are labelled following Don (2016).

Table 3.5 Inscription examples

Utterance (Chinese)	Utterance (English translation)	Attitude signal	Attitude
他越对我这样...我心情越..低落(Wife_W02_WW)	The more he treats me like this... **the lower my mood**	inscription	inscribe -ve Affect; emoter: self; trigger: antagonist
因为我..知道他这个人..心眼小啊(Wife_W03_WW)	Because I...know he is..**oversuspicious**	inscription	inscribe -ve Judge antagonist
她...太冲动了...就是(Husband_W03_AH)	She... (was) too **impulsive**... that's it	inscription	inscribe -ve Judge antagonist

3.2.4.3 Tracking Co-textual Cues

In family dispute resolution exchanges, not all utterances contain an explicitly evaluative item or attitudinal token signalling an attitude. There are situations when the speaker provides no obvious attitude signal in the immediate text but makes the evaluative meaning traceable from the co-text. A co-textual cue can be, for example, a contrast between the speaker's proposition and the antagonist's proposition in previous turns. Tracking the invocations afforded by such co-textual cues was particularly important for my analyses of these family dispute resolution exchanges because these interactions frequently involved interruptions, overlappings, and multiparty exchange. It was very frequently the case that a disputant produced an utterance in response to what has been proposed by other interactants without making it explicit that they were responding in this way. It was also commonplace for a speaker to have more than one layer of attitudinal positioning in one utterance. Thus, to sum up, some attitudinal positionings in the dataset could be identified within the utterance per se, whereas some layers of attitudinal positioning needed to be tracked by considering the co-text.

Excerpt 3.5 provides an example of annotating attitude with co-textual cues. The utterances are extracted from an episode featuring a wayward husband and an aggrieved wife. The discussion focuses on the husband's utterances in Turn 7, where he provided a detailed description of his behaviour when the wife was sick. Given that the husband's utterances did not stand alone but were responses to the wife's accusation in Turn 2, the attitudes or the husband's attitudinal positioning need to be unpacked by also considering the wife's utterances.

The annotations for Turn 7 show that the husband's utterances involve what I chose to treat as 'double assessments', that is, one utterance both positively assesses one target and negatively assesses another target. To my knowledge, expressions that work in this way (simultaneous activating different assessments of different targets) have not been widely noted or attended to in the Appraisal literature, a point I will return to below. The above extract just provided (Excerpt 3.5) illustrates this phenomenon. The husband's attitudinal ostensions (including pronouncement in Move 1 and quotations in Moves 2–4) signalled positive Judgements directed at the self. At the same time, his description of the caring behaviour functioned as a

Table 3.6 Attitude ostension examples in Episode_W02

Utterance (Chinese)	Utterance (English translation)	Attitude signal	Potential attitude(s)
他越对我这样...我心情越..低落(Wife_W02_WW)	The more he treats me like this... **the lower my mood**	attitudinal instance of inscribed Affect (potential invocation of -ve Judgement)	invoke -ve Judge antagonist
我是..要离婚 (Wife_W02_WW)	I.. want a **divorce**	attitudinal token of Appreciation	invoke -ve Judge marital relationship / the couple
那你可以现在来看 (Wife_W02_WW)	Then **you can** come and check my phone now	directive	invoke -ve Judge antagonist
拳头蹬我脚了没…你打我腿了没 (Wife_W02_WW)	Did your fist kick my feet… did you beat my leg	rhetorical question	invoke -ve Judge antagonist
一天三顿饭..都是我做 (Husband_W02_AH)	Three meals a day...**all** cooked by me	up-scaling	invoke +ve Judge self
你结果不给我发信息…你结果给人家发信息 (Husband_W02_AH)	it turned out that you **didn't send me** a message… it turned out that you **sent him** a message	contrast	invoke -ve Judge antagonist
不可能说了一个小时..两个小时..在谈的 (Husband_W02_AH)	It's **impossible** to talk for an hour.. two hours.. talking	denial	invoke -ve Judge antagonist
他们还去到..宾馆..开过房间 (Husband_W02_AH)	They **even** went to...hotel... checked in hotel rooms	counter-expectancy	invoke -ve Judge antagonist
很多事情..我也想做…也想维护 (Husband_W02_AH)	Many things.. I also **want to** do… also **want to** maintain	irrealis Affect	invoke +ve Judge self
她跟..人家说嘛(1.0)我私底下给你弄点钱…她说...我们的感情没处理完之前..我不能明目张胆地跟着你 (Husband_W02_AH)	**She said.. to the guy** (1.0) I'll manage to get you some money in private… **She said**...before our relationship is finished *[Translator's note: before I have my divorce settled]*...I can't openly date with you	quotation: other	invoke -ve Judge antagonist
她生了病..都是我询问她很详细的…哪个地方不舒服…吃什么药	When she was sick.. I was the one who asked her for her details … **what's wrong with you**… **what medicine to take**	quotation: self	invoke +ve Judge self

Excerpt 3.5 Tracking attitude by co-textual cues

Turn	Speaker	Move #	Utterance (Chinese)	Utterance (English translation)	Attitude signal	Potential attitude
2	Wife_ H01_AW	1	我诉求..拒绝过那种表里不一.. 阳奉阴违的日子	I request.. (I) refuse to live a life that is **duplicitous..** and **deceitful**	inscription	inscribe -ve Appreciation life
		2	他现在嘴上说他在乎夫妻感情	He only **pays lip service** when saying that he cares about the relationship	inscription	inscribe -ve Judge antagonist
……						
7	Husband_ H01_WH	1	她生了病…都是我询问她很详细的	Whenever she was sick… **I was the one who** asked her for details [*of how she was feeling*]	pronouncement	invoke +ve Judge self; invoke -ve Judge antagonist
		2	哪个地方不舒服	What's wrong with you	quotation: self	invoke +ve Judge self; invoke -ve Judge antagonist
		3	吃什么药	What medicine to take	quotation: other	invoke +ve Judge self; invoke -ve Judge antagonist
		4	都是我去买	**I was the one who** went out to buy the medicine	pronouncement	invoke +ve Judge self; invoke -ve Judge antagonist

counteraccusation against the wife and/or invoked negative Judgement of the wife. By providing counterevidence to the wife's prior accusations, the husband showed that the wife had spoken unfairly without having a basis for her negativity toward the husband. Hence, the husband's utterances have multiple layers of attitudinal positioning. In addition to positive Judgement of self, he counteracted the wife's negative positioning of the husband and/or invoked negative Judgement directed at the wife.

As just suggested, tracking 'double assessments' or multi-layered attitudinal positioning is arguably a development of prior practices in Appraisal annotation. No one, to my knowledge, has proposed such a multi-layered attitudinal assessment annotation. The phenomenon of having more than one layer of attitudinal positioning arises from the interactive and adversarial nature of family dispute resolution data, where by one utterance, a disputant aims not only to present the 'self' per se but also to counteract the prior utterances proposed by their antagonist. Thus, a spouse may offer a positive assessment of themself by challenging a prior negative assessment of them advanced by their partner, thereby casting the partner in a negative light. The multi-layered attitudinal positioning unpacks the linguistic mechanism regarding how a disputant constructs a 'self', the 'other' (particularly the antagonist), and a 'self' in relation to the 'other'.

In brief, this section has outlined the strategies by which the explicitness of attitudinal assessments was annotated in the text. Although the attitude signals potentially give rise to attitudinal meaning-making, whether an attitude and what kind of attitude will be eventually activated in the audience's end depends on the recipients' reading position. Nevertheless, the attitude signals point the recipients into the speaker's attitudinal direction (White, 2012, 2020b, 2021, 2025).

The above four strategies were used when annotating the Appraisal resources to best serve this research's purpose. Besides these strategies, two more annotation principles were followed when annotating the Appraisal resources in the data. One involved maintaining a consistent reading position during the annotation—to be discussed below. The other was to settle on an appropriate unit of analysis so that tendencies in the disputants' language choices could be quantitively processed via the computational tools mentioned in Chap. 1 and discussed later in this chapter.

3.2.5 Reading Position

Specifying one's reading position is crucial in Appraisal analysis, especially for analysing invoked evaluations. An analysis of the speaker's use of evaluative language is ultimately ideological (White, 2006). Any consumption of the text is a creation of 'subjectified meaning' (Martin & White, 2005, p. 25), which is influenced by the particular reading position adopted by the reader/hearer. Declaring the analyst's reading position can also manage the issue of inter-rater reliability (White, 2025). This research used two strategies to maintain a consistent reading position during the annotation. One was for me, the annotator, to adopt a 'tactical' (Martin & White, 2005, p. 75) reading position when undertaking the annotation process. The other was to specify the particular value positions or cultural frames by which attitudinal instances would be interpreted.

By 'tactical' reading position, I mean that the annotator (i.e., I) approached the texts as a linguist without any attitudinal involvement with the disputants or mediators. I analysed the texts tactically as a female, middle-aged, native Mandarin speaker with decades of living experience in China's northern and southern parts. Being an insider of the Chinese language, the Chinese culture, and family relationship practice within contemporary Chinese society, I was able to track the disputants' evaluative meaning-making preference as reflected by the linguistic configurations in the text.

The other strategy was to systematically consider the value positions or cultural frames underlying my reading of the extracts. This strategy is particularly relevant when annotating invocations. Despite the attitude signals, specific attitudes to be

Excerpt 3.6 Specify the underlying value positions

Turn	Speaker	Utterance (Chinese)	Utterance (English translation)
7	Husband_H01_WH	她生了病…都是我询问她很详细的	Whenever she was sick… **I was the one who** asked her for her details
		哪个地方不舒服	What's wrong with you
		吃什么药	What medicine to take
		都是我去买	**I was the one who** went out to buy the medicine

activated rely very much on the shared knowledge and cultural frames between the interactants. Excerpt 3.6 (reproduced from Excerpt 3.5) illustrates the indeterminacy of attitudinal meaning-making. The husband's utterances, in which he provided a detailed account of his behaviour when the wife was sick, can be interpreted in multiple ways. For the audience holding a value position that 'Attending a sick person in detail is a laudable behaviour', the husband's utterances invoke positive Judgements directed at the self. For the audience holding a value position that 'Taking care of a sick partner is a basic duty', the husband's utterances will not invoke any attitudinal assessment. As well, for the audience holding a value position that 'Taking care of a sick partner is nothing praiseworthy. It is weird for a man to mention such details in public', the husband's accounts invoke negative Judgement directed at the husband.

The indeterminacy of attitudinal meaning-making may be especially true for family dispute resolution interactions. It is highly possible that the disputing spouses, the mediators, and the programme audience hold divergent value positions. If the speaker does not make the attitudinal positioning explicit, multiple attitudinal interpretations of the text are possible, although there might be a reading position '"naturalised" by the overall trajectory of the meanings in a text' (Martin & White, 2005, p. 25).

To sum up, my analyses involved me in identifying the value positions underlying any annotation for invoked attitudes. In this monograph, the value positions that are presumably less obvious to the reader are noted in the footnotes.

3.2.6 Unit of Analysis

Unit of analysis is another methodological issue that requires specification. According to the existing Appraisal literature, it is necessary, albeit challenging, to adopt a principled approach to the unit of analysis when conducting Appraisal-based studies (Macken-Horarik & Isaac, 2014; Thompson, 2014). Being consistent with the unit of analysis is especially pivotal if quantitative data are to be derived from the annotation (Fuoli, 2018). Because my project involved quantitative methods to identify recurrent patterns in the speakers' deployment of evaluative meaning-making resources, it was critical for me to have specified the unit of analysis of the annotation and the subsequent quantifications of uses of attitude-associated meaning.

I chose 'move' as the unit of analysis following Eggins and Slade (1997). Move is 'a discourse unit whose **unmarked** realisation is as a clause selecting independently for MOOD' (Martin, 1992, p. 59, emphasis in original). It is the rank below 'exchange' (Martin, 1992; Sinclair & Coulthard, 1975b).

The reasons were threefold. Firstly, move is a unit of discourse organisation rather than a grammatical unit (Eggins & Slade, 1997, p. 186). Because Appraisal, or the language of evaluation, is concerned with meaning-making resources on the discourse semantics stratum, the unit of analysis should be a unit of 'proposition or proposal, or a sequence of interconnected propositions or proposals' (White, 2020a), rather than individual lexical or grammatical items. Accordingly, the discourse unit of move fitted nicely into the overall linguistic conceptualisation of this research. Secondly, move is the 'quantum of interaction' (Halliday & Matthiessen, 2014, p. 21), the basic unit for analysing the exchange of interpersonal meanings in the interaction. Setting move as the unit of analysis kept the evaluative text span under control and worked well in connection with my objective of identifying a disputant's overall evaluative profile. Finally, move can capture the more nuanced meaning-making mechanism in conversational data than other exchange boundary identifiers, such as turn, exchange, or act (Martin, 1992; Sinclair & Coulthard, 1975a). According to Martin (1992, p. 57), in situations of multiple moves within one turn, it is possible to have moves being identical in ideational meaning but different in interpersonal meaning. Taking move as the unit of analysis enabled me to track the disputants' deployment of Appraisal resources in a delicate and principled manner. Excerpt 3.7 exemplifies how attitudinal meaning-making resources were annotated in my analyses based on move. The wife verifies the chat history between her and an alleged intruder in four moves. In the first three moves, she admits that she and the man have chatted. In the final move, she denies the existence of flirtatious chats.

Defining a principled unit of analysis enabled me to track the division of labour among the three systems of the Appraisal resources—ATTITUDE, ENGAGEMENT, and GRADUATION—in the disputant's enactment of attitudinal disposition. In the existing Appraisal literature, the three systems inter-connect. According to Martin and White, GRADUATION is central to the Appraisal system because it scales both the meanings of ATTITUDE and ENGAGEMENT (2005, p. 136). ENGAGEMENT and GRADUATION can function both as local signals of preference acting to signal an attitude (Don, 2016, p. 16) and as linguistic framing devices for scaling, monoglossing or heteroglossing the attitudinal instance. As well, one linguistic item can realise both ENGAGEMENT and GRADUATION (illustrated by the wife's utterance in Excerpt 3.8). The interconnection and cross-realisation among the three systems require a principled annotation method to track the Appraisal resources vis-à-vis their functionality in the text. Having an explicit unit of analysis made the principled annotation achievable.

In my analysis, the ATTITUDE, ENGAGEMENT, and GRADUATION choices were annotated based on their contribution to the construal of the speaker's authorial

Excerpt 3.7 Move as the unit of analysis

Turn	Speaker	Move #	Utterance (Chinese)	Utterance (English translation)	Attitude signal	Potential attitude	Engagement
64	Wife_ W01_ WW	1	聊天是会有	We do have chatted			
		2	有聊天	We chatted			
		3	有过聊天	We have chatted			
		4	但是那些亲密的那些聊天是没有	But we don't have those flirtatious chats[a]	denial (realised by 没有 *don't have*)[b]	invoke +ve Judge self; invoke -ve Judge antagonist	Contract: disclaim (realised by 但是 *but*)

[a]According to the corpora, when used to describe extramarital relationships, '亲密的' inscribes a negative evaluation and can accordingly be translated into 'flirtatious'.
[b]Although '亲密的flirtatious' is a negative inscription of Appreciation about the chats, the evaluation of the chats was not the main communicative concern of this move. The immediate concern of this move was to deny the existence of 'flirtatious chats' between the wife and the alleged intruder. The ultimate concern was to invoke a negative Judgement directed at the person who argued for the existence of the 'flirtatious chats', which was the antagonist. Therefore, the attitude signal in this move is not the inscription 'flirtatious' but the denial '没有don't have'.

Excerpt 3.8 One item realises both ENGAGEMENT and GRADUATION

Turn	Speaker	Utterance (Chinese)	Utterance (English translation)	Potential attitude	Engagement	Graduation
1	Hostess_ H03	两位今天来到金牌调解要解决什么问题	What problems do you want to resolve by coming to Gold Medal Mediation today			
2	Wife_ H03_AW	就我老公老是触犯我的底线	It's that my husband **crosses the line** all the time	inscribe -ve Judge antagonist (realised by 触犯底线 *cross the line*)	Heterogloss: contract: disclaim: counter-expectancy (realised by 老是 *all the time*)[a]	Up-scaling (realised by 老是 *all the time*)[b]

[a]The adverb '老是 *laoshi (all the time)*' entails a meaning of dissatisfaction or disgust (Chinese Academy of Social Sciences Institute of Linguistics, 2017, p. 785)
[b]When prefix '老*lao-*' is used as an adverb, it means 'all the time, keeps … -ing' (Chao, 1965, p. 236)

attitudinal orientation. Specifically, the speaker's deployment of ATTITUDE resources was of primary concern. ENGAGEMENT and GRADUATION choices were annotated according to the following lines of inquiry. In each move, the analysis started by determining if there were attitude signals (either explicit or implicit) flagging the speaker's attitudinal orientation. If yes, the ENGAGEMENT and GRADUATION choices would be examined vis-à-vis their functions in framing the attitudinal orientation—whether the GRADUATION choice adjusted the degree of the attitude and whether the ENGAGEMENT choice presented the attitude categorically (i.e., 'monoglossing' so as not to acknowledge the possibility of alternative viewpoints) or, alternatively, recognising actual or potential alternative voices and viewpoints (i.e., 'heteroglossing' according to the terminology of the Appraisal framework). If no attitude signals were identified, the ENGAGEMENT and GRADUATION choices would be examined to determine if they functioned as attitude signals invoking specific attitudinal assessments. If the ENGAGEMENT or GRADUATION choices had the potential to invoke an attitudinal assessment, the choices would be annotated as attitude signals. Otherwise, they would not be annotated. Excerpt 3.9 illustrates the annotations made following the above lines of categorisations.

The above sections have introduced how attitudinal meaning-making resources were annotated in this research. The findings following from these analyses are reported and discussed in Chaps. 4–6. The annotations for each episode can be found in the book's GitHub repository.[4]

3.3 Measuring Disputants' Evaluative 'Preferences'

The disputants' discursive self-presentation was analysed and characterised by tracking the recurrent patterns in disputants' preference/dis-preference for a particular type of evaluative meaning: either a disputant using or not ever using a particular meaning-making resource, or a tendency to use a resource more often than other disputants or less often than other disputants. The analysis of disputants' preference/dis-preference (tendencies in their deployment of the different attitude-associated options) was pivotal to my objective of reaching conclusions and offering insights as to the attitudinal dispositions of the disputants. This section outlined the method used for measuring disputants' preference/dis-preference for specific meaning-making resources in later chapters (i.e., tendencies in their deployment of these resources).

For this aspect of the analysis, I drew on Martin and White's (2005) notion of 'frequency' to measure the disputants' preferences and map tendencies in their deployment of these resources. When exploring evaluative key in journalist discourse, they define 'frequency' as 'both a matter of whether or not any instances of the meaning occur in a text of a given key, and of the number of instances of that

[4] https://github.com/xu-qingxin/Appraisal-Approach-to-Conflict-Styles.git

Excerpt 3.9 Annotating ATTITUDE, ENGAGEMENT, and GRADUATION resources based on their contribution to the construal of authorial attitudinal stance

Turn	Speaker	Utterance (Chinese)	Utterance (English translation)	Attitude		Engagement	Graduation
				Attitude signal	Potential attitude		
9	Husband_ W02_AH	我那时是..出去去..要账	I was.. went out.. to collect debts				
		回来的路上一直在打电话	On my way back home I kept calling her all the time	up-scaling (realised by一直 *all the time*)	invoke +ve Judge self	Monogloss	
		打了一个多小时	I had called her for more than an hour	up-scaling (realised by 一个多小时for more than an hour)	invoke +ve Judge self	Monogloss	
		结果呢人家一直在通话中	The result was her line had been busy all the time	contrast ('I kept calling her' versus 'her line had been busy')	invoke -ve Judge antagonist	Heterogloss: contract: disclaim: counter-expectancy (realised by 结果*The result was*)	Up-scaling (realised by 一直 *all the time*)
		甚至我到家了..她马上给我挂..挂了	Even that when I got home.. she immediately hung up.. hung up the phone	contrast ('her line had been busy on my way home' versus 'she hung up the phone when I got home')	invoke -ve Judge antagonist	Heterogloss: contract: disclaim: counter-expectancy (realised by 甚至*even*)	Up-scaling (realised by 马上 *immediately*)

meaning in a given text' (Martin & White, 2005, p. 166). Accordingly, my analyses tracked the disputants' preference/dis-preference for a particular type of evaluative meaning, for example, inscribed positive self-Judgement, along two lines of inquiry: 'occurrence' and 'ratio'.

This first line of inquiry—'occurrence'—attended to the existence of the designated type of evaluative meaning in the sample of text under consideration (for example, the total of one disputant's contributions to one stage of the episode). In other words, it tracked whether there were any instances at all of this evaluative meaning in the disputant's speech. If so, it was noted that the disputant used this resource at least once. This might lead to them being grouped with any other disputants who also used this resource at least once. In contrast, when a disputant was observed to make no use at all of the resources in question, they would be classified as avoiding (dis-preferring) this meaning and, accordingly, might be grouped with any other disputants who similarly 'avoided' this particular resource. The proposition underlying this line of analysis was that the disputants who, for example, deployed instances of inscribed positive self-Judgement can be seen as different from those who had zero instance of such attitudinal assessments.

The other line of inquiry undertaken was what I term 'ratio', which was about the degree of the disputants' preference for the designated evaluative meaning. For example, while both disputant A and disputant B have instances of negative Judgement of their antagonist, they might differ in how often they advance this attitude. If disputant A deploys the attitude more often than B does, A would be interpreted as having an attitudinal disposition more antagonistic than B.

Then, as I developed my methodology, one question arose as to how to measure the degree of the speaker's preference. Methodologically, the degree of preference can be analysed via the ratio of a specific type of evaluative meaning in a disputant's talk. The following three methods can measure the ratio: 1) per 1000 words (Don, 2007; Pounds, 2011); 2) rate per minute; and 3) percentage. I chose not to use the per 1000 words method because it 'conflates two separate ideas: *How evaluative is the writer as a whole?* and *How much do they favour particular Attitude types?*' (O'Donnell, 2014, p. 103, emphasis in original). A disputant who overall sparingly appraises and only positively appraises the self, for example, might have a similar per 1000 words frequency of inscribed positive self-Judgement to a disputant who appraises frequently but only occasionally self-praises. Obviously, the evaluative construal of the self is different between the two disputants. Thus, for the purpose of this research, the per 1000 words method was not used. As well, I chose not to use the method of rate per minute because the disputants' speech rates differed considerably, making the method unreliable in comparing the speakers' use of evaluative meaning across the dataset. The average speech rate of all disputants in the dataset was 279.15 syllables per minute, with the slowest speaker's rate being 236.22 and the fastest speaker's rate being 339.30. Because the average length of Chinese clause is 6.63 syllables (Lin, 2011), the differences in speech rate means that the slowest speaker produced about seven clauses per minute fewer than the dataset average, and nearly sixteen clauses per minute fewer than the fastest speaker. The wide variation in speech rate means that it would be misleading to use rate per minute to measure variation in the use of these attitude-related resources across the speech of the different disputants.

I ended up choosing to use the percentage, or 'mean frequency' (O'Donnell, 2014), to analyse the disputants' degree of preference for the various attitude-related meaning-making resources under investigation. The ratio of a designated evaluative meaning was calculated by determining the percentage of the designated attitude-related meaning in the total number of attitudinal assessments in a disputant's speech (for example, the total number of attitude-related expressions in a disputant's contribution to one stage of the episode). A disputant, for example, for whom

60% of their total attitudinal assessments are negative Judgements of their spouse can plausibly be seen as operating with a different attitudinal disposition from a disputant for whom only 10% of their total attitudinal assessments are of this same type.

In short, this research adopted two lines of inquiry to map a disputant's deployment of these attitude-related resources and thereby to determine their preference/dis-preference for a designated evaluative meaning: 'occurrence' and 'ratio'. The following chapters will present findings concerning the disputants' attitudinal arrangements emerging from these two lines of inquiry.

3.4 Data Processing in a Computing Environment

A final note on methodology is that this research deployed a programming language and associated packages for data analysis and pattern recognition. As previewed in earlier chapters, the use of this particular computing environment for discovering recurrent patterns in linguistic annotations of complexity is one of the original contributions to the scholarship made by this research. This method's background is a 'two-culture' phenomenon in semantic studies within the SFL paradigm (Matthiessen, 2015): a culture focusing on manual discourse analysis and a culture engaging with computational modelling. Such a 'two-culture' phenomenon is sometimes perceived as a 'trade-off' between annotation delicacy and data size in Appraisal-based discourse analysis (Bednarek, 2008; Fuoli, 2018; Fuoli & Bednarek, 2022; Yu et al., 2024). A descriptive and interpretive Appraisal-based analysis can map a comprehensive and highly delicate profile of the Appraisal resources in the text. However, such an analysis is based on nuanced manual annotations, which can only be conducted on a small text set. If the patterns were not identified by systematic and principled scrutiny, some hidden or unexpected patterns might be overlooked due to the unavoidable human cognition limitations. In a similar vein, quantitative, even automated, Appraisal-based analysis can handle a big dataset, but with the sacrifice of not being able to track the more delicate Appraisal resources, especially the implicitly construed evaluative meanings. According to the algorithms underlying several Appraisal-informed sentiment analysis models (Wiebe et al., 2005; Taboada et al., 2011; Taboada, 2016; e.g., Goddard et al., 2019), this approach can only operate on the lexicogrammar stratum, unable to track resources on the discourse semantic stratum.

The tension between this research's purpose and its dataset size also posed a problem. My objective was to investigate how the disputants in my dataset discursively presented themselves via the use of evaluative language by identifying and characterising patterned variations among multiple disputants in the dataset. The dataset consisted of 12 disputants, which might sound small. However, considering the dataset's duration was 230 minutes, with 1147 turns and 5282 moves, the dataset was large. The multiple variables involved in the analysis augmented the complexity of pattern recognition. There were 15 simple variables of conversation features (e.g., turn holder or addressee), the disputants' choice of what attitudes to convey (e.g., attitude type or attitude polarity), and the disputants' choice of how to frame the attitudes (e.g., the scaling and/or dialogical framing options). Combining the simple variables gave rise to hundreds of possible compound variables (e.g., Judgement targeting the self or the husband's inscribed positive Judgement targeting the self when addressing the mediator). Theoretically, all the simple or compound variables can be used as a parameter of variation to identify similarities and differences among the disputants. There is no doubt that systematic identification of the repeated patterns in such a large dataset goes beyond manual capacity.

Against the backdrop of the 'two-culture' issue and my research objectives, I decided to explore the possibilities of pattern recognition (especially cluster analysis) made available via computational tools. The method I chose drew on Data Science, especially its concepts of data structure, pipeline (workflow), and reproducibility (Ozdemir, 2016; Wickham & Grolemund, 2017; Xu, 2024; Xu & Chen, 2020). Broadly speaking, data structure means that to process data in a computing environment, it is a prerequisite to structure the data in a machine-readable format, usually a rectangular structure composed of observations and variables. Because my concerns were with the meanings being conveyed by the disputants (a semantic/discourse semantic orientation) rather than with their wordings (a lexicogrammatical orientation), my texts were not in the form of structured, machine-readable data. (While advances in computational Sentiment Analysis continue, that are not yet at a level which would make possible automated classification of the nature of the attitudes in such texts or how the attitudes were activated.) Accordingly, I transformed the raw data into structured data by treating the disputants' talk (segmented in moves) as rows of observations and the Appraisal features as columns of variables. Secondly, the pipeline concept refers to the set of processing and analysis steps to convert raw data into actionable answers to research questions. In this research, the pipeline referred to the workflow from the transcription of the disputants' talk (raw data) to identifying and characterising attitudinal dispositions found in the dataset (actionable answers). Finally, the concept of reproducibility means that once I had written scripts in a programming language, the scripts could be saved, edited, and run in parts or as a whole on the same or different data files unlimitedly. The scripts and/or the data files could also be made available for other researchers—a response from discourse analysis or humanities researchers to the call for 'open science' (UNESCO, 2020). That being said, the data processing method in this research was based on manual annotations of Appraisal resources conducted at the discourse semantic stratum, aiming at tracking all the evaluative meaning-making resources at all delicacy levels. Hence, this research is fundamentally a linguistic study instead of a computational one. By deploying programming language in the pattern recognition stage, the method could handle large dataset and recognise patterns systematically.

More specifically, I used *R* (R Core Team, 2025) in RStudio (Posit team, 2025) as the computing environment. *R* has increasingly become a popular software environment because of its functionality in statistical analysis and visualisation (Gries, 2021; Wickham & Grolemund, 2017). It is free and open-sourced, with a wide range of library packages and a very supportive online community. In linguistic studies specifically, *R* has been deployed as an efficient tool for corpus linguistics (Desagulier, 2017; Gries, 2017, 2023) and sociolinguistics (Johnson, 2009), which are concerned with linguistic patterns on the lexicogrammar stratum. Previous research has employed *R* to analyse Appraisal patterns across diverse datasets. For example, Cavasso and Taboada (2021) examined variation in attitudinal types and polarity in online news comments; Xu and White (2021), Jing and Xu (2023), and Xu and Jing (2024) explored attitudinal disposition (type, polarity and target) variations in social media data; while Xu and Xiao (2024) examined dialogic positioning patterns (engagement) in deaf translators' textual identity. In addition, Almutairi (2013, 2021a, 2021b) utilised computational statistical methods to visualise Appraisal patterns. However, these studies primarily focused on pattern recognition with limited 'attitudinal axes' (White, 2008), lacking a comprehensive analysis of evaluative meaning-making resources within their datasets.

In contrast, my research took a wholistic view of 'attitude' and considered four attitudinal axes as an attitudinal complex (including attitudinal type, polarity, target, and explicitness). (To avoid overloading this chapter, details of the analysis have been held over until Chap. 4. There I explain my reasons for going beyond attitude type and polarity to include the nature of the 'appraised', the attitudinal target, in the patterns being recognised computationally.) When I sought to identify Appraisal patterns in the disputants' talk, my analysis was interested in the patterns in the attitudinal complexes among multiple disputants, as well as in the co-occurrence between the attitudinal complexes and the ENGAGEMENT/GRADUATION framings of the attitudinal complexes. The most complicated analysis I undertook recognised patterns among 24 attitude-related options (to be presented in Chap. 4). Hence, it is fair to argue that my research contributes to the existing linguistics literature by conducting a multivariate discourse analysis at the discourse semantics level in a computing environment.

Specifically, the data wrangling and pattern recognition were processed in the following steps. First, the disputants' talks were manually annotated by following the aforementioned annotation methods.

Then the transcription, annotation, and metadata of the disputants (e.g., gender, waywardness, and outcome of the resolution) were transformed from unstructured linguistic annotations into machine-readable structured data. The third step was to write *R* scripts to identify patterns and recurrent configurations in the disputants' deployment of evaluative meaning-making resources. Similarly, as Appraisal offers analysts a linguistically principled taxonomy to track evaluative meaning-making resources, the *R* scripts identify patterns in a systemic and principled matter. Pattern recognition methods used in this research include statistical analysis, visualisation, and correlation analysis with metadata. Because the raw data for the pattern recognition was the Appraisal annotations manually done at all levels of delicacy, the systemic and principled pattern recognition performed in the computing environment could identify all the evaluative meaning-making patterns in the dataset. Several *R* packages were used and will be introduced and described during the discussion when necessary. The *R* scripts for each chapter's analysis are in the book's GitHub repository.

The fourth step was to relate the patterns to the text and examine what the patterns indicated about the disputants' use of evaluative language. Notably, I did not take the patterns emerging from the computational methods as givens. Lacking the cushion of linguistic knowledge and socio-cultural experience to understand the patterns' implications, the computational methods cannot directly tell us what is going on in the disputants' use of evaluative language. The patterns require a human to interpret them. The strategy taken by this research was to have a human review (i.e., by me) of each pattern and to bring the patterns back to the disputants' talk. Each pattern was interrogated by considering the text and the context for its possible interpretations. The patterns were meaningful in the sense that they revealed things that might not be expected or raised new questions about the data.

One of the major pattern recognition methods I used in this project was the clustering (or cluster analysis) methods from data mining. The details of the specific methods will be introduced where necessary in later chapters. Nonetheless, a general description of clustering is provided here. The basic application for clustering is to partition a set of data points into a set of groups that are as similar as possible (Larose, 2005). Clustering analysis is frequently exploratory in nature, so it is a method particularly relevant for 'data-driven' instead of 'hypothesis-driven' studies (Aggarwal & Reddy, 2014). Each clustering method deploys multiple statistical measures underlying its algorithms. According to Aggarwal (2015), multiple research communities, including statistics, data mining, and machine learning, have significant overlaps but nevertheless approach the same problem from different perspectives. The clustering methods in data mining offered me useful tools to explore the similarities and differences across the disputants' use of attitude-associated resources. These methods are 'unsupervised learning', unsupervised 'because of the lack of a special training database to "teach" the model about the notion of an appropriate grouping' (Aggarwal, 2015, p. 19). To a certain degree, the clustering methods in data mining are similar to Michael Halliday's methods in discovering the inherent functional organisation of language—that is, his theory of metafunction (Halliday, 1969; Halliday & Matthiessen, 2004; Matthiessen, 2015). When developing a systemic description of English, Halliday manually noticed that certain systems clustered together and interpreted the clusters as revealing the intrinsic functional organisation of language. The clustering in data mining and Halliday's studies have a similar underlying research philosophy in the sense that both are hypothesis-generating explorations rather than hypothesis-driven experiments. While Halliday identified the clustering of systems in system networks manually and then arrived at the theory of metafunction, I used the computational clustering methods to identify the hidden tendencies in the disputants' use of evaluative language and their attitudinal positioning.

In short, the data processing process I used in this project is a human-computer integrated research method. It processes data via, firstly, 'human annotation' and then via 'computerised pattern recognition', then to 'human review and interpretation'. This data processing process optimises both the human and the computer potential in discourse analysis at a semantics level. It can be seen from the discussions in the following chapters that many patterns recognised by the computer offer fresh insights into the subtle or unexpected patterns in the data, which might be otherwise undetectable by the researchers' human intuition or traditional manual methods. Under this integrated research method, the two cultures in the 'two-culture' phenomenon are not binary oppositions. They can be incorporated into one research so that both cultures' advantages can be utilised to contribute to our understanding of the data.

4 Chapter Summary

This chapter has introduced the data and the research methods. It explained the socio-cultural background of the data source and the composition of the dataset. It provided a detailed account of the contextual features of the data, particularly the Tenor relations in the family dispute resolution exchanges. This chapter also explained the transcription and annotation principles in tracking the disputants' deployment of evaluative meaning-making resources. The nuanced linguistic annotations serve as the basis for pattern recognition reported and discussed in the following chapters. The chapter finally introduced the data processing method by which I sought to identify recurrent patterns among multiple disputants regarding their discursive self-presentation. This method takes the manual annotations as the raw data and conducts pattern recognition in a computing environment. The following chapters will demonstrate that the method arguably enables interpretative multivariate linguistic analysis on a large-scale dataset.

In the following chapters, the exploration of the disputants' discursive self-presentation will be attended to via two lines of inquiry: a synoptic view of attitudinal disposition in Chaps. 4 and 5 and a dynamic view of attitudinal disposition in Chaps. 6 and 7.

As a final note, it might be convenient to end this chapter with some definitions required for what is to follow. For this monograph, 'addressee' refers to the person whom the speaker directly addresses, for example, the other spouse or the hostess. The addressee can be inferred from the pronouns in the utterance or the speaker's gaze or body position in the video. 'Audience' or 'hearer' is used as a cover term to refer to all parties involved in the communicative context, including the immediate interactants, the family relationship expert panel, and the TV programme viewers. Finally, 'assessment' and 'evaluation' are used interchangeably, with the phrase 'attitudinal assessment' used to designate positive or negative assessments.

References

Aggarwal, C. C. (2015). *Data mining: The textbook*. Springer.
Aggarwal, C. C., & Reddy, C. K. (2014). *Data clustering: Algorithms and applications*. CRC Press.
Almutairi, B. A. A. (2013). Visualizing patterns of appraisal in texts and corpora. *Text & Talk, 33*(4–5), 691–723. https://doi.org/10.1515/text-2013-0031
Almutairi, B. A. A. (2021a). Quantifying systemic coupling and syndrome using multivariate statistical methods: An SFL corpus example. *Linguistics and the Human Sciences, 15*(1), 1–38. https://doi.org/10.1558/lhs.19983
Almutairi, B. A. A. (2021b). Towards estimating global probabilities of evaluation in English based on automatic extraction of least delicate Appraisal in large corpora. *Language Sciences, 88*, 101432. https://doi.org/10.1016/j.langsci.2021.101432
Bednarek, M. (2008). *Emotion talk across corpora*. Palgrave Macmillan. https://doi.org/10.1057/9780230285712
Berry, M. (2016). On describing contexts of situation. In W. L. Bowcher & J. Y. Liang (Eds.), *Society in language, language in society: Essays in honour of Ruqaiya Hasan* (pp. 184–205). Palgrave Macmillan.
Bowcher, W. L. (1999). Investigating institutionalization in context. In M. Ghadessy (Ed.), *Text and context in functional linguistics* (pp. 141–176). John Benjamins Publishing. https://www.jbe-platform.com/content/books/9789027299673-cilt.169.09bow. Accessed 12 April 2021.
Cavasso, L., & Taboada, M. (2021). A corpus analysis of online news comments using the appraisal framework. *Journal of Corpora and Discourse Studies, 4*(0), 1–38. https://doi.org/10.18573/jcads.61
Chao, Y. R. (1965). *A grammar of spoken Chinese*. University of California Press.
Chinese Academy of Social Sciences Institute of Linguistics. (2017). 现代汉语词典 *Xiandai Hanyu Cidian [Modern Chinese dictionary]*. Commercial Press.
Desagulier, G. (2017). *Corpus linguistics and statistics with R: Introduction to quantitative methods in linguistics* (Quantitative methods in the humanities and social sciences). Springer International Publishing. https://doi.org/10.1007/978-3-319-64572-8_1
Don, A. (2007). An approach to the analysis of textual identity through profiles of evaluative disposition. In *ASFLA 2007 proceedings*.
Don, A. (2016). "It is hard to mesh all this": Invoking attitude, persona and argument organisation. *Functional Linguistics, 3*, 9. https://doi.org/10.1186/s40554-016-0033-1
Du Bois, J. W. (2006). *Transcription convention updates*. http://transcription.projects.linguistics.ucsb.edu/A05updates.pdf.
Eggins, S., & Slade, D. (1997). *Analysing casual conversation*. Cassell.
'ELAN'. (2020). Nijmegen: Max Planck Institute for Psycholinguistics. *The Language Archive*. https://archive.mpi.nl/tla/elan
Fuoli, M. (2018). A stepwise method for annotating appraisal. *Functions of Language, 25*(2), 229–258. https://doi.org/10.1075/fol.15016.fuo
Fuoli, M., & Bednarek, M. (2022). Emotional labor in webcare and beyond: A linguistic framework and case study. *Journal of Pragmatics, 191*, 256–270. https://doi.org/10.1016/j.pragma.2022.01.016
Goddard, C., Taboada, M., & Trnavac, R. (2019). The semantics of evaluational adjectives: Perspectives from natural semantic metalanguage and appraisal. *Functions of Language, 26*(3), 308–342. https://doi.org/10.1075/fol.00029.god
Goffman, E. (1974). *Frame analysis: An essay on the organization of experience*. Northeastern University Press.
Gries, S. T. (2017). *Quantitative corpus linguistics with R: A practical introduction*. Routledge. https://doi.org/10.4324/9781315746210
Gries, S. T. (2021). *Statistics for linguistics with R: A practical introduction* (3rd ed.). De Gruyter Mouton. https://doi.org/10.1515/9783110307474

Gries, S. T. (2023). Statistics in corpus linguistics. In *Readings in corpus linguistics: A teaching and research guide for scholars in Nigeria and beyond* (pp. 78–114).

Halliday, M. A. K. (1969). Options and functions in the English clause. *Brno Studies in English, 8*, 82–88.

Halliday, M. A. K. (1978). *Language as a social semiotic: The social interpretation of language and meaning*. University Park Press.

Halliday, M. A. K. (1989). *Spoken and written language*. Oxford University Press.

Halliday, M. A. K., & Hasan, R. (1985). *Language, context, and text: Aspects of language in a social-semiotic perspective*. Deakin University.

Halliday, M. A. K., & Matthiessen, C. M. I. M. (2004). *An introduction to functional grammar*. Routledge.

Halliday, M. A. K., & Matthiessen, C. M. I. M. (2014). *Halliday's introduction to functional grammar* (4th ed.). Routledge.

Hao, J., & Humphrey, S. (2012). The role of "coupling" in biological experimental reports. *Linguistics and the Human Sciences, 5*(2), 169–194.

Hasan, R. (2014). Towards a paradigmatic description of context: Systems, metafunctions, and semantics. *Functional Linguistics, 1*(9), 1–54. https://doi.org/10.1186/s40554-014-0009-y

Hasan, R. (2020). Tenor: Rethinking interactant relations. *Language, Context and Text, 2*(2), 213–333.

Hawes, C. (2024). Moral transformation in the Chinese legal system: Contradiction or complementary relationship? In Y. Guo (Ed.), *Jiaohua: Chinese ideas and practices of moral transformation* (pp. 85–101). Springer Nature. https://doi.org/10.1007/978-981-97-9487-4_5

Hawes, C., & Kong, S. (2013). Primetime dispute resolution: Reality TV mediation shows in China's "harmonious society". *Law & Society Review, 47*(4), 739–770. https://doi.org/10.1111/lasr.12046

Hood, S., & Martin, J. R. (2007). Invoking attitude: The play of graduation in appraising discourse. In R. Hasan, C. M. I. M. Matthiessen, & J. J. Webster (Eds.), *Continuing discourse on language: A functional perspective* (pp. 739–764). Equinox Publishing Ltd. Available at: https://journals.equinoxpub.com/books/article/view/25351

Hood, S., & Zhang, D. (2020). GRADUATION in play with other systems of meaning in the enactment of interpersonal relations. *Journal of Foreign Languages, 43*(6), 21–41.

Jing, Y., & Xu, Q. (2023). Danmu video as the resemiotised: An attitudinal analysis of Home Visit. *Media, Culture & Society, 45*(4), 753–768. https://doi.org/10.1177/01634437231158514

Johnson, D. E. (2009). Getting off the GoldVarb standard: Introducing Rbrul for mixed-effects variable rule analysis. *Language and Linguistics Compass, 3*(1), 359–383. https://doi.org/10.1111/j.1749-818X.2008.00108.x

Larose, D. T. (2005). *Discovering knowledge in data: An introduction to data mining*. John Wiley & Sons.

Lin, C.-J. C. (2011). Chinese and English relative clauses: Processing constraints and typological consequences. In Z. Jing-Schmidt (Ed.), *Proceedings of the 23rd North American conference on Chinese lingusitics. NACCL-23* (pp. 191–199). University of Oregon.

Lukin, A., et al. (2011). Halliday's model of register revisited and explored. *Linguistics and the Human Sciences, 4*(2), 187–213. https://doi.org/10.1558/lhs.v4i2.187

Macken-Horarik, M., & Isaac, A. R. (2014). Appraising appraisal. In G. Thompson & L. Alba-Juez (Eds.), *Evaluation in context* (pp. 67–92). John Benjamins Publishing Company. https://doi.org/10.1075/pbns.242.04mac

Martin, J. R. (1991). Intrinsic functionality: Implications for contextual theory. *Social Semiotics, 1*(1), 99–162. https://doi.org/10.1080/10350339109360331

Martin, J. R. (1992). *English text: System and structure*. John Benjamins Publishing Company.

Martin, J. R. (2009). Language, register and genre. In C. Coffin, T. Lillis, & K. O'Halloran (Eds.), *Applied linguistics methods: A reader* (1st ed., pp. 1–27). Routledge. https://www.routledge.com/Applied-Linguistics-Methods-A-Reader-1st-Edition/Coffin-Lillis-OHalloran/p/book/9780415545457. Accessed 4 June 2019.

Martin, J. R., & White, P. R. R. (2005). *The language of evaluation: Appraisal in English*. Palgrave Macmillan.
Matthiessen, C. M. I. M. (2015). Halliday on language. In J. J. Webster (Ed.), *The Bloomsbury companion to M.A.K. Halliday* (pp. 137–202). Bloomsbury Publishing.
O'Donnell, M. (2014). Exploring identity through appraisal analysis: A corpus annotation methodology. *Linguistics and the Human Sciences, 9*(1), 95–116. https://doi.org/10.1558/lhs.v9i1.95
Ozdemir, S. (2016). *Principles of data science*. Packt Publishing. https://www.packtpub.com/au/big-data-and-business-intelligence/principles-data-science. Accessed 11 April 2020.
Posit Team. (2025). *RStudio: Integrated development environment for R*. Posit Software, PBC. http://www.posit.co/
Pounds, G. (2011). "This property offers much character and charm": Evaluation in the discourse of online property advertising. *Text & Talk - An Interdisciplinary Journal of Language, Discourse & Communication Studies, 31*(2), 195–220. https://doi.org/10.1515/text.2011.009
Poynton, C. M. (1989). *Language and gender: Making the difference*. Oxford University Press.
Poynton, C. M. (1990). *Address and the semiotics of social relations*. PhD Thesis, University of Sydney. https://ses.library.usyd.edu.au/handle/2123/2297. Accessed 6 January 2020.
R Core Team. (2025). *R: A language and environment for statistical computing*. R Foundation for Statistical Computing. http://www.r-project.org/
Sinclair, J. M., & Coulthard, M. (1975a). *Towards an analysis of discourse: The English used by teachers and pupils* (1st ed.). Oxford University Press.
Sinclair, J. M., & Coulthard, M. (1975b). *Towards an analysis of discourse: The English used by teachers and pupils*. Oxford University Press.
Taboada, M. (2016). Sentiment analysis: An overview from linguistics. *Annual Review of Linguistics, 2*(1), 325–347. https://doi.org/10.1146/annurev-linguistics-011415-040518
Taboada, M., et al. (2011). Lexicon-based methods for sentiment analysis. *Computational Linguistics, 37*(2), 267–307. https://doi.org/10.1162/COLI_a_00049
Thompson, G. (2014). Affect and emotion, target-value mismatches, and Russian dolls: Refining the appraisal model. In G. Thompson & L. Alba-Juez (Eds.), *Evaluation in context* (Pragmatics & beyond new series) (pp. 47–66). John Benjamins Publishing Company.
UNESCO. (2020). *Open science movement | United Nations Educational, Scientific and Cultural Organization*. http://www.unesco.org/new/en/communication-and-information/portals-and-platforms/goap/open-science-movement/. Accessed 30 July 2020.
White, P. R. R. (1998). *Telling media tales: The news story as rhetoric*. Doctoral Thesis, University of Sydney.
White, P. R. R. (2003). Beyond modality and hedging: A dialogic view of the language of intersubjective stance. *Text, 23*(2), 259–284. https://doi.org/10.1515/text.2003.011
White, P.R.R. (2006) 'Evaluative semantics and ideological positioning in journalistic discourse: A new framework for analysis', in I. Lassen, J. Strunck, and T. Vestergaard (eds) Mediating ideology in text and image. John Benjamins Publishing Company, pp. 37–67. https://benjamins.com/catalog/dapsac.18. Accessed 2 November 2020.
White, P. R. R. (2008). Praising and blaming, applauding and disparaging - Solidarity, audience positioning and the linguistic of evaluative disposition. In G. Antos, E. Ventola, & T. Weber (Eds.), *Handbook of interpersonal communication* (pp. 567–594). Mouton de Gruyter. (Handbooks of applied linguistics.
White, P. R. R. (2012). Exploring the axiological workings of "reporter voice" news stories—Attribution and attitudinal positioning. *Discourse, Context & Media, 1*(2–3), 57–67. https://doi.org/10.1016/j.dcm.2012.10.004
White, P.R.R. (2020a) *Appraisal theory homepage. The Appraisal Website*. https://www.grammatics.com/appraisal/. Accessed 27 September 2025.
White, P. R. R. (2020b). The putative reader in mass media persuasion – Stance, argumentation and ideology. *Discourse & Communication, 14*(4), 404–423. https://doi.org/10.1177/1750481320910512

White, P. R. R. (2021). Textual anticipation and the putative reader in persuasive discourse. *Journal of Foreign Languages, 44*(1), 2–20.
White, P. R. R. (2025). Appraisal theory and the analysis of point of view in news and views journalism – Unpacking journalistic "persuasiveness". *Language & Communication, 100*, 95–107. https://doi.org/10.1016/j.langcom.2024.11.005
Wickham, H., & Grolemund, G. (2017). *R for data science: Import, tidy, transform, visualize, and model data* (1st ed.). O'Reilly Media.
Wiebe, J., Wilson, T., & Cardie, C. (2005). Annotating expressions of opinions and emotions in language. *Language Resources and Evaluation, 39*(2), 165–210. https://doi.org/10.1007/s10579-005-7880-9
Xu, Q. (2024). Identifying disputants' attitudinal variations in family mediations: A data mining approach. *Discourse Studies, 26*(5), 693–719. https://doi.org/10.1177/14614456241237378
Xu, Q., & Chen, J. (2020). Appraisal-based discourse analysis through the lens of Data Science: Identifying evaluative styles in adversarial interactions [数据科学视角下的评价话语分析: 以冲突话语中会话者评价风格识别为例]. *Journal of Tianjing Foreign Studies University, 27*(6), 24–38. https://doi.org/10.13140/RG.2.2.22634.34246
Xu, Q., & Jing, Y. (2024). Ambient identity construction via massive anonymous danmu comments. *Language Sciences, 104*, 101631. https://doi.org/10.1016/j.langsci.2024.101631
Xu, Q., & White, P. R. R. (2021). "My husband always crosses the line": Textual identity and presentation of "the self" in family conflict communication. *Journal of Research in Applied Linguistics, 12*(2), 52–73. https://doi.org/10.22055/RALS.2021.17009
Xu, Q., & Xiao, X. (2024). Deaf translator's visibility in political discourse: A dialogic positioning perspective. *Perspectives, 32*(2), 242–260. https://doi.org/10.1080/0907676X.2022.2130080
Yu, D., et al. (2024). Assessing the potential of LLM-assisted annotation for corpus-based pragmatics and discourse analysis: The case of apology. *International Journal of Corpus Linguistics, 29*(4), 534–561. https://doi.org/10.1075/ijcl.23087.yu
Zappavigna, M. (2019). Ambient affiliation and #Brexit. In V. Koller, S. Kopf, & M. Miglbauer (Eds.), *Discourses of Brexit* (pp. 48–68). Routledge. https://doi.org/10.4324/9781351041867-4
Zappavigna, M., Dwyer, P., & Martin, J. R. (2008). Syndromes of meaning: Exploring patterned coupling in a NSW youth justice conference. In A. Mahboob & N. K. Knight (Eds.), *Questioning linguistics* (pp. 103–117). Cambridge Scholars Publishing.
Zappavigna, M., & Martin, J. R. (2018). *Discourse and diversionary justice*. Palgrave Macmillan.
Zhang, Y., & Chen, L. (2017). Exploration of factors leading to successful mediation: A regression analysis of reality TV mediation show episodes in China. *International Journal of Conflict Management, 28*(1), 24–49. https://doi.org/10.1108/IJCMA-12-2015-0087

Chapter 4
Attitudinal Cartography: Mapping Style Preferences

Contents

1 Introduction

This chapter and the following chapter report findings arising from the project's first line of inquiry into the disputants' discursive self-presentation: a synoptic view of attitudinal disposition. As indicated previously, by 'synoptic view' of attitudinal disposition, I mean tendencies that can be observed when a speaker's deployment of attitude-associated resources was tracked across an entire text or a complete textual stage. In this project, the texts analysed synoptically were comprised of the 'Problem Discussion' segment of the family dispute resolution programmes which constituted my dataset (as described in Chap. 3). As noted in Chap. 1, in this project, the disputants' attitudinal dispositions were explored from two perspectives: (1) a perspective focusing on the tendencies in the nature of the attitudes the disputants

Q. Xu, *Appraisal Approach to Conflict Styles*, The M.A.K. Halliday Library Functional Linguistics Series, https://doi.org/10.1007/978-981-95-6256-5_4

conveyed and (2) a perspective examining the tendencies in the disputants' framing of these attitudes. In this chapter, I report findings that emerged under the first perspective—when I focused on the attitudes the disputants advanced in the 'Problem Discussion' stage: what attitudes they conveyed, in what combinations, and at what frequencies.

In this analysis, I identified, classified, and quantified all attitudinal expressions (expressions explicitly or implicitly conveying or activating positive or negative assessments). The analysis was directed at identifying similarities and differences in the disputants' use of these attitudinal expressions, opting for the same types of attitudes and at similar rates. In this case, it would be possible to view this group of disputants as operating with the same attitudinal disposition. Since it is proposed that a speaker's attitudinal disposition constitutes a key aspect of their presentation of the 'self' (or their 'persona' or 'identity' as conceptualised in the Appraisal-based studies cited in the previous chapters), a basis would be provided for concluding that this group of disputants was associated with similar discursive self-presentation, at least with respect to those aspects of self-presentation grounded in evaluative meaning-making. (This proposition is dealt with in detail in this chapter and the next.) Based on this finding, it might be possible to identify and characterise certain sub-types of attitudinal disposition and group the disputants by reference to these sub-types. If alternatively, it turned out that *all* the disputants opted to convey the same types of attitudes at largely similar rates, this would be a basis for concluding that there was a common or uniform attitudinal disposition across the dataset, and, accordingly, that all the disputants offered the same self-presentation (at least with respect to the attitudinal aspect of 'self'). It might be hypothesised that this was an attitudinal disposition and, hence, an aspect of self-presentation that might be observed more widely in family dispute resolution situations. (Of course, for this hypothesis to be tested, an analysis of a substantially larger dataset of personal conflict resolution exchanges would be required.) Should it turn out, by way of one further possibility, that it was not possible to identify any patterns of similarity between the disputants in the nature and frequency of the attitudes they advanced, this would indicate that each disputant enacted unique and idiosyncratic attitudinal dispositions, and hence that there was no commonality with respect to their attitudinal self-presentation. Therefore, this analysis was directed at determining whether it might be possible to group these disputants in a family mediation television programme vis-à-vis some form of classification of attitudinal disposition. Any such classification could be interpreted as pointing to different discursive 'selves'.

It perhaps necessary to reiterate (as mentioned earlier in Chaps. 1 and 2) that the purpose of this analysis was not to explore any potential correlation between these sub-categories and external, socio-demographic characteristics of personal identity, including gender, age, and education background. Nevertheless, one pre-given feature of the disputants' 'self' was taken into consideration. The term 'pre-given' refers to a characteristic identified before initiating a detailed, bottom-up analysis of how disputants employed attitude-related resources. This feature was whether a disputant was classified as 'wayward' (being accused of some marital infidelity) or 'aggrieved' (the disputant making accusations of infidelity). The classification of the disputants in these categories was straightforward and easily achieved during the transcription process, as the accusations of infidelity were consistently stated explicitly. For clarity, it may be helpful to indicate at the outset that the analysis did not uncover a direct correlation between being classified as 'wayward' or 'aggrieved' and specific attitudinal tendencies. However, at some points in the analysis, some limited correlations were observed. These findings are further discussed below in greater detail, where appropriate.

This chapter starts with an overview of the analysis (Sect. 2), including an introduction to the focus of the analysis, the staging of the analysis, and a preview of key findings. It then reports the findings of each stage of analysis (Sects. 3 and 4). The chapter concludes with a summary of findings.

2 An Overview of the Analysis

2.1 The Focus of the Analysis

Within the current perspective—a perspective focusing on the tendencies in disputants' attitudes, I concentrated on similarities and differences in their preference for resources specifically attitudinal, that is, wordings that directly involve conveying or activating positive or negative assessments. This perspective was adopted on the basis that tendencies in the types of attitudes employed by a disputant were likely to play an influential role in that disputant's presentation of the self. For instance, a disputant who frequently utilises Judgement while rarely reporting their own Affectual responses to their spouse's behaviour plausibly enacts a different persona from one who frequently reports their Affectual assessments and has a substantially lower ratio of instances of Judgement.

The analysis employed in this perspective was generally similar to those used in a multitude of prior Appraisal-based textual identity studies (Coffin, 2006; Don, 2007a, 2016; Martin, 2008a; White, 1998, 2008; Zappavigna & Martin, 2018). It compared and contrasted the disputants' verbal contributions regarding their tendencies to use different types and subtypes of attitude (Judgement, Appreciation, Affect), taking into account whether these attitudes are positive or negative (attitude polarity) and whether they are directly expressed or implied (attitude explicitness).

The analysis extends the existing literature by examining patterns in the phenomena that are either the targets of the attitude or its trigger (the 'appraised'). This approach builds upon Don's (2007a, 2007b) work, where she analysed posts to an email discussion list not only for attitude type, polarity, and explicitness but also for whether the 'appraised' was the poster themselves, another person being addressed directly, some other contributor to the list, or the list community as a whole. Her findings highlighted how one of the posters stood out from others in their tendency not only to repeatedly report their own negative Affectual responses but also to use this device to imply wrongdoing on the part of other email list members who were the cause of their negative emotions.

Given my dataset—spouses being critical of each other and defending themselves—I adopted a taxonomy of sub-types of attitudinal target/trigger outlined in the previous chapter: self, antagonist, other participants in the marital situation, and the marital situation itself. These targets were overwhelmingly central to what went on attitudinally within these family dispute resolution interactions. The way the speaker evaluated themselves and their spouse (and other interested parties) was closely tied to how they presented themselves through discourse. Such a taxonomy accommodates a substantial proportion of the attitudinal assessments being advanced and enables the discovery of more general patterns of attitudinal orientation across the dataset. Therefore, in the annotation stage, all instances of attitudinal expressions were tagged with four attitude-associated features: attitude type, polarity, explicitness, and sub-type of appraised (self, antagonist, other, or marital situation).

I use the term 'attitudinal complex' to refer to this combination of features. An example of analysing such 'attitudinal complexes' is presented below (Table 4.1).

Table 4.1 Attitudinal complex (example)

Turn	Speaker	Utterance (Chinese)	Utterance (English translation)	Attitudinal features				Attitudinal complex
				Type	Polarity	Appraised/ target	Explicitness	
2	Wife_ H01_AW	他现在嘴上说他在乎夫妻感情	He **pays lip service** when saying that he cares about our marriage	Judgement	-ve	Antagonist	Inscription	Inscribe -ve Judge antagonist
		他在乎他的家庭	He **cares about his family**	Judgement	-ve	Antagonist	Inscription	Inscribe -ve Judge antagonist
3	Hostess_ H01	嗯						
4	Wife_ H01_AW	但是我从来没有感受到	But I've **never felt** it	Affect (triggered: Antagonist)	-ve	Self	Inscription	Inscribe -ve Affect self (triggered by the antagonist)
				Judgement	-ve	Antagonist	Invocation	Invoke -ve Judge antagonist
		我希望他真心对待	I **hope** he treats it sincerely	Affect (triggered: Antagonist)	+ve	Self	Inscription	Irrealis Affect self (triggered by the antagonist)
				Judgement	-ve	Antagonist	Invocation	Invoke -ve Judge antagonist

To a certain degree, the notion of 'attitudinal complex' is related to the concept of 'coupling' as described in the existing SFL literature, where 'coupling' is defined as 'the ways in which meanings combine, as pairs, triplets, quadruplets or any number of coordinated choices from system networks' (Martin, 2008b, p. 39). The most examined form of coupling is ideation-attitude coupling (Hao & Humphrey, 2012; Knight, 2013; Zappavigna, 2019; Zappavigna et al., 2008). Within this context, the term 'ideation' element from the 'coupling' concept is equivalent to what I define as the attitudinal target/trigger (the 'appraised'), aligning with Martin and White's (2005) definition.

Given this background, the present line of analysis focused on identifying patterns in disputants' use of attitudinal complexes. Which types of attitudinal complexes did they employ? In what combinations and at what frequencies? Were there any discernible grounds for grouping the disputants into sub-types of attitudinal disposition based on the similarities and differences in their deployment of these complexes? Moreover, were these aspects of 'self' associated with the deployment of attitudinal complexes broadly similar for all 'aggrieved' or 'wayward' spouses? The attempt to answer such questions involved two stages of analysis, with the relevant findings being presented in greater detail below.

2.2 *The Staging of the Analysis: 'Occurrence' Versus 'Ratio'*

The current synoptic analysis, exploring the tendencies in the disputants' preference for attitudinal complexes, was performed in two stages. These stages were related to the two complementary methods of measuring 'preference' (frequency of use) as foreshadowed in Chap. 3: 'occurrence' and 'ratio'. Each stage of this analysis yielded distinct insights into the above questions surrounding the disputants' preference for which attitudes to convey during the exchanges.

2.2.1 Stage One: The 'Occurrence' Analysis

The first stage involved an analysis of what I have termed the 'occurrence' of attitudinal complexes. As previewed in Chap. 3, the 'occurrence' analysis focused on whether a disputant employed a given attitudinal complex at least once within this segment of the episode. If so, it was interpreted that the disputants favoured, or at least did not avoid, using that specific attitudinal complex. On the other hand, if the disputants did not use an attitudinal complex even once, they were understood as avoiding or having no preference for that type of attitudinal meaning. This analysis was motivated by the proposition that differences between disputants in the attitudinal complexes they deployed at least once might indicate crucial differences in their textually performed identity. For example, those disputants who expressed positive Judgement towards the antagonist during a family dispute resolution interaction, thereby construing a more conciliatory 'self', are plausibly different from those who did not employ any such attitude in their responses.

I investigated the disputants' variations with respect to the 'occurrence' of attitudinal complexes through two steps. (Further details will be presented in Sect. 3.) Initially, I examined which attitudinal complexes were available for consideration under this 'occurrence' method. Different preference measurement methods necessitate distinct treatment of attitudinal meaning. The 'occurrence' analysis focused on the presence or absence of specific attitudinal orientations—such as positive self-Judgement or negative self-Judgement. These attitudinal orientations are determined by the speaker's co-selection of options across three attitudinal axes: attitude type (Judgement, Appreciation, or Affect)+polarity (positive or negative), and target/trigger (self, antagonist, other individuals involved in the relationship, or the marriage situation). Whether the attitudinal expression was conveyed via inscription or invocation does not influence the overall attitudinal orientation of the expression. Therefore, in the 'occurrence' analysis, attitudinal expressions with identical 'target + polarity + type' features were treated as instances of the same attitudinal complex, regardless of whether they involved inscription or invocation. By tracking instances of these complexes, I was able to draw up a list of all attitudinal orientations that could be observed in the dataset—a 'reservoir', so to speak, of what was available to each disputant.

The subsequent step in the 'occurrence' analysis was to explore the tendencies in the disputants' use of these available attitudinal complexes: whether they employed the same subset of the attitudinal complexes and if they clustered into groups based on deploying identical subsets of this array of attitudinal complexes, indicating that they were enacting a similar attitudinal disposition in the interaction. To analyse this, I used computational tools, particularly the clustering methods in data mining, to identify patterns in the occurrence of these attitudinal complexes. I interpreted the patterns from a linguistic perspective. The findings from this analysis stage will be presented in Sect. 3.

2.2.2 Stage Two: The 'Ratio' Analysis

As mentioned, the second stage of the analysis involved what I have referred to as the 'ratio' analysis. This entailed determining each disputant's degree of 'preference' for attitudinal complexes—whether they used a given complex frequently or less often in comparison with the other disputants. For reasons outlined below, the set of attitudinal complexes employed in this 'ratio' analysis was slightly different from that used in the 'occurrence' analysis discussed earlier. Chap. 3 detailed that the 'ratio' of use was calculated by determining what percentage of a disputant's total attitudinal expressions were comprised of the attitudinal complex being considered at any given time. For example, did their use of inscribed negative Judgement of the antagonist account for 10%, 50%, or 80% of all attitudinal instances observed in their speech? Underlying this analysis is the proposition that a disputant's degree of preference for a particular attitudinal complex or subset of attitudinal complexes would result in an attitudinal disposition different from those with different degrees of preference for the same set of attitudinal complexes. Consequently, disputants who, for instance, had 60% of their total attitudinal instances of inscribed positive self-Judgement could plausibly be seen as construing a distinct attitudinal disposition in comparison to those who had 20% such attitudinal complexes.

I explored the disputants' variation regarding the 'ratio' of attitudinal complexes in the following two steps. The first step was to examine what attitudinal complexes were available under the 'ratio' method. This 'ratio' method necessitated a different treatment of the attitudinal meaning from the 'occurrence' method. It was a sharper focus on the disparities across disputants regarding their deployment of attitude-associated resources than the 'occurrence' analysis, hence requiring a more precise measurement of disputants' attitudinal choices. (More details will be provided in the later sections.) In essence, attitudinal expressions having identical features ('target + polarity + type + explicitness') were considered as instances of the same attitudinal complex before making a distinction between those that were explicitly articulated and those that were not inscribed. Following this step, I compiled a list of all attitudinal complexes present in the dataset.

The second step was to explore the tendencies in the disputants' use of these attitudinal complexes. This step was complicated because my pilot studies indicated that each attitudinal complex could serve as one parameter of variation on its own, and it was also possible for two, three, four, or more attitudinal complexes to be combined to examine similarities and differences across the disputants. Therefore, the second step—which involved exploring tendencies among the disputants—followed this procedure. First, I employed each attitudinal complex as an individual parameter of variation or variable, distilling those that were most frequently used from those less frequently selected. This revealed commonalities among the disputants in the dataset: which attitudes were they consistently using at similar rates, and which did they regularly avoid in a similar fashion? Then, I combined the attitudinal complexes in pairs to find that the disputants tended to cluster into groups due to their similar ratios in using the designated attitudinal complexes, while differing from others. These groupings were suggestive of different attitudinal dispositions enacted by the disputants if ratios of multiple attitudinal complexes were considered simultaneously. Finally, I treated all the available attitudinal complexes as one bundle of parameters of variation and used clustering methods in the *R* data mining packages to perform a multivariate analysis. I then interpreted the findings from a linguistic perspective. The findings of the 'ratio' analysis will be presented in Sect. 4.

The above two stages of analysis—'occurrence' and 'ratio' of the attitudinal complexes—are summarised in Table 4.2. The findings of these analysis stages are set out in detail in a series of sections below.

Table 4.2 The staging of the analysis focusing on attitudes

Stage	Analysis	Steps	Section
1	Occurrence of the attitudinal complex	• Explore available attitudinal complexes • Explore the tendencies in the disputants' deployment of these attitudinal complexes – Find the clustering of the disputants and interpret the clustering from a linguistic perspective	Section 3
2	Ratio of the attitudinal complex	• Explore available attitudinal complexes • Explore the tendencies in the disputants' deployment of these attitudinal complexes – Explore variations vis-à-vis single attitudinal complex – Explore variations vis-à-vis attitudinal complex pairs – Explore variations vis-à-vis all the available attitudinal complexes Find the clustering of the disputants and interpret the clustering from a linguistic perspective	Section 4

2.3 *A Preview of Findings*

By way of a preview, broadly speaking, the findings reveal substantial variations in the disputants' preference for certain attitudinal complexes (with regards to which ones they use, their frequency, and in what combinations), leading to considerable variations in self-presentations associated with the expression of attitude. It is a somewhat more complex question as to whether, nevertheless, these findings provide a foundation for taxonomies of attitudinal disposition subtypes and hence for attitude-related presentations of the self.

This complexity arises from the fact that it was not typical for disputants to be similar or dissimilar in absolute terms regarding their preference for a particular attitudinal orientation or combination of attitudes. Instead, differences or similarities were often found to lie in relative frequency of use rather than one disputant using a particular attitude or a combination of attitudes while another disputant did not employ that resource at all (although this difference was evident in some cases). In such cases, this raised questions about how similar the usage patterns of two disputants need to be for them to be considered communicatively similar, such as construing the same attitudinal disposition.

More fundamental was the complication resulting from my decision (as outlined in the previous chapters) to explore findings facilitated by cluster analysis packages in *R*, as described earlier. In the case of my study, when determining degrees of similarity or difference in the disputants' use of these attitude-related resources, the computational packages simultaneously not only considered frequencies of use but also frequencies of combinations of these resources. This meant that the packages compared disputants not just on whether they, for example, advanced a positive assessment directed at the antagonist (in contrast to, e.g., advancing a negative assessment of their spouse) but also examined how frequently, for example, they inscribed a negative Judgement of their spouse in comparison with, for instance, a negative self-Judgement or a positive Judgement of their spouse. This resulted in a pattern of use being situated on a multidimensional map of possible variations, where one disputant's pattern of attitudinal resources deployment might coincide with another disputant's pattern along none, one, several, many, or even all axes of variation.

While such an analysis can provide deep insights into degrees of similarity and difference in the disputants' use of these resources, it does not always lead to the production of the kinds of simple taxonomies or sub-classifications that arise when comparisons are made across just a few axes of variation. All these findings and the complex insights thereby derived with respect to attitudinal disposition and the discursive presentation of the self (when viewed synoptically with a focus on the attitudes being expressed) will be explored in detail below.

3 Stage One: The 'Occurrence' Analysis of Tendencies in the Use of Attitudinal Complexes

In this and the following sections, I provide a more detailed discussion of the analyses outlined above and report key findings. I begin with what I have termed the 'occurrence' method. Recall that this method focused on the attitudinal orientations and examined whether each disputant made any use of the attitudinal complexes observed across the dataset. For example, was there at least one instance of positive self-Judgement or negative self-Judgement in the person's speech?

As noted in the previous section, different exploration methods require different treatment of the meaning-making resources: which system or subsystem of options should be selected and foregrounded in the analysis. Considering that the 'occurrence' method emphasises the existence of a particular attitudinal orientation (such as positive self-Judgement or negative self-Judgement), which is realised by the speaker's choices in the ATTITUDE systems of target, type, and polarity, I considered the attitudinal axes of 'sub-type of attitude + polarity + target/trigger' as compulsory in determining the orientation of an attitudinal expression. Subsequently, although all the attitudinal instances were annotated regarding all the attitudinal axes, including the explicitness of the expression (i.e., either inscribed or invoked), for this analysis, I grouped the attitudinal expressions (including both inscriptions and invocations) having the same 'sub-type of attitude + polarity + target/trigger' features as one type of attitudinal complex. An example can be found in Table 4.3, where an *inscribed* positive Judgement of the antagonist and an *invoked* positive Judgement of the antagonist are presented to exemplify the same attitudinal complex: positive Judgement of the antagonist.

This treatment allowed me to gain a more wholistic view of the tendencies regarding which types of attitudes were being deployed, whether positive or negative, and at whom/what were they directed (i.e., what was being appraised). In future analyses when, in contrast, the concern went beyond the attitude itself to the

Table 4.3 'Occurrence' analysis: Attitudinal complex annotation

Attitudinal complex		Attitudinal axes				
Assessment	Abbr.	Type	Polarity	Appraised/ target	Explicitness	Example
Positive Judgement of the antagonist	PJA	Judgement	+ve	Antagonist	Inscription	他之前是很负责任的一个男人He used to be a very **responsible** man (Wife_H01_AW)
					Invocation	他会把几天的菜都给我弄好He would prepare make-ahead meals **for a few days** for me (Wife_H01_AW)

mechanism or linguistic means by which the attitude was advanced or activated (and other potential communicative effects which thereby follow), the distinction between implicit and explicit attitude would be attended to (e.g., the 'ratio' analysis to be reported later in this chapter). In putting aside this distinction (for this analysis stage), I was able to achieve more of an overview with respect to the overall attitudinal orientation of the disputants—what attitudes did they tend to advance with respect to the targets central to these hostile exchanges. (Of course, an analysis along similar lines which did attend to the distinction between inscribed and invoked attitudes would have been insightful, but space limitations meant it was not practical to include this, given all the other lines of analysis I wanted to report.)

3.1 Available Attitudinal Complexes

As indicated, by way of the first step in this analysis, I identified all the different types of attitudinal complex observed across the dataset. Nine were found (summarised in Table 4.4). It is plausible that all these complexes, as options for targeted attitudinal assessment, were available to all the disputants and hence are the reservoir of resources on which they drew as they enacted a particular attitudinal self.

Six of the complexes were assessments of humans or human behaviour. These are the attitudinal assessments relating to the Appraisal resource of Judgement:

(1) positive Judgement of the antagonist (PJA);
(2) negative Judgement of the antagonist (NJA);
(3) positive Judgement of the self (PJS);
(4) negative Judgement of the self (NJS);
(5) positive Judgement of people outside of the marriage relationship (PJO); and
(6) negative Judgement of people outside of the marriage relationship (NJO).

Table 4.4 'Occurrence' analysis: The nine attitudinal complexes found in the dataset

	Attitudinal complex		Attitudinal axes				
	Assessment	Abbr.	Type	Polarity	Appraised/ target	Explicitness	Example
(1)	Positive judgement of the antagonist	PJA	Judgement	+ve	Antagonist	Inscription	他之前是很负责任的一个男人He used to be a very **responsible** man (Wife_H01_AW)
						Invocation	他会把几天的菜都给我弄好He would prepare make-ahead meals for a few days for me (Wife_H01_AW)
(2)	Negative judgement of the antagonist	NJA	Judgement	-ve	Antagonist	Inscription	他是道貌岸然的He is **hypocritical** (Wife_H01_AW)
						Invocation	所有公司的账目..我老公基本上不管All the company's income and expenditure.. my husband basically doesn't care (Wife_W01_WW)
(3)	Positive judgement directed at the self	PJS	Judgement	+ve	Self	Inscription	我坦坦然然的I am **honest and calm** (Husband_H01_WH)
						Invocation	公司里面没钱…都是我去跟我娘家借If the company ran out of money… I was the person who went to borrow money from my natal family (Wife_W01_WW)
(4)	Negative judgement directed at the self	NJS	Judgement	-ve	Self	Inscription	是..这点欠缺Yes.. I'm **not good** enough on this (Husband_H01_WH)
						Invocation	可能我没有方法吧Maybe I don't have a method (to communicate with the kids) (Husband_H03_WH)
(5)	Positive judgement directed at people outside of the marriage relationship	PJO	Judgement	+ve	Other	Inscription	这男同学一开始..开导效果还比较好一点 in the beginning.. this male high schoolmate.. **did a** pretty **good job** (Husband_H02_WH)
						Invocation	他都会跟我说..该怎么走该怎么做He[a] will talk to me.. tell me how to make a decision and what to do (Wife_W02_WW)
(6)	Negative judgement directed at people outside of the marriage relationship	NJO	Judgement	-ve	Other	Inscription	因为我知道她不是个正经女人Because I knew she[b] was **not** a **responsible** woman (Wife_H01_AW)
						Invocation	他就是不还He[c] just didn't want to return the money (Wife_W01_WW)

(continued)

Table 4.4 (continued)

	Attitudinal complex		Attitudinal axes				
	Assessment	Abbr.	Type	Polarity	Appraised/ target	Explicitness	Example
(7)	Negative affectual response triggered by the antagonist or antagonist's behaviour	NATA	Affect	-ve	Self (emoter)/ (eventually the antagonist)	Inscription of affect, invoking a negative judgement of the trigger	当时我看到这里我就已经气得忍不住When I read this..[d] I was so **angry** that I couldn't hold my anger (Wife_H01_AW) (invoking a negative judgement of the antagonist)
						Invocation of affect, invoking a negative judgement of the trigger	我吃饭都不能I couldn't even eat (because of my anger) (Wife_H03_AW) (invoking a negative judgement of the antagonist)
(8)	Observed other people's affectual response	OAO	Affect	-ve	Emoter (antagonist / other)	Inscription of affect, invoking a judgement of the emoter/ trigger	很害怕失去 She **is** very **afraid of losing** (Husband_H01_WH) (invoking a judgement of the antagonist on the basis that the 'fear' is irrational and excessive)
						Invocation of affect, invoking a judgement of the emoter/ trigger	她刚才哭成那个样子She cried that badly just now (Husband_H03_WH) (invoking a judgement of the antagonist on the basis that the 'sad' is irrational and excessive)
(9)	Appreciation	APP	Appreciation	+ve/-ve	Thing	Inscription	我诉求..拒绝过那种表里不一.. 阳奉阴违的日子 I request.. I refuse to live a life that is **duplicitous and deceitful** (Wife_H01_AW)
						Invocation	已经起诉离婚 I have sued for divorce (Wife_W02_WW)

Note that the distinction between inscribed and invoked Attitude is recorded here. However, as already indicated, this difference was put aside for this 'occurrence' analysis so as to provide a more wholistic view of the disputant's attitudinal orientation

[a]'*他He*' refers to a man with whom the wife had an allegedly flirtatious relationship

[b]'*她She*' refers to a female neighbour: the woman with whom the husband had an allegedly flirtatious relationship

[c]'*他He*' refers to a friend of the husband who borrowed money from the couple

[d]'*这里This*' refers to the husband's chat messages with a female neighbour, with whom the husband had an allegedly flirtatious relationship

These six types of attitudinal propositions reveal the speakers' attitudinal positioning of the self, the antagonist, and the others in the dispute negotiation. Their assessments directed at people outside of the marriage relationship (e.g., an alleged third party, the children, or the in-laws), if there were any, reflect their conceptualisation of the relationship dispute: whether considering the dispute as a matter implicating just the couple or as a matter involving a third party.

Besides attitudinal complexes of Judgement, there were the attitudinal expressions reporting Affectual responses or states. As foreshadowed in Chap. 3, the instances of reporting Affect very largely served two purposes for these disputants. Firstly, the disputant may describe their own past or present Affectual state to invoke an assessment of the antagonist as a trigger—as the party who is held to be responsible for, or the cause of, the negative emotion. Such instances typically activate negative Judgement of the antagonist (whose untoward behaviour or attitude was being referenced). However, they may also activate a positive Judgement of the trigger of the positive emotion (if the antagonist's triggering behaviour was assumed to be praiseworthy). Secondly, a disputant may report the antagonist's past Affectual state or responses, typically also to invoke an assessment of the antagonist as an emoter. This is possible because of the cultural frames associated with emotions—for example, being angry is often sanctioned negatively in many cultures, whereas being confident is often positively sanctioned. The two Affect-centred attitudinal complexes found in the dataset were:

(7) authorial negative Affectual response triggered by the antagonist or the antagonist's behaviour (NATA); and
(8) observed other people's Affectual response (OAO).

The final attitudinal complex type found in the dataset involved assessment of situations, happenings, or objects—the attitudinal complex of.

(9) Appreciation (APP).

In family dispute resolution exchanges, instances of Appreciation, if there are any, are usually found to be the speakers' assessments of the relationship.

The first point of interest emerging from the analysis was that, although these nine types of attitudinal complex were found in the dataset, they did not occur in every disputant's speech. Some disputants deployed all nine types, while others deployed a smaller subset. Presumably, these nine attitudinal complexes constitute a reservoir of attitudinal meaning-making resources available to all the disputants, and yet there is variation regarding the range of the resources deployed by different disputants. By identifying the recurrent patterns in the range of the resources deployed by the disputants, it became possible to reveal the commonalities and variations across the disputants' deployment of this reservoir.

3.2 *Findings: Tendencies in the Deployment of Attitudinal Complexes*

The objective of the current analysis was to discover how similar or different the 12 disputants were regarding their deployment of these attitudinal complexes and thereby to discover whether enough similarities in this deployment could be observed to provide a basis for the clustering of the attitudinal disposition they enacted.

This occurrence analysis determined which of these nine attitudinal complexes each disputant deployed at least once. In other words, for each of the nine attitudinal complexes found in the dataset, the analysis determined whether each disputant did or did not use that resource. For example, did every disputant at least once positively judge themself (PJS)? The proposition motivating this line of analysis was that differences between disputants in the attitudinal complexes they used at least once might be communicatively salient and hence would point to substantive differences in their self-presentation. Of course, this point of difference may be more marked or less marked. Should two disputants deploy entirely different subsets of the nine attitudinal complexes (for example, by way of a hypothetical case, disputant A using only complexes 1–4 as listed above and disputant B using only complexes 5–9), presumably the difference would be associated with a marked difference in attitudinal disposition and hence in the 'self' thereby being discursively construed? This would plausibly also be the case vis-à-vis a comparison between a disputant who used all or most of these attitudinal complexes and one who used a narrow range. In contrast, should two disputants only differ with respect to one attitudinal complex (for example, disputant A deploying all nine at least once and disputant B deploying only eight of the complexes), we would be more cautious in reaching conclusions as to whether this would result in a salient difference in attitudinal disposition and the 'self' being presented.

3.2.1 Commonalities in the Disputants' Deployment of the Attitudinal Complexes

I turn now to a discussion of the findings arising from this 'occurrence' analysis. As just discussed, this involved determining, for a given attitudinal complex, which of the disputants deployed this complex at least once and which did not. It enabled the clustering together of disputants who deployed the same or similar subset of the attitudinal complex combination—for example, clustering together those who used the same or similar combination of attitudinal complexes and, alternatively, those who deployed a different combination. It then became possible to identify and characterise the clustering according to the range of the attitudinal complexes the disputants deployed.

As might have been anticipated, given the nature of the dataset (communications around marital conflict), all the disputants advanced assessments of negative Judgement against their antagonist and positive self-Judgement (via both inscription and invocation). This is perhaps an unsurprising point of commonality. Perhaps not so predictable, and hence of interest, is the finding that these are the only two attitudinal complex types used by all 12 disputants. As far as the other attitudinal complexes are concerned, two attitudinal complexes were shared by most disputants: negative Judgment of people outside of the marriage relationship (11 out of 12 disputants) and negative Affectual response triggered by the antagonist (10 out of 12 disputants). The remaining attitudinal complexes were only used by some disputants. Accordingly, the four most widely deployed attitudinal complexes—(1)

negative Judgement of the antagonist, (2) positive self-Judgement, (3) negative Judgement of people outside of the relationship, and (4) the reporting of negative Affectual response triggered by the antagonist—would appear to be key resources for the negotiation of marital conflict and key elements of the disputants' attitudinal orientation. Certain common tendencies in deploying these attitudinal complexes were revealed across the disputants. They all criticised their spouses and the people outside of the marriage relationship (usually the alleged third party), presented their spouses as having caused them emotional pain, and commended their own behaviour or character.

This, then, was observed to be a central point of commonality in the attitudinal dispositions of most of the disputants and hence a common feature of their self-presentation. Variability and hence differences were revealed once patterns of use of the remaining attitudinal complexes were attended to. It emerged that disputants differed in how many attitudinal complex types they deployed and which of the attitudinal complex types they deployed. For example, as indicated, one disputant stood out from the rest in offering no negative Judgement directed at the people outside of the relationship (Husband_H01_WH, a wayward husband). Four of the disputants advanced positive Judgements of their antagonists (Husband_H03_WH, Wife_H01_AW, Wife_H01_AW, and Wife_W02_WW; two wayward spouses and two aggrieved spouses), meaning that eight never did this. This, of itself, might be seen as pointing to a salient difference in the disputants' self-presentation, with the disputants who presented as prepared at least sometimes to praise their spouse standing apart from those who were only critical. Eight disputants did at least once seek to put themselves in an unfavourable light by negatively assessing their own behaviour and therefore potentially accepted some responsibility for the marriage breakdown, while four never did this (Husband_H01_WH, Husband_W02_AH, Wife_H02_AW, and Wife_H03_AW; one wayward spouse and three aggrieved spouses)—again a potentially significant difference in terms of the discursively presented 'self'. Eight disputants used instances of Appreciation (to activate a negative Judgement of the antagonist) while four did not (all being husbands, two wayward and two aggrieved). Seven of the disputants opted for reporting the observed Affectual responses of other people (usually the antagonist or the children of the marriage) to invite the audience to Judge the emoter or trigger of the Affects in a certain way.

In addition, a certain degree of covariation was also observed in the dataset with respect to their 'waywardness' or 'aggrievedness'. Undoubtedly, a dataset with 12 speakers was far too small to conclude what might be more generally the case in terms of any correlations between tendencies in the deployment of these attitudinal complexes and whether a spouse was 'wayward' or 'aggrieved'. The findings, nonetheless, showed suggestive similarities within the wayward and the aggrieved groups regarding their shared preferences for some attitudinal complexes. Table 4.5 summarises the number of disputants deploying or not deploying a designated attitudinal complex in the wayward and aggrieved groups. The resources used by a majority of disputants (five and above) are highlighted. It can be observed that the wayward spouses in the dataset had similarities in choosing five attitudinal

Table 4.5 Number of disputants choosing a particular attitudinal complex (wayward versus aggrieved)

		Who used		Who did not use	
	Dataset sum	wayward	aggrieved	wayward	aggrieved
Positive self-judgement (PJS)	12	6	6		
Negative judgement of the antagonist (NJA)	12	6	6		
Negative judgement of others (NJO)	11	5	6	1	
Negative affectual responses triggered by the antagonist (NATA)	10	4	6	2	
Negative self-judgement (NJS)	8	5	3	1	3
Appreciation (APP)	8	4	4	2	2
Positive judgment of others (PJO)	7	4	3	2	3
Observed other people's affect (OAO)	7	5	2	1	4
Positive judgement of the antagonist (PJA)	4	2	2	4	4

complexes: (1) positive self-Judgement, (2) negative Judgement of the antagonist, (3) negative Judgement of other people outside of the relationship, (4) negative self-Judgement, and (5) observed other people's Affect. The similarities in these attitudinal complexes indicate that wayward spouses tended to consistently present the self as antipathetic towards the antagonist (both via Judgement and observed Affect) but, at the same time, willing to reconcile, or least willing to admit some fault on their own part (via negative self-Judgement). While the aggrieved spouses were similar to the wayward spouses in regularly judging their partner negatively, they differed in that the aggrieved spouses also uniformly construed the 'self' as an 'emotional victim' of the antagonist's behaviour (all six did this, compared with only four of the wayward spouses). Additionally, only three of the aggrieved spouses indicated a willingness to accept some responsibility for the marital breakdown (via negative self -Judgement), whereas five of the wayward spouses were willing to do this. Obviously, the correlation between waywardness/aggrievedness is not an absolute one. It is not the case, for example, that none of the aggrieved spouses judged themselves negatively and that, in contrast, all the wayward spouses did so. Nevertheless, the findings are still suggestive of a tendency, for example, for wayward spouses to take some blame for the marriage breakdown. At the same time, there is also the interesting finding that being an aggrieved spouse (the one making the accusations of marital infidelity) did not prevent a spouse from judging themself negatively. As just indicated, three out of the six aggrieved spouses did this at least once. Even though being aggrieved, they were apparently prepared to take some blame for the marital breakdown.

These insights emerged when the use of each attitudinal complex was considered in isolation. Clustering could thus be identified in association with each attitudinal complex, such as a grouping of disputants who self-criticised versus a grouping of those who did not; similarly, a grouping of disputants who praised their antagonist versus a grouping of those who did not. Whether the disputants used a particular attitudinal complex or not would reflect a particular attitudinal disposition or a specific aspect of the 'self' enacted by the speaker in the interaction.

3.2.2 Clusters Emerging from Co-Selection of Multiple Attitudinal Complexes

Different insights emerged when the analysis turned to consider patterns across all the attitudinal complexes. Here those disputants who, at least once, used a similar subset of multiple attitudinal complexes would be grouped, and those who never used this subset of multiple complexes would not be grouped. The more attitudinal complexes shared by disputants, the more closely they would be associated.

For this, I employed cluster analysis methods from Data Science and used the programming language *R* to identify and visualise the variations among the disputants. As noted in Chap. 3, in Data Science, clustering is a method of unsupervised learning for classifying data points into a specific group (Jain & Dubes, 1988; Xu & Tian, 2015). My analysis was carried out in three steps: (1) determine how many clusters to identify, (2) identify the clusters, and (3) explore what the clustering informs us about the disputants' preference for the attitudinal complexes.

In the first step, I determined the number of clusters. Intuitively, for a dataset with N samples, the cluster numbers can range from 1 to N. That means, for a dataset of 12 disputants, 1 to 12 clusters can be identified. My analysis used the average silhouette method (Batool & Hennig, 2021; Kaufman & Rousseeuw, 1990) to determine the optimal number of clusters in the dataset. This method provides a simple and popular solution to measure the quality of a clustering. Briefly, it measures how similar an object is to the other objects in its own cluster versus objects in the neighbouring clusters. The result of the measurement is a silhouette value, which ranges from −1 to +1. Positive silhouette values indicate that the object is well matched to its own cluster, and negative values mean that the object might be misclustered because it is more similar to a neighbouring cluster. If most objects have a high

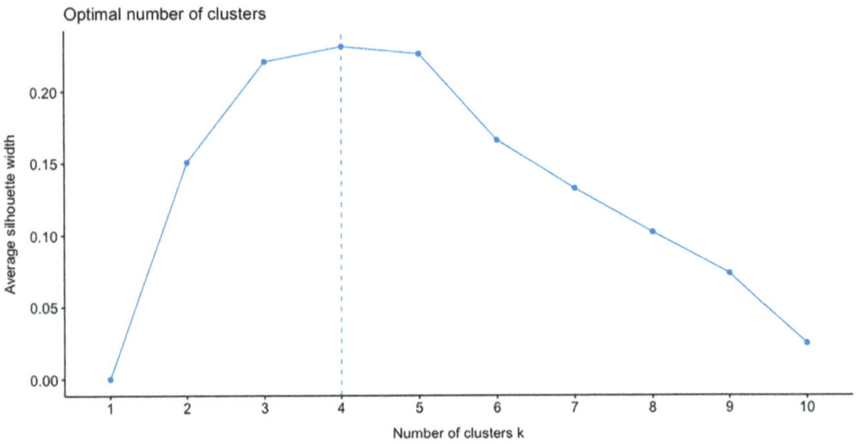

Fig. 4.1 'Occurrence' analysis: Optimal number of clusters (co-selection of multiple attitudinal complexes)

value, the clustering is appropriate. A high average silhouette width indicates a good clustering. Thus, the average silhouette method provides a way to assess the optimal number of clusters in the dataset. In my analysis, the average silhouette was done using the 'fviz_nbclust' function from the 'factoextra' package (v1.0.7; Kassambara & Mundt, 2020) in *R*. The optimal number of clusters was found to be four (visualised in Fig. 4.1), indicating four clusters would provide the highest quality of clustering in the dataset.

In the second step, I identified the four clusters using the 'complete linkage clustering' method in hierarchical cluster analysis to find clusters among the disputants. In this method, the similarity of two clusters is the similarity of their most dissimilar members (Colman, 2009; Upton & Cook, 2008). The method was chosen because it has been used in hierarchical clustering on categorical data in *R* (Dinh et al., 2019; Rezankova et al., 2011), and the occurrence of the attitudinal complexes in a disputant's speech is categorical data (used versus not used). In simple words, this method computes a distance between every pair of objects to create a distance matrix. Then any two units having the smallest distance will be grouped together as a new object, giving a new distance matrix. The same progress will continue until all objects end up being in the same cluster. The clustering among the disputants was done using the 'hclust' function from the 'cluster' package (v2.1.0; Maechler et al., 2019) in *R*. The disputants were clustered into four groups.

In the third step, I contextualised the clustering with the disputants' deployment of the attitudinal complexes and explored the insights the clustering might bring to light. I found that the disputants in each group used a similar number and a similar co-selection of attitudinal complexes by which they were distinct from the disputants in other groups, who used a different number and co-selected different attitudinal complexes. Roughly speaking, the grouping reveals variability in the range of attitudinal complexes deployed by the disputants. Specifically, group one has one disputant, who used a minimal number (three out of nine) of attitudinal complexes and hence can be characterised as having a 'narrow range' of attitudinal complex deployment. Group two have four disputants, who used more than half (six to seven) of the nine attitudinal complexes available and used a similar combination of attitudinal complexes, so can be characterised as having a 'middle range' of selection. Group three, with four disputants, also used more than half (six to eight) of the nine attitudinal complexes but with a different combination from that of group two. Hence, they can also be characterised as having a 'middle range' of attitudinal complex deployment but with a different selection. Finally, with three disputants, group four chose almost all (eight to nine) of the attitudinal complexes found in the dataset, which means they deployed a 'wide range' of available resources. Therefore, the cluster analysis informed me that the disputants in each group chose a similar number of attitudinal complexes and selected similar subsets of attitudinal complex types. Accordingly, the disputants in the same group demonstrated a similar discursive disposition type in terms of the occurrence of the attitudinal complexes they deployed. Details of each disposition type can be found in the following sections.

3.2.2.1 Attitudinal Disposition Type 1: Narrow Range

The first attitudinal disposition type vis-à-vis the occurrence of the attitudinal complex is 'narrow range'. The speaker of this type selected a minimal range of the available attitudinal complex options and repeatedly deployed these options in the interaction. By doing so, they managed to portray a highly salient authorial intersubjective positioning.

Only one speaker in the dataset is associated with this 'narrow range' disposition, suggesting that the speaker was an outlier among all the disputants in the dataset. This is Husband_H01_WH, a wayward husband. In the dispute exchanges, he deployed only three types of the attitudinal complex: positive Judgement directed at the self, negative Judgement of the antagonist, and observed Affectual responses of others which invoke negative Judgement of these others, on the basis of the observed Affect being in some way 'untoward' (in his utterances, the antagonist). He could be characterised as highly combative concerning his focus on these attitudinal complexes, which cast his spouse in a negative light while also defensive in seeking to cast himself in a positive light. He did not have any instances of other types of attitudinal assessment at all. Because he never attitudinally commented on people outside of the relationship, he portrayed the relationship dispute as intrinsically an issue between himself and his wife, making him highly focused in terms of attitudinal target. Additionally, because he never revealed his authorial emotions or offered Appreciations of happenings or things, he was highly focused on the attitude type of Judgement. Moreover, because he never conveyed a negative assessment directed at the self or a positive assessment directed at the antagonist, he was highly focused in terms of attitudinal polarity. All these facets suggest that although the 'narrow range' speakers only opted for a limited range of the available attitudinal resources, their attitudinal positioning was highly focused. The occurrence of attitudinal complex types in the husband's speech is summarised Table 4.6. The attitudinal complexes chosen by the husband are highlighted with a tick.

Table 4.6 Attitudinal disposition type 1: Narrow range

		Occurrence of attitudinal complex								
		Judgement						Affect		
		self		antagonist		Other		self	other	Appreciation
		+ve	-ve	+ve	-ve	+ve	-ve	-ve	+ve/-ve	+ve/-ve
Speaker	Waywardness	PJS	NJS	PJA	NJA	PJO	NJO	NATA	OAO	APP
Husband_ H01_WH	Wayward	Y			Y				Y	

Key: Husband's attitudinal complexes: *PJS* positive Judgement directed at the self, *NJA* negative Judgement of the antagonist, *OAO* observed other people's Affectual response. Complexes not used by this husband: *NJS* negative Judgement of self, *PJA* positive judgement of antagonist, *PJO* positive Judgement of others, *NJO* negative Judgement of others, *NATA* negative Affectual responses triggered by the antagonist, *APP* Appreciation

The attitudinal disposition type of 'narrow range' is exemplified by Husband_ H01_WH's utterances in one turn in Excerpt 4.1. In this excerpt, the husband articulated his purpose of coming to the mediation. (The extract is typical of all this disputant's language use regarding options for attitudinal expression—which of the attitudinal complexes he chose. See the book's GitHub repository for the complete analysis of his contributions to this segment of the episode.)

It can be seen from Table 4.6 that this speaker, with his 'narrow range' attitudinal disposition, opted for only a limited range of attitudinal resources but relied on these resources to make their attitudinal positioning prominent and fixed. In Excerpt 4.1, the husband relied heavily on the attitudinal complexes of positive self-Judgement and negative Judgement of the antagonist, nothing else. The attitudinal arrangements of this 'narrow range' attitudinal disposition distinguished it from the dispositions of the other three disputant groups.

3.2.2.2 Attitudinal Disposition Type 2: Middle Range

The second attitudinal disposition type identified is what I term 'middle range'. As the label suggests, speakers exhibiting this disposition chose a broader range of attitudinal complexes than the 'narrow range' disposition speakers, yet they did not fully use all the available resources. Interestingly, their co-selection patterns were such that all the attitudinal complexes they employed ultimately construed the same attitudinal positioning. As mentioned above, two disputant groups demonstrate a 'middle range' deployment of attitudinal complex resources with different co-selections of the resources. Specifically, all the eight speakers in the two 'middle range' groups used the four common attitudinal complexes (discussed in previous sections) found in the dataset: (1) positive self-Judgement, (2) negative Judgement of the antagonist (3) and the people outside of the marital relationship, and (4) negative Affectual response triggered by the antagonist which potentially invokes negative assessment directed at the antagonist. The two groups differ regarding their deployment of the other attitudinal complexes. Group 2 (consisting of three aggrieved and one wayward spouse) all had instances of Appreciation, which means

Excerpt 4.1 Example of the 'narrow range' attitudinal disposition (Husband_H01_WH's utterances in Turn 7)

Turn	Move	Utterance (Chinese)	Utterance (English translation)	Attitude signal	Attitudinal complex	
					Assessment	Abbr.
7	1	我的诉求就是希望改正她的心态吧	My request is that I hope (the mediation) can correct her mentality	Irrealis affect	Invoke -ve Judge antagonist[a]	NJA
	2	经过这个调解啊..让大家评判一下..到底是她的心态没摆正..还是我做的事是她所谓的表里不如一	By this mediation.. I would like to let everyone comment on it.. Ultimately.. is it that her mentality is not correct.. or what I did was her so-called 'duplicitous'	Contrast	Invoke -ve judge antagonist[b] (see footnotes throughout for discussion of attitudinally more complex or subtle expressions)	NJA
	3	我是每天对这个家庭是添砖加瓦的..对吧	I AM **making a contribution** to this family every day.. right	Inscription	Inscribe +ve Judge self	PJS
	4	她却说我看不到	But she says I can't see	Counter-expectancy	Invoke -ve Judge antagonist[c]	NJA
	5	她生了病..都是我询问她很详细的	Whenever she was sick.. I was the one who asked her for her details	Up-scaling	Invoke +ve Judge self; invoke -ve Judge antagonist[d]	PJS; NJA
	6	哪个地方不舒服	What's wrong with you	Quotation: Self	Invoke +ve Judge self; invoke -ve Judge antagonist	PJS; NJA
	7	吃什么药	What medicine to take	Quotation: Self	Invoke +ve Judge self; invoke -ve Judge antagonist	PJS; NJA
	8	都是我去买	I was the one who went out to buy the medicine	Up-scaling	Invoke +ve Judge self; invoke -ve Judge antagonist	PJS; NJA
		茶水递她手上	(and me who) put the tea in her hand	Evoke	Invoke +ve Judge self; invoke -ve Judge antagonist[e]	PJS; NJA

(continued)

Excerpt 4.1 (continued)

[a]The Chinese word '心态 mentality' refers to a person's mental attitude towards the world. In this utterance, the husband stated his intention to '改正她的心态 correct her mentality', thereby implying that the wife's mentality was wrong

[b]In earlier turns, the wife explicitly characterised her life as 'duplicitous', thereby implying that the husband was duplicitous. In this utterance, the husband re-presented the wife's words through a negative dialogic framing—'所谓的 so-called', which challenged her veracity. This negative dialogic framing opened up the possibility of negative Judgement directed at the wife

[c]In previous turns, the wife accused the husband of paying lip service. In this turn, the husband explicitly assessed the self as '添砖加瓦 making a contribution' and used a counter-expectancy device '却 but' to frame the wife's words '我看不到 I can't see'. His explicit self-praise stood in sharp contrast to the wife's earlier accusation. Hence, through this contrast and the counter-expectancy, the husband's utterance potentially implied a negative Judgement of the wife's veracity

[d]In this utterance, and in those that followed till the end of the turn, the husband recounted his behaviour when the wife was sick. His account invoked a cultural norm that 'Attending to a sick person in detail is laudable'. Under this cultural norm, the husband presented the self as highly attentive, hence invoking a positive self-Judgement. Meanwhile, this account also had the potential to activate negative Judgement directed at the wife. Because the wife had accused him of paying lip service in previous turns, his detailed narrative functioned to counter her accusation and to position her as having misrepresented him—thereby invoking a negative judgement of her veracity

[e]Some Chinese people have the practice of taking medicine with tea. In this utterance, the husband sought to demonstrate his care for the wife by providing detailed accounts of his behaviour when the wife was ill

they opted for attitudinally evaluating their life, the relationship, or the situations they are in, which eventually had the potential to invoke a negative Judgement of the antagonist. In contrast, Group 3 (consisting of two aggrieved and two wayward spouses) chose another three attitudinal complexes: (1) negative self-Judgement, (2) positive Judgement of other people, and (3) observed other people's Affectual response. Although both Groups 2 and 3 deployed a similar number of attitudinal complexes, their differences are twofold. One difference lies in their overall attitudinal positioning of the self. Group 3 disputants had both positive and negative Judgement directed at the self, so the two attitudes possibly balanced each other out, whereas the disputants in Group 2 were purely self-commending (no negative assessment of their own behaviour). The second difference is in that their strategy in invoking attitudinal assessments. The disputants in Group 2 chose to assess things, whereas Group 3 speakers preferred to evaluate other people. Nevertheless, the two groups deployed six to eight out of nine attitudinal complexes, a 'middle range', rather than all the resources available. The occurrence of attitudinal complexes in these groups is summarised in Table 4.7, with the attitudinal arrangement of the 'narrow range' group for comparison. The shared attitudinal complexes of each group are highlighted with a tick.

A typical example of a 'middle range' disputant is the attitudinal complex choices of Wife_H01_AW, an aggrieved wife. She is the wife of Husband_H01_WH presented in Excerpt 4.1's discussion of 'narrow range' disposition, so her attitudinal arrangements can be contrasted with that of the husband. In the dispute exchanges, while both speakers adopted an overall combative attitudinal positioning—positively assessing the self and negatively assessing the antagonist, they were

Table 4.7 Attitudinal disposition type 2: Middle range

			Occurrence of attitudinal complexes									
			Judgement						Affect			
			Self		Antagonist		Other		Self	Other	Appreciation	Num. of Attitudinal complex
			PJS	NJS	PJA	NJA	PJO	NJO	NATA	OAO	APP	
Disposition	Speaker	Waywardness	+ve	-ve	+ve	-ve	+ve	-ve	-ve	+ve/-ve	+ve/-ve	
Narrow range (Group 1)	Husband_H01_WH	Wayward	Y			Y				Y		3
Middle range (Group 2)	Wife_H03_AW	Aggrieved	Y		Y	Y		Y	Y		Y	6
	Husband_W02_AH	Aggrieved	Y			Y	Y	Y	Y		Y	6
	Wife_W01_WW	Wayward	Y	Y		Y		Y	Y		Y	6
	Wife_H01_AW	Aggrieved	Y	Y	Y	Y		Y	Y		Y	7
Middle range (Group 3)	Husband_W01_AH	Aggrieved	Y	Y		Y	Y	Y	Y			6
	Husband_W03_AH	Aggrieved	Y	Y		Y		Y	Y	Y		6
	Husband_H02_WH	Wayward	Y	Y		Y	Y	Y	Y	Y		7
	Wife_W03_WW	Wayward	Y	Y		Y	Y	Y	Y	Y	Y	8

Key: *PJS* positive Judgement directed at the self, *NJS* negative Judgement directed at the self, *PJA* positive Judgement of the antagonist, *NJA* negative Judgement of the antagonist, *PJO* positive Judgement of others, *NJO* negative Judgement of others, *NATA* negative Affectual response triggered by the antagonist or antagonist's behaviour, *OAO* observed other people's Affectual response, *APP* Appreciation remarkably different in terms of which of the attitudinal complexes they deployed to be combative. As discussed above, the husband only used positive self-Judgement and negative antagonist-Judgement. In contrast, the wife's attitudinal arrangement was more complicated. In addition to positively judging herself and negatively judging her husband, she deployed a range of the other attitudinal complexes that indirectly cast her husband in a negative light (consistent with her overall combative orientation). The additional attitudinal complexes she deployed included negative Judgement directed at the antagonist's friend (by association casting her husband in a negative light), her own negative Affectual responses triggered by the antagonist and negative Appreciation of antagonist related happenings or situations. The wife's utterances in Excerpt 4.2 are illustrative of this tendency—as can be observed across all her turns in this segment of the episode. (See the book's GitHub repository for the full analysis of her language.)

In Excerpt 4.2, the wife articulated her purpose of coming to the mediation. Her utterances and the attitudinal assessments were concerned with multiple attitudinal targets, including life, the couple, the antagonist, and her own emotion. Accordingly, the attitudinal types involved Judgement, Appreciation, and Affect. Nevertheless, the wide range of attitudinal meaning-making resources deployed by the wife ultimately served one attitudinal orientation: to position the audience to assess the antagonist (her husband) negatively.

3.2.2.3 Attitudinal Disposition Type 3: Wide Range

The last attitudinal disposition type as to the attitudinal complex occurrence is 'wide range'. The three speakers of this type, two wayward spouses and one aggrieved spouse, deployed almost all (eight to nine) of the attitudinal complex types found in the dataset. They assessed a wide range of attitudinal targets, including the self, antagonist, people outside of the relationship, and happenings or things. When reporting Affectual responses, they reported both their own Affect triggered by the antagonist and the observed others' Affectual responses/states. As far as the attitudinal polarity is concerned, they had both positive and negative assessments. In family dispute resolution exchanges, the communicative effects of such a mixture of attitudinal arrangements are complicated. For one thing, because the disputants conveyed both positive and negative Judgement directed at the antagonist and the self, their authorial attitudinal orientation towards the self and the antagonist were in sharp contrast with the 'narrow range' or 'middle range' ones (i.e., foregrounding positive self-Judgement and negative antagonist-Judgement). The 'wide range' disputants can be interpreted as discursively presenting the self as willing to conciliate, negotiable, and ready to reconcile. However, on the other hand, if the disputants did not make their attitudinal positionings explicit when deploying the wide range of attitudinal meaning-making resources, the complicated attitudinal arrangements might make the authorial attitudinal positioning vague and ambiguous to the audience. Hence, the disputants potentially demonstrated a multiplex of attitudinal positionings by deploying a 'wide range' of attitudinal complexes. The attitudinal complexes deployed by the 'wide range' speakers are summarised in Table 4.8.

Excerpt 4.2 Example of the 'middle range' attitudinal disposition (Wife_H01_AW's utterances in Turn 2–4)

Turn	Speaker	Move	Utterance (Chinese)	Utterance (English translation)	Attitude signal	Attitudinal complex	
						Assessment	Abbr.
1	Hostess_H01	1	到金牌调解来是为了解决什么问题	What problem do you want to solve by coming to the Gold Medal Mediation			
2	Wife_H01_AW	1	我诉求..拒绝过那种表里不一..阳奉阴违的日子	I request.. I refuse to live a life that is **duplicitous..** and **deceitful**	Inscription	Inscribe -ve Appreciation life; invoke -ve Judge antagonist[a]	APP; NJA
		2	既然是夫妻..就应该全心全意坦诚面对	Since we are husband and wife.. we should treat each other faithfully and wholeheartedly	Directive	Invoke -ve Judge couple; invoke -ve Judge antagonist[b]	NJA
		3	他现在嘴上说他在乎夫妻感情.. 他在乎他的家庭	He only **pays lip service** when saying that he cares about the relationship.. He cares about his family	Inscription	Inscribe -ve Judge antagonist	NJA
3	Hostess_H01	1	嗯	Mhm			
4	Wife_H01_AW	1	但是我从来没有感受到	But I never felt it	Denial	Invoke -ve Affect self (triggered by the antagonist); invoke -ve Judge antagonist[c]	NATA; NJA
		2	我希望他真心对待	I hope he will treat me with sincerity	Irrealis affect	Invoke -ve Judge antagonist	NJA

[a]This utterance contains two instances of Judgement that are construed as Appreciation. The lexical items '表里不一 duplicitous' and '阳奉阴违 deceitful' are typically used to judge a person's behaviour. However, in this utterance, the wife used them to convey negative Appreciation about her life, an abstract entity. By explicitly and negatively appreciating the life, she attempted to invoke negative Judgement directed at the antagonist

[b]This utterance involved a modulation of obligation—'应该 should', which implied that the couple did NOT treat each other faithfully and wholeheartedly. The wife used this assertion of obligation to invoke a negative Judgement directed at the husband

[c]In the previous turn (Turn 2), the wife reported that the husband said he cared about the relationship and the family. In this utterance, the wife reported her that she had never felt the husband's caring. Although '没有感受到 never felt it' is a mental process of cognition, it has the potential to invoke a negative assessment of the wife's emotional status. She was dissatisfied because she did not feel the husband's caring. Her negative emotion of dissatisfaction was based on the husband's behaviour of paying lip service

Table 4.8 Attitudinal disposition type 3: Wide range

Disposition	Speaker	Waywardness	Occurrence of attitudinal complexes									Num. of Attitudinal complex
			Judgement						Affect		Appreciation	
			self		antagonist		other		self	other		
			PJS	NJS	PJA	NJA	PJO	NJO	NATA	OAO	APP	
			+ve	-ve	+ve	-ve	+ve	-ve	-ve	+ve/-ve	+ve/-ve	
Narrow range (Group 1)	Husband_H01_WH	Wayward	Y			Y				Y		3
Middle range (Group 2)	Wife_H03_AW	Aggrieved	Y		Y	Y		Y	Y		Y	6
	Husband_W02_AH	Aggrieved	Y			Y	Y	Y	Y		Y	6
	Wife_W01_WW	Wayward	Y	Y		Y		Y	Y		Y	6
	Wife_H01_AW	Aggrieved	Y	Y	Y	Y		Y	Y		Y	7
Middle range (Group 3)	Husband_W01_AH	Aggrieved	Y	Y		Y	Y	Y	Y			6
	Husband_W03_AH	Aggrieved	Y	Y		Y		Y	Y	Y		6
	Husband_H02_WH	Wayward	Y	Y		Y	Y	Y	Y	Y		7
	Wife_W03_WW	Wayward	Y	Y		Y	Y	Y	Y	Y	Y	8
Wide range (Group 4)	Wife_H02_AW	Aggrieved	Y		Y	Y	Y	Y	Y	Y	Y	8
	Husband_H03_WH	Wayward	Y	Y	Y	Y	Y	Y		Y	Y	8
	Wife_W02_WW	Wayward	Y	Y	Y	Y	Y	Y	Y	Y	Y	9

Key: *PJS* positive Judgement directed at the self, *NJS* negative Judgement directed at the self, *PJA* positive Judgement of the antagonist, *NJA* negative Judgement of the antagonist, *PJO* positive Judgement of others, *NJO* negative Judgement of others, *NATA* negative Affectual response triggered by the antagonist or antagonist's behaviour, *OAO* observed other people's Affectual response, *APP* Appreciation

A typical example from the dataset is the attitudinal arrangements of Wife_W02_WW, a wayward wife. (For the full analysis of her contributions to this segment of the episode, see the book's GitHub repository.) In the family dispute resolution exchange, she deployed all the nine attitudinal complex types, as exemplified in Excerpt 4.3. Given that the previous examples of 'narrow range' (Husband_H01_WH in Excerpt 4.1) and 'middle range' (Wife_H01_AW in Excerpt 4.2) both illustrate the speakers' purpose statements of attending the mediation, I also present the 'wide range' disputants' attitudinal arrangement with a purpose statement, allowing readers to grasp the distinctions between these three attitudinal dispositions. Excerpt 4.3 specifically features Wife_W02_WW's purpose statement of coming to the mediation.

In Excerpt 4.3, the wife deployed a wide range of resources, including negative Appreciation about the relationship and the life, observed negative Affect of her child, observed irrealis Affect of the antagonist, and authorial negative Affect triggered by the child's words and the life. Although some of the attitudinal instances of Appreciation and Affect have the potential to invoke attitudes of Judgement directed at the self and the antagonist, the wife did not make the human target clear. For example, for her utterances in Turn 4, she reported two instances of negative authorial Affect triggered by the life—'我对这段生活很恐惧 I am terrified by this life' and '很绝望 Very desperate'. These Affectual responses had the potential to invoke negative assessments directed at the trigger of the emotions—the life. However, because she did not clarify the source of the negativity of the life—the human agent who made her life 'terrified' and 'desperate', her negative Appreciation of the life did not further invoke any Judgements directed at the antagonist, nor someone else. She attitudinally positioned the audience to view her life negatively and view her as an emotional victim of the relationship. Her positionings of the self and the antagonist remained unspecified.

3.2.2.4 Summary

The above sections have outlined three attitudinal disposition types derived from an analysis of the 'occurrence' of the attitudinal complexes deployed in the disputants' utterances (their contributions to the Problem Discussion stage). The analysis has revealed that it is possible to cluster the disputants into four groups and characterise three attitudinal disposition types based on the similarities and differences in the disputants' deployment of the nine attitudinal complexes.

By way of hopefully making clearer what has been established here, the clustering of the disputants is visualised in Fig. 4.2. The visualisation can add value to the language descriptions provided so far, especially for the readers who favour more science-based and visual techniques besides descriptive linguistic analysis. In Fig. 4.2, under the method of 'complete linkage clustering' (see Sect. 3.2.2 for details), the clustering of the 12 speakers into four groups is depicted, highlighted by the red squares. Briefly, the closer the speakers, the more similarities they have in terms of the occurrence of the attitudinal complexes in the utterances. It is

Excerpt 4.3 Example of the 'wide range' attitudinal disposition (Wife_W02_WW's utterances in Turn 2–4)

Turn	Speaker	Move	Utterance (Chinese)	Utterance (English translation)	Attitude signal	Attitudinal complex	
						Assessment	Abbr.
1	Hostess_ W02	1	两位今天来到金牌调解...要解决什么问题	You two come to the Gold Medal Mediation today…to resolve what problems			
2	Wife_ W02_WW	1	我是..要离婚	I.. want a divorce	Irrealis affect	Invoke -ve Appreciation relationship	APP
		2	已经起诉离婚	(I) Have sued for divorce	Evoke	Invoke -ve Appreciation relationship	APP
		3	他不愿意离婚	He is **not willing** to divorce	Irrealis affect	Inscribe -ve Affect (observed antagonist)	OAO
		4	就在前几天(1.05)小孩的一句话	Just a few days ago (1.05) my child said a sentence			
		5	小孩说妈妈我不想...别人说我没有爸妈的孩子	My child said that mom I don't want...others to say that I am a child without parents	Quotation: Other	Invoke -ve Affect (observed child); invoke -ve Appreciation relationship[a]	OAO; APP
		6	所以...我心里也...犹豫起来了	So... in my heart… I start to **hesitant**	Attitudinal instance of inscribed affect (potential invocation of -ve judgement)	Inscribe -ve Affect (triggered by child); invoke +ve Judge self[b]	Triggered affect; PJS
		7	呃想让各位老师...帮我...分析…看我这段婚姻...有必要再...继续吗	Eh I want to let the teachers... help me... analyse… to see if my marriage... is it necessary to... continue	Irrealis affect	Invoke -ve Appreciation relationship; invoke +ve Judge self[c]	APP; PJS
3	Hostess_ W02	1	那你觉得你们的婚姻走到今天最大的原因是什么	What do you think is the biggest reason for your marriage to end up like this today			

(continued)

Excerpt 4.3 (continued)

Turn	Speaker	Move	Utterance (Chinese)	Utterance (English translation)	Attitude signal	Attitudinal complex	
						Assessment	Abbr.
4	Wife_ W02_WW	1	我...对这段生活很恐惧	I am… very **terrified** by this life	Attitudinal instance of inscribed affect (potential invocation of -ve judgement)	Inscribe -ve Affect (triggered by life); invoke -ve Appreciation life	Triggered affect; APP
		2	很绝望	Very **desperate**	Attitudinal instance of inscribed affect (potential invocation of -ve judgement)	Inscribe -ve affect (triggered by life); invoke -ve appreciation life	Triggered affect; APP

[a]In this utterance, the wife quotes her child. The child's words imply a negative emotion of unhappiness the child might have if the couple divorce. By quoting the child, the wife invokes an observed negative Affect, with the child being the Emoter. This observed Affect, in turn, potentially activates a negative Appreciation of the couple's relationship, which is construed as the trigger for the child's unhappiness

[b]Feeling '犹豫 hesitant' implies a negative emotion associated with anxiety and uncertainty. Because this negative emotion is triggered by the child's words, by reporting this emotion, the wife indicates that she considers the child's best interest before rushing into divorce. The wife's behaviour references a common practice in the Chinese communities—parental sacrifice. Chinese parenthood is closely associated with the notion of 'responsibility for children' and 'making sacrifice for the benefit of children'(Leung et al., 2016). In this utterance, the wife presents the self as a responsible and moral parent through her expressed concern for the child's welfare. Her hesitation thus has the potential to invoke a positive Judgement directed at the self

[c]The wife's behaviour of seeking dispute resolution consultation implies a negative Appreciation of the marital relationship. At the same time, her choice to pursue consultation, rather than rush into divorce, highlights both her willingness to sacrifice for the child and her readiness to conciliate. Her behaviour has the potential to position the audience to positive judge her

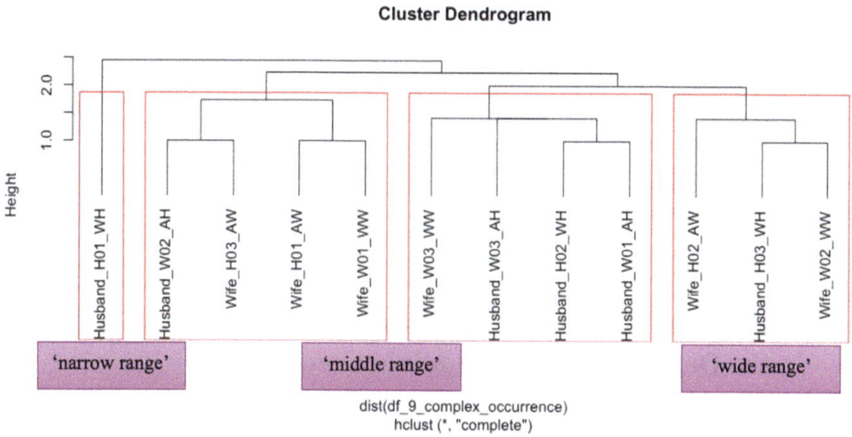

Fig. 4.2 Attitudinal disposition clustering as to the occurrence of attitudinal complex

observable that the disputants having a 'middle range' attitudinal disposition constitute most of the speakers in the dataset, which might suggest a higher probability of this disposition occurring in similar text types. Only one speaker demonstrates a 'narrow range' attitudinal disposition, perhaps suggestive that this disposition would be less likely to occur in similar contexts of family conflict communication. Obviously, an analysis of a much larger dataset would be needed if these possibilities were to be confirmed.

A certain degree of correlation between the range of attitude-associated resources deployed by a disputant and their waywardness can be observed in Table 4.8. Five out of six wayward spouses are found to deploy 'middle range' or 'wide range' of the available attitudinal complexes. Three wayward spouses used eight or nine attitudinal complexes. In other words, when defending the self against the accusation from the antagonist regarding an allegedly cheating behaviour, a wayward spouse tends to make full use of the attitudinal resources available to present the 'self' in front of the mediators. The deployment of a broader range of resources also reveals that the wayward spouses tend to maintain an arguably balanced attitudinal stance (both positive and negative) towards the self and the antagonist. Comparatively, five out of six aggrieved spouses fall into the 'middle range' attitudinal disposition, with four aggrieved spouses deployed six (out of nine) attitudinal complexes. Half of the aggrieved spouses had no instance of negative self-Judgement nor positive antagonist-Judgment. The difference in the range of the deployed attitudinal complexes between wayward and aggrieved spouses might suggest that the aggrieved spouses tend to be more focused and salient in their attitudinal positioning of the self and the antagonist than the wayward spouses.

It is worth noting that there are no clear-cut boundaries among the three proposed attitudinal disposition types, and there is observable in-group variation within each disposition type. From 'narrow range' to 'middle range' to 'wide range', it is better to view the three types as different vantage points along a continuum rather than three boxes of features. What distinguishes the three attitudinal disposition types is not the specific number of attitudinal complexes or the particular attitudinal complexes favoured by the speakers. What sets the speakers apart is the similarity in the range of the attitude-associated resources deployed by the speakers. When having the same attitudinal positioning resources at their disposal, some speakers make full use of all the options available, while some speakers only deploy a minimal range of resources. Therefore, the variation vis-à-vis the attitudinal complex occurrence is about the variability in the range of the resources deployed by the language user in functionally comparable situations.

4 Stage Two: The 'Ratio' Analysis in Tendencies in the Deployment of Attitudinal Complexes

The discussion so far has been about tendencies in the 'occurrence' of the nine attitudinal complexes in a disputant's speech—that is, by reference to whether speakers deployed each of attitudinal complex at least once. This section reports on the 'ratio' stage of the analysis. This analysis attended to tendencies in the disputants' degree of 'preference' (frequency of use) for an array of attitudinal complexes. As outlined earlier in the chapter, the similarities and the differences across the disputants were explored vis-à-vis the ratio of each attitudinal complex in the total attitudinal instances of a person's speech. The proposition motivating this line of analysis was that the disputants who more frequently advanced—for example, positive self-Judgement—present a different 'self' from those who infrequently or not deployed this complex.

As noted above, different exploration methods require different treatment of the meaning-making resources. The 'ratio' analysis operates on the percentage of the number of instances involving a designated attitudinal expression in the total attitudinal instances in a person's speech. It provides a sharper focus on the differences across the disputants' attitudinal arrangements than the 'occurrence' analysis (as discussed above), hence requiring precise measurement of the disputants' attitudinal choices—the exact number of instances (as opposed to just tracking whether a complex was deployed at least once). Accordingly, for this analysis, I tracked a list of attitudinal complexes which were classified not only by reference to attitude type, polarity, and target/trigger, but also by reference to explicitness (inscribed versus invoked). This was done to enable me to separate all expressions where the attitude was only invoked from those which involved lexis inscribing an attitudinal assessment. I chose to do this so that, for computational cluster analysis purposes, I could treat all invoking attitudinal complexes as a single attitudinal complex, regardless of the nature of the attitude, thereby potentially implied of the target. The invoked attitudes were all treated as a bundled attitudinal complex under the umbrella of 'invocation'. Examples of this treatment can be found in Table 4.9 and justifications for this methodology are provided below.

The justifications for this treatment are twofold. Firstly, inscriptions have a much higher degree of attitudinal stability than invocations, so an attitudinal assessment advanced via inscription conveys the speaker's attitudinal orientation unambiguously, leaving little room for alternative interpretations. The precise number of inscribed attitudinal expressions—such as five instances of inscribed positive self-Judgement—provides a definite profile for the speaker's attitudinal positioning towards the appraised (e.g., positive positioning of the self). By comparison, as noted in Chap. 3, there might be double coding or multiple layer interpretations for an attitudinal assessment activated via invocation, depending on the reading position of the audience. Although the invocations might signal the speaker's attitudinal positioning or 'naturalise' (Martin & White, 2005, p. 62) a reading position, the eventual interpretation of the speaker's attitudinal signal is often highly audience-dependent. The unpredictability of invocation is augmented by the immediate interactional and adversarial nature of my data. In family dispute resolution, what a disputant says does not stand by itself. It also has the potential to reference or counteract what was proposed by the other interactants in previous turns. In such cases, the specific attitudinal type, polarity, and target for an invocation are highly indeterministic. Therefore, in this analysis, the invocations were counted in the speaker's total number of attitudinal instances but were not treated as advancing a particular

Table 4.9 'Ratio' analysis: Grouping the attitudinal expressions (example)

	Attitudinal complex		Attitudinal axes				
	Assessment	Abbr.	Type	Polarity	Appraised/ target	Explicitness	Example
Attitudinal inscriptions having the same attitudinal orientation were grouped together.	Inscribed positive self-judgement	PJS	Judgement	+ve	Self	Inscription	我还是..比较...公认的一个..比较**好**的人I am nevertheless.. more or less... everyone agrees.. more or less a **good** person (Husband_W03_AH)
			Judgement	+ve	Self	Inscription	我..我是个**追求浪漫**..**追求**那个**激情**的人I.. I am a person who **pursues romance**.. **pursues** that kind of **passion** (Husband_H03_WH)
Invocations were group as a bundle attitudinal complex.	Invocation	INVO	Judgement	-ve	Antagonist	Invocation	她还喊对方..那个她的初恋..开车去拉东西She even called that man.. that her first love.. to drive his car and deliver some goods (Husband_W03_AH) (signalled by the counter-expectancy and evocation)
			Judgement	+ve;-ve	Self; Antagonist	Invocation	最后是我..追了他三天In the end it was me..who chased his friend for three days (and got our money back) (Wife_W01_WW) (signalled by the upscaling)

attitudinal orientation. Secondly, the attitudinal instances advanced via invocation were grouped as an attitudinal complex bundle because they had the same attitudinal meaning-making mechanism. It is only in cases of inscribed attitude that the speaker directly calls on or challenges the addressee to accept the specific attitudinal assessment. By inscribing an attitudinal assessment, the speaker potentially puts speaker-addressee rapport at risk, should they disagree or view the assessment as unfair or unfounded. In contrast, in cases of invocation, the risk to rapport is not so deliberate or direct since an assessment has only been suggested or implied rather than overtly asserted. Although the invocations might signal the speaker's attitudinal positioning, the signal is often highly dependent on the 'reading position' applied when interpreting the utterance in question, thereby allowing multiple interpretations. Therefore, in this analysis, I treated all the implicit attitudinal assessments as an attitudinal complex bundle under the umbrella term of 'invocation'. In this, I foregrounded the fact that for a speaker to invoke rather than to inscribe was a choice not to be attitudinally direct, to rely on the addressee to supply the necessary attitudinal inferences. It seemed valid to recognise the communicative significance of this choice by bundling all invocations of attitude into this single attitudinal complex, for the purpose of the computational cluster analysis. (This, of course, is not to suggest that an analysis which did assign invoked and inscribed assessment to different attitudinal complexes would not be entirely valid and able to produce important findings. It was just that, given the limitations of this monograph, it was not possible to offer an analysis along these lines.)

In short, this treatment allowed me to map out the degree of the disputants' attitudinal complex preferences in an accurate manner—tendencies in how often they advanced a particular type of attitudinal orientation, whether they advanced it more frequently or less frequently than other disputants in the dataset. As outlined earlier in the chapter, the 'ratio' analysis was conducted in two steps. The first step was to identify the attitudinal complexes available in the dataset. The second step was to explore the tendencies in the disputants' use of the available attitudinal complexes. What are the similarities and differences regarding the disputants' deployment of one attitudinal complex? What are the similarities and differences regarding the disputants' deployment of two or multiple attitudinal complexes?

4.1 *Available Attitudinal Complexes*

Via the recognition/classificatory principles just outlined, ten types of attitudinal complex were found in the dataset. These attitudinal complexes constitute the resources available for speakers in family-dispute-resolution settings to draw upon. The speakers may, in principle, deploy any or all of these attitudinal complexes to construe their attitudinal positioning.

Among the ten attitudinal complexes found in the dataset, six types are explicit assessments of human and human behaviour, with the attitudinal targets being the self, the antagonist, or the other(s). These are the attitudinal assessments construed by the Appraisal resource of Judgement (summarised in Table 4.10). The six attitudinal complex types are:

(1) Inscribed positive Judgement directed at the antagonist (PJA);
(2) Inscribed negative Judgement directed at the antagonist (NJA);
(3) Inscribed positive Judgement directed at the self (PJS);
(4) Inscribed negative Judgement directed at the self (NJS);
(5) Inscribed positive Judgement directed at people outside of the marriage relationship (PJO); and
(6) Inscribed negative Judgement directed at people outside of the marriage relationship (NJO).

These six types of attitudinal expressions reveal the speakers' attitudinal positioning of the self, the antagonist, and the others in the dispute negotiation. Their assessments directed at people outside of the marriage relationship (e.g., an alleged third party, the children, or the in-laws), if there are any, reflect their conceptualisation of the relationship dispute—whether considering the dispute as a matter implicating just the couple or as a matter involving a third party.

Besides attitudinal complexes of Judgement, there were also complexes involving inscribed Affect. The emotions, or the Appraisal resources of Affect, are

Table 4.10 'Ratio' analysis: Six Judgement-oriented attitudinal complexes found in the dataset

	Attitudinal complex		Attitudinal axes				
	Assessment	Abbr.	Type	Polarity	Appraised/ target	Explicitness	Example
(1)	Inscribed positive judgement of the antagonist	PJA	Judgement	+ve	Antagonist	Inscription	他之前是很负责任的一个男人..一个老公He used to be a very **responsible** man.. and husband (Wife_H01_AW)
(2)	Inscribed negative judgement of the antagonist	NJA	Judgement	-ve	Antagonist	Inscription	你就是撒谎You ARE **lying** (Wife_H01_AW)
(3)	Inscribed positive judgement directed at the self	PJS	Judgement	+ve	Self	Inscription	好多地方就是去照顾他In a lot of aspects, I **take care of him** (Wife_H03_AW)
(4)	Inscribed negative judgement directed at the self	NJS	Judgement	-ve	Self	Inscription	我不会沟通I am **not good at** communication (Husband_H03_WH)
(5)	Inscribed positive judgement directed at people outside of the marriage relationship	PJO	Judgement	+ve	Other	Inscription	这男同学一开始..开导效果还比较好一点 at the beginning.. this male high schoolmate.. **did a** pretty **good job** (Husband_H02_WH)
(6)	Inscribed negative judgement directed at people outside of the marriage relationship	NJO	Judgement	-ve	Other	Inscription	说实话..后来我这个男同学..也能说..他说话水平也有限 to be honest.. later on.. this male high schoolmate.. or we can say that.. he **had limited communicative skills** (Wife_H02_WH)

annotated by tracking the origin of the Affectual response (summarised in Table 4.11). As already discussed in connections with the 'occurrence analysis', there were two types of Affectual assessments found in the dataset:

(7) Inscribed negative Affectual response triggered by the antagonist (NATA); and
(8) Inscribed observed other people's Affectual response (OAO).

As foreshadowed in Chap. 3, these two types of Affectual assessments have different evaluative meaning-making mechanisms in the dispute exchanges. Generally speaking, when the speaker reports having had a negative emotion triggered by the antagonist (an instance of NATA), they attempt to invoke a negative assessment of the antagonist—that is, for having caused the speaker to feel bad. (In a sense, they

Table 4.11 'Ratio' analysis: Two Affect-oriented attitudinal complexes found in the dataset

	Attitudinal complex		Attitudinal axes				
	Assessment	Abbr.	Type	Polarity	Appraised/ target	Explicitness	Example
(7)	Inscribed negative affectual response triggered by the antagonist	NATA	Affect	-ve	Self (as the emoter) (eventually antagonist as the trigger)	Inscription of affect, invoking a negative judgement of the trigger	他越对我这样... 我心情越..低落the more he treats me like this…the more I **feel..down** (Wife_W02_WW) (invoke a negative judgement of the husband)
(8)	Inscribed observed other people's affectual response	OAO	Affect	-ve/+ve	Emoter (antagonist /other)	Inscription of affect, invoking a judgement of the emoter/ trigger	她就气得不得了 She just became terribly **angry** (Husband_H03_ WH) (invoke a negative judgement of the wife on the basis that the 'anger' is irrational and excessive)

Table 4.12 'Ratio' analysis: Appreciation-oriented attitudinal complex found in the dataset

	Attitudinal complex		Attitudinal axes				
	Assessment	Abbr.	Type	Polarity	Appraised/target	Explicitness	Example
(9)	Appreciation	APP	Appreciation	+ve/-ve	Thing	Inscription	这日子没办法过了 This life is **unbearable** (Wife_W01_WW)

are instances of inscribed Affect which simultaneously act as tokens of Judgement—so both inscription and invocation. For the purposes of this analysis, they were treated as inscriptions, rather that as invocations.) Likewise, when a disputant reports other peoples' emotions (instances of OAO), there is the potential for this to invoke an assessment of the emoter, according to whether the observed Affect is viewed as socially appropriate or inappropriate. For example, reporting that someone was angry potentially invokes a negative Judgement, on the basis that being angry is often socially deprecated. This potential for observed Affect to act as a token of Judgement in this way is, obviously, very much dependent on the context.

Besides attitudinal complexes of Judgement and Affect, there was the attitudinal complex involving assessment of situations, happenings, or objects—(9) appreciation (APP). In the dataset, instances of Appreciation were usually found to be the speakers' assessments of the relationship (example in Table 4.12).

The final attitudinal complex type found in the dataset is attitudinal assessment advanced via invocation. As noted and explained above, the attitudinal complex labelled 'invocation' consists of all the attitudinal expressions where the disputant

Table 4.13 'Ratio' analysis: Invocations as an attitudinal complex bundle

	Attitudinal complex		Attitudinal axes				
	Assessment	Abbr.	Type	Polarity	Appraised/target	Explicitness	Example
(10)	Invocation	INVO	Judgement	+ve	Self	Invocation	二月初一过生日我是提前到她那个做生意的那个地方去On the first day of the second lunar month I went to the place where she did business in advance to celebrate her birthday (Husband_W03_AH) (signalled by the upscaling)
			Judgement	-ve	Antagonist	Invocation	她跟..人家说嘛(1.0) 我私底下给你弄点钱 She.. told him (1.0) I'll secretly give you some money (Husband_W02_AH) (signalled by the quotation)

chose not to inscribe—that is, chose not to include explicitly attitudinal lexis (see Table 4.13 for examples).

Although these ten attitudinal complex types were found in the dataset, they did not occur in every disputant's speech. Some disputants deployed all ten types. Some disputants only had instances of some attitudinal complex types. That is to say, when having available the same reservoir of attitudinal meaning-making resources, the disputants varied regarding the range of the resources they deployed.

4.2 *Findings: Tendencies in the Deployment of Attitudinal Complexes*

The current analysis aimed to discover how similar or different the 12 disputants were regarding the frequency in their deployment of these attitudinal complexes, and thereby whether enough similarities in this deployment could be observed to provide a basis for the clustering of the attitudinal disposition subtypes they enacted. As noted above, this exploration was carried out in the following steps. I first treated each available attitudinal complex as an individual parameter of variation and arrived at commonalities of the disputants in the dataset: what attitudes did all or most disputants use at comparable ratios? Then I combined the attitudinal complexes in pairs and explored if disputants formed subgroups regarding their similar ratios in using the designated attitudinal complexes while differing from others. Finally, I treated all available attitudinal complexes as a single bundle of parameters of variation and applied clustering methods to perform a multivariate analysis. I subsequently interpreted the findings from a linguistic perspective. The findings are discussed in detail below.

4.2.1 Tendencies When Each Attitudinal Complex Was Considered Individually

Strictly speaking, each of the ten attitudinal complex types can be one parameter of variation to explore variability among the disputants. For example, the attitudinal complex of 'observed other people's Affectual response' can be used to distinguish the disputants who frequently conveyed such attitudes from those who seldom made use of this resource. When each attitudinal complex type is treated as an independent parameter of variation, it is possible to find the particular resources favoured by all or most of the disputants in the dataset. The commonalities among the disputants, if there are any, can reveal a certain degree of predictability as to how people discursively present the self in similar situations.

With respect to family dispute resolution settings, it might be anticipated that all the disputants would frequently advance negative Judgement directed at the antagonist via inscription. The dataset verified this assumption. All the 12 disputants had inscriptions of negative Judgement of the antagonist and used this attitudinal complex at a relatively high ratio. The dataset average ratio is 11.10% of total attitudinal expressions (SD = 3.99, max = 17.39%, min = 5.32%[1]), the highest average ratio among the inscribed attitudinal complexes. As well, all the 12 disputants had instances of invocation, with an average ratio of 80.49% (SD = 8.13, max = 91.49%, min = 66.3%), the highest average ratio among all the ten attitudinal complexes. Note, of course, that these were undifferentiated with respect to attitude type and target. This tells us that all the disputants more often chose not to inscribe than they chose to inscribe—they 'preferred' to invoke and hence to be attitudinally indirect, to rely on the address to supply the specific attitudinal assessment. As far as the other attitudinal complexes are concerned, two attitudinal complexes were shared by a majority of disputants—inscribed positive self-Judgement (used by 11 out of 12 disputants, M = 3.10%, SD = 3.06, max = 10.83%, min = 0.73%) and inscribed negative Affectual response triggered by the antagonist (10 out of 12 disputants, M = 6.12%, SD = 3.94, max = 11.48%, min = 1.09%). The remaining attitudinal complexes are only used by a minority of disputants (3 to 8 out of 12 disputants) and with relatively lower ratios. The least favoured attitudinal complex is inscribed

[1] When reporting findings in the ratio analysis, I provide the following descriptive statistics to offer the readers basic information about the variables in the dataset: (1) average (or mean, abbr. M) ratio; (2) standard Deviation (SD), measuring how spread-out the data is. A low SD means that most numbers are close to the average, whereas a high SD means that the numbers are more lied apart; (3) max (i.e., the highest ratio in the dataset); and (4) min (i.e., the lowest ratio in the dataset).

positive Judgement of the antagonist, only deployed by 3 out of 12 disputants and with an average ratio of 0.55% (SD = 1.41, max = 4.92%, min = 0.83%).

The commonalities among the disputants suggest that being both invocative and explicitly antagonistic with respect to a subset of the attitudinal complexes is a shared attitudinal disposition for all the speakers in this situation of publicly broadcast conflict resolution. When relying on invocations, which they frequently did, the disputants construed 'like-minded' putative mediators (White, 2020), who presumably shared the same norms and reading positions as the speaker. Meanwhile, by frequently advancing the other three attitudinal inscriptions—(1) inscribed negative Judgement of the antagonist, (2) inscribed positive self-Judgement, and (3) inscribed negative Affectual response triggered by the antagonist, the disputants consistently foregrounded an antagonistic attitudinal positioning. The disputants made their accusation of the antagonist explicit and unambiguously clear.

Apart from the commonalities, the disputants varied in many aspects. For example, their attitudinal positioning directed at the antagonist is not universally negative: three disputants had instances of inscribed positive Judgement of the antagonist (max = 4.92%, min = 0.83%). It means that these three disputants, compared to the other disputants who were purely antagonistic, had relatively 'balanced' attitudinal orientation towards the antagonist. Additionally, the disputants also varied concerning their positioning of the self. There was just one disputant who never praised himself. Six disputants overtly blamed the self (max = 5%, min = 0.79%), indicating that some disputants preferred to present a 'conciliatory' aspect of the self by admitting their faults.

Additionally, there were also observable in-group variations among the disputants. Consider the attitudinal complex of inscribed negative Judgement of the antagonist. Although all disputants picked up this option with an average ratio of 11.11%, one disputant (Husband_H02_WH, a wayward husband) had up to 17.39% of his total attitudinal instances being negative antagonist-oriented inscriptions. In contrast, one disputant (Husband_H01_WH, a wayward husband) had only 5.43% of his attitudes being negative inscription directed at the antagonist. These two ratios mean that the high-ratio disputant was three times more frequent than the low-ratio disputant when explicitly advancing their condemnations of the spouse. For the rest of the disputants, their ratios spread along the continuum between 5.43% to 17.39% (illustrated by Fig. 4.3). The ratio difference reveals an in-group divergence in the speakers' hostility towards the antagonist. While all the disputants were overall hostile towards the antagonist, the disputants varied significantly with respect to the degree of their hostility. The different degree of hostility constructed a completely different attitudinal disposition. The higher ratio of the inscribed negative inscription directed at the antagonist, the more hostile the speaker's attitudinal stance was.

Similar observable in-group variations were found in other attitudinal complex types. The patterns reveal that despite a commonality in the disputants' preference for certain attitudinal complex, there are observable individual differences among

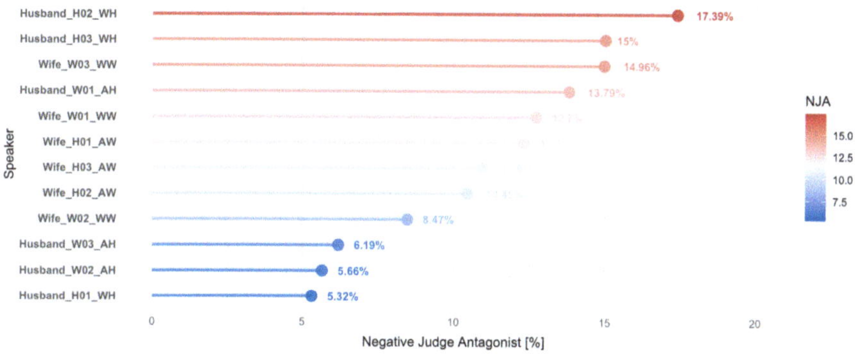

Fig. 4.3 Ratio of inscribed negative Judgement of the antagonist

the disputants. When each attitudinal complex option is used as a parameter of variation, the disputants disperse along a continuum between the disputant with the highest ratio and the disputant with the lowest ratio. In one sense, the disputants can be classified into two or multiple groups in terms of the similarity of their ratios—for example, groups of disputants with high-ratio /mid-ratio /low-ratio of inscribed negative Judgement of the antagonist. The disputants in each group arguably construct a similar attitudinal disposition. Meanwhile, in another sense, there is no abrupt change or discontinuity among the disputants regarding their ratios. This pattern is represented visually by the colour of the bars in Fig. 4.3. The disputants with lower ratios are illustrated with yellowish bars: the lower the ratio, the yellower the bar is. In contrast, the disputants having higher ratios are illustrated with purplish bars. The higher the ratio, the more purple the bar. The colours from yellow to purple are different shades of yellow or purple. There is nothing absolute nor definite. The continuous feature of the groupings of the disputants—for example, as high-ratio, mid-ratio or low-ratio groups—indicate that the attitudinal disposition identified vis-à-vis single attitudinal complex type was a matter of quantitative relativity, rather than a matter of qualitative difference.

As far as the relationship between the disputants' choice and their waywardness/aggrieveness is concerned, one interesting finding emerged. This finding is related to who were more overtly antagonistic, the wayward spouses or the aggrieved spouses. Before looking at the results, one might speculate that the aggrieved spouses, who were assumingly victim of the counterparts' allegedly cheating behaviour, might advance their negative inscriptions of the antagonist more frequently than the wayward spouses, whom we might expect to be defensive. However, the findings proved that the opposite was true. As illustrated in Fig. 4.4, the wayward spouses (blue) were relatively more frequent in advancing explicit condemnations of the aggrieved spouses (orange). It seems that for the wayward spouses, attacking was the best form of self-defence.

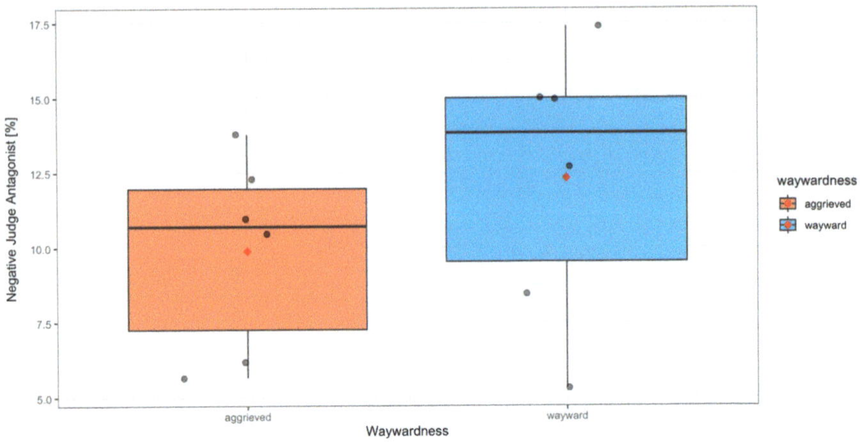

Fig. 4.4 Ratio of inscribed negative Judgement of the antagonist (wayward versus aggrieved)

4.2.2 Tendencies When Two Attitudinal Complexes Were Considered Together

The above analysis has shown that the ratio of each attitudinal complex can be used as a parameter of variation. Along this line of thinking, I continued to explore any patterns when a pair of attitudinal complex types were considered together. In other words, did some disputants have similar ratios when co-selecting two attitudes? For example, were there two or more disputants who all had relatively high ratios of inscribed negative Judgement of the antagonist and high ratios of inscribed negative Affectual response triggered by the antagonist? If so, the attitudinal profile for these disputants might stand out because of their foregrounding of judgemental hostility towards their spouse and the tendency to present their spouse as having made them feel bad.

When pairs of attitudinal complex types were examined, patterned variations were likewise identified among the disputants. I will illustrate with a simple case when the two attitudinal complex types under consideration are—(1) inscribed negative Judgement of the antagonist and (2) inscribed negative Affectual response triggered by the antagonist. Both attitudinal complexes eventually convey the speaker's antipathy directed at the antagonist but via different attitudinal meaning-making mechanisms. The attitudinal complex of inscribed negative Judgement of the antagonist constructs an attitudinal disposition of being 'hostile' towards the antagonist or a 'combatant' of their spouse. The attitudinal complex of negative Affectual response triggered by the antagonist construct an attitudinal disposition of an 'emotional victim' of the antagonist's behaviour, which might eventually activate a negative assessment of the antagonist, albeit not explicitly. High ratios in these two attitudinal complexes would reflect the speaker's overall negativity towards the antagonist. It turned out that the disputants cluster into two groups (visualised in Fig. 4.5). The disputants in the red group (upper section of the figure) had relatively

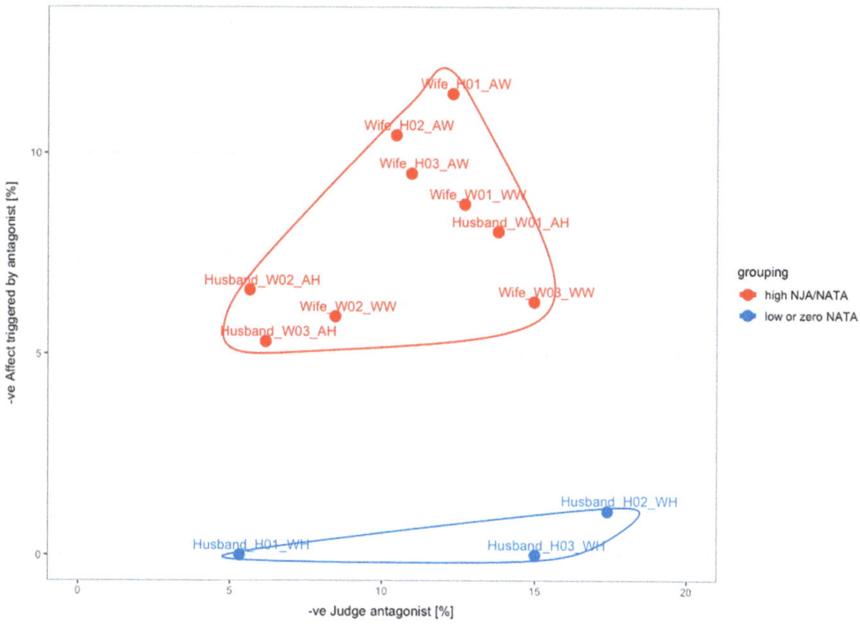

Fig. 4.5 Ratios of two attitudinal complex types: inscribed negative Judgement of the antagonist (abbr. NJA) (x-axis) and inscribed negative Affectual response triggered by the antagonist (abbr. NATA) (y-axis)

high ratios of both attitudinal complexes. That is to say, they presented themselves as both 'combatant' and an 'emotional victim'. Their choices appear to be in sharp contrast to that of the blue group (bottom section of the figure). The disputants in the blue group had zero or a very low ratio of inscribed negative Affectual responses triggered by the antagonist. It means that they avoided construing an attitudinal disposition of an 'emotional victim'. Meanwhile, the disputants in the blue group varied significantly regarding their ratio of inscribed negative Judgement of the antagonist, suggesting the disputants of the blue group had variations vis-à-vis their hostility towards the antagonist. They presented themselves as being 'combatants' but not as 'emotional victims'.

A certain degree of correlation between the speakers' preference for these two types of attitudinal complex and their waywardness could also be observed. As presented in Fig. 4.6, there is a tendency for the aggrieved spouses (the red group) to have higher ratios of these two attitudinal complexes than the wayward spouses (the blue group). It means that the aggrieved spouses tended to favour construing an attitudinal disposition that was of being both a 'combatant' and an 'emotional victim'. In contrast, the wayward spouses tended to focus more on the 'hostile' self-presentation.

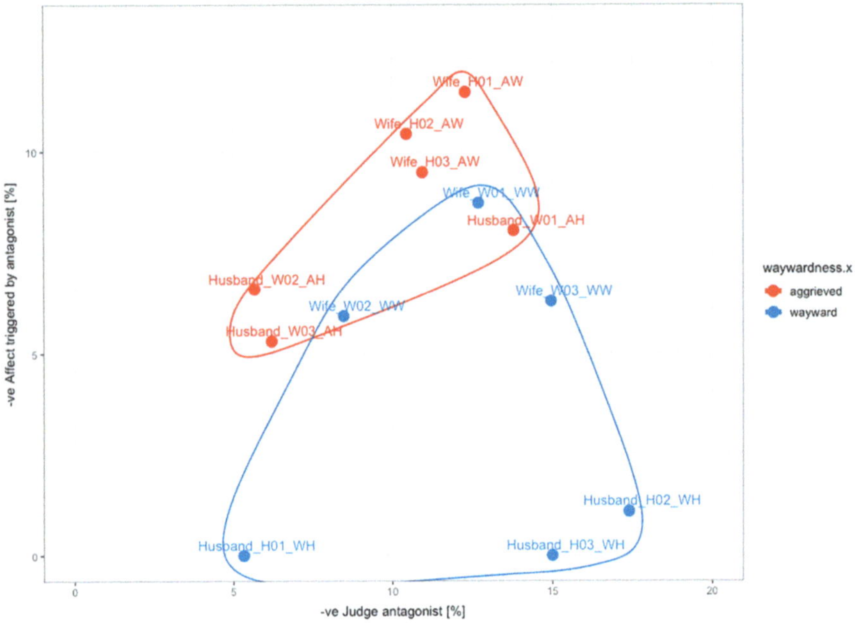

Fig. 4.6 Ratios of two attitudinal complex types: inscribed negative Judgement of the antagonist (abbr. NJA) (x-axis) and inscribed negative Affectual response triggered by the antagonist (abbr. NATA) (y-axis) (wayward versus aggrieved)

Exploration along this line of inquiry can lead to patterned variations in other parings of attitudinal complex types. Strictly speaking, any two attitudinal complexes can be combined to form a parameter set for variation exploration. Similarly, combinations of three or four or even more attitudinal complex types can be considered as distinct parameter sets to explore lines of variation among the speakers in the dataset. The parameters—or the attitudinal complex types—in a parameter combination can be carefully selected to foreground a particular aspect of the speakers' use of evaluative language, such as the speakers' attitudes directed at the self or the speakers' assessment of human behaviours. Such zoomed-in inquiries will be particularly valuable when the research focuses on a particular aspect of the speakers' attitudinal orientation.

Because the research objective for this study was to explore the variability among the disputants' use of attitude-associated resources in general, the following step of my analysis took a very bold step and put all the ten available attitudinal complex types together. In other words, I took the ten attitudinal complexes as one parameter combination to explore the tendencies among the disputants—whether some disputants had a similar degree of preference for multiple complex types, which gave rise to a particular type of attitudinal disposition. Obviously, this was only possible on account of my use of the computational tools discussed previously.

4.2.3 Clusters Emerging from Co-Selection of Multiple Attitudinal Complexes

Different insights emerged when the analysis turned to consider patterns across all the attitudinal complexes. Here those disputants who used a similar subset of attitudinal complexes with similar ratios would be grouped together, and those who used a different subset with similar ratios would be grouped together. The more similar ratios shared by disputants, the more closely they would be associated.

Methodologically, ratios of ten attitudinal complex options are ten independent parameters of variation. Combining all of them together as one parameter creates high dimensional data, where multiple values are needed to identify a data point uniquely. Say, for example, a disputant's position or identity in a ten-parameter data can only be identified by the ratios of their choice in all the ten attitudinal complex options. If variations regarding one attitudinal complex or two complexes can be identified manually, variations vis-à-vis a parameter combination with ten options become too complex to be explored by hand.

As indicated previously, for this, I employed cluster analysis methods from Data Science and used the programming language *R* to identify and visualise the variations among the disputants. The procedure for carrying out this analysis was similar to that in the aforementioned 'occurrence' analysis, consisting of three steps: (1) determine how many clusters to identify, (2) identify the clusters, and (3) explore what the clustering informs us about the disputants' preference for the attitudinal complexes.

In the first step, I determined the number of clusters. I used the average silhouette method (see Sect. 3.2.2 for details) to determine the optimal number of clusters in the dataset. The optimal number was two (visualised in Fig. 4.7), indicating that two clusters can best represent the clustering in the dataset.

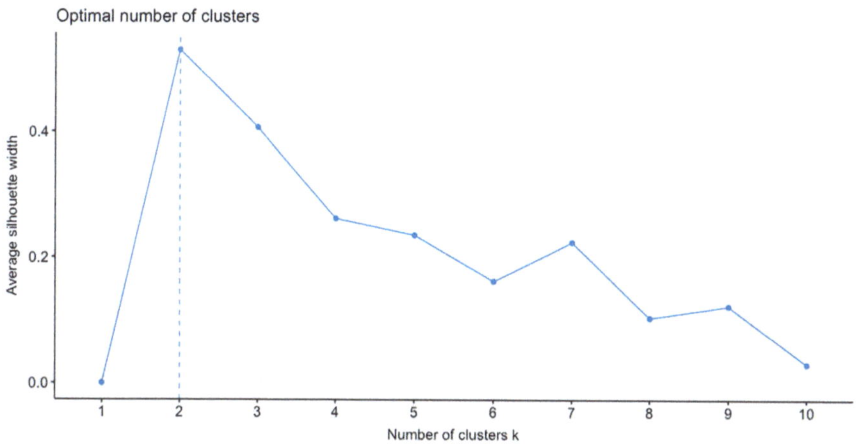

Fig. 4.7 'Ratio' analysis: Optimal number of clusters (co-selection of multiple attitudinal complexes) (Figure adapted from Xu and White (2021), pp. 52–73. Reused with permission)

In the second step, I identified the two clusters using the 'Principal Component Analysis' (PCA), method (Jolliffe, 2002; Mardia et al., 1979). According to the data mining literature (Hayden, 2018; Jolliffe & Cadima, 2016; Metsalu & Vilo, 2015), the PCA method is particularly helpful in 'wide' datasets or multivariate analysis, where there are multiple continuous variables for each sample. According to the previous discussions, the 'ratios' of attitudinal complexes—that is, the percentage of instances of a designated attitudinal complex in the total number of attitudinal instances in a person's speech—are continuous variables. The PCA method identifies the combinations of highly correlated variables, which together account for the most variance in the data. These combinations of variables are called 'principal components', with the total number of principal components being equal to the original number of variables. It means that in my dataset of 10 attitudinal complex types, there would be 10 'principal components'. Usually, the first few principal components contribute to the majority of the possible variance in the dataset. The first principal component accounts for the most significant possible variance in the dataset, followed by the second principal component. Therefore, the findings of the PCA were not to identify the variations in the disputants' use of one particular attitudinal complex option, but a combination of correlated attitudinal complex options which account for the most significant possible variance among the disputants. Notably, in her seminal 'semantic variation' studies, Hasan (1989, 2009) used PCA as a statistical method, although she used it to explore the correlations between the social factors of class and sex on the one hand and the orientation towards certain patterns of semantic choice on the other, rather than to identify hidden patterns in the dataset.

It is worth noting that many data mining studies have used PCA as a dimensionality-reduction method—to reduce the number of variables in a dataset, sometimes at the expense of accuracy. I used this method for its effectiveness in identifying patterns and visualising the variation present in a dataset with many variables, rather than with an aim to remove any attitudinal complex types from the analysis. In my study, every attitudinal complex option was meaningful in unpacking the disputants' attitudinal self-presentation, regardless of the particular option's specific contribution to the overall variations in the dataset. In this analysis, I used the 'PCA' and 'get_pca_ind' functions from the 'FactoMineR' (Lê et al., 2008; v 2.4; Husson et al., 2020) and 'factoextra' package (v 1.0.7; Kassambara & Mundt, 2020) in *R*. This visualisation of the PCA can be found later in Sect. 4.2.3.4.

In the third step, I contextualised the clustering with the disputants' deployment of the attitudinal complexes and explored the insights the clustering might bring to light. I found that the disputants in each group used a similar co-selection of attitudinal complexes at similar ratios by which they were distinct from the disputants in the other group, who used a different subset of attitudinal complexes at similar ratios. Roughly speaking, the grouping revealed variability in the disputants' 'expressiveness' when advancing the attitudinal orientations that were of their primary concern. Specifically, group one has two disputants with similar and relatively high ratios in attitudinal inscriptions involving negative Judgements of the antagonist and positive self-Judgement. Their preference made their overall antagonistic attitudinal orientation unambiguously clear and foregrounded, and hence they can be characterised as having a 'more expressive' attitudinal disposition. Group two have ten disputants with similar and relatively low ratios in their explicit condemnation of the antagonist and self-praise. In contrast, they had relatively high ratios in attitudinal complexes that did not explicitly construe an 'antagonistic' attitudinal positioning, having the potential to more indirectly position the audience to view the antagonist in a negative light (for example, via reporting their own negative emotions as presumably caused by the antagonist, or negatively appreciating the situation of the marriage and thereby indirectly blaming the antagonist). Therefore, they could be characterised as being 'less expressive' in their positioning. After zooming into the attitudinal complexes favoured by the second group, I realised that there were two sub-groups within the 'less expressive' cluster. That is to say, while all these ten disputants were relatively more indirect than the 'more expressive' group, the ten disputants diverged regarding their preferred attitudinal complexes. Specifically, four disputants had similarly high ratios in the attitudinal bundle of 'invocation', suggesting that these disputants favoured relying solely on presenting ideational meanings to invoke attitudinal assessments from the audience rather than inscribing the assessments. The other six disputants opted for attitudinal inscriptions, such as negative Affectual response triggered by the antagonist and Appreciations, to activate particular attitudinal assessments from the audience. In other words, the two sub-groups, both being 'less expressive', favoured different meaning-making mechanism when building the speaker-audience rapport. The disputants favouring 'invocation' could be characterised as being 'least expressive'—that is, even further down the scale of 'expressiveness' or not expressive at all.

Subsequently, based on the findings that emerged from the computational clustering methods, I identified and characterised three attitudinal disposition groups. The three groups demonstrate different degrees of 'expressiveness', as discussed in detail in the following sections.

4.2.3.1 Attitudinal Disposition Type 1: More Expressive

The first attitudinal disposition type identified through this line of inquiry is given the label 'More expressive'. The two disputants of this type had a relatively high ratio of inscriptions, which means, compared with speakers of the 'less expressive' and 'least expressive' groups, they preferred to articulate their attitudinal assessments explicitly. Generally speaking, the higher the ratio of the attitudinal proposition, the more salience is given to that specific attitudinal value. The inscriptions favoured by 'more expressive' speakers usually centred around the attitudinal complexes of central concern in the speakers' attitudinal positioning. That is to say, whatever attitudinal values the speakers aimed at foregrounding, they would present them via inscription. Such explicit attitudinal positioning explicitly presented the speakers' central concern as such, without any ambiguity. Such explicit attitudinal arrangements also positioned the mediators to attitudinally assess the attitudinal

Table 4.14 Ratios making the 'more expressive' disposition different from the other groups[a]

			Ratio of attitudinal complex (%)					
			Inscribe –ve Judge antagonist	Inscribe +ve Judge self	Inscribe -ve/ +ve Affect (observed)	Inscribe +ve Judge others	Inscribe –ve Judge self	Invocation
Disposition	Speaker	Waywardness	NJA	PJS	OAO	PJO	NJS	INVO
'More expressive'	Husband_ H02_WH	Wayward	17.39	6.52	10.87	3.26	1.09	66.30
	Husband_ H03_WH	Wayward	15.02	10.83	4.17	0.80	5.05	66.67
	Group average		16.20	8.68	7.52	2.05	3.05	66.49
'Less expressive' group average			12.11	1.74	1.17	1.00	0.84	79.48
'Least expressive' group average			7.05	2.35	0.75	0.24	0.22	89.01

Key: *NJA* negative Judgement of the antagonist, *PJS* positive Judgement directed at the self, *OAO* observed other people's Affectual response, *PJO* positive Judgement of others, *NJS* negative Judgement directed at the self, *INVO* invocation

[a]Table adapted from Xu and White (2021), pp. 52–73. Reused with permission

targets in the same way as the speakers did. Hence, such attitudinal arrangements were interpreted as demonstrating a 'more expressive' attitudinal disposition.

Specifically, the two 'more expressive' disputants had an average of 35% of their total attitudinal instances being inscriptions, twice as much as that of the 'less expressive' group and three times the 'least expressive' group. Among the inscriptions, they had noticeably higher ratios in three attitudinal complex types than the other group. They had 16.20% of inscribed negative Judgement of the antagonist, 8.68% of inscribed positive self-Judgement, and 7.52% of observed Affectual responses of the antagonist. They had relatively a lower degree of preference for invocations than the other two groups. The ratios of the attitudinal complexes that made the 'more expressive' disputants distinct from other disputants are summarised in Table 4.14. Both 'more expressive' disputants were wayward husbands.

Accordingly, as illustrated in Table 4.14, the disputants of this disposition type had a high ratio of inscribed assessments on attitudinal complexes of negative Judgement directed at the antagonist and others, as well as positive and negative Judgement directed at the self. The high ratios of inscriptions on observed other people's Affects can serve as attitude signals inviting the mediators to assess the emoters in a certain way, for example, negative Judgement of the antagonist. The foregrounding of these attitudinal complex types reveals a salient focus in the speakers' attitudinal positioning—to accuse the antagonist.

A typical example from the dataset is demonstrated by Husband_H03_WH, a wayward spouse who consistently expressed negative judgments toward his wife throughout the dispute interactions, positioning the mediators to negatively assess the wife accordingly. This pattern is exemplified in Excerpt 4.4, where, in one single turn, he advanced six instances of negative judgment directed at his wife through inscription, critiquing her perceived character traits. Similarly, as demonstrated in Excerpt 4.5, the husband made his attitudinal positioning regarding both self and other parties explicitly evident in the exchange, manifesting his strongly negative

Excerpt 4.4 Example of the 'more expressive' attitudinal disposition (Husband_H03_WH's utterances in Turn 103)[a]

Turn	Speaker	Move	Utterance (Chinese)	Utterance (English translation)	Attitude signal	Attitudinal complex	
						Assessment	Abbr.
102	Hostess_ H03	1	所以这个事在柯先生看来也无伤大雅	So this thing is also innocuous in Mr. Ke's opinion			
103	Husband_ H03_WH	1	那肯定的喽	That's for sure			
		2	她要自己找自己难受	She wants to **find troubles for herself**	Inscription	Inscribe -ve Judge antagonist	NJA
		3	我跟她无法沟通..你知道吗	I can't communicate with her.. you know	Denial	Invoke inscribe -ve Judge antagonist	INVO
		4	我跟她说了几句话她就犟起来..吱吱吱	If I say a few words to her she will **pick up an argument with me defiantly**.. blah blah blah	Inscription	Inscribe -ve Judge antagonist	NJA
		5	还发脾气了	Also she will even **lose her temper**	Inscription	Inscribe -ve Judge antagonist	NJA
		6	骂我..骂死你	She will **curse at** me.. cursing at me to death	Inscription	Inscribe -ve Judge antagonist	NJA
		7	她祖宗十八代都骂	She will **curse at** all my ancestors.. Ancestors of eighteen generations	Inscription	Inscribe -ve Judge antagonist	NJA
		8	她骂你一个人都不算	She doesn't **curse at** you alone	Inscription	Inscribe -ve Judge antagonist	NJA

[a]Example adapted from Xu and White (2021), pp. 52–73. Reused with permission

evaluative stance. (See the book's GitHub repository for the full analysis of his language.)

From the above two excerpts, it could be observed that, regardless of the specific target or polarity of the attitude, 'more expressive' disputants generally favoured assessing human and human behaviour rather than things and happenings. The high ratio of inscriptions tended to be deployed to advance assessments of Judgement, either targeted at the self, the antagonist, or any other persons outside of the marital relationship. In contrast, they did not favour inscriptions of Appreciation. In family dispute resolution exchanges, regardless of the cause of the disputes, the central attitudinal concern for any disputant is presumably people's behaviour. The 'more expressive' disputants' attitudinal preference for focussing directly on humans and human behaviours reinforced the characterisation of the attitudinal disposition type—expressively foregrounding the speakers' attitudinal central concern.

Excerpt 4.5 Example of the 'more expressive' attitudinal disposition (Husband_H03_WH's utterances in Turn 207–209)[a]

Turn	Speaker	Move	Utterance (Chinese)	Utterance (English translation)	Attitude signal	Attitudinal complex	
						Assessment	Abbr.
207	Husband_ H03_WH	1	对我这么..对我**照顾**得这么**好**	Of me so.. she takes care of me so well	Inscription	Inscribe +ve Judge antagonist	PJA
		2	来..拥抱一下	Come on.. let's hug			
208	Wife_ H03_AW	1	嗯	Mhm			
209	Husband_ H03_WH	1	起来	Stand up			
		2	我..我是个**追求浪漫**..**追求**那个**激情**的人	I.. I am a person who **pursues romance.. pursues** that kind of **passion**	Inscription	Inscribe +ve Judge self	PJS
		3	**不**是那种**死板**的人	I am **not** the kind of **rigid** person	Inscription	Inscribe +ve Judge self	PJS
		4	你看..她一点都**不热情**	You see.. she is **not enthusiastic** at all	Inscription	Inscribe -ve Affect antagonist	OAO
		5	怎么回事啊	What's the matter	Rhetorical question	Invoke -ve Judge antagonist	INVO
		6	不接受..是吧	You are not accepting me.. right	Denial	Invoke -ve Judge antagonist	INVO
		7	再来一次	Let me try again			

[a]Example adapted from Xu and White (2021), pp. 52–73. Reused with permission

4.2.3.2 Attitudinal Disposition Type 2: Less Expressive

The second attitudinal disposition type is 'less expressive'. Compared with speakers of the 'more expressive' type, the six 'less expressive' speakers favoured invocation over inscription and chose not to make their central attitudinal concerns foregrounded. That is to say, speakers of this type not only had a relatively lower ratio of inscriptions than the 'more expressive' speakers but also when deploying inscription, the inscriptions tended not to be used on attitudinal complexes that were presumably of the central attitudinal concerns of the speakers—that is, to directly condemn the antagonist or explicitly assess human or human behaviours. The inscriptions were associated with some other attitudinal values that seemingly were not immediately related to the condemnation.

The 'less expressive' group demonstrated distinct patterns in their attitudinal arrangements. They had a higher proportion of invocations compared to the 'more expressive' group, with an average of 80% of total attitudinal instances being

Table 4.15 Ratios making the 'less expressive' disposition different from the other groups

			Ratio of attitudinal complex (%)				
			Inscribe –ve Affect (triggered by the antagonist)	Inscribe +ve Judge antagonist	Inscribe -ve Appreciation relationship	Inscribe –ve Judge antagonist	Invocation
Disposition	Speaker	Waywardness	NATA	PJA	APP	NJA	INVO
'Less expressive'	Husband_ W01_AH	Aggrieved	8.05	0	0	13.8	75.86
	Wife_ H01_AW	Aggrieved	11.48	4.92	1.64	12.3	77.05
	Wife_ H02_AW	Aggrieved	10.45	0	1.49	10.5	80.6
	Wife_ W01_WW	Wayward	8.73	0	3.17	12.7	80.95
	Wife_ W02_WW	Wayward	5.93	0.85	2.54	8.5	80.51
	Wife_ W03_WW	Wayward	6.3	0	1.57	15.0	81.89
	Group average		8.49	0.96	1.74	12.11	79.48
'More expressive' group average			0.55	0.42	0.84	16.20	66.49
'Least expressive' group average			5.37	0	0.42	7.05	89.01

Key: *NATA* negative Affectual response triggered by the antagonist or antagonist's behaviour, *PJA* positive Judgement of the antagonist, *APP* Appreciation, *NJA* negative Judgement of the antagonist, *INVO* invocation

invocations (15% more than the 'more expressive' group). In terms of inscriptions, this group particularly favoured negative Affectual responses triggered by the antagonist, with an average ratio of 8.49% (significantly higher than the 'more expressive' group's 0.55%, SD = 2.21). While they also expressed negative Judgements about the antagonist, averaging 12.11% (compared to the 'more expressive' group's 16.20%), their explicit condemnations were relatively lower. These patterns suggest that the 'less expressive' group maintained a more restrained approach to explicitly articulating negative evaluations toward the antagonist. The implicit nature of their attitudinal positioning proved crucial, as the communicative outcomes heavily depended on the reading positions of other participants, particularly the mediators. The attitudinal arrangements of this subset are summarised in Table 4.15, where I find three wayward spouses and three aggrieved spouses."

A representative case is demonstrated through Wife_H01_AW, an aggrieved party who showed the highest frequency of negative Affectual responses triggered by the antagonist in our dataset. This pattern is clearly illustrated in Excerpt 4.6, which demonstrates the wife's attitudinal profile (See the book's GitHub repository for the full analysis of her contributions to this segment of the episode). In this excerpt, the wife recounted her experience with her husband's perceived infidelity with a neighbor, describing her negative emotions—anger, discomfort, and insecurity—all triggered by his behaviour. Rather than making direct accusations, she chose to express these feelings indirectly, maintaining a restrained stance while allowing the mediators to interpret her attitudinal position.

Excerpt 4.6 Example of the 'less expressive' attitudinal disposition (Wife_H01_AW's utterances in Turn 98)[a]

Turn	Speaker	Move	Utterance (Chinese)	Utterance (English translation)	Attitude signal	Attitudinal complex	
						Assessment	Abbr.
96	Wife_ H01_AW	1	我打过那个女人的电话	I called the woman on the phone			
97	Hostess_ H01	1	你求证到了什么结果没有	Did you prove something			
98	Wife_ H01_AW	1	没有..他们双方都不承认	No.. neither of them admitted it			
		2	都认为这只是一个玩笑而已	Both of them thought this was just for fun			
		3	我打那个女人电话是因为出于心头很**气愤**	I called the woman because I was extremely **angry**	Attitudinal instance of inscribed affect (potential invocation of -ve judgement)	Inscribe -ve Affect self (triggered by the antagonist) (invoke -ve Judge antagonist)	NATA
		4	打过去**骂**她的	I called her **to curse at** her	Evoke	Invoke -ve Affect self (triggered by the antagonist)	INVO
		5	当时她和我**对骂**	She **cursed back at** me on the phone	Inscription	Inscribe -ve Judge other	NJO
		6	所以我更相信他们之间更**不正常**	So I believed more firmly that there was something **abnormal** between them	Inscription	Inscribe -ve Appreciation relationship b/t the husband and the woman (invoke -ve Judge antagonist)	APP
		7	让我感觉很**不踏实**	They made me **feel** very **unsettled**	Attitudinal instance of inscribed affect (potential invocation of -ve judgement)	Inscribe -ve Affect self (triggered by the antagonist) (invoke -ve Judge antagonist)	NATA
		8	很没安全感	Very **insecure**	Attitudinal instance of inscribed affect (potential invocation of -ve judgement)	Inscribe -ve Affect self (triggered by the antagonist) (invoke -ve Judge antagonist)	NATA

[a]Example adapted from Xu and White (2021), pp. 52–73. Reused with permission

From the above excerpt, it could be observed that the 'less expressive' disputants generally favoured reporting their own emotions and appreciating situations or things rather than directly assessing human and human behaviour. The high ratio of negative Affectual responses triggered by the antagonist positioned the audience to view the speakers as being emotionally victimised by their counterparts' allegedly cheating behaviours, hence eventually activating condemnations directed at their counterparts.

4.2.3.3 Attitudinal Disposition Type 3: Least Expressive

The final attitudinal disposition type is characterised as 'least expressive'. The four disputants in this group predominantly favoured the attitudinal complex of 'invocation', with an average ratio of 89.03% (SD = 1.70, max = 91.49%, min = 87.61%) of their individual total attitudinal instances being advanced through attitudinal signals or pure ideational meanings rather than direct inscription. In comparison, for the attitudinal complex of inscribed negative Judgment of the antagonist, which was the most favoured attitudinal complex in the dataset, the 'least expressive' group showed an average ratio of 7.05% (SD = 2.64, max = 10.95%, min = 5.32%), significantly lower than both the 'less expressive' group (12.11%) and the 'more expressive' group (16.20%). This preference for invocations by the 'least expressive' group indicated their construal of a highly 'like-minded' audience—that is, they assumed the mediators shared the same cultural norms and value positions as themselves, making attitudinal signals (e.g., contrast or self-quotation) or pure ideational meanings (e.g., a description of a past event) sufficient to activate the intended mediator assessment. The detailed ratios for the four disputants exhibiting 'least expressive' disposition are summarised in Table 4.16. Of these four disputants, one was a wayward spouse and three were aggrieved spouses.

Husband_H01_WH's attitudinal arrangements in Excerpt 4.7 examplifies a typical 'least expressive' disposition. (Refer to the book's GitHub repository for the full analysis of his language.) He had the highest ratio of invocation in the dataset, with 91.49% of his total attitudinal instances taking the form of invocations—that is, nine out of ten of his attitudinal instances did not involve explicit attitudinally stable

Table 4.16 Ratios making the 'least expressive' disposition different from the other groups[a]

			Ratio of attitudinal complex (%)		
			Invocation	Inscribe –ve Judge antagonist	Inscribe –ve Affect (triggered by the antagonist)
Disposition	Speaker	Waywardness	INVO	NJA	NATA
'Least expressive'	Husband_H01_WH	Wayward	91.49	5.32	0.0
	Husband_W02_AH	Aggrieved	88.68	5.66	6.6
	Husband_W03_AH	Aggrieved	87.61	6.19	5.31
	Wife_H03_AW	Aggrieved	88.24	10.95	9.56
	Group average		89.03	7.05	5.37
'More expressive' group average			66.49	16.20	0.55
'Less expressive' group average			79.48	12.11	8.49

Key: *INVO* invocation, *NJA* negative Judgement of the antagonist, *NATA* negative Affectual response triggered by the antagonist or antagonist's behaviour

[a]Table adapted from Xu and White (2021), pp. 52–73. Reused with permission

Excerpt 4.7 Example of the 'least expressive' attitudinal disposition (Husband_H01_WH's utterances in Turn 28–30)[a]

Turn	Speaker	Move	Utterance (Chinese)	Utterance (English translation)	Attitude signal	Attitudinal complex	
						Assessment	Abbr.
28	Husband_H01_WH	1	当时对我来说.. 才开始玩这个微信	At that time.. for me.. I was a new user of WeChat	Evoke	Counteract -ve Judge wife[a]	INVO
		2	很多==都不==懂	There were many things I ==didn't== understand	Denial	Invoke -ve Judge self; counteract -ve Judge wife[b]	INVO
29	Hostess_H01	1	==嗯==	==Mhm==			
30	Husband_H01_WH	1	感觉好奇嘛	I simply felt curious	Attitudinal token	Counteract -ve Judge wife[c]	INVO
		2	然后**无聊**的情况下..就加她微信	Then when I **felt bored..** I added her to my WeChat	Attitudinal token	Inscribe -ve Affect, self; counteract -ve Judge wife[d]	INVO
		3	然后就这样聊下天	Then we chatted briefly	Evoke	Counteract -ve Judge wife[e]	INVO
		4	实际上这个女人都不在重庆	In fact.. This woman was not even in Chongqing	Denial	Counteract -ve Judge wife[f]	INVO
		5	外面做生意	She did business elsewhere	Evoke	Counteract -ve Judge wife[g]	INVO
		6	我怎么解释她都不相信	No matter how hard I explained that to her.. She would not believe it	Denial	Invoke +ve Judge self; invoke -ve Judge antagonist[h]	INVO
		7	快一年了她都说我继续跟那个女的在保持联系	Almost a year has passed.. she is still saying that I continue to keep in touch with that woman	Up-scaling	Invoke -ve Judge antagonist[i]	INVO
		8	我可以说.. 现在根本就没有记对方的那个电话号码	I can say.. now I don't have that woman's phone number at all	Denial; upscaling	Invoke +ve Judge self; counteract -ve Judge wife[j]	INVO

[a]Example adapted from Xu and White (2021), pp. 52–73. Reused with permission

[b]Following the wife's disclosure of alleged WeChat communications between her husband and a female neighbour, she positioned the mediators to adopt a negative assessment of the husband's conduct. In this turn, however, the husband repositioned himself as a 'new user of WeChat', offering an explanation that would be comprehensible to audiences adhering to cultural norms such as 'It is common for a new user to explore all the functions of an application' or 'It is understandable that a new user might temporarily misuse certain features'. Through this strategic self-positioning and explanation, the husband countered his wife's negative characterisation of his behaviour

[c]In this turn, the husband expressed his lack of familiarity with WeChat's features and functions, offering a self-assessment that positions himself as having insufficient knowledge about proper usage. This self-directed Judgement of capacity serves as an attitudinal resource that would resonate with audiences holding cultural norms such as 'It is understandable when someone makes mistakes due to lack of knowledge' or 'A person should not be judged for what they do not know how to do'. Through this strategic self-positioning, the husband attempts to counter his wife's negative characterization of his conduct

[d]Curiosity as 'a feeling of deprivation reflects feelings of uncertainty and tension' (Litman & Jimerson, 2004, p. 147). In his response, the husband positions himself as having acted out of curiosity rather than with deliberate intent, explaining his decision to add and chat with the female neighbour. In Appraisal terms, this strategic deployment of curiosity functions as an attitudinal token that counters his wife's negative characterisation of his behaviour, aligning with cultural understandings where 'curiosity-driven actions are seen as natural rather than suspicious'

[e]The husband's feeling of boredom in this exchange can be interpreted as an Affect of dissatisfaction, with its trigger unspecified. For audiences who hold cultural positions such as 'When someone feels bored, it is natural to initiate conversation' or 'A person should not be judged for seeking social interaction', the husband's expression of feeling 'boring' serves as an attitudinal token to counteract his wife's negative positioning directed at him

[f]The husband's deployment of 'briefly' functions as a downscaling device to diminish the significance of his interactions with the female neighbour. This modification serves to counter his wife's negative characterisation, aligning with cultural understandings where 'casual chats between opposite-sex individuals are considered normal and typically harmless'. Through this downscaling, the husband qualifies the nature of these communications while challenging his wife's previous accusations

[g]The husband's revelation that he and the female neighbour reside in different cities serves to counter his wife's underlying assumptions and those of potential mediators. This geographical separation functions as a counter-expectancy resource, dismissing any possibility of intimate involvement between himself and the female neighbour. The counter-expectancy formulation 'not even' emphasises this physical impossibility, thereby undermining his wife's accusations

[h]Through the juxtaposition of Chongqing (his residence) against 'elsewhere' (where the female neighbour resides), the husband positions the mediators to recognise the physical impossibility of intimate involvement between himself and the neighbour. This geographical contrast serves as an attitudinal signal, countering his wife's concerns

[i]The husband's explanation may potentially invoke two attitudinal positionings. From a self-directed perspective, it positions the mediators to evaluate him positively when viewed through cultural norms of 'good personal traits' like patiently explaining misunderstandings. Simultaneously, his explanation to the wife is positioned through a counter-expectancy formulation ('no matter how... she would not...'), potentially prompting mediators to negatively assess her lack of understanding

[j]Through upscaling, the husband positions the mediators to evaluate his wife's response as disproportionate or excessive. This attitudinal signal counters his wife's concerned reactions while inviting mediator assessment of her behaviour as potentially overreactive

[k]Through denial and upscaling, the husband positions the mediators to evaluate his conduct as appropriately maintaining boundaries with the opposite sex, which eventually counteracts his wife's previous accusations

linguistic items. He extensively relied on the mediators to infer from his utterances the attitudinal propositions he aimed to convey. In Excerpt 4.7, Husband_H01_WH defended himself against his wife's accusations regarding alleged flirtatious WeChat communications with a female neighbour.

In this excerpt, the husband's counteraccusation was advanced by invocations of relevant background context without inscriptions in his self-defense. He positions mediators through attitudinal signals that may influence their interpretation of events. While his response could potentially counteract the wife's previous accusations or even lead to negative assessment of the wife, the final evaluation remains contingent upon mediator interpretation. The husband's reserved demeanor maintains an 'least expressive' attitudinal profile throughout the interaction.

4.2.3.4 Summary

Up to this point, this section has reported the variability among the disputants vis-à-vis ratio of attitudinal complex options. With the ten options found in the dataset, three attitudinal disposition types were identified and characterised. The disputant clusters indicate a certain degree of commonality of the disputants' self-presentation and observable variations of the disputants' attitudinal positioning preference.

Figure 4.8 visualises the clustering of the disputants in the dataset under this investigation (PCA) method (see Sect. 4.2.3 for details). This visualisation serves as an additional presentation of the findings to the language descriptions provided so far. This figure is a Principal Component Analysis biplot illustrating the variations among the speakers in the dataset.

Three explanations are presumably needed of the figure. (See Jolliffe and Cadima (2016) for more details of PCA biplot.) First, about the speakers. The disputants in the dataset are mapped on the figure regarding the ratios of the attitudinal complex types in their speech. The further from the centre of the figure, the higher ratio the speaker had. Roughly illustrated in the figure, the 12 disputants cluster into three groups. The blue cluster on the right represents the 'more expressive' disposition group (two disputants). The green cluster on the top-left portion represents the 'less expressive' disposition group (six disputants), and the purple group on the bottom right corner is the 'least expressive' disposition group (four disputants). In simple words, the closer the speakers, the more similarities they have in terms of the ratio of the attitudinal complexes. Second, about the attitudinal arrangement. The red arrows represent different attitudinal complex types. The longer the arrow, the more influence it has on identifying the variations among the speakers—the closer the distance between two arrows, the stronger the correlational co-occurrence between the two options. The arrows point in the direction of the variables (which are the attitudinal complex options in this case), as projected into the 2-dimensional plane of the biplot. Finally, about the two axes and the four quadrants. The two axes represent the top two dimensions that account for the most variance in the data. The horizontal axis illustrates the first dimension, accounting for 38.6% of the variation in the dataset. The vertical axis represents the second dimension, accounting for

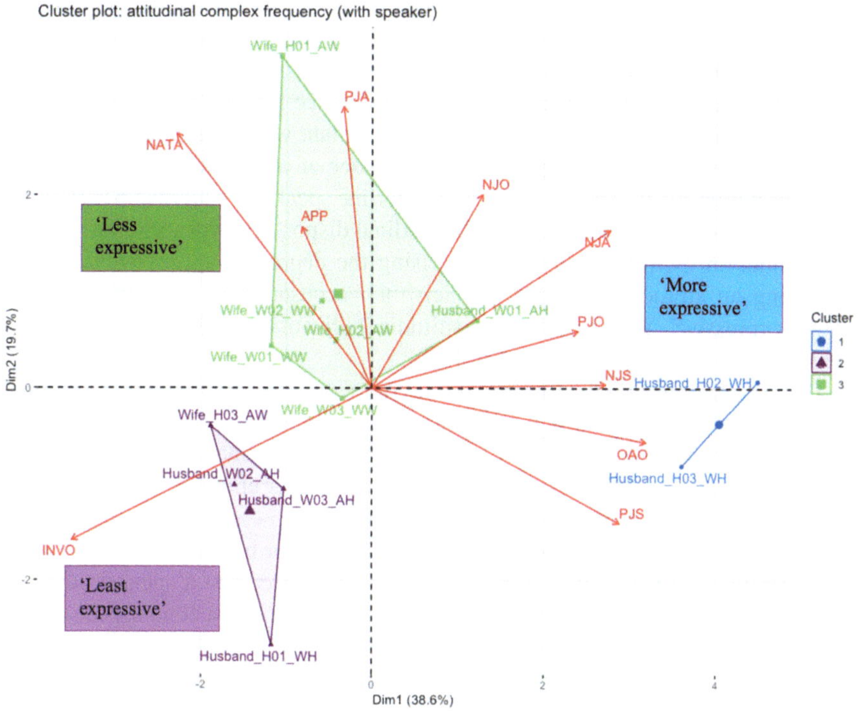

Fig. 4.8 Disputant clustering as to the ratios of the ten attitudinal complex types (Figure adapted from Xu and White (2021), pp. 52–73. Reused with permission)

19.7% of the variation in the dataset. Therefore, this clustering method captures a total of 58.3% of the variation for an analysis of ten different variables. The two axes divide the graph into four quadrants. The disputants locating in the same quadrant have similar choices, whereas disputants locating at opposed quadrants have opposing choices.

It can be observed that the disputants deploying 'less expressive' or 'least expressive' attitudinal dispositions constitute the majority of the speakers in the dataset. It suggests that being implicit and relying on the co-participants to infer assessment is an attitudinal profile picked up by most disputants in the dataset. The high proportion of 'less expressive' and 'least expressive' speakers in the dataset might be indicative as to how disputing spouses converse in similar family dispute resolution exchanges. Based on the findings discussed above, there is also a broad tendency for the wayward spouses to be 'more explicit' and the aggrieved spouses to be 'less explicit' or 'not explicit'.

Additionally, it is worth noting that there are no clear-cut boundaries among the three proposed attitudinal disposition types. As discussed previously, the computational clustering methods suggest two groups as the optimal number of clusters in the dataset. This initial grouping pointed me to discover a variability among the disputants that the existing SFL/Appraisal literature has not identified—variability vis-à-vis the language user's degree of 'expressiveness' when advancing attitudinal assessments. This initial grouping also motivated me to identify two subgroups within the broad 'less expressive' category—a subgroup that is even more 'less expressive' than the other because of their preference for invocations. This whole exploration process suggests that whether a disputant was 'more expressive', 'less expressive', or even 'least expressive' is a matter of quantitative relativity rather than qualitative absoluteness. There are borderline speakers in all disposition types. It is better to view the three proposed attitudinal disposition types as different vantage points on a cline, a cline characterising the degree of expressiveness when advancing an attitude. The more explicit their accusation of the antagonist, the 'more expressive' is the speaker's attitudinal disposition. Similarly, the more implied the attitudes, the 'less expressive'.

The exportations and the findings in the 'ratio' analysis pointed me to propose a 'cline of expressiveness', which can be used to systematically identify and describe the variations regarding the ratios of the disputants' deployment of attitudinal complexes. 'Expressiveness' refers to the overtness a speaker employs when advancing an attitudinal orientation. Three aspects can be used to consider how 'explicit' a speaker is. The first aspect is their overall preference for inscription or invocation. As illustrated by the findings in my dataset, the more frequent a speaker advances attitudinal inscriptions, the more explicit they would be. The second aspect considers how the speaker constructs an attitudinal stance that is of their central communicative concern. For the disputants in family dispute resolution, as verified by the commonalities in the dataset, their central communicative concern is attacking the antagonist and defending the self. Accordingly, if a speaker frequently inscribes their negative Judgement of the antagonist and positive self-Judgement, they could be characterised as being 'expressive' because they foreground their primary attitudinal positioning via inscriptions. Conversely, if a speaker frequently advances other types of attitudes or seldom advances any explicit attitudes at all, their primary attitudinal orientation would not be made clear to the audience, hence being 'less expressive' or 'least expressive'. The final aspect is related to the speakers' preferred attitude type. That is to say, according to the existing Appraisal framework, Affect, Judgement, Appreciation, which attitude type(s) does the speaker favour? Based on the findings in my dataset, the family dispute resolution register foregrounds the attitude type of 'Judgement', which expects the resolution participants to assess humans or human behaviours frequently. Previous studies have shown that other registers tend to foreground other attitude types, for example, Appreciation for advertisement (Hommerberg & Don, 2015; Pounds, 2011) and academic discourse (Hood, 2010), but mixed attitude types for movie reviews (White, 2008) or journalist discourse (White, 1998). In my analysis, the disputants who favoured explicitly assessing each other's behaviours were interpreted as more 'expressive' than the disputants who relatively preferred to report personal feelings or appreciate things and happenings. This 'cline of expressiveness' is illustrated in Fig. 4.9, illustrated by the disputants' choices in my dataset.

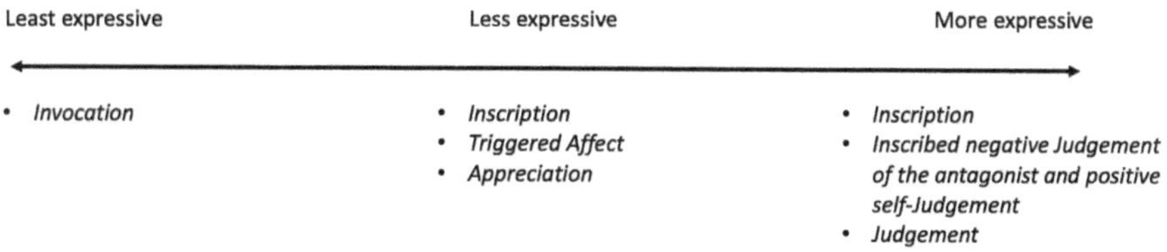

Fig. 4.9 Cline of expressiveness (illustrated by the disputants' choices in my dataset)

5 Chapter Summary

This chapter has presented findings related to the project's first line of inquiry into the disputants' attitudinal self-presentation. The analyses adopted a synoptic view of attitudinal disposition and explored how the disputants present themselves through their preferences in using attitudinal expressions across an entire textual stage—specifically, the Problem Discussion stage. The chapter has reported tendencies among the disputants vis-à-vis their attitudinal meaning-making choices from two perspectives: (1) the occurrence of attitudinal expressions and (2) the ratio of attitudinal expressions. The exploration attended to similarities and differences across the dataset regarding which attitudes the disputants used, in what combinations, and at what frequencies.

The analyses were carried out in two stages. The first stage was concerned with the first perspective, focusing on the occurrence of the attitudinal complexes—that is, whether the disputants used a designated attitudinal expression at least once. The findings from this perspective identified nine types of attitudinal complexes, which mostly involved the disputants' Judgement of human and human behaviours. It was found that four attitudinal complex types were deployed by all or most of the disputants, suggesting a certain degree of commonalities among the disputants in the dataset. Variations were observed when each attitudinal complex was considered as an individual parameter of variation. Tendencies were also discovered concerning the different preferences between the wayward spouse group versus the aggrieved spouse group. The final step of this line of analysis was to consider all nine attitudinal complexes together, identifying clusters arising from the tendencies in disputants' co-selection of multiple attitudinal complexes. These clusters were interpreted as revealing variability in the range of the attitudinal complexes deployed by the disputants, with the disputants diverging along a cline of using either a 'wide range', a 'middle range' or a 'narrow range' of available attitudinal complexes. Notably, the disputants within each group utilised a similar number and subset of the attitudinal complexes, thus being characterised as enacting a similar attitudinal disposition.

The second stage of analyses attended to the degree of the disputants' preference for a designated type of attitudinal complex. The exploration used 'ratio' as the metric for measuring speakers' degree of preference, defined by the relative frequency of their use of each complex within their speech. This analysis operated with ten attitudinal complexes. It was found that four of these complexes were used by

Table 4.17 Summary of the two-stage analysis

Stage	Perspective	Key findings
1	Occurrence of the attitudinal complex	1. Nine types of attitudinal complex (both via inscription and invocation) 2. Four shared attitudinal complexes: Negative Judgement of antagonist; positive self-Judgement; negative Judgement of people outside of the relationship; negative Affectual response triggered by the antagonist 3. Observable in-group variation per single attitudinal complex 4. Wayward spouses tend to reconcile. Aggrieved spouses tend to emotional victimise the self. 5. Clustering vis-à-vis co-selection of multiple attitudinal complexes: Variability in the range of the resources deployed: Narrow range; Middle range; Wide range
2	Ratio of the attitudinal complex	1. Ten types of attitudinal complex 2. Four shared attitudinal complexes: Inscriptions of negative Judgement of the antagonist; invocation; inscribed positive self-Judgement; inscribed negative Affectual response triggered by the antagonist 3. Observable in-group variation per single attitudinal complex 4. Observable in-group variation and clustering per attitudinal complex pairs 5. Clustering vis-à-vis co-selection of multiple attitudinal complexes: Variability in the expressiveness of the disputants' construal of their overall attitudinal positioning: More expressive; Less expressive; Least expressive 6. Wayward spouses tend to be more expressive than aggrieved spouses.

all or most disputants at similar frequency ratios. This suggests a tendency among the disputants to construe 'like-minded' putative audiences and foreground an antagonistic attitudinal positioning. Variations emerged when individual attitudinal complexes or pairs of complexes were examined as parameters of variation within the dataset, leading to the identification of in-group differences and disputant clustering patterns. When all ten attitudinal complexes were considered collectively, the clustering analysis revealed variations in the disputants' 'expressiveness' in advancing their overall attitudinal positioning, whether they were relatively 'more expressive', 'less expressive', or 'not expressive'. It was observed that wayward spouses tended to be more expressive in these contexts compared to aggrieved spouses.

The findings reported in this chapter are summarised in Table 4.17.

The findings indicate substantial variation in the disputants' preference for attitude-associated resources, specifically, these attitudinal complexes. The disputants differ regarding which resources they employ, in what combinations, and at what frequencies. Notably, there was no straightforward answer to whether certain subsets of disputants exhibit similar choices while distinct from others. It was generally observed that the disputants are neither identical nor distinctly different in their preferences for a given attitudinal complex or co-occurrences of multiple attitudinal complexes. Instead, similarities and differences across the dataset reveal quantitative variations rather than qualitative distinctions. It cannot be overemphasized that there are no clear-cut boundaries among these proposed variation patterns or attitudinal disposition types. Although some disputants exhibit relative similarities via specific parameters of variation, it is impossible to find two disputants with identical attitudinal arrangements. Within each attitudinal disposition type (e.g., 'narrow range', 'middle range', and 'wide range' or 'more expressive', 'less expressive', and 'least expressive'), some speakers are more typical and representative than others, with a few speakers being relatively positioned at the intersection of multiple attitudinal disposition types. Therefore, instead of categorising attitudinal dispositions definitively, it is preferable to view proposed tendencies or patterns as various vantage points on a continuum. There is a certain degree of fluidity among different attitudinal disposition types.

Thus far, I have detailed the findings arising from the first line of inquiry: the disputants' construction of attitudinal dispositions in relation to tendencies in their deployment of different types of attitudinal complexes. The forthcoming chapter will present the results emerging under the second line of inquiry, which broadens the analysis scope by exploring tendencies in the disputants' framing of these attitudinal complexes. This expanded focus entailed analyses that went beyond options within the ATTITUDE system to also encompass choices from the ENGAGEMENT and GRADUATION systems within the Appraisal framework. The next chapter is particularly concerned with how these attitudinal expressions were upscaled or downscaled, as well as how they were positioned dialogically.

References

Batool, F., & Hennig, C. (2021). Clustering with the average Silhouette width. *Computational Statistics & Data Analysis, 158*, 107190. https://doi.org/10.1016/j.csda.2021.107190

Coffin, C. (2006). *Historical discourse: The language of time, cause and evaluation*. Continuum (Continuum discourse series).

Colman, A. M. (2009). Complete linkage clustering. In *A dictionary of psychology*. Oxford University Press. Available at: https://www.oxfordreference.com/view/10.1093/acref/9780199534067.001.0001/acref-9780199534067-e-1704 (Accessed: 14 December 2020)

Dinh, D.-T., Fujinami, T. and Huynh, V.-N. (2019) 'Estimating the optimal number of clusters in categorical data clustering by Silhouette coefficient', in J. Chen et al. (eds) Knowledge and systems sciences.: Springer (Communications in Computer and Information Science), pp. 1–17. https://doi.org/10.1007/978-981-15-1209-4_1.

Don, A. (2007a) *A framework for the investigation of interactive norms and the construction of textual identity in written discourse communities: The case of an email list* (Unpublished Ph.D Thesis). University of Birmingham.

Don, A. (2007b). An approach to the analysis of textual identity through profiles of evaluative disposition. In *ASFLA 2007 Proceedings*.

Don, A. (2016) "It is hard to mesh all this": Invoking attitude, persona and argument organisation. *Functional Linguistics, 3*, 9(9). https://doi.org/10.1186/s40554-016-0033-1

Hao, J., & Humphrey, S. (2012). The role of "Coupling" in biological experimental reports. *Linguistics and the Human Sciences, 5*(2), 169–194.
Hasan, R. (1989). *Linguistics, language and verbal art*. Deakin University.
Hasan, R. (2009) Semantic variation; meaning in society and in sociolinguistics. Edited by J.J. Webster. Equinox (The Collected Works of Ruqaiya Hasan).
Hayden, L. (2018) *Principal Component Analysis in R, DataCamp Community*. Available at: https://www.datacamp.com/community/tutorials/pca-analysis-r. Accessed: 16 December 2020
Hommerberg, C., & Don, A. (2015). Appraisal and the language of wine appreciation: A critical discussion of the potential of the appraisal framework as a tool to analyse specialised genres. *Functions of Language, 22*(2), 161–191. https://doi.org/10.1075/fol.22.2.01hom
Hood, S. (2010). *Appraising research: Evaluation in academic writing*. Palgrave Macmillan.
Husson, F., et al. (2020). FactoMineR: Multivariate Exploratory Data Analysis and Data Mining. *Available at*. http://factominer.free.fr
Jain, A. K., & Dubes, R. C. (1988). *Algorithms for clustering data*. Prentice Hall.
Jolliffe, I. T. (2002). *Principal component analysis* (2nd ed.). Springer Science & Business Media.
Jolliffe, I. T., & Cadima, J. (2016). Principal component analysis: A review and recent developments. *Philosophical Transactions. Series A, Mathematical, Physical, and Engineering Sciences, 374*(2065). https://doi.org/10.1098/rsta.2015.0202
Kassambara, A., & Mundt, F. (2020). *Factoextra: Extract and visualize the results of multivariate data analyses*. http://www.sthda.com/english/rpkgs/factoextra
Kaufman, L., & Rousseeuw, P. J. (1990). *Finding groups in data: An introduction to cluster analysis*. Wiley-Interscience.
Knight, N. K. (2013). Evaluating experience in funny ways: How friends bond through conversational hum. *Text & Talk, 33*(4–5), 553–574. https://doi.org/10.1515/text-2013-0025
Lê, S., Josse, J., & Husson, F. (2008). FactoMineR: A package for multivariate analysis. *Journal of Statistical Software, 25*(1), 1–18. https://doi.org/10.18637/jss.v025.i01
Leung, J. T. Y., Shek, D. T. L., & Ma, C. M. S. (2016). Measuring perceived parental sacrifice among adolescents in Hong Kong: Confirmatory factor analyses of the Chinese parental sacrifice scale. *Child Indicators Research, 9*(1), 173–192. https://doi.org/10.1007/s12187-015-9313-7
Litman, J. A., & Jimerson, T. L. (2004). The measurement of curiosity as a feeling of deprivation. *Journal of Personality Assessment, 82*(2), 147–157. https://doi.org/10.1207/s15327752jpa8202_3
Maechler, M. et al. (2019) '*cluster: Cluster Analysis Basics and Extensions*. Available at: https://cran.r-project.org/web/packages/cluster/citation.html. Accessed 12 December 2020
Mardia, K., Kent, J., & Bibby, J. (1979). *Multivariate analysis*. Academic.
Martin, J. R. (2008a). Innocence: Realisation, instantiation and individuation in a Botswanan town. In A. Mahboob & N. K. Knight (Eds.), *Questioning linguistics* (pp. 32–76). Cambridge Scholars Publishing.
Martin, J. R. (2008b). Tenderness: Realisation and instantiation in a Botswanan town. In N. Nørgaard (Ed.), *systemic functional linguistics in use. (Odense Working Papers in Language and Communication)* (pp. 30–62).
Martin, J. R., & White, P. R. R. (2005). *The Language of Evaluation: Appraisal in English*. Palgrave Macmillan.
Metsalu, T., & Vilo, J. (2015). ClustVis: A web tool for visualizing clustering of multivariate data using principal component analysis and heatmap. *Nucleic Acids Research, 43*(W1), W566–W570. https://doi.org/10.1093/nar/gkv468
Pounds, G. (2011). "This property offers much character and charm": Evaluation in the discourse of online property advertising. *Text & Talk - An Interdisciplinary Journal of Language, Discourse & Communication Studies, 31*(2), 195–220. https://doi.org/10.1515/text.2011.009
Rezankova, H., Loster, T., & Husek, D. (2011). Evaluation of categorical data clustering. In E. Mugellini et al. (Eds.), *Advances in Intelligent web mastering – 3* (pp. 173–182). Springer (Advances in Intelligent and Soft Computing). https://doi.org/10.1007/978-3-642-18029-3_18

Upton, G., & Cook, I. (2008). Complete linkage clustering. In *A dictionary of statistics* (2 rev. ed.). Oxford University Press. Available at: https://www.oxfordreference.com/view/10.1093/acref/9780199541454.001.0001/acref-9780199541454-e-317. Accessed 14 December 2020

White, P. R. R. (1998). *Telling media tales: The news story as rhetoric* (Doctoral Thesis). University of Sydney.

White, P. R. R. (2008). Praising and blaming, applauding and disparaging - solidarity, audience positioning and the linguistic of evaluative disposition. In G. Antos, E. Ventola, & T. Weber (Eds.), *Handbook of interpersonal communication* (pp. 567–594). Mouton de Gruyter (Handbooks of applied linguistics).

White, P. R. R. (2020). The putative reader in mass media persuasion—Stance, argumentation and ideology. *Discourse & Communication, 14*(4), 404–423. https://doi.org/10.1177/1750481320910512

Xu, D., & Tian, Y. (2015). A comprehensive survey of clustering algorithms. *Annals of data science, 2*(2), 165–193. https://doi.org/10.1007/s40745-015-0040-1

Xu, Q., & White, P. R. R. (2021). 'My husband always crosses the line': Textual identity and presentation of 'the self' in family conflict communication. *Journal of Research in Applied Linguistics, 12*(2), 52–73. https://doi.org/10.22055/RALS.2021.17009

Zappavigna, M. (2019). Ambient affiliation and #Brexit. In V. Koller, S. Kopf, & M. Miglbauer (Eds.), *Discourses of Brexit* (pp. 48–68). Routledge. https://doi.org/10.4324/9781351041867-4

Zappavigna, M., Dwyer, P., & Martin, J. R. (2008). Syndromes of meaning: Exploring patterned coupling in a NSW youth justice conference. In A. Mahboob & N. K. Knight (Eds.), *Questioning linguistics* (pp. 103–117). Cambridge Scholars Publishing.

Zappavigna, M. and Martin, J.R. (2018) Discourse and diversionary justice.: Palgrave Macmillan.

Chapter 5
Framing the Conflict: Graduation & Engagement Strategies

Contents

1 Introduction

The preceding chapter presented the results of a synoptic analysis, focusing on tendencies in the disputants' deployment of resources for conveying and activating attitudinal assessments. This chapter reports findings arising when this synoptic analysis was expanded to encompass not just tendencies in the use of attitudinal

Q. Xu, *Appraisal Approach to Conflict Styles*, The M.A.K. Halliday Library Functional Linguistics Series, https://doi.org/10.1007/978-981-95-6256-5_5

complexes but also to investigate how these attitudinal complexes were 'framed' in various ways. Specifically, I report findings that emerged when I (1) recorded whether the attitudinal expressions (expressions explicitly or implicitly conveying or activating positive or negative assessments targeting self, antagonist, some other party, or the marital situation) were intensified, mitigated, or left unscaled (the scaling options in the GRADUATION system as outlined in Appraisal); (2) recorded how these attitudinal expressions were framed dialogistically (the dialogistic options in the ENGAGEMENT system in Appraisal, for example, 'monoglossed', 'proclaimed', 'disclaimed', 'entertained', or 'attributed'); and also (3) tracked tendencies in how the attitudinal complexes were simultaneously scaled and dialogistically positioned.

The underlying premise of this perspective was that disputants' preferences regarding the framing of their attitudinal expressions allow them to enact a particular aspect of the 'self'. For example, for disputants who share similar attitudinal complex preference (such as an overall praising stance towards the self and a condemning stance towards the antagonist), differences in how they frame these stances can lead to different discursive self-presentation styles being perceived. This includes variations in whether they tend to monogloss their attitudinal assessments categorically, heterogloss them through some form of modulation, or mitigate them by downscaling the intensity of the utterance. In essence, this chapter presents findings on the tendencies disputants exhibit in framing attitudes.

This analysis shared similar research objectives with that of the previous chapter. The aim was to uncover similarities and differences in how disputants used these framing resources, specifically focusing on their use of scaling and dialogistic positioning options when expressing attitudes: which of these they chose for a given type of attitudinal expression, in what combinations, and at what frequencies. It involved tracking tendencies in the disputants' use of what I term 'framed attitudinal complexes'. For the purposes of this tracking, attitudinal expressions which involved the same attitudinal values and the same 'framing' option were treated as instances of the same framed attitudinal complex—for example: framing[upscaled/monogloss] + attitude type[Judgement] + polarity[negative] + target[antagonist] + explicitness[inscribed] (as in 'He was really disloyal' or 'She completely crossed the line').

The questions addressed were as follows: Were the patterns of use broadly similar across the disputants in the dataset, suggesting a uniform or consistent attitudinal disposition being verbally enacted by all? Alternatively, might these patterns suggest sub-types of attitudinal disposition among subsets of the disputants, differing from others? Or would each disputant employ resources for scaling and dialogistic positioning of attitudinal complexes in an idiosyncratic manner, without apparent basis for grouping into sub-types of attitudinal disposition? And then, taking the discussion further, how might such findings be interpreted within the context of discursive self-presentation? Do the findings suggest that aspects of the 'self' associated with attitudinal meaning-making are broadly similar for all 'aggrieved' or 'wayward' spouses—all making similar use of these resources and hence presenting a similar discursive self? Or do the findings imply the enactment of particular socio-culturally established or conventionalised attitudinal dispositions and hence ways of self-presentation by individuals in conflictual situations?

This chapter begins with an overview of the analysis (Sect. 2), introducing the focus of the analysis, the staging of the analysis, and providing a preview of key findings. The subsequent sections report the findings from each stage of analysis (Sects. 3–5). The chapter concludes b summarising the main findings.

2 An Overview of the Analysis

2.1 The Focus of the Analysis

As previously noted, this chapter extends the analysis focus to explore tendencies in how disputants framed their attitudinal expressions. Building upon Chap. 4's discussion, the term 'attitudinal expression' refers specifically to the attitudinal instances tagged with four attitude-related features: attitude type, polarity, explicitness, and sub-type of appraised (self, antagonist, other, or marital situation). The term 'attitudinal complex' is used to describe this combination of four features. Accordingly, as indicated above, this chapter's focus on the 'framing of the attitudinal expressions' involves examining how disputants employed options for 'scaling' or 'dialogistic positioning' in conjunction with these attitudinal complexes.

To summarise, as outlined earlier, two key aspects were analysed: (1) tendencies in the scaling of the attitudinal complexes (i.e., intensifying, tempering the force of attitudinal complexes, or leaving attitudes unscaled—reflecting options from the Appraisal's system of GRADUATION) and (2) tendencies regarding the dialogistic positioning of these attitudinal complexes (i.e., presenting the attitudes as being unarguable and categorical, or as being negotiable or open to question, and so on—drawing upon options from Appraisal's system of ENGAGEMENT). An example illustrating this analysis is presented in Table 5.1.

For this analysis, I chose to focus on how disputants framed only a subset of the attitudinal complexes discussed in the previous chapter. This subset comprised six attitudinal complexes that featured either the disputant themselves or their antagonist as the target/trigger (excluding those directed at third parties or the marital situation). This choice was motivated by both practical considerations regarding data management and a desire to prioritise analysis of assessments targeting self and antagonist, given these were crucial components in the disputants' attitudinal stance (Cf. the 'two concerns' approach ('concern for self' and 'concern for other') in conflict management studies as outlined in Blake and Mouton, 1964; Rahim, 2023). It was expected that tendencies in framing attitudes directed towards the self and the adversary would significantly impact a disputant's discursive self-presentation. An analysis focusing on these core attitudinal expressions could provide valuable insights into a disputant's broader attitudinal orientation.

Table 5.1 Framing of an attitudinal complex (example)

Turn	Speaker	Utterance (Chinese)	Utterance (English translation)	Attitudinal complex	Framing	
					Scaling	Dialogistic framing
2	Wife_ H03_ AW	就我老公老是触犯我的底线	It's that my husband **crosses the line** all the time	Inscribe -ve Judge antagonist (realised by 我老公触犯底线 my husband crosses the line)	Upscaling (realised by 老是 *all the time*)[a]	Heterogloss: Contract: Disclaim: Counter-expectancy (realised by 老是 *all the time—More often than would be expected*)[b]
		特别不好受	I feel extremely **uncomfortable**	Inscribe -ve Affect self (triggered by the antagonist) (realised by 不好受 *feel uncomfortable*)	Upscaling (realised by 特别 *extremely*)	Monogloss
				Invoke -ve Judge antagonist (realised by (不好受 *feel uncomfortable*)[c]	Upscaling (realised by 特别 *extremely*)	Monogloss

[a]According to Chao (1965, p. 236), when prefix '老lǎo-' is used as an adverb, it means 'all the time, keeps… -ing'
[b]The adverb '老是 lǎoshì (all the time)' entails a meaning of dissatisfaction or disgust (Chinese Academy of Social Sciences Institute of Linguistics, 2017, p. 785)
[c]This instance is double coded. The first layer of coding is an inscribed negative Affect triggered by the antagonist, as the speaker reports her insecurity. This Affectual inscription, in turn, invokes a second layer of coding, which is to negatively assess the trigger of that insecurity. The invocation draws on a reading position that 'Making people feel bad is wrong'

The specific attitudinal complexes examined within this framing analysis (those involving attitudes towards oneself and one's antagonist) are listed below.

(1) Inscribed positive Judgement of the antagonist (PJA);
(2) Inscribed negative Judgement of the antagonist (NJA);
(3) Inscribed positive Judgement of the self (PJS);
(4) Inscribed negative Judgement of the self (NJS);
(5) Inscribed authorial negative Affectual response triggered by the antagonist or the antagonist's behaviour (invoking an assessment of the antagonist) (NATA); and.
(6) Inscribed observed antagonist's Affectual response (i.e., the disputant attributes emotional responses to their antagonist, typically intending to invoke a negative assessment of the antagonist; OAO).

As a second step with a view to manageability, this analysis only dealt with inscribed attitudinal assessments (excluding instances where attitudes were merely hinted or invoked).[1] This treatment is justifiable on the basis that inscriptions have a much higher degree of attitudinal stability compared to invocations. This feature of invocations was addressed in previous chapters and is revisited here for ease of reference. Only in cases of inscribed attitudes, the speaker directly calls on or challenges the addressee to accept the specific attitudinal assessment. By inscribing an attitudinal assessment, the speaker potentially puts speaker-addressee rapport at risk, should they disagree or view the assessment as unfair or unfounded. Conversely, invocation involves suggesting rather than asserting an attitude explicitly. The risk of damaging rapport is less direct and deliberate in invocations because they rely on interpretation rather than direct assertion. Although invocations might signal the speaker's attitudinal positioning, the signal can be interpreted differently depending on how the 'reading position' are applied (a concept explored further in Chap. 3), thereby allowing multiple interpretations. Therefore, there are theoretically principled reasons for limiting the analysis to instances of inscribed attitude in this particular line of inquiry.

It is worth highlighting that all attitudinal complexes in the dataset were treated as involving some 'choice' of framing. This stems from the observation that every expression carrying an explicit or implicit attitudinal assessment always involves either upscaling, downscaling, or a decision not to scale at all (with the absence of scaling considered a choice). Additionally, these expressions invariably select one or more options simultaneously from the ENGAGEMENT system, which encompasses both monogloss or heterogloss options (and may involve more than one of the options from the heterogloss sub-system). Consequently, each annotation for an attitudinal complex (consisting of attitude type, polarity, target/trigger, and explicitness) is accompanied by annotations for scaling type (upscaled, downscaled, or non-scaled) and ENGAGEMEN choice (monogloss or sub-type of heterogloss).

The analysis explored the variability in the degree to which disputants preferred specific framed attitudinal complexes, focusing on their relative frequency of use. The methodology employed here was based on the 'ratio' analysis (as opposed to the 'occurrence' analysis), as discussed in Chaps. 3 and 4. In this context, by 'frequency', I mean the proportion or ratio of use. For each disputant, a ratio of framing for each of the six attitudinal complexes was calculated. For example, if a disputant had a total of 100 attitudinal complexes in the Problem Discussion stage (which would be 'framed' in various ways) and they used 'upscaling' to frame the attitudinal complex of 'inscribed positive Judgement of self' ten times, the ratio for this particularly framed complex (i.e., upscaled inscribed positive self-Judgement) would correspond to a ratio of 10%. The ratios were then compared across all disputants to determine whether similarities or differences in their use patterns could be identified as grounds for clustering. For instance, two disputants with similar

[1] A sister analysis published in Xu (2024) includes attitudinal invocations in the analysis, alongside the inscriptions. The invocations in that analysis incorporate positive and negative invocations directed at the self and the antagonist.

ratios of upscaling and inscribed positive self-Judgement framing (e.g., both used it 10% of the time) would appear closer together in the clustering analysis than those whose ratios differ substantially. If two disputants had similar ratios across more than one framed attitudinal complex (for instance, they both used upscaled inscribed positive self-Judgement and downscaled inscribed negative Judgement of the antagonist at similar rates), their closeness in the clustering would increase further due to these additional similarities in framing choices. In essence, the more disputants agreed on the proportion of different framing devices used for specific attitudinal complexes (i.e., had similar ratios across those complexes), the closer they were likely to cluster together based on their use patterns. This ultimately led to the formation of groups among the disputants based on their shared preferences in framing and self-presentation.

As such, the analysis did not aim at identifying a preference for a specific framing device (such as upscaling or downscaling) in isolation from its application to particular attitudinal complexes. Instead, it sought to examine how disputants preferred to frame specific attitudinal complexes in distinct ways (for instance, upscaled positive self-Judgement versus downscaled positive self-Judgement versus upscaled negative self-Judgement). In the context of Appraisal theory within SFL, this analysis was particularly interested in exploring the co-selection of multiple features from across the Appraisal systems and subsystems.[2]

As foreshadowed in Chap. 1, a substantial body of research within SFL/Appraisal literature (White, 1998, 2003, 2012, 2016; Hood & Martin, 2007; Macken-Horarik & Isaac, 2014; Thompson, 2014; Don, 2016) has been dedicated to exploring the interplay between the three key Appraisal systems—ATTITUDE, GRADUATION, and ENGAGEMENT. A significant portion of this work has centred around investigating how the deployment of grading or dialogistic positioning formulations have the potential to invoke attitudinal assessments—in other words, how choices from the GRADUATION system and the ENGAGEMENT system can function as implicit signals of choices in the ATTITUDE system. However, no previous study to my knowledge aimed to uncover patterns in the use of these scaling and dialogistic positioning options in connection with the expression of attitudes, specifically examining how these resources might be employed to either reinforce or temper expressions of attitude or to indicate different degrees of openness to negotiating the attitude being advanced.

To recapitulate, the line of analysis being reported here focused on identifying tendencies in the disputants' use of the framing resources when expressing attitudes. Specifically, it examined: Which of the framing options did they use when

---

[2] This treatment of Appraisal resources aligns with Martin's (2010, p. 19) conceptualisation of 'coupling', which refers to 'the way in which meanings combine—across strata, meta-functions, ranks, and simultaneous systems (and across modalities)'. This approach attends to the simultaneous co-selection of options across all aspects of the Appraisal systems and subsystems, distinguishing itself significantly from the dominant approach in existing research on Appraisal resources. This latter has focusesd primarily on identifying patterns in the relationship between ideational meaning and attitudinal expressions.

advancing a particular attitudinal complex? In what combinations, and at what frequencies? Was there any observable basis for grouping the disputants into sub-types of attitudinal disposition? Furthermore, how were these aspects of 'self' associated with framing the attitudinal complexes broadly similar for all spouses labelled as 'aggrieved' or 'wayward'? This analysis consisted of three key stages, which will be discussed in detail below.

2.2 The Staging of the Analysis

The current synoptic analysis, exploring the tendencies in the disputants' use of the resources that framed these attitudinal complexes, was conducted in the following three stages: (1) the scaling of the attitudinal complex, (2) the dialogistic framing of the attitudinal complex, and (3) the co-occurrence of scaling and dialogistic framing of the attitudinal complex.

In the first two stages, I attended separately to tendencies in the disputants' use of the scaling resources (by reference to the GRADUATION system in Appraisal) and to tendencies in their use of the resources for dialogistic positioning (by reference to the ENGAGEMENT system in Appraisal). For each stage, the analysis was concerned with the co-articulation of the framing device with a particular attitudinal complex, such as tendencies with respect to 'upscaling (scaling) inscribed negative Judgement of the antagonist (attitudinal complex)' or tendencies with respect to 'monoglossing (dialogistic positioning) inscribed positive Judgement of the self (attitudinal complex)'. The analyses explored the similarities and differences in the disputants' deployment of a particular scaling or dialogistic positioning option to frame a specific attitudinal complex.

In the third stage, I treated tendencies in the disputants' deployment of these two framing resources (resources of scaling and dialogistic positioning) as interconnected and as factors which could mutually contribute to a raising or lowering of a disputant's attitudinal presence. Relying on White (2019), I use the term 'attitudinality' for this quality of the text. Under this analysis, a speaker's 'attitudinality' may be raised/heightened either by a tendency to intensify their attitudinal assessments or to categorically assert them, with the heightening of the 'attitudinality' maximised if a disputant combines these tendencies—frequently using categorical assertion and intensification when conveying attitudinal assessments. Likewise, this 'attitudinality' may be weakened or lowered by a tendency to downscale attitudinal assertions or 'entertain' them, with the weakening maximised if the tendencies in downscaling and entertaining are simultaneous.

For each of the three stages, I first tracked the 'framing + attitudinal complex' options found in the dataset, that is, what were the resources available at the disputants' disposal. I then explored the tendencies in the disputants' deployment of these options. Specifically, the exploration was carried out in the following three steps: (1) What 'framing + attitudinal complex' options were the most 'popular' in the dataset (i.e., used by all or most disputants and with the highest average ratios)? (2)

What kind of variations could be identified when a particular 'framing + attitudinal complex' option was attended to as one parameter of possible variation between the disputants? (3) What kind of variations could be observed between the disputants when two of these 'framing + attitudinal complex' options were considered together? And (4) What kind of clustering would emerge if all the available options were considered together, and what linguistic insights did the clustering provide?

Given the space limitations of this book, I selectively report the findings from the above three stages of analysis. For the first two stages, I report findings arising from the first three steps—the steps concerning the commonalities in the dataset and the variations when one or two 'framing (scaling or dialogistic framing) + attitudinal complex' options were considered. For the last stage, I focused on reporting the final step—findings that emerged from a cluster analysis when all the available options were considered a bundle of variation parameters. The above three stages of analysis are summarised in Table 5.2. Each stage offers a unique insight into the disputants' deployment of attitude-associated resources, that is, their enactment of attitudinal disposition. The findings of these analysis stages are set out in detail in a series of sections below.

Table 5.2 The staging of the analysis focusing on the framing of the attitudes

Stage	Analysis	Steps	
1	Focus on the scaling of the attitudinal complex	• Explore available 'scaling + attitudinal complex' options • Explore the tendencies in the disputants' deployment of these options – Explore the most popular options – Explore variations vis-à-vis single option – Explore variations vis-à-vis two options	Section 3
2	Focus on the dialogistic framing of the attitudinal complex	• Explore available 'dialogistic framing + attitudinal complex' options • Explore the tendencies in the disputants' deployment of these options – Explore the most popular options – Explore variations vis-à-vis single option – Explore variations vis-à-vis two options	Section 4
3	Focus on the scaling and dialogistic framing of the attitudinal complex	• Explore available 'scaling + dialogistic framing + attitudinal complex' options • Explore the tendencies in the disputants' deployment of these options – Explore the most popular options – Explore variations vis-à-vis all the available options Find the clustering of the disputants and interpret the clustering from a linguistic perspective	Section 5

2.3 A Preview of Findings

Similar to findings discussed in the previous chapter (i.e., tendencies in the disputants' use of attitudes), complications emerged as to 'what kind of attitudinal disposition did the disputants enact' or 'what subtypes of attitudinal dispositions were found in the dataset'. The disputants could be interpreted as demonstrating different aspects of the 'self' when their use of the framing options was examined from different angles. As well, the similarities or differences among the disputants were not absolute or categorical. Nonetheless, the inquiry into the framing of the attitudinal complexes has proved valuable in discovering more delicate variations among the disputants in the dataset. As will be demonstrated below, for disputants in these family dispute resolution interactions, how they framed these attitudinal complexes played a critical role in their presentation of the 'self'.

3 Stage One: Focus on the Scaling of the Attitudinal Complexes

This stage was concerned with the tendencies in how the disputants scaled the six attitudinal complexes. Three scaling options were identified by to the GRADUATION system in the Appraisal framework tracking—whether the disputants (1) upscaled (i.e., to intensify the attitudinal assessment), (2) downscaled (i.e., to tempered or mitigated the attitudinal assessment), or (3) did not scale (i.e., conveyed the attitudinal assessment without either up or scaling—itself also an option) a particular attitudinal complex. The three scaling options and six attitudinal complexes afford, in theory, 18 'scaling + attitudinal complex' options. Examples of such options include 'upscaled inscribed positive self-Judgement' or 'unscaled observed antagonist's negative Affectual responses'. The analysis explored similarities and differences in the disputants' use of the 18 options: which they used, in what combinations, and at what frequency.

3.1 Available 'Scaling + Attitudinal Complex' Options

Sixteen 'scaling + attitudinal complex' options were found in the dataset (summarised in Table 5.3 below), indicating that although 18 options were presumably at a disputant's disposal in the given situation, two options were not deployed by any of the disputants in the dataset. The two options which did not occur were: (1) upscaled negative self-Judgement and (2) downscaled observed antagonist's Affectual response. The first of these findings might well be anticipated. Given that the purpose of the disputants was typically to cast the antagonist in a negative light and themselves in a positive light, there would be little reason to intensify any

Table 5.3 Sixteen 'scaling + attitudinal complex' options found in the dataset

	'Scaling + attitudinal complex' options	Attitudinal complex	Scaling	Example
(1)	Upscaled negative judgement of the antagonist	Inscribe -ve Judge antagonist	Upscaling	他太不尊重我了He is too **disrespectful** to me (Wife_H03_AW)
(2)	Non-scaled negative judgement of the antagonist		No-scaling	她脾气不好 She **has a bad temper** (Husband_H03_WH)
(3)	Downscaled negative judgement of the antagonist		Downscaling	心智不是很成熟的那一种She is **not** quite mentally **mature** (Husband_H01_WH)
(4)	Upscaled positive judgement of the antagonist	Inscribe +ve Judge antagonist	Upscaling	他之前是很负责任的一个男人He used to be a very **responsible** man (Wife_H01_AW)
(5)	Non-scaled positive judgement of the antagonist		No-scaling	你是辛苦You **endured hardship** (Husband_H03_WH)
(6)	Downscaled positive judgement of the antagonist		Downscaling	勤奋这一块应该是说还是可以In terms of diligence I would say he is so-so with **diligence** (Wife_W01_WW)
(7)	Upscaled positive self-judgement	Inscribe +ve Judge self	Upscaling	我是每天对这个家庭是添砖加瓦的I AM **making a contribution** to this family every day (Husband_H01_WH)
(8)	Non-scaled positive self-judgement		No-scaling	所以要替她想一下So I **was considerate of her** (Husband_H03_WH)
(9)	Downscaled positive self-judgement		Downscaling	以前都是出于我一种包容吧I was sort of **tolerant** in the past (Wife_H02_AW)
(10)	Downscaled negative self-judgement	Inscribe -ve Judge self	Downscaling	我可能在这个夫妻感情方面..沟通方面..是有点欠缺I may be sort of **not good** enough in terms of couple relationship.. in term of communication (Husband_H03_WH)
(11)	Non-scaled negative self-judgement		No-scaling	这个我欠缺I was **not good** in this respect (Husband_H02_WH)

Table 5.3 (continued)

	'Scaling + attitudinal complex' options	Attitudinal complex	Scaling	Example
(12)	Upscaled negative affect triggered by the antagonist	Inscribe -ve Affect (triggered by the antagonist)	Upscaling	特别不好受I feel extremely **uncomfortable** (Wife_H03_AW)
(13)	Non-scaled negative affect triggered by the antagonist		No-scaling	让我感觉到没有安全感He made me **feel no sense of security** (Wife_H01_AW)
(14)	Downscaled negative affect triggered by the antagonist		Downscaling	这两年当中..我不是太高兴I was **not** very **happy** during these 2 years (Wife_H02_AW)
(15)	Upscaled observed antagonist's affect	Observed antagonist's Affect	Upscaling	她就气得不得了She just became terribly **angry** (Husband_H03_WH)
(16)	Non-scaled observed antagonist's affect		No-scaling	置气啊(she) became **angry** (Husband_H02_WH)

negative assessments of themselves, if they ever criticised themselves at all. Similarly, there do seem to be plausible reasons why the disputants might refrain from downscaling their reports of their partners' emotional reactions. As discussed at several points previously, such reports typically functioned to cast the antagonist in a negative light and present them as being subject to excessive, inappropriate, or socially deprecated emotions. The upscaling of such a response (e.g., 'she got *really* angry') or the unscaled reporting of such a response ('she got angry') would appear to be compatible with such a purpose—in contexts where being angry would be viewed negatively. However, downscaling does not seem so compatible with this purpose—for example, 'she was *somewhat* angry'. Such a downscaling would seem likely to weaken the potential of such a report to activate a negative Judgement of the antagonist for being subject to the socially deprecated emotional reaction. Thus, the downscaling of an observed antagonist's Affectual response potentially cancels out the invocatory potential of the Affectual recount. This seems a plausible explanation of why no such instances were observed in the dataset.

3.2 *Findings: Tendencies in the Scaling of the Attitudinal Complexes*

Each of the 16 'scaling + attitudinal complex' options can provide a specific focus for the investigation of similarities and differences in the attitudinal dispositions of the disputants. For example, ratios of upscaled negative inscribed Judgements of the antagonist can be tracked to distinguish the disputants who deployed high ratios of this option from those with relatively low ratios. When each 'scaling + attitudinal complex' option was treated as an independent parameter of variation, patterns of commonalities and in-group variations were identified.

3.2.1 The 'Most Popular' Options

When each option was treated as an independent parameter of variation, two commonalities among the disputants emerged with respect to the 'most popular' 'scaling + attitudinal complex' options. As noted earlier in this chapter, for easy reference, I use the term 'popular' to refer to the options with the highest dataset average ratios and were used by all or most disputants. The three 'most popular' options were used by most disputants (10–11 disputants) and also had the highest dataset average ratios, indicating that they were deployed by most of the disputants in a similar fashion. The consistency in the disputants' opting for the same set of options plausibly revealed commonalities in the dataset, that is, how most people might scale their attitudinal expressions in similar adversarial situations. (Given that the focus of the current analysis was on the commonalities among the disputants, I would not discuss the other options—the options chosen by some disputants or with relatively lower dataset average ratios—at the present stage. These options were beyond doubt significant in identifying the variability among the disputants and will be discussed in later analyses.) The commonalities derived from these 'most popular' options provided reference points to explore specific similarities and differences across the disputants in the later stages of the analysis.

The top three 'most popular' options revealed two commonalities among the disputants in the dataset. The first commonality was in connection with the scaling of inscribed negative Judgement of the antagonist (the most frequently deployed inscribed attitudinal complex across the dataset.) The analysis revealed that the disputants favoured two ways of framing this antagonist-oriented inscribed negative Judgement—either upscaling this assessment or simply asserting it without either up or downscaling. Eleven of the disputants deployed the first option at least once—unscaled inscribed negative Judgement of the antagonist. The ratios of use across these 11 disputants ranged from 1.89% to 8.73%, resulting in an average ratio of 5.28%, the highest average ratios of use in the dataset. Eleven of the disputants deployed the second option at least once—upscaled negative inscribed Judgement of the antagonist—and with the second-highest dataset average ratio. The ratios of use across these 11 disputants ranged from 2.54% to 8.7%, resulting in its average ratio of use being the second-highest of all the 'scaling + attitudinal complex' options in the dataset (M = 5.07%). Examples of these two options are provided above in Table 5.3 (see items numbered 1 to 2). The fact that each of these options was deployed by 11 out of the 12 disputants and with the highest dataset ratios indicates that not softening/mitigating negative Judgement of the antagonist was a common feature of the disputants' attitudinal disposition. By refraining from any softening of their accusations directed against their partners, all the 11 disputants in these two groupings presented themselves as sharply antipathetic of their antagonists. The commonality with respect to these two options reflects the adversarial nature of these exchanges.

Besides this commonality in the framing these inscribed negative Judgements of the antagonist, a consistent tendency was observed in the disputants' scaling of their own negative emotions, as triggered by the antagonist. Because this type of Affectual assessment has the potential to ultimately activate negative assessments directed at the antagonist, the framing of the Affectual response reveals how the disputants implicitly condemned the antagonist. The findings show that 10 out of 12 disputants presented the negative Affectual response triggered by the antagonist with no scaling device. Their ratios of use ranged from a low of 0.74% to a high of 10.45%, resulting in an average ratio of use of 3.17%, one of the highest across the dataset. Chapter 4 has argued that by deploying the attitudinal complex 'negative Affectual response triggered by the antagonist', the disputants enacted an 'emotional victim self'. Accordingly, by consistently presenting this attitudinal complex without either up or downscaling, the disputants presented the 'emotional victim self' as unmitigated. Notably seven disputants also favoured upscaling this complex, with an average dataset ratio of 2.55% (max = 8.82%, min = 1.57%). These seven disputants chose to augment the force of the 'emotional victim self'.

The disputants' shared preferences for augmenting their condemnation of the antagonist or asserting the condemnation and their negative emotional responses triggered by the antagonist without either up or downscaling can be illustrated by Wife_W01_WW's utterances in Excerpt 5.1. (See the book's GitHub repository for the complete analysis of her language.) In this excerpt, the wayward wife upscaled most instances of negative inscription of the antagonist. She also sometimes presented the negative Judgements and her negative emotions triggered by the husband's behaviours as it is. Her frequent deployment of the upscaling and no-scaling devices when presenting these two attitudinal complexes augmented or maintained the force of her accusation against the husband.

Apart from developing findings regarding the 'popular' options, the analysis also attended to tendencies in those 'scaling + attitudinal complex' options which were deployed only by a minority of the disputants. These options—which I term the 'least popular' options—had the lowest average ratios in the dataset and were used only by the fewest disputants. While the 'most popular' options revealed what most people in similar situations might do, the 'least popular' options showed what they might NOT do, which was also suggestive of the commonalities among the people. The least chosen options were (1) upscaling with inscribed positive Judgement of the antagonist and (2) downscaling with inscribed positive Judgement of the antagonist. Both options were only used by one disputant and had the lowest average ratios. Option 1 (upscaled inscribed positive Judgement of the antagonist) represented just 0.83% of this one disputant's total attitudinal expressions. Option 2 (downscaled positive Judgement of the antagonist) represented just 0.82% of this one disputant's total attitudinal expressions. Of course, the disputants' preference for the attitudinal complex per se was a matter of concern here. The attitudinal complex of these two 'least popular' options—positive inscription of the antagonist—as

Excerpt 5.1 All/most disputants preferred to upscale/no-scale NJA and no-scale NATA (exemplified by Wife_W01_WW's utterances)

Turn	Speaker	Move	Utterance (Chinese)	Utterance (English translation)	Attitude signal	Attitudinal complex		Scaling
						Assessment	Abbr.	
13	Wife_W01_ WW	1 2 3	如果人家来我们这边喝茶来我们这边坐..他看到朋友来了他所有的事情不做	If someone visited our company to drink tea and came to our office.. when he saw a friend coming he would stop doing everything	Upscaling	Invoke -ve Judge antagonist	INVO	
			他也就一直跟着屁股后面	He just **followed behind the ass** of the friend	Inscription	Inscribe -ve Judge antagonist	NJA	Upscaling
			再重要的事情他都可以丢下不管	No matter how important the business he was doing he would just **abandon it**	Inscription	Inscribe -ve Judge antagonist	NJA	Upscaling
14	Hostess_W01	1	来的这个朋友是什么人	Who was this visiting friend				
15	Wife_W01_ WW	1	当然是跟我们公司有业务来往的	Of course it was someone who had a business relationship with our company	Evoke	Invoke -ve Judge antagonist	INVO	
		2	男的	A male person				
16	Hostess_W01		他这样子放下==手中==的活不干过来是陪客人呢还是来干嘛呢	He put down the work ==left the work behind== like this did he do this to host the guest or to do something else				

17	Wife_W01_ WW	1	==他==	==He==				
		2	他不跟人家讲话的	He didn't talk to the guest	Denial	Invoke -ve Judge antagonist	INVO	
		3	基本上是不跟人家讲话的	He almost never talked to the guest	Denial	Invoke -ve Judge antagonist	INVO	
		4	就是坐在那里	He just sat there				
		5	就是反正看你们两个聊天	Anyway he just sat there and watched you two (us) talking	Counter-expectancy	Invoke -ve Judge antagonist	INVO	
		6	听你们聊天啊	He just listened to what you two (us) were talking	Counter-expectancy	Invoke -ve Judge antagonist	INVO	
		7	他这种行为我不能接受	His behaviours like this I **can't accept**	Attitudinal instance of inscribed Affect (potential invocation of -ve judgement)	Inscribe -ve Affect self (triggered by the antagonist) (invoke -ve Judge antagonist)	NATA	No-scaling
		8	我就认为他不信任的一种态度呀	I just think he has an attitude of **distrust**	Attitudinal instance of observed inscribed Affect (potential invocation of -ve judgement)	Observed inscribed -ve Affect antagonist; inscribe -ve Judge antagonist	OAO	No-scaling

discussed in the previous chapter, was not used by most disputants in the first place. Thus, the fact that almost all disputants chose not to upscale or not-scale their positive Judgement of the antagonist might be the result of there being not much such assessment overall.

The above selection of the most popular and the least popular options show that when each 'scaling + attitudinal complex' option was examined as a single parameter of variation, the deployment of this option enacted a unique aspect of the 'self' for the disputants, for example, an augmented 'combatant' self or an unmitigated 'emotional' self. Along this line of thinking, the deployment of the other options (e.g., tendencies in the use of the options which were used by a midrange of disputants—for example, deployed by five, six, seven of disputants) would have a role to play in the discursive performance of other aspects of the 'self'. With the multiple options at the disputants' disposal, the disputants could deploy any resources as they wish, either with or without their conscious awareness, to present a particular aspect of the 'self' in the family dispute resolution. Multiple facets of the 'self' can potentially be constructed, and multiple facets of the 'self' are constructed when the disputants' talk is examined from different angles. There is a multifacetedness of the disputants' discursive self-presentation vis-à-vis their preferences in how they scaled these attitudinal complexes. Limitation of space (and the need to address other issues in the presentation of the self) prevent a presentation of analyses of tendencies in deploying these other 'scaling + attitudinal complex' options. It is hoped, however, that the discussion in the above sections provides some pointers to the nature of the findings which can emerge from such analyses.

3.2.2 Tendencies Observed When the Analysis Attended to One Scaling Option

When each of the 16 'scaling + attitudinal complex' options was used as one parameter of variation to explore the variability among the disputants, observable in-group variations among the disputants emerged. Consider the 'popular' option—up-scaled negative Judgement of the antagonist. As noted, this is an option deployed by 11 out of the 12 disputants. As already indicated, there was a wide variation among the disputants regarding the ratio of this option in their speeches. The disputant having the highest ratio (Husband_H02_WH, a wayward husband) had 8.7% of his total attitudinal instances being upscaled negative inscription towards the antagonist. In sharp contrast, the disputant having the lowest ratio (Wife_H02_AW, an aggrieved wife) had zero instances. (She was the 12th disputant, so to speak, the one who did not make any use of this option.) The other disputants were located along the continuum between 8.7% and zero (illustrated in Fig. 5.1). The ratio difference reveals an in-group divergence regarding the speakers' forcefulness when advancing an explicit condemnation against the antagonist. Although all the disputants were overall assertive and confrontational, the disputants varied significantly as to how much additional force they invested in the antagonist-oriented condemnation. The different degrees of forcefulness constructed completely different attitudinal dispositions.

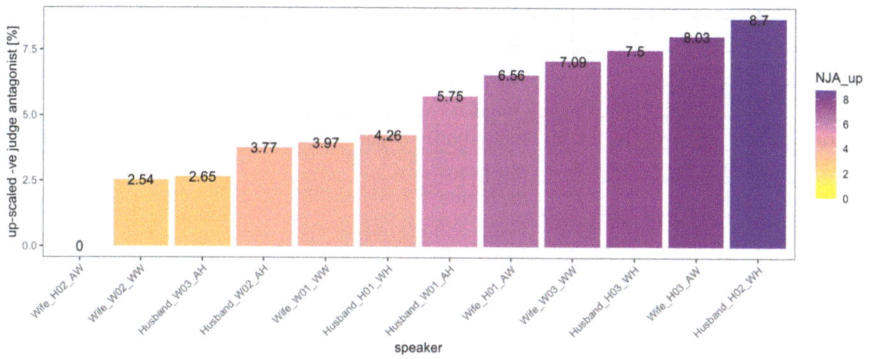

Fig. 5.1 Ratios of upscaled inscribed negative Judgement of the antagonist

Arguably, the higher ratio of the upscaled negative inscription of the antagonist, the more forceful was the speaker's confrontational stance.

The difference in forcefulness between the speakers having a higher ratio of upscaling explicit condemnation of the antagonist and the speakers having a relatively lower ratio of doing so is illustrated by Excerpt 5.2 and Excerpt 5.3, respectively. Excerpt 5.2 features the speaker (Husband_H02_WH) who had the highest ratio in the dataset, whereas Excerpt 5.3 a speaker (Wife_H02_AW) who did not use this 'scaling + attitudinal complex' option at all. These two disputants happened to be a couple, with the wife accusing the husband of having an allegedly cheating relationship with a female high schoolmate. Both excerpts involve the disputants' direct accusation of the antagonist. In Excerpt 5.2, the husband reported the wife's excessive reaction upon hearing the phrase—'high schoolmate gathering'. The husband used infused intensification to accuse the wife of overreaction, thereby augmenting the force of his condemnation. By contrast, in Excerpt 5.3, the wife recounted past events when the husband was consistently late for the family business and explicitly assessed him as irresponsible. She did not use any upscaling to frame her accusations, so the force of her condemnation was more moderate than his.

Similar in-group variations could be identified in other 'scaling + attitudinal complex' options. The patterns revealed that despite a commonality in the disputants' preference for specific options, there were observable individual differences among the disputants. When each option was used as a parameter of variation, the disputants disperse along a continuum between the disputant with the highest ratio and the disputant with the lowest ratio. In one sense, the disputants could be assigned to two or more groups in terms of the similarity of their ratios—for example, groups of disputants with high-ratio /mid-ratio /low-ratio of upscaled negative Judgement of the antagonist. The disputants in each group arguably constructed a similar 'self' by reference to forcefulness in their advancement of a specific attitudinal complex. Meanwhile, in another sense, there is no abrupt change or discontinuity among the disputants regarding their ratios. This pattern is visualised by the colour of the bars

Excerpt 5.2 Speaker having a higher ratio of upscaling negative Judgement of the antagonist (exemplified by Husband_H02_WH's utterances)

Turn	Speaker	Move	Utterance (Chinese)	Utterance (English translation)	Attitude signal	Attitudinal complex: Assessment	Attitudinal complex: Abbr.	Scaling
8	Husband_H02_WH	1	她在市场就是出摊的邻居吧..说了一句话..同学聚会这几个词	She heard the phrase.. high schoolmate gathering.. from a neighbour vendor in the market				
		2	到家跟我生了场气	She came home and got **angry** with me	Attitudinal instance of inscribed Affect (potential invocation of -ve Judgement)	Observed inscribe -ve Affect antagonist (invoke -ve Judge antagonist)	OAO	No-scaling
9	Hostess_H02	1	你说连这四个字都不能提	You mean that you can't even mention these words				
10	Husband_H02_WH	1	别人提了就那次因为别人说一个同学聚会..跟我开始生气	(Even when) someone else mentioned it once because someone else talked about a high schoolmate gathering.. she started to get **angry** with me	Attitudinal instance of inscribed Affect (potential invocation of -ve Judgement)	Observed inscribe -ve Affect antagonist (invoke -ve Judge antagonist)	OAO	Upscaling[a]
		2	开始发飙	(She) started to **lash out** (at me)	Inscription	Inscribe -ve Judge antagonist	NJA	Upscaling
		3	晚上怒骂	(She) **roared at** me at night	Inscription	Inscribe -ve Judge antagonist	NJA	Upscaling
		4	哎呀	Oh my god				

[a]The husband indicated that the wife got angry more often than one would expect

Excerpt 5.3 Speaker having a lower ratio of upscaling negative Judgement of the antagonist (exemplified by Wife_H02_AW's utterances)

Turn	Speaker	Move	Utterance (Chinese)	Utterance (English translation)	Attitude signal	Attitudinal complex		Scaling
						Assessment	Abbr.	
111	Wife_ H02_ AW	1	这两年给我的感觉就是对家庭不负责任	In these 2 years I have the feeling that he is **not responsible** for the family	Inscription	Inscribe -ve Judge antagonist	NJA	No-scaling
Voiceover								
112	Wife_ H02_ AW	1	我们家是做生意的嘛..在外头	Our family is doing business.. outside				
		2	让他帮我儿子看摊的时候..我儿子去的时候..就是说七点就可以到那儿	When it's his turn to help my son take care of the trade.. when it's my son's shift.. that is to say.. my son can get there at seven o'clock				
		3	让他的去的时候到八点半九点才到	When it's his turn to go he won't arrive until eight thirty or nine	Contrast	Invoke -ve Judge antagonist	INVO	
		Voiceover						
113	Wife_ H02_ AW	1	对..总是晚去	Yes.. he is always late	Contrast	Invoke -ve Judge antagonist	INVO	
		Voiceover						
114	Wife_ H02_ AW	1	说明他对家庭不负责任	That shows that he is **not responsible** for the family	Inscription	Inscribe -ve Judge antagonist	NJA	No-scaling

in Fig. 5.1 above. The disputants with lower ratios are illustrated with yellowish bars, with the disputant having a zero instance in the designated feature being white—the lower the ratio, the yellower the bar. In contrast, the disputants having higher ratios are illustrated with purplish bars. The higher the ratio, the more purple the bar. The colours from white to yellow to purple are different shades of yellow or purple, with bar colours absolute nor definite. The continuous feature of the groupings of the disputants—for example, as high-ratio, mid-ratio, or low-ratio groups—indicates that the in-group variation among the disputants is a matter of quantitative relativity, rather than a matter of qualitative difference.

In short, when each 'scaling + attitudinal complex' option was used as a single parameter of variation, there were observable similarities among the disputants because some options were used frequently by all the disputants, and some were used by a majority of disputants. Whether a disputant used a given 'scaling + attitudinal complex' option not at all, infrequently (with a low ratio of use), or more frequently (with a higher ratio of use) plausibly has implications for their attitudinal disposition and hence for some facet of the 'self' they were in the process of discursively enacting. Hence, there are multiple aspects of attitudinal disposition or multiple facets of the attitudinal 'self' associated with these different tendencies.

3.2.3 Tendencies Observed When More Options Were Considered

The above analysis has shown that each 'scaling + attitudinal complex' option can be used as a parameter of variation in each disputant's attitudinal disposition and hence as a basis for identifying similarities and differences between disputants. Along this line of thinking, I continued to explore what patterns might be discovered when more than one of the 'scaling + attitudinal complex' options were used. The question being addressed was: Did some disputants have similar ratios when co-selecting the same set of framing options?

I started with a simple case when two scaled attitudinal complex options were considered together: (1) upscaled negative Judgement of the antagonist and (2) upscaled negative Affectual response triggered by the antagonist. As reported in the previous chapter, both attitudinal complexes eventually convey the speaker's negativity towards the antagonist, but via different attitudinal meaning-making mechanisms. The attitudinal complex of negative Judgement of the antagonist constructs a 'self' who is antipathetic towards the antagonist. The attitudinal complex of negative Affectual response triggered by the antagonist enacts a 'self' who is an 'emotional victim' of the antagonist's behaviour. When framed with upscaling devices, high ratios in these two attitudinal complexes would reflect the speaker's foregrounding of negativity, forcefulness, and emotional invocation. It turned out that the disputants clustered into three groups (visualised in Fig. 5.2). The disputants in the red group (top right corner of the figure) had relatively high ratios in both framing options. They presented themselves as both 'combatant' and 'emotional victim', and they chose to amplify this self-presentation with additional upscaling devices. Their framing choices and attitudinal positioning appear to be in sharp contrast to that of the green group (bottom of the figure). The disputants in the green group had zero instances of upscaled negative Affectual responses triggered by the antagonist. They might have this attitudinal complex in the speech but never upscaled their negative emotions. Meanwhile, the disputants in the green group varied significantly in their ratio of upscaled negative Judgement of the antagonist. Hence, the disputants of the green group had variations in terms of their upscaled explicit negativity of the antagonist. They presented themselves as operating with an amplified

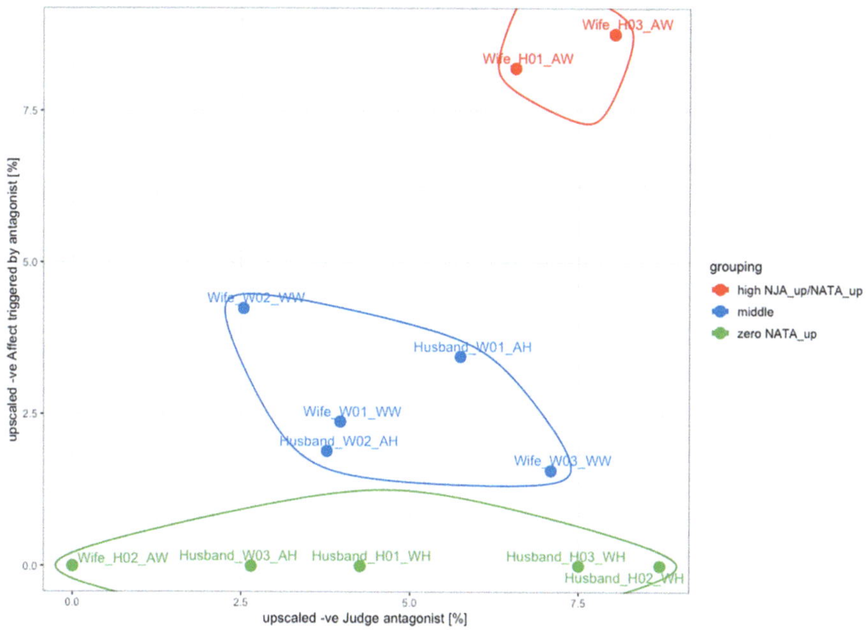

Fig. 5.2 Ratios of two framing options: upscaled negative Judgement of the antagonist (x-axis) and upscaled negative Affectual response triggered by the antagonist (y-axis)

antipathy, but not as an amplified 'emotional victim'. The last group is the blue group (centre of the figure), which had relatively middle ratios in the two framing formulations.

The above pair of framing options are related to one's attitudinal positioning of the antagonist, and both involve the framing device of upscaling. One might argue that the high ratio of the co-selection in these two options can be reflective of the speaker's preference for upscaling an attitudinal complex in general or can be expected because augmenting negativity against the antagonist aligns with the overall attitudinal positioning of any disputant in such a conflictual setting. Subsequently, one might wonder if patterned variations can also be found in the 'scaling + attitudinal complex' options directed at different targets and involve different scaling devices. It turned out that patterned variations could be found in any other framing option, regardless of the attitudinal target and the specific scaling devices. The variability in how the disputants scaled a specific attitudinal complex revealed variability in the degree of forcefulness when they advanced the attitude. They differed regarding whether they favoured adding additional force to or even mitigating the force of their attitudinal positioning. They also differed in what types of attitudes they favoured foregrounding or backgrounding by deploying relevant scaling devices.

4 Stage Two: Focus on the Dialogistic Framing of the Attitudinal Complex

Up to this point, I have outlined findings regarding the tendencies in the disputants' use of scaling resources in connection with a particular attitudinal complex. I turn now to the second type of 'framing', as introduced above—framing associated with the deployment of the resources for dialogistic positioning (from the ENGAGEMENT system in the Appraisal framework). These are the options by which, for example, an attitudinal assessment of some target can be asserted in a way not to recognise any alternative voices or viewpoints (what is termed 'monogloss' in the Appraisal literature) or, in contrast, to ground the assessment in the speaker's own contingent subjectivity and thereby recognise the possibility of alternative views and views (what the Appraisal literature terms heterogloss/entertain). I carried out this line of inquiry in a similar manner as what I did for the scaling resources. Specifically, I first investigated the available 'dialogistic framing + attitudinal complex' options in the dataset, then explored the variability among the disputants concerning their deployment or preference for these options. I used the same subset of attitudinal complexes—the six types of attitudinal inscriptions I used for the scaling analysis. Three dialogistic framing features were drawn from the ENGAGEMENT system in the Appraisal framework to track whether the disputants (1) monogloss (i.e., to present the attitudinal assessment as a bare assertion), (2) entertain (i.e., to recognise the possibility of alternatives to the attitude), or (3) contract (i.e., to proclaim or disclaim the attitude by fending off alternatives) a particular attitudinal complex. The three dialogistic framing options and six attitudinal complexes afford, in theory, 18 'dialogistic framing + attitudinal complex' options. Examples of such an option include 'monoglossed positive self-Judgement' or 'entertained observed antagonist's Affectual responses', and so on.

Space precludes a detailed discussion of every aspect of this line of inquiry—as was also the case for my discussion of tendencies in the use of the scaling options. In the following sections, I will report briefly a few key findings that are pivotal in our understanding of the disputants' construal of attitudinal 'self' via how they presented their attitudes dialogistically.

4.1 Available 'Dialogistic Framing + Attitudinal Complex' Options

Seventeen 'dialogistic framing + attitudinal complex' options were found in the dataset (summarised in Table 5.4). The only option that, in theory, should be available to the disputants but was used by none was to present the inscribed positive Judgement of the antagonist as 'entertained', that is, presenting the stance of praising the antagonist as potentially open to question and thereby negotiable. The

Table 5.4 Seventeen 'dialogistic framing + attitudinal complex' options

	'Dialogistic framing + attitudinal complex' options	Attitudinal complex	Dialogistic framing	Example
(1)	Monoglossed negative judgement of the antagonist	Inscribe -ve Judge antagonist	Monogloss	她脾气不好 she **has a bad temper** (Husband_H03_WH)
(2)	Entertained negative judgement of the antagonist		Entertain	这两年给我的感觉就是对家庭不负责任In these 2 years I have the feeling that he is **not responsible** for the family (Wife_H02_AW)
(3)	Contracted negative judgement of the antagonist		Contract	因为我..知道他这个人..心眼小啊 Because I...know he is.. **oversuspicious** (Wife_W03_WW)
(4)	Monoglossed positive judgement of the antagonist	Inscribe +ve Judge antagonist	Monogloss	很体贴的一个男人 (He is) A very **considerate** man (Wife_H01_AW)
(5)	Contracted negative judgement of the antagonist		Contract	他其实是很好一个人 He was actually a very **good person** (Wife_H01_AW)
(6)	Monoglossed positive self-judgement	Inscribe +ve Judge self	Monogloss	我对全世界所有的女人都好I am **nice** to all women in the world (Husband_H03_WH)
(7)	Entertained positive self-judgement		Entertain	我给你一个所谓的安全感..对吧 I **gave you** a so-called **sense of security**.. is that right (Husband_H01_WH)
(8)	Contracted positive self-judgement		Contract	都是我一手操持I am the person who **handles everything** (Wife_W01_WW)
(9)	Monoglossed negative self-judgement	Inscribe -ve Judge self	Monogloss	以前都是我的错It was all **my fault** in the past (Husband_W01_AH)
(10)	Entertained negative self-judgement		Entertain	我可能在这个夫妻感情方面..沟通方面..是有点欠缺I may be sort of **not good** enough in terms of couple relationship.. in term of communication (Husband_H03_WH)
(11)	Contracted negative self-judgement		Contract	对她确实有一些意识不到的错误I really **made** some **mistakes** that I was unaware of (Husband_W01_AH)

(continued)

Table 5.4 (continued)

	'Dialogistic framing + attitudinal complex' options	Attitudinal complex	Dialogistic framing	Example
(12)	Monoglossed negative affect triggered by the antagonist	Inscribe -ve Affect (triggered by the antagonist)	Monogloss	特别不好受 (I) Feel extremely **uncomfortable** (Wife_H03_AW)
(13)	Entertained negative affect triggered by the antagonist		Entertain	我就说..看着她..跟任何人有笑..有说的..就是在我心里来说..是一种打击I am saying that.. seeing her.. laughing with anyone.. talking with them.. it is that **in my heart**...it's a sort of **blow** (Husband_W01_AH)
(14)	Contracted negative affect triggered by the antagonist		Contract	就是特别地气愤It's that I was extremely **angry** (Wife_H01_AW)
(15)	Monoglossed observed antagonist's affect	Observed antagonist's Affect	Monogloss	置气啊(She) Became **angry** (Husband_H02_WH)
(16)	Entertained observed antagonist's affect		Entertain	这句话对于她来说也是个打击This sentence from her point of view was also a **blow** (Husband_H02_WH)
(17)	Contracted observed antagonist's affect		Contract	她就气得不得了She just became terribly **angry** (Husband_H03_WH)

disputants preferred to present the positive inscription as categorical assertion (via monoglossing) or via dialogistically contractive formulations (via disclamation or proclamation).

4.2 Findings: Tendencies in the Dialogic Framing of the Attitudinal Complexes

Each of the 17 dialogic positioning + attitudinal complex options can be one parameter by which the attitudinal dispositions of the disputants might be seen to vary and by which similarities and differences can be identified between the disputants. For example, those disputants who have low ratios of use of the monoglossed positive self-Judgement can be distinguished from those with high ratios of use of this option. When each option was treated as an independent parameter of variation, patterns of commonalities and in-group variations were found.

4.2.1 The 'Most Popular' Options

Two 'dialogistic framing + attitudinal complex' options stood out in that each was used by most or all of the disputants, and each had a high average ratio of use, relative to other options. The most frequently used 'dialogistic framing + attitudinal complex' option was monoglossed inscribed negative Judgement of the antagonist. It was used by all the disputants at least once and had the highest average ratio of usage in the dataset—at 4.79% of total attitudinal complexes (max 14.13%, min = 1.64%). The second most frequently used 'dialogistic framing + attitudinal complex' option was contracted negative Judgement of the antagonist, with 11 disputants using this option and with an average ratio of use of 4.66% (max = 10.63%, min = 1.06%), the second-highest ratio of use in the dataset. Examples of the two options can be found in Table 5.4 (items (1) and (3)). The disputants' preference for these two options reveals a commonality in foregrounding their negativity against the antagonist via formulating the assessments as dialogistically unproblematic (associated with the monogloss option), highly warrantable, and at odds with any alternative positions (associated with the heterogloss/contract option).

Besides the commonality in dialogistically framing the negative inscription towards the antagonist, there was a commonality in framing the speakers' negative Affectual response triggered by the antagonist. The third most popular option involved using dialogistically contractive formulation to frame this type of Affectual assessment (used by 9 out of 12 disputants, M = 2.83%, max = 7.38%, min = 1.09%). The fourth most frequently deployed option was to categorically assert this attitudinal complex (used by 7 out of 12 disputants, M = 2.33%, max = 10.45%, min = 1.59%). These statistics revealed that presenting the speakers' authorial emotions categorically or contractively was an attitudinal meaning-making strategy favoured by most disputants. By doing so, the speakers explicitly invited the audience to share their negative emotions directed at the trigger of the feelings: the antagonist. The speakers positioned the audience to treat the disputants' 'emotional victim self' as a proposition that was unproblematic (monoglossed) or at least highly warranted (formulated via options for dialogistic contraction).

The disputants' shared preferences for monogloss and contracting their condemnation of the antagonist and their negative emotional responses triggered by the antagonist can be illustrated by Wife_W01_WW's utterances in Excerpt 5.4. (See the book's GitHub repository for the full analysis of her language.) In this excerpt, the wayward wife presented every instance of negative inscription of the antagonist as bare assertions or framed the attitude with additional authorial investment. She also presented an Affectual instance relating to her negative emotions triggered by the husband's behaviours in categorical terms (monoglossed). Her frequent deployment of the monoglossing and contracting devices when presenting these two attitudinal complexes augmented the assertiveness of her accusation against the husband. Although the disputants varied regarding their specific ratios for the above four 'dialogistic framing + attitudinal complex' options, the wife's utterances

Excerpt 5.4 Most disputants preferred to monogloss/contract NJA and NATA (exemplified by Wife_W01_WW's utterances)

Turn	Speaker	Move	Utterance (Chinese)	Utterance (English translation)	Attitude signal	Attitudinal complex: Assessment	Attitudinal complex: Abbr.	Dialogistic framing
92	Hostess_W01	1	这件事情会让你对这个男人有什么看法	What does this incident make you think of this man				
93	Wife_W01_WW	1	没有担当呀	**Not responsible**	Inscription	Inscribe -ve Judge antagonist	NJA	Monogloss
		2	当时我就不同意借啊	I didn't agree to lend his friend the money at that time	Contrast	Invoke +ve Judge self; invoke -ve Judge antagonist	INVO	
		3	他对家里的所有事情都没有==担当==	He **doesn't have responsibility** towards anything in the family ==at all==	Inscription	Inscribe -ve Judge antagonist	NJA	Heterogloss: Contract: Proclaim
94	Hostess_W01	1	==明白==了	==I see==				
		2	这件==事情==	For ==this matter==				
95	Wife_W01_WW	1	==我要离开==他的主要原因就是我在他的面前得不到自尊	==I want to leave== the main reason is that I **don't get self-esteem** in front of him	Inscription	Inscribe -ve Affect self (triggered by the antagonist) (invoke -ve Judge antagonist)	NATA	Monogloss
		2	没有担当	**Not responsible**	Inscription	Inscribe -ve Judge antagonist	NJA	Monogloss
		3	再有就是怀疑	Then (he has) **suspicion**	Inscription	Inscribe -ve Judge antagonist	NJA	Monogloss

nevertheless exemplify the options most frequently deployed by most of the disputants in the dataset to frame their overall negativity towards the antagonist.

Meanwhile, three options were the treated as 'least popular' on the basis that they were used by only one disputant and had the lowest ratios of use of all the complexes in the dataset. These options were (1) monoglossed positive Judgement of the antagonist (2.46%), (2) entertained observed antagonist's Affect (1.09%), and (3) monoglossed negative self-Judgement (0.83%). In later sections, I explored if these less popular options were useful in distinguishing the speakers who frequently deployed such options from the majority of disputants who never used them.

The above discussions show that when each 'dialogistic framing + attitudinal complex' option is examined as a single parameter of variation, the deployment of this option enacted a unique aspect of the 'self' for the disputants, for example, an assertive 'enemy' self or a highly warranted 'emotional' self.

4.2.2 Tendencies Observed When the Analysis Attended to One Option for Dialogistic Positioning

When each of the 17 'dialogistic framing + attitudinal complex' options were used as one parameter of variation to explore the variability among the disputants, observable in-group variations among the disputants emerged. Consider the 'most popular' option—monoglossed negative Judgement of the antagonist. As noted, this was an option taken up by all disputants with an average ratio of 4.79%. However, there was a wide variation among the disputants regarding the ratio of this option in their speeches. The disputant having the highest ratio (Husband_H02_WH, a wayward husband) had 14.13% of his total attitudinal instances being monoglossed negative Judgements of the antagonist. In contrast, Wife_H01_AW (an aggrieved wife) had 1.64% of her total attitudinal instances being this attitude, the lowest ratio in the dataset. These two ratios mean that the high-ratio disputant had a ratio of use which was eight times higher than the ratio of the low-ratio disputant. The other disputants were located along a continuum between 14.13% and 1.64% (illustrated in Fig. 5.3). The ratio difference reveals an in-group divergence regarding the speakers' assertiveness when advancing an explicit condemnation against the antagonist. While all the disputants were overall assertive and confrontational, they varied significantly regarding the degree of their assertiveness in the antagonist-oriented condemnation. The different degrees of assertiveness constructed different attitudinal dispositions. The higher ratio of the monoglossed negative inscription of the antagonist, the more categorical the speaker's confrontational stance was.

Similar to the findings reported in the discussion about 'scaling + attitudinal complex' options, besides the framing option of monoglossing the negative antagonist-oriented inscriptions, there were similar in-group variations patterns in other 'dialogistic framing + attitudinal complex' options. The patterns revealed that despite a commonality in the disputants' preference for specific options, there were observable individual differences among the disputants and a certain degree of continuity in the disputants' preference for a particular option. The in-group variation

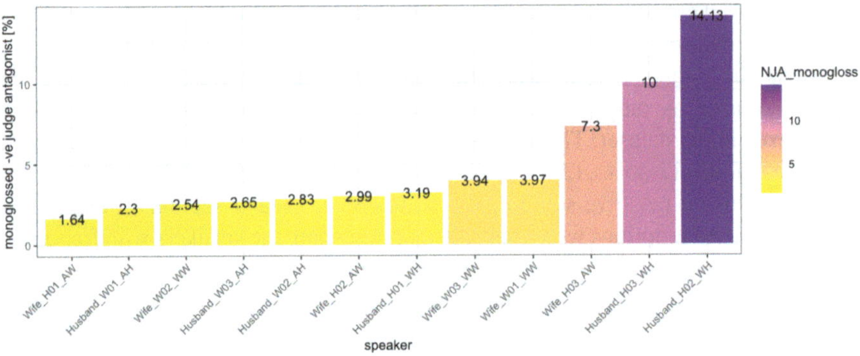

Fig. 5.3 Ratios of monoglossed negative Judgement of the antagonist

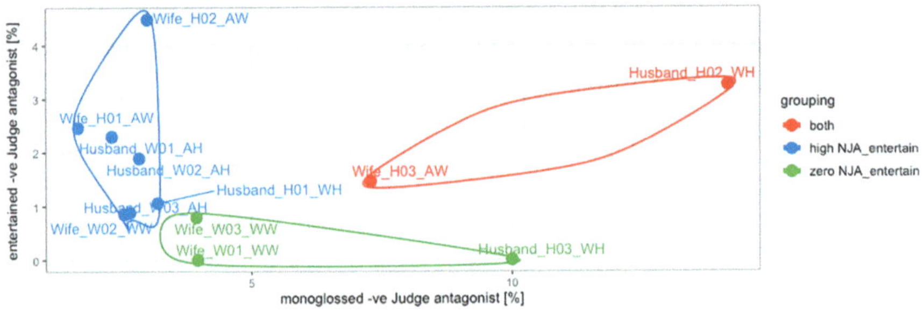

Fig. 5.4 Ratios of two framing options: monoglossed negative Judgement of the antagonist (x-axis) and entertained negative Judgement of the antagonist (y-axis)

among the disputants is a matter of quantitative relativity rather than qualitative difference. Each disputant's patterns of use of each of these options have potential implications for their attitudinal disposition and, hence, some facet of their discursive performance of 'self'.

4.2.3 Tendencies Identified When More Options Were Considered

When more than one dialogistic framing formulations were considered together, there were also observable variations among the disputants. Consider the two 'popular options': (1) monoglossed negative Judgement of the antagonist (the most 'popular' option) and (2) entertained negative Judgement of the antagonist (the fifth most 'popular' option). This pair has the same target type, but the first option involves a categorical assertion of the assessment (i.e., a formulation by which the attitudinal proposition is treated as uncontentious, not in tensions with alternatives or rival viewpoints). In contrast, the second option construes the attitudinal proposition as open to question, as not necessarily agreed upon. The distribution of the disputants by reference to their ratios of these two options are visualised in Fig. 5.4.

With respect to these options, the disputants broadly cluster into three observable groups, with each group having similar ratios in using the two options but different from the other two groups. The green group on the bottom of the figure have zero instances entertained negative Judgement of the antagonist, which means that the three disputants (all wayward spouses) always categorically blamed their counterparts without tempering this blame in any way. In contrast, the blue group on the left portion of the figure opted for entertaining their negative Judgment of the antagonist, presenting their condemnation as contingent and open for negotiation. Two other speakers (the red group in the middle portion of the figure) tended to do both. While they relatively favoured blaming the antagonist categorically, they also had a relatively high ratio of the option by which the negative judgment was presented as open to question and potentially contentious. This finding suggests that although explicitly blaming the antagonist is a uniform choice for all the disputants in the dataset, there was variability regarding how the disputants dialogistically position their condemnation.

Excerpt 5.5 illustrates speakers having a relatively high ratio of use of the option by which negative Judgement of the antagonist was entertained. Wife_H02_AW, in this excerpt, reported an allegedly flirtatious relationship between her husband and a female high schoolmate. The wife quoted a WeChat message the husband sent to the woman, by which the wife positioned the audience to assess the husband negatively. For the two inscribed negative Judgements directed at the husband (Move 2 in Turn 61 and Move 1 in Turn 63), the wife framed the assessments as entertained. She presented her condemnation of the husband as her own perspective and recognised the possibility of alternatives views of what had happened. (See the book's GitHub repository for the full analysis of her language.)

Wife_H02_AW's preference for entertaining the condemnation is in sharp contrast to Husband_H03_WH exemplified in Excerpt 5.6. The wayward husband opted for framing his condemnation of the antagonist via monoglossing, presenting the criticisms as categorically unproblematic. (See the book's GitHub repository for the full analysis of his language.)

Up to this point, I have reported findings arising from the analysis concerning two aspects of the disputants' framing of the attitudinal complexes—framing the attitudinal expressions via scaling devices (options from the GRADUATION system) or dialogistic framing devices (options from the ENGAGEMENT system). The findings revealed tendencies or patterned variations regarding how the disputants framed their attitudes. Strictly speaking, any one or any pair of scaling/dialogistic framing formulations can be used as one parameter for variation exploration. Similarly, any three or four or even more framing formulations can be different parameter combinations by which to explore variations among the speakers in the dataset. The parameters—or the scaled/dialogistically framed attitudinal complex options—can be carefully selected to foreground a particular aspect of the speakers' use of evaluative language, for example, the speakers' attitudes directed at the self or the speakers' preference in upscaling devices. Such zoomed-in inquiries will be particularly useful when the research objective is focused on a particular aspect of the speakers' attitudinal arrangement.

Excerpt 5.5 Speakers having a high ratio of entertaining but low ratio of monoglossing when advancing negative Judgements of the antagonist (exemplified by Wife_H02_AW's utterances)

Turn	Speaker	Move	Utterance (Chinese)	Utterance (English translation)	Attitude signal	Attitudinal complex		Dialogistic framing
						Assessment	Abbr.	
56	Hostess_H02	1	你认为这些话都是有关联的..==是吗==	You think these words are all related.. ==don't you==				
57	Wife_H02_AW	1	==嗯==	==Mhm==				
		2	就是说虽然不联系…但是你在我内心里的一角	That is to say although we don't contact each other… but there's a corner of my heart that is yours	Quotation: Other	Invoke -ve Judge antagonist	INVO	
		3	==这==一句话	==This== was the sentence				
58	Hostess_H02	1	==嗯==	Mhm==				
59	Wife_H02_AW	1	他们==没有联系==了吗	Did they ==stop contacting== each other				
60	Hostess_H02	1	==所以..你==	==So.. you==				
61	Wife_H02_AW	1	他在这里头不联系	He didn't contact her in the group				
		2	他用这种暗示..我感觉是	He used this **flirting sign**.. I feel	Inscription	Inscribe -ve Judge antagonist	NJA	Heterogloss: Expand: Entertain
62	Husband_H02_WH	1	没有	No		Invoke +ve Judge self; invoke -ve Judge antagonist	INVO	
		2	这都属于很正常	This was very **normal**	Inscription	Inscribe +ve Judge self; invoke -ve Judge antagonist	PJA	Monogloss
63	Wife_H02_AW	1	我看来不正常	In my view it was **not normal**	Inscription	Inscribe -ve Judge antagonist	NJA	Heterogloss: Expand: Entertain

Excerpt 5.6 Speakers having a high ratio of monoglossing but no entertaining when advancing negative Judgement of the antagonist (exemplified by Husband_H03_WH's utterances)

Turn	Speaker	Move	Utterance (Chinese)	Utterance (English translation)	Attitude signal	Attitudinal complex		Dialogistic framing
						Assessment	Abbr.	
125	Hostess_H03	1	柯先生..确实发誓没有用	Mr. Ke.. it's true that vow doesn't prove anything				
		2	但是事实很有用	But facts are very useful				
		3	她刚刚说的那两==那个==事情是真的吗	Are the two incidents she just ==said = really true				
126	Husband_ H03_WH	1	==诶==	==Eh==				
		2	是..是一起吃饭	Yes.. we ate together				
127	Hostess_H03	1	那为什么	Then why				
128	Husband_ H03_WH	1	我那天下午没吃饭	I didn't eat that afternoon				
		2	她吃饭了	She had her meal already				
129	Hostess_H03	1	那为什么要要跟她撒那个慌	Then why did you did you lie to her				
130	Husband_ H03_WH	1	我说跟女人一起吃饭..她她受得了吗	If I had said that I were to eat with a woman.. could she stand it	Rhetorical question	Invoke -ve Judge antagonist	INVO	
		2	她本来心心眼那么小	She was so **mean** in her heart	Inscription	Inscribe -ve Judge antagonist	NJA	Monogloss
		3	又又容易生气	She was so easy to get **angry**	Inscription	Inscribe -ve Judge antagonist	NJA	Monogloss

Exploration along this line of thinking can lead to an even more complicated line of inquiry: are there tendencies in the disputants' preference for both the scaling and the dialogistic framing devices? To put this another way, when the two framing resources (resources of scaling and dialogistic positioning) are treated as interconnected and as factors that could mutually contribute to raising or lowering a disputant's attitudinal presence, what are the similarities and differences across the disputants in the dataset? As indicated earlier in this chapter, this complicated line of inquiry is the final stage in the second perspective—a perspective focusing on the framing of attitudinal complexes.

5 Stage Three: Focus on the Scaling and Dialogistic Framing of the Attitudinal Complex

The final stage of analysis—the final stage in the framing of the attitudinal complex and final stage for the whole chapter's analysis—took a very bold attempt to put all the scaling, dialogistic framing, and attitudinal complex options together, treating all the features as mutually contributive to a speaker's attitudinal disposition. Specifically, the final analysis was concerned with the co-occurrence of both the scaling and the dialogistic framing devices by which the attitudinal complexes might be 'framed'. It explored tendencies in the disputants' deployment simultaneously of both options of scaling and dialogistic positioning—how often, for example, they might both upscale and monogloss a negative Judgement of the antagonist, or both downscale and monogloss a negative Judgement of the antagonist, and so on. That is to say, this line of analysis explored what scaling and dialogistic framing options the disputants used when advancing a particular attitudinal complex, what options they used together, and at what frequencies they used these options. The analysis also investigated if the disputants clustered into observable groups with sub-sets of the disputants using these combinations of the two types of framing options in a similar fashion while differing from other disputants in their use of these options.

5.1 Available Scaling and Dialogistic Framing Options

The analysis used the same scaling options (i.e., upscale, downscale, and not scale) and dialogistic framing options (i.e., monogloss, contract, and entertain) as dealt with in the previous discussion. However, the analysis focused on the co-selection of the features, for example, 'upscale + monogloss', 'downscale + monogloss', 'downscale + contract', and so on. The three scaling options, three dialogistic framing options, and six attitudinal complex options, in theory, afford 54 scaling and dialogistic framing options. One example would be 'monoglossed and upscaled negative Judgement of the antagonist'.

Forty 'scaling + dialogistic framing + attitudinal complex' options were found in the dataset, with 14 options, which, in theory, would be possible but was not used by any disputant in the dataset. Given the space limitations of this monograph, I present the four 'most popular' options (used by most disputants and with the highest average ratios) with examples in Table 5.5 rather than providing a list of 40 options with 40 examples.

5.2 *The 'Most Popular' Options*

Strictly speaking, each of the 40 'scaling + dialogistic framing + attitudinal complex' options can be one parameter of possible variation by which a disputant's attitudinal disposition can be characterised and by which similarities and differences between disputants can be tracked. For example, the ratio of entertained and upscaled positive self-Judgement can be used to distinguish the disputants who have conveyed such attitudes at relatively high ratios from those who make use of this resource with a relatively low ratio. When each option was treated as an independent parameter of variation, patterns of commonalities and in-group variations emerged.

Table 5.5 'Scaling + dialogistic framing + attitudinal complex' option examples

	'Scaling + dialogistic framing + attitudinal complex' options	Attitudinal complex	Scaling	Dialogistic framing	Example
(1)	Monoglossed non-scaled negative Judgement of the antagonist	Inscribe -ve Judge antagonist	No-scaling	Monogloss	他是这样侮辱我He **humiliated** me like this (Wife_W03_WW)
(2)	Monoglossed upscaled negative Judgement of the antagonist		Upscaling	Monogloss	你说出来的话..就是伤我一辈子What you have said.. can **hurt me** for a lifetime (Wife_W03_WW)
(3)	Contracted non-scaled negative Judgement of the antagonist		No-scaling	Contract	因为我..知道他这个人..心眼小啊Because I... know he is.. **oversuspicious** (Wife_W03_WW)
(4)	Contracted upscaled negative Judgement of the antagonist		Upscaling	Contract	她其实有很多东西都在瞒着我She is actually **hiding** a lot of things **from me** (Husband_W03_AH)

There was wide variation regarding the disputants' preference for these 40 'scaling + dialogistic framing + attitudinal complex' options. No option was used by all the 12 disputants in the dataset, indicating a relatively lower degree of commonality than previous analyses regarding the variabilities in attitudinal complex, scaling of the attitudinal complex, or dialogistic framing of the attitudinal complex. The top four 'most popular' options were deployed by nine disputants. These all involved framings of negative Judgements of the antagonist. The option having the highest average ratio in the dataset was that involving upscaling and dialogistic contraction (M = 2.39%, max = 5.12%, min = 1.06%), followed by that involving upscaling and monoglossing (M = 2.36%, max = 8.7%, min = 0.79%). The other two top popular options are to present the negative Judgement of the antagonist as a dialogistical contraction and with no-scaling (M = 2.14%, max = 5.56%, min = 0.88%) or monogloss and with no-scaling (M = 2.04%, max = 5.43%, min = 0.82%). These top four options reveal that most disputants, albeit not all, preferred foregrounding their explicit negativity of the counterpart by intensifying and assertively advancing (via monoglossing or dialogistic contraction) this negative assessment of the antagonist. This tendency was particularly true for the wayward spouse because the disputants having the highest ratios in these four options were all wayward spouses. By presenting the attitudinal value of negative Judgement towards the antagonist as a bare assertion and with additional intensification, rather than framing it with downscaling devices or presenting it as open to question, most disputants attitudinally presented the self as in sharp opposition to their counterparts. Consequently, the disputants enacted an identity of a 'combatant' against the antagonist. The commonality of the degree of preference in these four framing options reflects the adversarial nature of such marital conflict interactions.

Besides a commonality in the augmented forcefulness and assertiveness in the disputants' negative Judgement of the antagonist, a majority of disputants (six to eight) also had a similar preference in how they advanced reports of their own negative affectual responses, as triggered by the antagonist. As discussed previously, this was an important attitudinal meaning-making strategy for the disputants to invoke negative assessments of the antagonist. These disputants presented their authorial negative emotions via dialogistic contraction without scaling (eight disputants, M = 1.28%, max = 4.76%, min = 0.74%), contraction plus upscaling (seven disputants, M = 1.55%, max = 5.74%, min = 0.79%), and monoglossing without scaling (six disputants, M = 1.48%, max = 10.45%, min = 0.82%). It means that while a majority of disputants chose to reference their personal emotions to condemn the antagonist implicitly, they also repeatedly chose to present their emotions as unproblematic, highly warrantable, and sometimes with additional intensifications. This tendency was particularly relevant to the wives because all the disputants having the highest ratios in these three options were wives, two aggrieved wives and one wayward wife. These favoured framing devices elevate the forcefulness and assertiveness of the negative emotions, making the Affectual invocation more powerful and salient.

As what was discussed in the analysis about the tendencies in 'scaling + attitudinal complex' and 'dialogistic framing + attitudinal complex' options, each 'scaling

+ dialogistic framing + attitudinal complex' option or each pair of options can be used as parameters to explore the variation among the disputants in the dataset. The following analysis took a bold attempt to consider the 40 framing formulations as one parameter combination and explore any patterned variations among the disputants. Would the patterns of use be broadly similar across the disputants in the dataset, suggesting a uniform or consistent attitudinal disposition enacted by the disputants? Or might these patterns suggest sub-types of attitudinal disposition, with sub-sets of the disputants similarly using the resources while differing from others? And then, taking this further, do the findings suggest that those attitudinal aspects of discursive self-presentation are broadly similar for all 'aggrieved' or 'wayward' spouses—they all made similar use of the resources and hence presented a similar discursive 'self'? Details of this final analysis are now presented.

5.3 *Clusters Emerging from Co-Selection of Multiple Framing Options*

Methodologically, 40 'scaling + dialogistic framing + attitudinal complex' options are 40 independent parameters of variation. Combining all of them together as one parameter creates high dimensional data, where multiple values are needed to identify a data point uniquely. Say, for example, a disputant's position or identity in a 40-parameter data can only be identified by the ratios of their choice in all the 40 framing options. If variations vis-à-vis a parameter combination with two or three options can be identified manually, variations vis-à-vis a parameter combination with 40 options become too complex to be explored by hand.

This analysis drew on clustering methods from data mining and used the programming language *R* to perform pattern recognition. The exploration procedure was similar to that in Chap. 4 and was conducted in the following steps: (1) determine how many clusters to identify, (2) identify the clusters, and (3) explore what the clustering informs us about the disputants' preference for the attitudinal complexes.

In the first step, I used the average silhouette method (see Chap. 4 for details) to determine the optimal number of clusters in the dataset. The optimal number was three (visualised in Fig. 5.5), indicating that three clusters can best represent the clustering in the dataset.

The analysis then used the 'Principal Component Analysis' (PCA). As introduced in Chap. 4, this method identifies the combinations of highly correlated variables, which together account for the most variance in the data. In my dataset of 40 'scaling + dialogistic framing + attitudinal complex' options, there would be 40 'principal components', or combinations of variables. The method helped identify the top two principal components that contribute to most of the possible variance in the dataset. In addition, similar to what was discussed in Chap. 4, I used this method for its effectiveness in visualising the variation present in a dataset with many

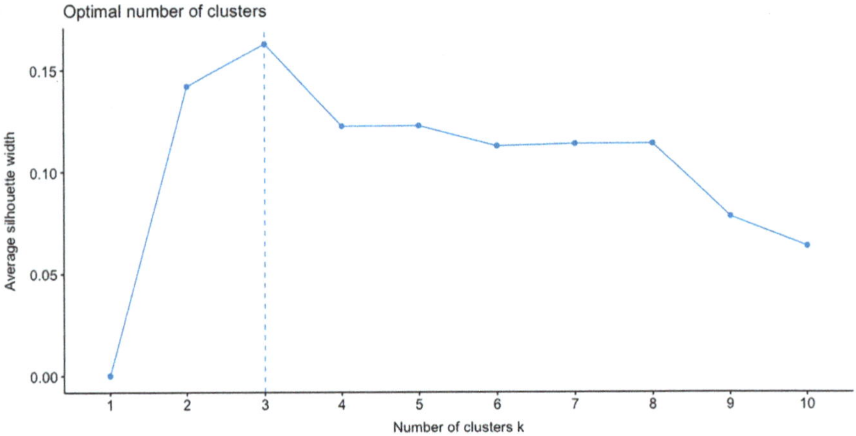

Fig. 5.5 Optimal number of clusters (co-selection of 40 'scaling + dialogistic framing + attitudinal complex' options) [Figure adapted from Xu (2024), pp. 693–719. Reused with permission]

variables, rather than with an aim to remove any 'scaling + dialogistic framing + attitudinal complex' options from the analysis. In my study, every option was understood to contribute in a meaningful way to the disputants' attitudinal self-presentation, regardless of the particular option's specific contribution to the overall variations in the dataset. This analysis used the 'PCA' and 'get_pca_ind' functions from the 'FactoMineR' (Lê, Josse & Husson, 2008; v 2.4; Husson et al., 2020) and 'factoextra' package (v 1.0.7; Kassambara & Mundt, 2020) in *R*. This visualisation of the PCA can be found later in Sect. 5.3.4.

The cluster analysis identified three disputant groups vis-à-vis the ratios of use of the 40 'scaling + dialogistic framing + attitudinal complex' options. Speakers in each group shared similar ratios in specific framing options but were distinct from speakers in the other groups. The grouping vis-à-vis the ratio of the options revealed three distinct attitudinal disposition types in the given situation. Roughly speaking, the disputants varied in terms of the 'attitudinality' (White, 2019)—the strength of an attitudinal complex. The 'attitudinality' includes at least two dimensions of strength—the assertiveness (realised by the dialogistic framing devices of ENGAGEMENT) and the forcefulness (realised by the scaling devices of GRADUATION). In this analysis, attitudinal complexes advanced via monogloss were understood to have a higher degree of assertiveness than those that were 'entertained' (modalised in some way). Similarly, attitudinal complexes advanced via upscaling were treated as having a higher degree of forcefulness than those advanced with downscaling or no-scaling.

The clustering of the disputants can be interpreted regarding the relationship between the disputants' 'attitudinality' and the attitudinal complexes which are of central attitudinal concern. Chapter 4 outlined that four attitudinal complexes construed the disputants' central concern: negative Judgement of the antagonist, positive self-Judgement, negative Affectual responses triggered by the antagonist, and negative Judgement of the people outside of the marriage relationship (usually the alleged third party). The disputants in group 1 had relatively weak attitudinality in the framing of most attitudinal complexes. The disputants in group 2 had relatively strong attitudinality in presenting their central concern, particularly in the Judgement-related attitudinal complexes. Finally, the disputants in group 3 also had a middle degree of attitudinality but a high degree of forcefulness in negative Affectual attitudinal complexes. The differences in attitudinality in each group are indicative of three distinct attitudinal disposition types.

5.3.1 Attitudinal Disposition Type 1: Weak Attitudinality

The first attitudinal disposition type involves advancing most attitudinal complexes with a weak attitudinality. Generally speaking, the speakers of this type favoured the GRADUATION resources of downscaling or no-scaling and the ENGAGEMENT resources of entertain when framing their attitudinal complexes. They had a relatively low preference for upscaling, monoglossing, or contracting their attitudinal complexes. Just one disputant was found to belong to this group: Wife_H02_AW, an aggrieved spouse.

Specifically, the wife's 'weak attitudinality' is reflected in three aspects. Firstly, she preferred downscaling or no-scaling over upscaling. She had a relatively low frequency of upscaled attitudinal complex across all attitudinal values, with only 13% of her total attitudinal complexes being additionally formulated via upscaling, compared to an average ratio of 30% in the dataset. Even for inscriptions of negative Judgement of the antagonist and positive self-Judgement, the two prominent attitudinal complexes favoured by the disputants in the dataset, this 'weak attitudinality' disputant had zero instance of upscaling these attitudinal inscriptions. Secondly, in sharp contrast to her avoidance of upscaling, the wife favoured the GRADUATION resource of downscaling and the ENGAGEMENT resource of entertain to frame her attitudinal complexes. She had a three times higher ratio of downscaled inscriptions of negative Judgement of the antagonist and positive self-Judgement than the dataset's average. Finally, when the 'weak attitudinality' wife did intensify or assert some attitudinal complexes, the complexes were found to be here own negative Affectual response, rather than direct Judgements targeting any parties in the dispute. For example, about 11% of the wife's total attitudinal instances were monoglossed and no-scaled negative Affectual response triggered by the antagonist, nine times as many as the average for the dataset. In short, the wife's preference in these three aspects softened her overall attitudinal positioning in the dispute interaction. Compared to other harsh and tough disputants, this 'weak attitudinality' disputants discursively present herself as soft, ready to be persuaded, and to a certain degree sentimental.

Wife_H02_AW's attitudinal arrangements can be exemplified by Excerpt 5.7,

where the wife recounted a past event between the husband and a female high schoolmate. According to the wife, the husband sent the schoolmate a red envelope of 520 RMB on Valentine's Day. The husband called the female schoolmate 'elder

Excerpt 5.7 Example of 'weak attitudinality' disposition (Wife_H02_AW's utterances in Turn 11–19)[a]

Turn	Speaker	Move	Utterance (Chinese)	Utterance (English translation)	Attitude signal	Attitudinal complex		Framing	
						Assessment	Abbr.	Scaling	Dialogistic framing
11	Wife_H02_AW	1	他回家的时候..跟同学聚完会以后	When he got home.. after meeting with his high schoolmates					
		2	从他回来以后我就发现	I found that after he came back					
		3	他跟那个女同学有些私聊	He had some sort of private chats with the female high schoolmate	Evoke	Invoke -ve Judge antagonist[b]	INVO		
		4	聚会回来的时候第二天嘛.. 是2月14号.. 情人节..情人节的晚上	The next day after the party.. It was on February 14th.. Valentine's Day.. Valentine's Day evening					
		5	他俩聊天	They chatted					
		6	聊天的时候他发给那女同学的红包是==520==	When they chatted.. he sent to the female high schoolmate a red envelope of ==520 RMB==	Evoke	Invoke -ve Judge antagonist	INVO		

12	Husband_ H02_WH	1	==哼==	==Humph==					
13	Wife_H02_ AW	2	然后我发现下边的记录.. 还有一些**暧昧**	Then I found in the chat history.. were sort of **flirtatious**	Inscription	Inscribe -ve Judge antagonist	NJA	Downscaling	Monogloss
		2	比如说他在里头跟那女同学	For example he said to the female high schoolmate					
		3	*[模仿丈夫的声音]* 姐姐啊..怎么啦	[mimicking the husband's voice] Elder sister.. what's wrong	Quotation: Other	Invoke -ve Judge antagonist	INVO		
		4	*[模仿丈夫的声音]* 你真想让我叫你姐姐吗	*[mimicking the husband's voice]* do you really want me to call you elder sister	Quotation: Other	Invoke -ve Judge antagonist	INVO		
		5	但是那种声音跟咱们平常这样的叫姐姐.. 那种不一样	But that kind of voice calling elder sister.. was not the same as what we do in normal situations	Contrast	Invoke -ve Judge antagonist	INVO		
14	Hostess_ H02	1	就语音聊天..是吧	They had voice chat.. right					
15	Wife_H02_ AW	1	嗯..对	Yep.. right					

(continued)

Excerpt 5.7 (continued)

Turn	Speaker	Move	Utterance (Chinese)	Utterance (English translation)	Attitude signal	Attitudinal complex		Framing	
						Assessment	Abbr.	Scaling	Dialogistic framing
16	Hostess_ H02	1	语气让你觉得==有点==暧昧	Does the tone make you feel they were ==a little== flirtatious					
17	Wife_H02_ AW	1	==哎==	==Yep==					
		2	对	Correct					
18	Hostess_ H02	1	然后又发了一个520的红包	And he sent a red envelope of 520 RMB					
19	Wife_H02_ AW	1	嗯..对我的感觉..我就是说他精神上**有问题**	Yes.. the feeling for me is.. I mean.. he **has** emotionally **cheated**	Inscription	Inscribe -ve Judge antagonist	NJA	Downscaling	Heterogloss: Expand: Entertain

[a]Example adapted from Xu (2024), pp. 693–719. Reused with permission

[b]Having private chats with a member of the opposite-sex can be considered as a cheating or betraying behaviour for some people. In this utterance, by reporting that the husband and the female schoolmate engaged in private chats, the wife indicates that their interaction extends beyond the scope of public schoolmate gatherings or communication within a public schoolmate social-group context. The relationship has entered a private sphere

sister' in the voice messages, the significance of which is discussed below. (See the book's GitHub repository for the full analysis of her language.)

Some explanations are needed for the readers to understand the attitudinal meaning-making mechanism in the ideational meaning of the wife's recounts. First, Chinese people celebrate western Valentine's Day on February 14th, albeit they also observe another traditional love festival—the Qixi Festival. Hence, the husband's private chats with the female schoolmate on Valentine's Day have the potential to invoke some attitudinal assessments directed at the husband's propriety. In addition, sending a red envelope has a rich evaluative meaning-making potential. Although giving a red envelope, or monetary gift, is common in Chinese culture, it is always seen during holidays or special occasions, such as Lunar New Year, weddings, or childbirth. The husband giving the female schoolmate a red envelop on Valentine's Day suggests that he considers the day, the recipient, or what happened on that day significant or unique. Most importantly, the amount of money in the red envelope—520 RMB—is not a casual amount for a Chinese culture insider. The number 520 has a connotative meaning of being a love message. When the number is read digit by digit, it is 'wǔ èr líng' in Pinyin. The pronunciation is very similar to that of the phrase '我爱你' (Pinyin: wǒ ài nǐ; I love you). Therefore, the number 520 has been widely regarded as a number to express love. In this excerpt, the wife provided three details of the husband's behaviour with the female high schoolmate—on Valentine's Day, sending a red envelope, and with an amount of 520. Even though the wife does not explicitly condemn the husband's behaviour, these three details are enough to invoke a negative Judgement directed at the husband's propriety. The final implicit strike from the wife is her recount of a voice message sent from the husband to the female schoolmate. In the message, he called her 'elder sister' with a voice, which the wife argues, different from what people do in normal situations. Notably, the addressing term '姐姐elder sister' also has a strong connotation. In contemporary China, the term can be used as a colloquial form for addressing women among friends, workmates, or even strangers. Whereas this addressing term can create a warm and familial environment, it can also be used to express interest in and flirt with a member of the opposite sex. In this excerpt, by mimicking the husband's voice message, the wife positions the audience to assess the husband's propriety negatively.

In this excerpt, there are seven attitudinal instances, all about negative Judgement of the antagonist, two via inscription ('暧昧flirtatious' in Turn 13 and '精神上有问题has emotionally cheated' in Turn 19) and five via invocation. No attitudinal instance is framed by up-scaling. However, two instances are framed by down-scaling devices ('有些私聊some sort of private chats' in Turn 11 and '有一些暧昧were sort of flirtatious' in Turn 13). The co-occurrence pattern between attitudinal complexes and GRADUATION resources to a certain degree weakens the wife's accusation of the husband. Meanwhile, one of the two negative assessments of the antagonist is entertained. This instance is in Turn 19 when the wife explicitly accuses the husband of '精神上有问题has emotionally cheated'. This accusation is framed with—'对我的感觉the feeling for me is' and '我就是说I mean'. By doing so, the wife presents the accusation as grounded in her own contingent subjectivity, allowing for dialogic alternatives, such as 'The husband's behaviours are acceptable' or 'The husband's behaviours do not prove anything'.

To wrap up, Wife_H02_AW's attitudinal arrangements concerning the framing of the attitudinal complexes presented herself as soft and mild when launching an accusation, potentially presenting here as associated with a 'weak attitudinality' attitudinal disposition. For her preference and the average ratios of the other two attitudinal disposition groups, see Table 5.6. Only the ratios of the 'scaling + dialogistic framing + attitudinal complex' options that made the wife different from the other disputants are presented.

As noted, Wife_H02_AW was the only speaker featuring a 'weak attitudinality' attitudinal disposition in the dataset. This might indicate that choosing to mitigate one's attitudinal complexes was not common for disputants in family dispute resolution interactions. Most disputants favoured adopting a more uncompromising tone in the accusation and defence. A more assertive, less accommodating attitudinal orientation can be found in the following two attitudinal disposition types.

5.3.2 Attitudinal Disposition Type 2: Strong Attitudinality

The second attitudinal disposition type is 'strong attitudinality'. Disputants of this type were in sharp contrast with the prior 'weak attitudinality' wife. 'Strong attitudinality' speakers preferred to upscale and assert all the attitudinal complexes in line with their central concerns. They generally avoided downscaling and 'entertaining' their assessments. There were two disputants in this group, both being wayward husbands.

Specifically, for the disputants in the dataset, the 'strong attitudinality' is reflected in three aspects. Firstly, these disputants had a relatively high degree of forcefulness with a higher ratio of upscaled inscriptions than the dataset average. For example, more than 8% of the 'strong attitudinality' disputants' total attitudinal instances were upscaled negative Judgement of the antagonist (either monoglossed or dialogistically contracted), twice that of the average. More than 5% were upscaled observed Affectual responses of the antagonist (either monoglossed or dialogistically contracted), five times the average. They were also twice more frequent in advancing contracted and upscaled positive self-Judgement than the average. They rarely downscaled these attitudinal complex types. Secondly, as to the deployment of ENGAGEMENT framing options, the 'strong attitudinality' disputants had a relatively high degree of assertiveness regarding their preference in monoglossing and dialogistic contraction. They had nearly 13% of all their attitudinal complexes as monoglossed inscriptions (either upscaled or unscaled) of negative Judgement of the antagonist, three times the dataset average. They also had 6.5% of their attitudinal instances being monoglossed or contracted inscriptions (either upscaled or unscaled) of observed Affectual responses of the antagonist (five times of the dataset average) and 3.5% being monoglossed or contracted (either upscaled or unscaled) inscriptions of positive self-Judgement (seven times of the dataset average). Finally, the 'strong attitudinality' speakers did not favour entertaining any attitudinal

Table 5.6 Ratios making the 'weak attitudinality' disposition different from the other two dispositions

	Speaker	Waywardness	NATA_monogloss_noscale	NJA_entertain_noscale	NJA_monogloss_down	NJA_contract_down	PJS_entertain_noscale	OAO_monogloss_noscale
'Weak attitudinality'	Wife_H02_AW	Aggrieved	10.45	4.48	2.99	1.49	1.49	1.49
'Strong attitudinality' group average			0	1.63	0.42	0	0.55	0.55
'Middle attitudinality' group average			0.53	0.18	0.09	0	0.10	0.09

(Key: *NATA* negative Affectual response triggered by the antagonist or antagonist's behaviour, *NJA* negative Judgement of the antagonist, *PJS* positive Judgement of the self, *OAO* observed other people's Affectual response)

complexes. They seldom reported their own Affectual responses, either. In short, the disputants' preference in these three aspects sharpens their overall attitudinal positioning in the dispute interaction. Compared to the 'weak attitudinality' disputants, the 'strong attitudinality' disputants discursively presented themselves as dogmatic, sharp, and straightforward.

Two disputants in the dataset were found to demonstrate this 'strong attitudinality' disposition, both wayward husbands. A summary of the ratios of their framed attitudinal complexes, in contrast with the average ratios of the other two groups, is presented in Table 5.7.

A typical example from the dataset is the attitudinal meaning-making arrangements of Husband_H03_WH, a wayward husband. His wife accused him of having flirtatious relationships with a female neighbour and a female business associate. In Excerpt 5.8, the husband defended himself by blaming the wife for her bad temper. (See the book's GitHub repository for the full analysis of his language.)

In Excerpt 5.8, the husband used a series of inscriptions to assess the wife negatively. The husband showed no reservation in investing authorial emphasis on the wife's 'impropriate' behaviours in his utterance. His use of upscaling devices augmented the forcefulness of his accusation. He used an infused intensification '犟 pick up an argument with someone defiantly' to describe how the wife responded to his words. He also used isolated intensifications—'骂死你curse at me to death', '祖宗十八代都骂 curse at all my ancestors of eighteen generations', and '骂你一个人都不算 does not curse at you alone'—to elevate the severity of the wife's impropriate verbal behaviour. Additionally, all these negative inscriptions were presented as bare assertions or dialogistic contractions, indicating the husband's authority in the validity of the assessments. In short, by frequently upscaling and monoglossing or contracting the accusations, the husband demonstrated very high degrees of forcefulness and assertiveness.

5.3.3 Attitudinal Disposition Type 3: Middle Attitudinality

The last attitudinal disposition type vis-à-vis the ratio of linguistically framed attitudinal complexes is 'middle attitudinality'. Speakers of this type had lower degrees of forcefulness and assertiveness than the 'strong attitudinality' speakers, but a much higher degree than the 'weak attitudinality' speaker. They tended to avoid downscaling and entertaining all inscribed attitudinal complexes. They frequently relied on invocations to activate attitudinal assessments. Nine disputants in the dataset operated with this disposition—four wayward and five aggrieved spouses.

Specifically, the 'middle attitudinality' is reflected in the following two aspects. First, concerning the attitudinal complexes of the disputants' central concern, the 'middle attitudinality' speakers favoured intensifying and asserting such attitudinal complexes, making them different from the 'weak attitudinality' group who favoured downscaling and entertain. However, the 'middle attitudinality' disputants had relatively lower ratios of upscaling and monoglossing these attitudes than the 'strong attitudinality' speakers. Take the two framing devices—upscaling and

Table 5.7 Ratios making the 'strong attitudinality' disposition different from the other two dispositions

	Speaker	Waywardness	NJA_ monogloss_up	NJA_monogloss_ noscale	PJS_contract_ noscale	PJS_ contract_up	PJS_monogloss_ noscale	OAO_ monogloss_up
'Strong attitudinality'	Husband_ H02_WH	Wayward	8.7	5.43	0	1.09	2.17	4.35
	Husband_ H03_WH	Wayward	4.17	5	5.83	1.67	0.83	1.67
	Group average		6.44	5.22	2.92	1.38	1.50	3.01
'Weak attitudinality' group average			0	0	0	0	0	0
'Middle attitudinality' group average			1.42	1.34	0.57	0.19	0	0.12

(Key: *NJA* negative Judgement of the antagonist, *PJS* positive Judgement of the self, *OAO* observed other people's Affectual response)

Excerpt 5.8 Example of 'strong attitudinality' disposition (Husband_H03_WH's utterances in Turn 103)[a]

Turn	Speaker	Move	Utterance (Chinese)	Utterance (English translation)	Attitudinal signal	Attitudinal complex		Framing	
						Assessment	Abbr.	Scaling	Dialogistic framing
102	Hostess_H03	1	所以这个事在柯先生看来也无伤大雅	So this thing is also innocuous in Mr. Ke's opinion					
103	Husband_H03_WH	1	那肯定的喽	That's for sure					
		2	她要自己找自己难受	She wants to **find troubles for herself**	Inscription	Inscribe -ve Judge antagonist	NJA	No-scaling	Monogloss
		3	我跟她无法沟通..你知道吗	I can't communicate with her.. you know	Denial	Invoke -ve Judge antagonist	INVO		
		4	我跟她说了几句话她就犟起来..吱吱吱	If I say a few words to her she will **pick up an argument** with me defiantly.. blah blah blah	Inscription	Inscribe -ve Judge antagonist	NJA	Upscaling	Monogloss
		5	还发脾气了	Also she will even **lose her temper**	Inscription	Inscribe -ve Judge antagonist	NJA	No-scaling	Heterogloss: Contract: Disclaim
		6	骂我..骂死你	She will **curse at** me.. curse at me to death	Inscription	Inscribe -ve Judge antagonist	NJA	Upscaling	Monogloss
		7	她祖宗十八代都骂	She will **curse at** all my ancestors.. ancestors of eighteen generations	Inscription	Inscribe -ve Judge antagonist	NJA	Upscaling	Monogloss
		8	她骂你一个人都不算	She doesn't **curse at** you alone	Inscription	Inscribe -ve Judge antagonist	NJA	Upscaling	Heterogloss: Contract: Disclaim

[a]Example adapted from Xu (2024), pp. 693–719. Reused with permission

monoglossing—for negative Judgement of the antagonist to illustrate. The average ratio of use of upscaled (either monoglossed or contracted) negative Judgement towards the antagonist for the 'middle attitudinality' group was less than 5%, whilst the average ratio for the 'strong attitudinality' group was 8.1%. Likewise, the average ratio for monoglossed (either upscaled or non-scaled) negative Judgement of the antagonist for the 'middle attitudinality' group was 3.4%, only one-third the rate of the 'strong attitudinality' group, whose ratio was more than 12%. Secondly, when negative Affectual responses triggered by the antagonist is concerned, the 'middle attitudinality' speakers had a relatively high frequency of upscaling (either monoglossed or contracted) such attitudinal complexes—the antagonist was presented as not only making the disputant feel bad but as responsible for making them feel *really* bad. The ratio of upscaled negative Affectual responses for a 'middle attitudinality' speaker was as high as nearly 9%, whereas the ratios for the 'strong attitudinality' and 'weak attitudinality' speakers were zero. By amplifying their negative Affectual responses, the 'middle attitudinality' speakers highlighted the emotional victimisation aspect of the 'self'.

There were nine disputants in the dataset demonstrating this 'middle attitudinality' disposition. This means that 'middle attitudinality' disputants represented three-quarters of the dataset, suggesting that being of 'middle attitudinality', rather than being 'strong' or 'weak' in attitudinality, is a highly probable attitudinal disposition type in family dispute resolution exchanges. A summary of the ratios of their linguistically framed attitudinal complexes in contrast with the average ratios of the other two groups is presented in Table 5.8.

A typical 'middle attitudinality' disputant is Wife_H03_AW, an aggrieved wife (wife of Husband_W03_AH in Excerpt 5.8), who accused her husband of having a flirtatious relationship with a female neighbour. In Excerpt 5.9, the wife reported the husband's behaviours during her pregnancy. According to the wife, the husband kept going to the female neighbour's house without attending to his wife. Triggered by the husband's coldness, the wife was so angry that she could not eat, had to receive medical treatment, and lost a significant amount of weight. (See the book's GitHub repository for the full analysis of her language.)

In this excerpt, the wife frequently used upscaling devices to intensify the degree of her anger and the severity of the ideational meanings. Among 16 attitudinal instances which involve invocations or negative Affectual responses triggered by the antagonist, ten were framed via upscaling. Although these attitudinal instances do not explicitly point the finger at the husband, they have the potential to invoke negative Judgement of the husband. By intensifying the force of these attitudinal assessments, the wife invited the audience to assess the husband attitudinally.

5.3.4 Summary

Up to this point, this section has reported the variability among the disputants vis-à-vis ratio of 'scaling + dialogistic framing + attitudinal complex' options. With the 40 options found in the dataset, three attitudinal disposition types were identified

Table 5.8 Ratios making the 'middle attitudinality' disposition different from the other two dispositions

	Speaker	Waywardness	NJA_contract_up	NJA_contract_noscale	NATA_contract_up	NATA_contract_noscale	NATA_monogloss_up
'Middle attitudinality'	Husband_H01_WH	Wayward	1.06	0	0	0	0
	Husband_W01_AH	Aggrieved	4.6	4.6	2.3	0	0
	Husband_W02_AH	Aggrieved	0	0.94	1.89	1.89	0
	Husband_W03_AH	Aggrieved	1.77	0.88	0	3.54	0
	Wife_H01_AW	Aggrieved	4.92	2.46	5.74	1.64	2.46
	Wife_H03_AW	Aggrieved	2.21	0	2.94	0.74	5.88
	Wife_W01_WW	Wayward	3.17	5.56	1.59	4.76	0
	Wife_W02_WW	Wayward	2.54	2.54	3.39	0.85	0.85
	Wife_W03_WW	Wayward	5.12	5.51	0.79	0.79	0
	Group average		**2.82**	**2.5**	**2.07**	**1.58**	**1.02**
'Weak attitudinality' group average			0	1.49	0	0	0
'Strong attitudinality' group average			1.67	0.84	0	0.55	0

(Key: *NJA* negative Judgement of the antagonist, *NATA* negative Affectual response triggered by the antagonist)

Excerpt 5.9 Example of 'middle attitudinality' disposition (Wife_H03_AW's utterances in Turn 34–38)[a]

Turn	Speaker	Move	Utterance (Chinese)	Utterance (English translation)	Attitude signal	Attitudinal complex: Assessment	Attitudinal complex: Abbr.	Framing: Scaling	Framing: Dialogistic framing
34	Wife_ H03_AW	1	他自己家里不呆就到她家去	He went to her house without staying at his own home	Contrast	Invoke -ve Judge antagonist	INVO	No-scaling	Heterogloss: Contract: Disclaim
		2	怀我女儿那年..我大着个肚子在在家里	When I was expecting my daughter.. I stayed at home with a big belly					
		3	他到她家去玩	He went to her house to play	Evoke	Invoke -ve Judge antagonist	INVO	No-scaling	Monogloss
		4	看电视	To watch TV	Evoke	Invoke -ve Judge antagonist	INVO	No-scaling	Monogloss
		5	你叫也叫不回来	Even if you called him he wouldn't come back	Denial	Invoke -ve Judge antagonist	INVO	Upscaling[a]	Heterogloss: Contract: Disclaim
		6	经常就是两个人有说有笑的在一起	You can always see those two talking and laughing together	Evoke[b]	Invoke -ve Judge antagonist	INVO	Upscaling	Monogloss
35	Hostess_ H03	1	他对你呢..那个时候	How was he to you.. at that time					

(continued)

Excerpt 5.9 (continued)

Turn	Speaker	Move	Utterance (Chinese)	Utterance (English translation)	Attitude signal	Attitudinal complex		Framing	
36	Wife_ H03_AW	1	他对我很平淡	He was very **cold** to me	Inscription	Inscribe -ve Jjudge antagonist	NJA	Upscaling	Monogloss
		2	我吃饭都不能	I couldn't even eat	Denial	Invoke -ve Affect (triggered by the antagonist); invoke -ve Judge antagonist[c]	INVO	Upscaling	Heterogloss: Contract: Disclaim
		3	几天都不能吃饭	For several days I couldn't even eat	Denial	Invoke -ve Affect (triggered by the antagonist); invoke -ve Judge antagonist	INVO	Upscaling	Monogloss
		4	我打..打那个那个救命针呢还给我	I had.. I had the life-saving injection.. they gave me	Evoke	Invoke -ve Affect (triggered by the antagonist); invoke -ve Judge antagonist	INVO	Upscaling	Monogloss
		5	我差点死了	I almost died	Evoke	Invoke -ve Affect (triggered by the antagonist); invoke -ve Judge antagonist	INVO	Upscaling	Monogloss
37	Hostess_ H03	1	为什么	Why					

38	Wife_ H03_AW	1	我气成那样啊	Because I was so **angry**	Attitudinal instance of inscribed affect (potential invocation of-ve judgement)	Inscribe -veAffect (triggered by the antagonist); invoke -ve Judge antagonist	NATA	Upscaling	Monogloss
		2	他不给我解释	He did not explain it to me	Denial	Invoke -ve Judge antagonist	INVO	No-scaling	Monogloss
		3	我跟他说的时候..他就跑	Whenever I talked to him.. he ran	Contrast	Invoke -ve Judge antagonist	INVO	Upscaling	Heterogloss: Contract: Disclaim
		4	跑..一天不着家的	He ran away.. without coming back home for a whole day	Denial	Invoke -ve Judge antagonist	INVO	Upscaling	Monogloss
		5	不着家	He didn't stay at home	Denial	Invoke -ve Judge antagonist	INVO	No-scaling	Monogloss
		6	不管你	He didn't care about you	Denial	Invoke -ve Jjudge antagonist	INVO	No-scaling	Monogloss
		7	我从一个女孩子120斤嫁到他家去	I was a girl of 60 kgs when I married him					
		8	一下子瘦成88斤	I suddenly lost my weight to 44 kgs	Contrast	Invoke -ve Affect (triggered by the antagonist); invoke -ve Judge antagonist[e]	INVO	Upscaling	Monogloss

[a]Example adapted from Xu (2024), pp. 693–719. Reused with permission

[a]The upscaling is realised by the adverb 也 (yě, too). Chao (1965, p. 781) proposes that也 can be used as an adverb of evaluation, meaning 'to one's unpleasant surprise'. Ding et al. proposes that (1999, p. 192) 也 can be used in a '连(lián) … 也' formulation to mean 'even', indicating a sense of counter-expectancy. The first lexicon 连(lián) can be omitted. Moreover, Lü (1999, pp. 596–597) argues that besides expressing counter-expectancy, when 也 is used before negation, it adds the force to the proposition. In this utterance, the 也 is used in a '连(lián) … 也 + negation' pattern, with 连(lián) being omitted, to realise the GRADUATION option of upscaling and the ENGAGEMENT option of contractive disclamation

(continued)

Excerpt 5.9 (continued)

[c]The attitude signal in this utterance is 'evoke' because the experiential meaning—'a married man and a woman talking and laughing together'—is suggestive for a flirtatious relationship between the two. For an audience holding that 'Playful flirting with an opposite sex brings harm to the intimate relationship', the experiential meaning has the potential to activate a negative Judgement directed at the husband for his crossing the line. Accordingly, the upscaling device—'经常 always'—amplifies this attitudinal positioning

[d]According to Turn 37–38, the wife was extremely angry with the husband's relationship with the female neighbour. In this turn, the wife provided details of her physical condition as a result of her anger. In this utterance, she reported that she was angry to such an extent that she couldn't eat. The experiential meaning of her not being able to eat has the potential to invoke her negative Affectual response to the husband's behaviour, which then invoke a negative Judgement directed at the husband. The same meaning-making mechanism applies to all the rest utterances in this turn

[e]In this utterance, the wife reports that she lost considerable amount of weight as a result of her anger towards the husband's behaviours. This experiential meaning has the potential to invoke her negative Affectual response to the husband's behaviour, which then invoke a negative Judgement directed at the husband

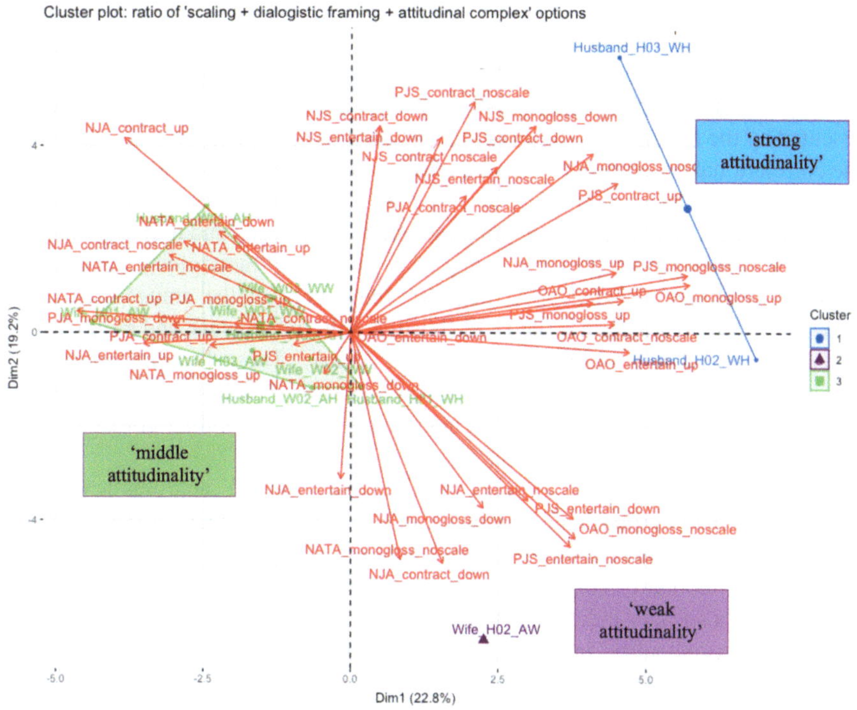

Fig. 5.6 Disputant clustering as to the ratios of 40 'scaling + dialogistic framing + attitudinal complex' options

and characterised. The disputant clusters indicate a certain degree of commonality of the disputants' self-presentation and observable variations of the disputants' attitudinal positioning preference.

Figure 5.6 visualises the clustering of the disputants in the dataset under this investigation (PCA) method (as discussed in previous sections). This visualisation serves as an additional presentation of the findings to the language descriptions provided so far. This figure is a Principal Component Analysis biplot illustrating the variations among the speakers in the dataset. A brief introduction to the key information presented in this type of PCA biplot—including the speakers and their clusters, the variables (i.e., the 'scaling + dialogistic framing + attitudinal complex' options), and the two axes and four quadrants—can be found in Chap. 4. In Fig. 5.6, the horizontal axis illustrates the first dimension, accounting for 22.8% of the variation in the dataset. The vertical axis represents the second dimension, accounting for 19.2% of the variation in the dataset. Therefore, this clustering method captures 42% of the variation for an analysis of 40 different variables.

There is a certain degree of covariation between the speakers' 'attitudinality' and their waywardness. Both disputants featuring 'strong attitudinality' were wayward spouses, and the 'weak attitudinality' disputant was an aggrieved spouse. Most disputants opted for construing a 'middle attitudinality'. Broadly speaking, there was a tendency for the wayward spouses to have stronger attitudinality and the aggrieved spouses weaker attitudinality.

Besides disputant clusters, Fig. 5.6 reveals some correlations among the framing options: which options tend to co-occur. In the figure, the framing options are represented by the red arrows. The closer the distance between two arrows, the stronger the correlational co-occurrence between the two attitudinal propositions is. It can be observed that some options tend to co-occur. For example, the nine red arrows pointing towards the bottom-right direction are monoglossed and non-scaled NATA (negative Affect triggered by the antagonist), contracted/monoglossed/entertained and downscaled/non-scaled NJA (negative Judgement of the antagonist), entertained and downscaled/non-scaled PJS (positive self-Judgement), and monoglossed and non-scaled OAO (observed antagonist's Affect). These framing options co-occur in the 'weak attitudinality' disputants' speech. Similarly, a bundle of red arrows pointing towards the top-right direction represent the options co-occurring in the 'strong attitudinality' disputants' speech.

The exportations and the findings in the above 'framing' analyses lead me to propose a 'cline of attitudinality', which can be used to systematically identify and describe the variations regarding the disputants' framing of attitudinal complexes. The term 'attitudinality', drawing on White (2019), refers to the degree of authorial involvement a speaker indicates when advancing attitudinal assessments. As noted above, the 'attitudinality' includes at least two dimensions of strength: (1) the assertiveness (realised by the dialogistic framing devices of ENGAGEMENT) and (2) the forcefulness (realised by the scaling devices of GRADUATION). Two aspects can be used to consider the degree of a speaker's degree of 'attitudinality'. The first aspect is their overall preference for the framing devices when presenting an attitudinal expression. As illustrated by the findings in my dataset, a speaker's 'attitudinality' may be raised or heightened either by a tendency to upscale their attitudinal assessments or categorically assert them. They could also choose to maximise the heightening of the 'attitudinality' by combining both tendencies—frequently using categorical assertion and intensification when conveying attitudinal assessments. Likewise, a speaker's 'attitudinality' may be weakened or lowered by a tendency to downscale attitudinal assertions or 'entertain' them, with the weakening maximised if the tendencies in downscaling and entertaining are deployed simultaneously. The second aspect considers which attitudinal assessments the speaker tends to invest with additional authorial involvement and whether the attitudinal assessments are arguably directly related to the speaker's primary concern. As discussed throughout this chapter and the previous chapter, the primary concern for the disputants in these interactions was to condemn the antagonist and commend their own behaviour or character. Accordingly, a speaker's 'attitudinality' may be raised or heightened by a tendency to intensify or categorically assert their negative Judgement of the antagonist and positive self-assessment. In a similar vein, their 'attitudinality' may be weakened or lowered if they tend to upscale or monogloss other types of attitudinal expressions (e.g., positive Judgement of other people or negative Affectual response triggered by the antagonist). Their 'attitudinality' would be maximised, either in

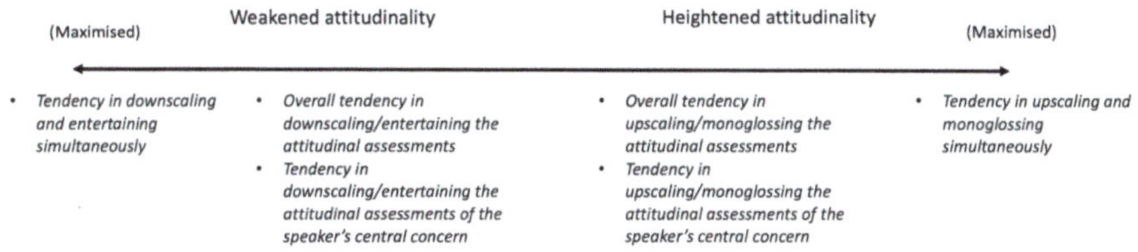

Fig. 5.7 Cline of attitudinality

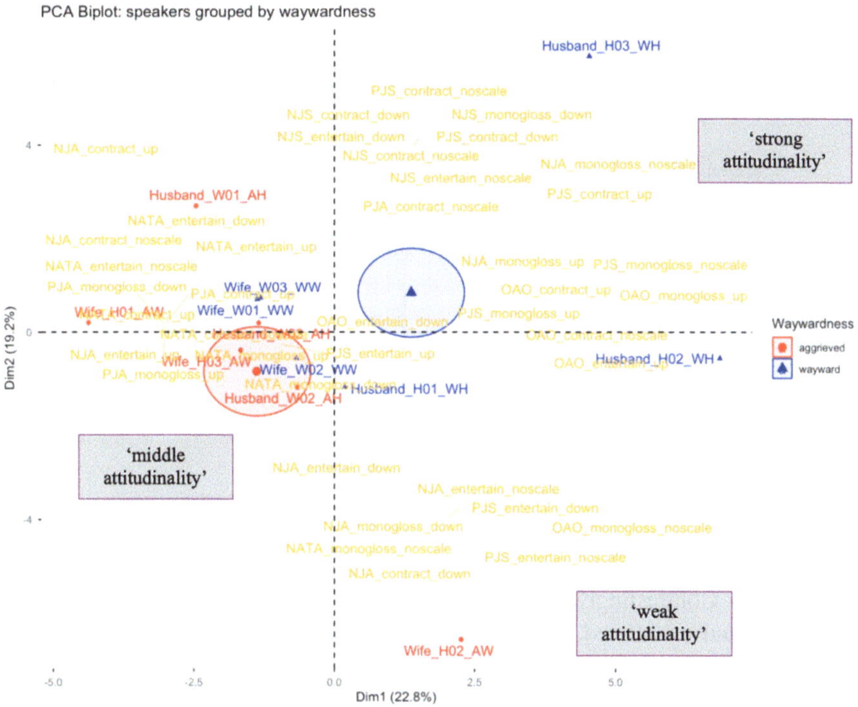

Fig. 5.8 Covariation between the speakers' attitudinality and waywardness

terms of heightening or weakening, by their tendencies in deploying the two resources simultaneously. This 'cline of attitudinality' is illustrated in Fig. 5.7.

Readers might be curious about the connection between the disputants' attitudinal variations and their metadata, particularly their waywardness and gender. For example, whether wayward spouses exhibit certain attitudinal tendencies while aggrieved spouses lean towards others, and whether the spouses' attitudinality correlates with their gender.

The covariation between the speakers' attitudinality and waywardness is illustrated in Fig. 5.8, a PCA biplot. Generally, wayward spouses (indicated by blue triangles) demonstrate stronger attitudinality, while aggrieved spouses (marked by red dots) display weaker attitudinality. In other words, wayward spouses tend to

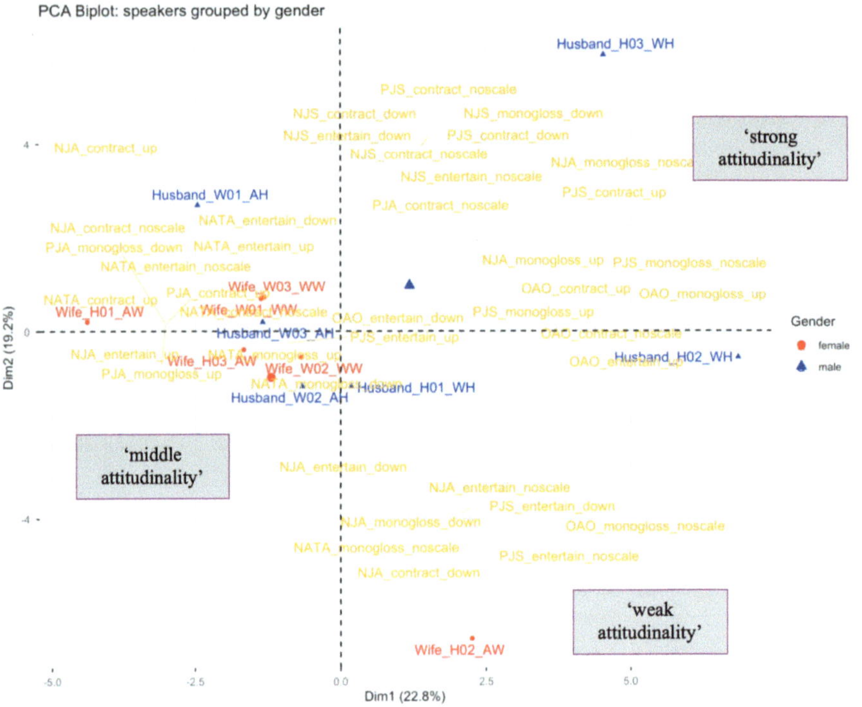

Fig. 5.9 Covariation between the speakers' attitudinality and gender

amplify and assert their attitudinal assessments, particularly those connected to their central concerns. As a result, they project a confrontational and defensive self-presentation. Contrastingly, aggrieved spouses typically present their evaluations as negotiable and moderated, avoiding direct negative assessments of their counterparts. Instead, they express their negative emotions triggered by the antagonists, inviting mediators to assign blame. This leads them to portray themselves as emotionally victimised and seeking reconciliation.

Regarding the covariation between attitudinality and gender, Fig. 5.9 reveals no clear patterns. The data shows a relatively even distribution of both male and female participants throughout the PCA biplot, with no notable distinctions between the two gender groups.

It should be noted that the sample size of 12 disputants in the dataset is relatively mall to draw definitive conclusions regarding the covariation between a disputant's linguistic choice, waywardness or gender. Nevertheless, these findings offer indicative insights into how disputing spouses convey attitudes in family mediation. These insights can inform mediators in adjusting their mediation strategies.

As a side note, it might be interesting to report that a sister study published in Xu (2024) also conducts a disputants' variation analysis on the same dataset with similar data mining methods, but with different treatment of the explicitness of attitudes.

While the analysis reported by the current book focuses exclusively on the framing of attitudinal inscriptions, Xu (2024) includes both attitudinal inscriptions and invocations. The invocations encompass positive and negative invocations directed at the self and the antagonist, identifying 43 possible 'scaling + dialogistic framing + attitudinal complex' combinations within the dataset. Although the clustering of the disputants and covariation patterns between attitudinal types and metadata remain consistent with the findings reported here, the similarities between the two studies demonstrate the 'prosodic structure of interpersonal meanings' (Halliday, 1979). Linguistic items having highly stable attitudinal value can attitudinally 'color the surrounding text, telling us how to interpret meanings that are not "emically" evaluative' (Martin, 2008, p. 117).

Up to this point, I have reported the findings concerning the tendencies in how the disputants framed their attitudinal expressions, findings arising from the second line of inquiry in exploring the disputants' attitudinal disposition construction from a synoptic view. In this synoptic exploration, I examined the similarities and differences in the disputants' use of attitudes (expressions explicitly or implicitly conveying or activating positive or negative assessments) and their framing of these attitudes (via any scaling and dialogistic positioning resources). The analyses tracked the variations in the speaker's construal of attitudinal positioning via the deployment of ATTITUDE, GRADUATION, and ENGAGEMENT resources as schematised by the Appraisal literature. The analyses identified and characterised multiple tendencies in the disputants' deployment of these attitude-associated resources, revealing commonalities in the dataset suggesting a certain degree of predictability of how people discursively present themselves in similar adversarial situations. Some patterns suggest a wide range of variations among the disputants. Some tendencies also lead to groupings of the disputants, indicating sub-types of attitudinal disposition. Synthesising all the findings arising from these two synoptic lines of inquiry, I arrived at the conclusion that discursive identity construction must be seen as multifaceted, which is discussed in detail in the following section.

6 A Multifacetedness of Attitudinal Disposition from a Synoptic View

Chapters 4 and this chapter have presented findings that underscore the multifaceted nature of attitudinal disposition from a synoptic perspective. The integration of two perspectives—the disputants' preference in attitudes and framing of attitudes—reveals that attitudinal disposition must be understood as complex.

The complexity is evident through the existence of multiple attitudinal disposition types within the dataset, which emerges from the various clusters observed across different lines of inquiry. The exploration into the disputants' self-presentation involves examination along multiple parameters of variation (e.g., negative judgement of the antagonist, upscaled negative judgement of the antagonist, and so on). Each attitudinal axis can operate independently as a parameter of variation. Additionally, bundles or combinations of multiple attitudinal axes are used to investigate the variability among disputants in the dataset (e.g., inscribed negative judgment of the antagonist and invoked positive self-judgement). The findings demonstrate that regardless of the chosen parameters, there is always potential for identifying and characterising multiple disputant clusters, although the boundaries between these clusters are not distinct. Some clusters include a significant proportion of speakers, suggesting commonalities in their meaning-making choices within this marital conflict reality television context, while others consist only of subsets of speakers, indicating patterned variations in their choice of meanings. The results provide evidence that while language choice is theoretically conditioned by situational variables, there remains considerable room for personal preference and the construction of different 'selves' or aspects of 'self' through the use of attitude-associated resources. Notably, despite being generally confrontational, disputants demonstrated multiple attitudinal dispositions in their interactions. This finding offers valuable insights to our understanding of discursive persona construction from a social semiotic perspective, highlighting how the same meaning potential conditioned by context can distribute unevenly among language users, leading to the construal of different types of discourse personas.

In addition to the multiplicity of attitudinal disposition types among disputants, our analysis also reveals the multifaceted nature of each individual's attitudinal disposition. Take, for instance, Husband_H02_WH. His deployment of attitude-associated resources can be interpreted as having a complex and dynamic representation of his attitudinal 'self'. When examined from the perspective of monoglossed negative Judgement of the antagonist, he stands out with an exceptionally high ratio of 14.2% in the dataset, signifying that he portrays himself as an assertive combatant. In contrast, when focusing on upscaled negative Judgement towards the antagonist, Husband_H02_WH's 8.7% share of attitudinal instances presents him as a forceful combatant. Furthermore, when the occurrence of the attitudinal complex is concerned, Husband_H02_WH is classified as a 'wide range' disputant, making full use of the meaning-making resources available. In terms of the framed attitudinal complex options, Husband_H02_WH is characterised as a 'strong attitudinality' speaker, exhibiting relatively higher levels of assertiveness and forcefulness compared to other participants in the dataset. The case of Husband_H02_WH exemplifies how one individual can be described as presenting different facets of their 'self' under varying analytical methods. There is no inherent superiority or authenticity attributed to any single facet; these diverse attitudinal dispositions are simply distinct aspects of a person and their linguistic choices. For a comprehensive understanding of someone's discursive self-presentation, it becomes imperative to approach the person's language use through multiple perspectives.

The above observations were made when the disputants' use of attitude-associated resources was examined from a synoptic perspective. Similar multifacetedness was also observed when their language use was explored from a dynamic perspective, the findings of which will be reported in Chap. 6 and 7.

7 Chapter Summary

This chapter has reported findings relating to the project's first line of inquiry into the disputants' attitudinal self-presentation—a synoptic analysis of attitudinal disposition which explored the disputants' preferences in framing the attitudinal expressions across a complete textual stage—the Problem Discussion stage. The chapter has reported tendencies among the disputants vis-à-vis the speaker's construal of attitudinal positioning via the deployment of ATTITUDE, GRADUATION, and ENGAGEMENT resources as schematised by the Appraisal literature.

The study was divided into three stages, focusing on the scaling (choices from the GRADUATION system in Appraisal), the dialogistic framing (choices from the ENGAGEMENT system in Appraisal), and the co-occurrence of scaling and dialogistic framing of the attitudinal complexes, respectively. In the first two stages, I detailed the available 'scaling/dialogistic framing + attitudinal complex' options found within the dataset, highlighting both frequent and less commonly used choices that showed a degree of commonality across the data. Variations emerged when considering each option or pair of options as parameters for analysis, along with differences in preferences observed between spouses categorised as wayward versus aggrieved.

The third stage examined how disputants simultaneously employed scaling and dialogistic framing devices to convey attitudinal orientations, identifying 40 possible 'scaling + dialogistic framing + attitudinal complex' combinations within the dataset and applying a multivariate analysis. The clustering arising from the analyses revealed variability in the 'attitudinality' where the disputants raised or heightened their attitudinal positioning by intensifying/categorically asserting the attitudinal complexes and weakened or lowered the positioning by downscaling or entertaining the attitudinal assertions. The disputants varied regarding whether they demonstrated a 'strong attitudinality', 'middle attitudinality', or 'weak attitudinality'.

The findings reported in this chapter are summarised in Table 5.9.

The findings revealed substantial variation in how the disputants' advanced their attitudinal assessments of the different targets: the framing resources they employed, the combinations they favoured, and the frequencies of these choices. Despite these variations, there was no straightforward answer regarding whether certain subgroups of disputants consistently used similar attitudinal constructs while differing from others. Rather, the disputants exhibited similarity or dissimilarity in relative rather than absolute terms.

The findings presented here and those from the preceding chapter contribute to our understanding of the synoptic perspective on the disputants' construction of discursive attitudinal disposition, which took the disputants' talk in the Problem Discussion stage as a complete text. The findings were synthesised as revealing the multifacetedness of discursive attitudinal disposition construction.

The following two chapters adopt a more dynamic view, examining how attitudinal dispositions evolve over time and across different mediation stages, when

Table 5.9 Summary of the three-stage analysis

Stage	Analysis	Key findings
2	Focus on the scaling of the attitudinal complex	1. Sixteen 'scaling + attitudinal complex' options 2. Three shared options: No-scaling/upscaling negative Judgement of the antagonist; no-scaling of negative Affect triggered by the antagonist 3. Observable in-group variation per single option/pair of options
3	Focus on the dialogistic framing of the attitudinal complex	1. Seventeen 'dialogistic framing + attitudinal complex' options 2. Four shared options: Monoglossed/contracted negative Judgement of the antagonist; Monoglossed/contracted negative Affect triggered by the antagonist 3. Observable in-group variation per single option/pair of options
4	Focus on the scaling and dialogistic framing of the attitudinal complex	1. Forty 'scaling + dialogistic framing + attitudinal complex' options 2. Clustering vis-à-vis co-selection of multiple options: Variability in the attitudinality of the disputants' construal of their overall attitudinal positioning: Weak attitudinality; Middle attitudinality; Strong attitudinality 3. The wayward spouses tended to have stronger attitudinality, and the aggrieved spouses had weaker attitudinality.

interacting with different addressees, and as the interaction unfolds within the Problem Discussion stage itself. They explore the stability and adaptability of disputants' attitudinal orientations in these contexts.

References

Blake, R. R., & Mouton, J. S. (1964). *The managerial grid*. Gulf Publishing.

Chao, Y. R. (1965). *A grammar of spoken Chinese*. University of California Press.

Chinese Academy of Social Sciences Institute of Linguistics. (2017). 现代汉语词典 *Xiandai Hanyu Cidian [Modern Chinese dictionary]*. Commercial Press.

Ding S. et al. (1999). 现代汉语语法讲话 *Xiandai Hanyu Yufa Jianghua* [Talks on modern Chinese grammar]. Commercial Press.

Don, A. (2016). "'It is hard to mesh all this": Invoking attitude, persona and argument organisation. *Functional linguistics*, *3*, 9(9). Available at: https://doi.org/10.1186/s40554-016-0033-1

Halliday, M. A. K. (1979). Modes of meaning and modes of expression: Types of grammatical structure and their determination by different semantic functions. In D. J. Allerton, E. Carney, & D. Holdcroft (Eds.), *Function and context in linguistic analysis: A festshrift for William Haas* (pp. 57–79). Cambridge University Press.

Hood, S., & Martin, J. R. (2007). Invoking attitude: The play of graduation in appraising discourse. In R. Hasan, C. M. I. M. Matthiessen, & J. J. Webster (Eds.), *Continuing discourse on language: A functional perspective* (pp. 739–764). Equinox Publishing Ltd. Available at: https://journals.equinoxpub.com/books/article/view/25351

Husson, F. et al. (2020) *FactoMineR: Multivariate exploratory data analysis and data mining*. Available at: http://factominer.free.fr

Kassambara, A., & Mundt, F. (2020). F*actoextra: Extract and visualize the results of multivariate data analyses*. Available at: http://www.sthda.com/english/rpkgs/factoextra

Lê, S., Josse, J., & Husson, F. (2008). FactoMineR: A package for multivariate analysis. *Journal of Statistical Software, 25*(1), 1–18. https://doi.org/10.18637/jss.v025.i01

Lü, S. (1999). 现代汉语八百词 *Xiandai Hanyu Babaici* [800 Words of modern Chinese]. Commercial Press.

Macken-Horarik, M., & Isaac, A. R. (2014). Appraising appraisal. In G. Thompson & L. Alba-Juez (Eds.), *Evaluation in context* (pp. 67–92). John Benjamins Publishing Company. https://doi.org/10.1075/pbns.242.04mac

Martin, J. R. (2008). What kind of structure?—Interpersonal meaning and prosodic realization across strata. *Word, 59*(1–2), 111–141. https://doi.org/10.1080/00437956.2008.11432583

Martin, J. R. (2010). Semantic variation: Modelling realisation, instantiation and individuation in social semiosis. In M. Bednarek & J. R. Martin (Eds.), *New discourse on language: Functional perspectives on multimodality, identity, and affiliation* (pp. 1–34). Bloomsbury Publishing.

Rahim, M. A. (2023). *Managing conflict in organizations* (5th ed.). Routledge. https://doi.org/10.4324/9781003285861

Thompson, G. (2014). Affect and emotion, target-value mismatches, and Russian dolls: Refining the appraisal model. In G. Thompson & L. Alba-Juez (Eds.), *Evaluation in context* (pp. 47–66). John Benjamins Publishing Company (Pragmatics & Beyond New Series).

White, P. R. R. (1998). *Telling media Tales: The news story as rhetoric* (Doctoral Thesis). University of Sydney.

White, P. R. R. (2003). Beyond modality and hedging: A dialogic view of the language of intersubjective stance. *Text, 23*(2), 259–284. https://doi.org/10.1515/text.2003.011

White, P. R. R. (2012). Exploring the axiological workings of "reporter voice" news stories—Attribution and attitudinal positioning. *Discourse, Context & Media, 1*(2–3), 57–67. https://doi.org/10.1016/j.dcm.2012.10.004

White, P. R. R. (2016). Evaluative contents in verbal communication. In *Verbal communication*. De Gruyter Mouton. https://doi.org/10.1515/9783110255478-006

White, P. R. R. (2019). Journalistic warrantability in the age of "fake news"? - developing a linguistics-based epistemology/axiology of news discourse. *2019 ASFLA*, Sydney, Australia, 2 October.

Xu, Q. (2024). Identifying disputants' attitudinal variations in family mediations: A data mining approach. *Discourse Studies, 26*(5), 693–719. https://doi.org/10.1177/14614456241237378

Chapter 6
Fluid Styles: Logogenesis of Attitudinal Positioning

Contents

1 Introduction

The previous two chapters have presented findings and insights arising from a focus on the construction of the disputants' attitudinal disposition from a synoptic perspective. This chapter and the next chapter will shift the study's focus to the construction of the disputants' attitudinal disposition from a dynamic perspective. Chapter 1 has foreshadowed that the dynamic perspective towards the disputants' discursive self-presentation situates the disputants' talk into a logogenetic time-frame. The dynamic perspective is concerned with the 'ongoing creation of meaning in the unfolding of text' (Halliday & Matthiessen, 2014, p. 63). The dynamic view on constructing attitudinal dispositions emphasizes the stability or fluidity in the disputants' deployment of attitude-associated resources and aims to elucidate the gradual development of the disputants' discursive self-presentation within an unfolding multiparty adversarial interaction. The research questions guiding the analysis were broad, focusing on the disputants' attitudinal positioning throughout the entire mediation episode: (1) Did the disputants employ the same set of attitude-associated resources across different mediation stages? (2) When interacting with various addressees? (3) Moreover, are there observable changes in the

Q. Xu, *Appraisal Approach to Conflict Styles*, The M.A.K. Halliday Library Functional Linguistics Series, https://doi.org/10.1007/978-981-95-6256-5_6

attitude-associated resources favoured (used more frequently or less frequently) as the 20- to 30-minute Problem Discussion stage unfolds within a constant situational context? In essence, the dynamic perspective treats the construction of attitudinal disposition as an emerging process rather than as a collection of static choices throughout the text. (The results pertaining to questions 1 and 2 are presented in this chapter, whereas the findings related to question 3 can be found in Chap. 7).

Before initiating the discussion proper, it is crucial to acknowledge that the stability of a disputant's attitudinal arrangement is a matter of the scope of attention. When considering a disputant's utterances within the entire mediation episode as a cohesive unit, the disputant's global preference in attitude-associated resources generates a synoptic view of the disputant's attitudinal profile: an attitudinal disposition based on the totality of the disputant's linguistic choices (as elaborated in Chaps. 4 and 5). On the other hand, a disputant's attitudinal orientation (which options for advancing attitudinal meanings were favoured and which were disfavoured) can also be examined more closely by focusing on specific segmented texts or phases of the interaction.[1] I employ the term 'local attitudinal disposition' to refer to recurring patterns in the disputant's attitudinal meaning-making arrangements within a particular span or shorter segment of text. It is this local sense of attitudinal disposition that is central to the current chapter. For convenience, the attitudinal disposition characterised by a disputant's global linguistic choices is labelled 'synoptic disposition' or 'regular disposition', and any local attitudinal disposition departing from their synoptic disposition will be termed a 'disposition shift'.

This chapter examines the stability of the disputants' attitudinal disposition from two angles when there is a change in the context of situation. Specifically, Sect. 2 reports findings on the stability of the disputants' attitudinal disposition across different mediation stages (different segments within the mediation episode), followed by Sect. 3 which is concerned with disposition shifts among the disputants in response to changes in their addressee. Due to space constraints, these two sections concentrate on attitudinal disposition stability with respect to the types of the attitudes advanced and the targets of the attitudes (without examining tendencies in the framing of these attitudes, as Chap. 5 did).

[1] In this monograph, the term 'phase' is used non-technically to denote segments or chunks of texts where a disputant tends to maintain relatively similar evaluative arrangements. It's worth noting that the divisions made between these phases are made in a somewhat loose sense, rather than being guided by a principled genre analysis, which is outside the scope of the present study.

2 Attitudinal Disposition Stability Across Different Mediation Stages

This section is concerned with the stability of the disputants' attitudinal disposition across different mediation stages. As mentioned in Chap. 3, there are five mediation stages within each family dispute resolution episode, and this section's analysis explored the disputants' attitudinal orientation in three specific stages: (1) Problem Discussion, (2) Private Mediation, and (3) Post-mediation. These stages were chosen because they are characterised by direct interactions between the disputing spouses and the mediators.

2.1 Describing the Three Stages

The three stages, having different registerial features, constitute different communicative contexts. Specifically, while all the stages share the same Mode of the text (face-to-face unscripted conversation), they differ in their Field and Tenor features.

The Problem Discussion stage involves a large TV studio setting where the disputants converse directly with their spouse and the hostess before the mediation panel, but without mediator intervention. Here, the Field of discourse comprises: (1) the disputants' outlines of their concerns, grievances, complaints, and versions of events; (2) confrontations between the disputants over accusations or defence of past actions; and (3) facilitation and elicitation by the hostess. The Tenor of discourse is characterised by the interpersonal relationships between the two disputing spouses and the hostess. Generally, the disputing spouses enjoyed equal 'status'[2] in that they participated equally in discussions and had equal access to meaning-making resources, refraining from adopting dominant or subordinate roles within their interactions with each other. Their language exchanges suggest they were in close 'contact' experientially—having many common experiences. In terms of attitude, they were largely disaligned at least regarding their views on personal behaviour but may have shared other values or attitudes. In contrast, the disputants and hostess had different status dynamics, with the hostess holding a dominant position in guiding the interaction's course.

In contrast, the Private Mediation stage takes place in a small mediation room where one disputant directly communicates privately with one mediator. The Field of the discourse involves (1) comments and advice from the mediator and (2) the disputant's response to these comments. In this context, Tenor reflects unequal and deferential status in terms of who controlled the conversation.

Finally, the Post-mediation stage occurs in the main TV studio where all participants (disputing spouses, hostess, and mediators) convers. The Field of discourse

[2] The notions of 'status' and 'contact' are borrowed from Martin's model of Tenor, as described in Martin (1992). For a more detailed discussion, please refer to Chap. 3.

includes (1) the disputants' declaring their decisions following the mediation (e.g., to make some changes and continue with the relationship or to divorce the partner); (2) concluding remarks by the master mediator; and (3) facilitation from the hostess. The Tenor is similar to that of the Problem Discussion stage.

Table 6.1 summarises the contextual characterisation for each of the three mediation stages.

2.2 *The Subset of Attitudinal Complexes to Explore the Disposition Shift*

Perhaps unsurprisingly, a key finding was that, across these three different segments of the episode, the disputants made different use of the attitude-associated resource available to them, and hence could be seen to be enacting distinct attitudinal dispositions in these different contextual settings. Due to space constraints, this section will focus on an analysis of the speakers' expressions of attitude, specifically examining a subset of attitudinal complexes used by the disputants. The seven attitudinal complexes examined for this purpose include:

(1) Inscribed positive Judgement of the antagonist (PJA);
(2) Inscribed negative Judgement of the antagonist (NJA);
(3) Inscribed positive Judgement of the self (PJS);

Table 6.1 The contextual characterisation of three mediation stages

<table>
<tr><th></th><th colspan="2">Problem Discussion</th><th colspan="2">Private Mediation</th><th colspan="2">Post-mediation</th></tr>
<tr><td>Field</td><td colspan="2">The disputants' outlines of their concern; confrontations between the disputants; the hostess's elicitation and facilitation</td><td colspan="2">The mediator's comments and advice; the disputant's response</td><td colspan="2">The disputants' decisions; the master mediator's concluding remarks; the hostess's facilitation</td></tr>
<tr><td rowspan="2">Tenor</td><td>Between the two disputing spouses:</td><td>Equal status/close social contact/attitudinally disaligned</td><td rowspan="2">Between the disputant and the mediator:</td><td rowspan="2">Unequal and deferential status/distant social contact/each disputant seeks attitudinal alignment with the mediators</td><td>Between the two disputing spouses:</td><td>Equal status/close social contact</td></tr>
<tr><td>Between the disputants and the hostess:</td><td>Unequal and deferential status/distant social contact/each disputant seeks attitudinal alignment with the hostess (eventually the mediators)</td><td>Between the disputants and the hostess/master mediator:</td><td>Unequal and deferential status/distant social contact</td></tr>
<tr><td>Mode</td><td colspan="6">Face-to-face unscripted conversation</td></tr>
</table>

(4) Inscribed negative Judgement of the self (NJS);
(5) Inscribed negative Affectual response triggered by the antagonist or the antagonist's behaviour (NATA);
(6) Inscribed observed Affectual response of the antagonist (OAO);
(7) Invocation.

The first six attitudinal complexes examined in this analysis are identical to those discussed in the framing analysis of the attitudinal disposition in the previous chapter. Justifying a narrower focus on these particular complexes is their pivotal role within the disputants' attitudinal orientation, as they primarily involve conveying assessments with both negative and positive valencies through criticisms of one's spouse and defences of personal behaviour. This analysis refers to the classification of the attitudinal complexes according to variations across four attitudinal axes: type of attitude, polarity (positive or negative), explicitness (whether the attitude is explicitly stated or not), and target/trigger. For a detailed explanation of these axes and their application in this context, please see Chap. 5.

In addition to the above six attitudinal complexes discussed, this disposition shift analysis also considered invoked attitudinal complexes. Here, un-inscribed attitudinal instances (assessments that were to be 'provoked' or 'evoked' by an attitudinal signal, rather than being explicitly articulated) were treated as a broader category of attitudinal complex under the umbrella term of 'invocation', primarily for three reasons. Firstly, this approach was particularly suitable for a dynamic analysis of the disputants' attitudinal disposition. In examining how disputants deployed attitudinal complexes within an evolving interaction, it was crucial to have a background or backdrop that against which their attitudinal profiles could be mapped, highlighted, and analysed. Ideally, this backdrop should encompass all attitudinal instances in a given turn or phase of the exchange, including both inscriptions and invocations. By incorporating invoked attitudinal instances into the analysis, it was possible to gain insight into the totality of attitudinal dynamics within the segment as it unfolded. Invoking expressions provided a backdrop for and context in which to understand primarily inscribed attitudinal expressions. Without referencing these invocations, it would be impossible to accurately chart the density of attitudinal meanings advanced at any point during the development of the given segment. Therefore, by incorporating this background of invoked attitude into the analysis, it became possible to track the stability or change in how disputants employed inscribed attitudinal complexes, which were central to their attitudinal stance.

Secondly, treating invoked attitudinal instances as a bundle under the category of 'invocation' was justified by their similar nature in terms of mechanism—using an attitudinal signal to invite interpretation rather than directly expressing an attitude with positive or negative polarity. As discussed in Chaps. 3 and 4, invocations are relatively less attitudinally stable than inscriptions and potentially afford multiple interpretations. This approach allowed for accurate recording of all attitudinally meaningful instances without assigning speculative attitudes to individual invocations, thereby respecting the speaker's intention and choice in constructing their attitudinal position.

Finally, from a dynamic perspective, including invoked attitudinal instances was significant because it revealed variations among disputants in their preferred methods of advancing attitudinal positioning. While some participants showed stability in their preference for invocation or inscription over time, others exhibited changes in their preferences across different phases of the interaction. For instance, they might shift from implicit to explicit expression of attitudes at certain points. This consideration of invoked attitudinal instances added depth to the dynamic analysis by highlighting the complexities and nuances in disputants' strategies for constructing and communicating their attitudinal dispositions.

As explored in Chap. 4, the attitudinal disposition deployed within a particular mediation stage can be characterised by the combinations of attitudinal complexes a disputant favours (used or used more often) or disfavour (not used or used less often) during that mediation stage. The number of attitudinal complexes present in the disputants' talk reflects the range of resources the disputant drawn upon for conveying attitude from the available repertoire. The more attitudinal complexes employed, the broader their attitudinal range. Additionally, the ratio of use of a particular attitudinal complex or combination (as a percentage of the total number of complexes deployed by a given disputant) indicates the degree to which that particular attitudinal complex or combination is preferred. For instance, the disputants with a high ratio of negative Affectual responses triggered by the antagonist can be seen as projecting themselves as emotional victims of their relationship issues. Those with a strong preference for inscribed positive self-Judgement can be characterised as self-promoting individuals. By examining the occurrence and preference for attitudinal complexes within a specific mediation stage, it is possible to describe and classify the attitudinal disposition constructed during that time frame. Any differences in these dispositions across different stages result in shifts in attitude between those stages.

2.3 General Patterns

Disposition shifts were found in all the disputants' speech. The was a general tendency across the disputants to 'favour' (use or use more often) one subset of attitudinal complexes in one stage of the mediation and opt for a different subset of attitudinal complexes in another stage. No disputant in the dataset enacted the same attitudinal disposition in all the three mediation stages. The disputants' attitudinal orientations at different mediation stages are illustrated in Fig. 6.1, which visualises the ratio of use of a particular attitudinal complex in a disputant's speech. The x-axis illustrates the three mediation stages in three columns. From left to right are the Problem Discussion, Private Mediation, and Post-mediation stages, respectively. The y-axis indicates the ratio of use of a specific attitudinal complex in the total attitudinal instances of a disputant's talk in that stage. The attitudinal complexes are coloured bars with the colour legend on the right hand of the figure.

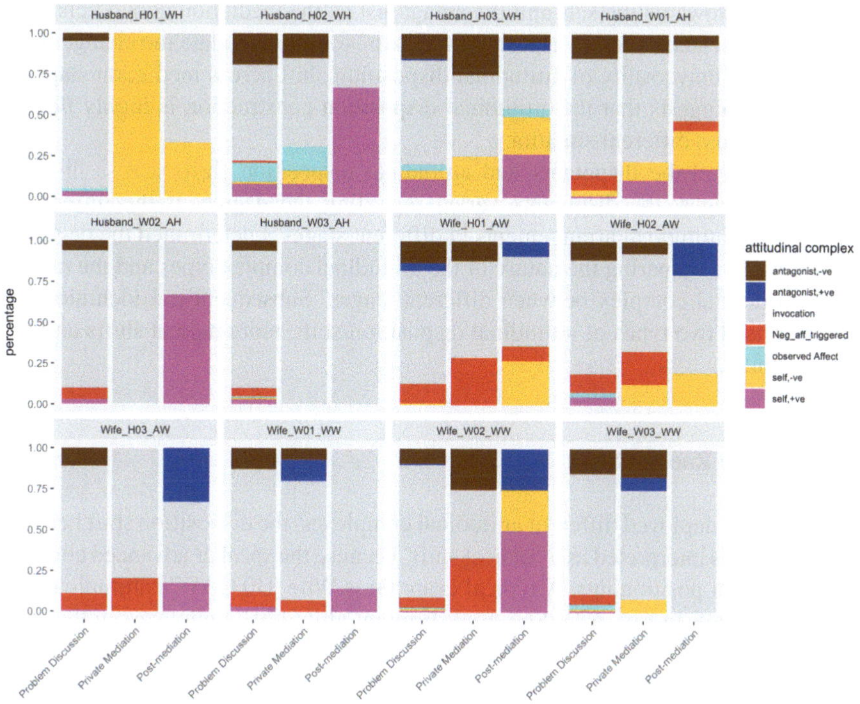

Fig. 6.1 Disputants' attitudinal orientations in different mediation stages

Take Husband_H01_WH's (top left in the figure) attitudinal profiles as a way of illustration. During the Problem Discussion stage (first column on the left), he heavily favoured invocations (grey bar) rather than inscriptions. He had only a few attitudinal inscriptions, including negative Judgement of the antagonist (brown bar), observed antagonist's Affect (cyan bar), and positive self-Judgment (pink bar). He presented an aspect of the 'self' that was not expressive in attitudinal positioning and construal a like-minded audience who would infer the husband's attitudes from his implicit signals. In contrast, when the husband spoke directly to the mediator in the Private Mediation stage (second column), he became very expressive by advancing only instances of inscribed negative self-Judgment (yellow bar). He construed another aspect of the 'self', a 'self' that frequently self-blamed and was therefore presented as willing to reconcile. Finally, in the Post-mediation stage (third column), two-thirds of the husband's attitudinal expressions were invocations (grey bar), and one-third were inscribed negative self-Judgement (yellow bar). He presented both the 'not expressive' and the 'self-blaming' aspects of the 'self' again, indicating his through these negatively assessing himself signalled an openness to conciliation. In short, Husband_H01_WH, as summarised in the figure, performed different aspects of the 'self' at different mediation stages.

It is observable from the figure that all the disputants have different attitudinal arrangements in different mediation stages. They deployed different attitudinal positionings towards the self and the antagonist as the mediation context changes, and they presented different aspects of the 'self' to accommodate the change in the context. The universality of attitudinal disposition shift across mediation stages in the dataset suggests that the attitudinal disposition construction is highly flexible and fluid across different situations.

Although all the disputants had attitudinal disposition shifts across different mediation stages, the disputants varied regarding the degree of the differences between the attitudinal arrangements in different stages. I determined the degree of difference by comparing the nature of the attitudinal complex types and the ratio of each attitudinal complex between different stages. Subsequently, I identified and characterised two types of attitudinal disposition shift: more radical shifts and less radical shifts.

2.3.1 More Radical Shift

If a disputant deployed different attitudinal complexes, the disposition shift between the stages was interpreted as a 'radical shift' because the speaker advanced contrasting attitudinal positionings. A typical example is Wife_H03_AW's attitudinal profile (bottom left in Fig. 6.1). She used different attitudinal complexes in the three mediation stages. She deployed a combination of three attitudinal complex types (inscribed negative Judgement directed the antagonist, negative Affectual responses triggered by the antagonist, and invocation) in the Problem Discussion stage, enacting a 'self' that was overwhelmingly confrontational and emotionally victimised (exemplified by Excerpt 6.1). In the Private Mediation stage, she only used invocations, relying on the mediator to infer her attitudinal stance (exemplified by Excerpt 6.2). In sharp contrast, in the Post Mediation stage, she had a number of instances of positive assessment—both inscribed positive Judgement of her spouse and positive self-Judgement. Her invocations had the potential to eventually activate positive assessments of the self and the antagonist (exemplified by Excerpt 6.3). Subsequently, she switched into what I term a 'praiser', a radical change from her 'self' in the other two stages. (See the book's GitHub repository for a full analysis of her language.)

2.3.2 Less Radical Shift

In contrast, if a disputant was observed deploying the same attitudinal complexes but with different ratios in different stages, the disposition shift between the stages was characterised as 'less radical'. The speaker advanced fundamentally the same attitudinal position or stance but with a different level of preference for that positioning. Take Husband_W01_AH's profile as an illustration (top right in Fig. 6.1). He deployed the same set of attitudinal complexes in the three stages (i.e., inscribed negative Judgement of the antagonist, inscribed negative/positive self-Judgement, negative Affectual responses triggered by the antagonist, and invocation) but with

Excerpt 6.1 Wife_H03_AW's attitudinal profile in the Problem Discussion stage

Turn	Speaker	Move	Utterance (Chinese)	Utterance (English translation)	Attitude signal	Attitudinal complex
1	Hostess_ H03	1	两位今天来到金牌调解要解决什么问题	What problems do you want to resolve by coming to gold medal mediation today		
2	Wife_ H03	1	就我老公老是触犯我的底线	It's that my husband **crosses the line** all the time	Inscription	Inscribe -ve Judge antagonist
		2	特别不好受	I feel extremely **uncomfortable**	Attitudinal instance of inscribed Affect (potential invocation of -ve judgement)	Inscribe -ve Affect self (triggered by the antagonist); invoke -ve Judge antagonist
		3	我跟他到现在结婚三十一年	I have been married to him for 31 years now		
		4	没有一天安全感*[哭泣]*	I **don't have a sense of security** in any single day *[cry]*	Attitudinal instance of inscribed Affect (potential invocation of -ve Judgement)	Inscribe -ve Affect self (triggered by the antagonist); invoke -ve Judge antagonist

different ratios. Progressing from the Problem Discussion stage to the Post-mediation stage, his ratios of use of the three attitudinal complexes gradually decreased (i.e., inscribed negative Judgement of the antagonist, negative Affectual responses triggered by the antagonist, and invocation), indicating he became less confrontational but more explicit in his attitudinal positioning. Meanwhile, his ratios of two other attitudinal complexes (i.e., inscribed positive/negative self-Judgement) steadily increased from less than 10% in the Problem Discussion stage to almost 50% in the Post-mediation stage. The changes in the ratios of these attitudinal complexes revealed a shift in the attitudinal focus of the husband's attitudinal positioning. He gradually shifted from a confrontational and antagonist-oriented positioning to a more self-oriented positioning. Nonetheless, his overall confrontational stance remained unchanged because he deployed the same set of attitudinal complexes in the three stages. The husband's attitudinal arrangements in the three stages are exemplified by Excerpts 6.4, 6.5, and 6.6, respectively. Thus, it could be determined that Husband_W01_AH's attitudinal disposition shift is relatively less substantive compared to that of Wife_H03_AW. (See the book's GitHub repository for a full analysis of Husband_W01_AH's language.)

The variations regarding the degree of attitudinal disposition shift among the disputants in the dataset suggest a cline of disposition shifting (illustrated in Fig. 6.2). Whereas attitudinal disposition shifts might be expected when the

Excerpt 6.2 Wife_H03_AW's attitudinal profile in the Private Mediation stage

Turn	Speaker	Move	Utterance (Chinese)	Utterance (English translation)	Attitude signal	Attitudinal complex
155	Mediator_ Zhu_H03	1	你刚刚说了一句话..我觉得让我有点警觉	Just now you said a sentence.. which I think sort of alerted me		
		2	就是你经常会一边发脾气的时候一边做事	That was you often continued working while losing your temper		
		3	这叫什么..这叫压抑	What is this.. this is called depression		
		4	为什么你一生气的时候..你的身体会特别不好	Why is that whenever you are angry.. you would get terribly sick		
		5	那个东西叫病由心生	That thing is called sickness from the heart		
		6	你心里面很多的负面情绪	You have a lot of negative emotions in your heart		
156	Wife_H03_ AW	1	*[哭泣]* 我不知道我做错了什么	*[cry]* I **don't know what I did wrong**	Denial	Invoke +ve Judge self; invoke -ve Judge antagonist[a]
		2	*[哭泣]* 让我的人生过得这么痛苦	*[cry]* (what) has made my life so **miserable**	Attitudinal instance of inscribed Appreciation (potential invocation of -ve affect/ judgement)	Invoke -ve Affect self (triggered by the antagonist); invoke -ve Judge antagonist

[a]The wife's rhetorical question might activate multiple attitudinal readings. For an audience holding that 'The wife did nothing wrong', the wife's utterance invokes a positive self-Judgement. For an audience holding that 'The husband is accountable for the relationship turmoil', the wife's utterance invokes a negative Judgement of the antagonist. Of course, it is also possible for an audience to hold both positions, positively assessing the wife and condemning the husband simultaneously.

mediation progresses from one stage to the next, the disputants varied in terms of the radicality of the attitudinal disposition shifts. From the more radical shifts to the less radical shifts, the disputants chose to perform radically different aspects of the 'self' or relatively less radically different aspects of the 'self' as the mediation unfolded. The variation of the attitudinal disposition shifts indicates an exchangeability among different attitudinal disposition types. No attitudinal disposition type was absolutely stable or unstable. The disputants were agentive, either consciously or subconsciously, in choosing which aspect of the 'self' to present as the mediation progressed through the different stages of the episode.

Excerpt 6.3 Wife_H03_AW's attitudinal profile in the Post-mediation stage

Turn	Speaker	Move	Utterance (Chinese)	Utterance (English translation)	Attitude signal	Attitudinal complex
215	Hostess_ H03	1	那你看今天这是不是你要的	Then you see what happens today is this what you want		
216	Wife_ H03_AW	1	是	Yes		
217	Hostess_ H03	1	你是的话你得告诉他啊	If it is what you want you need tell him		
218	Wife_ H03_AW	1	我一下子不适应. . 好像	I can't adapt to it all at once.. it seems		
		2	好像天上掉馅饼了一样	It seems **like a windfall**[a]	Metaphor	Invoke +ve/-ve Judge antagonist
219	Husband_ H03_WH	1	那个那个恋爱的时候..我每..看一场电影我追了你四次..你还不知道啊	When when we were dating..every movie.. to watch a movie.. I invited you **four times**.. didn't you remember	Upscaling	Invoke +ve Judge self
		2	是不是	Isn't it		
		3	我有那份激情..有那份热情	I **have** that **passion**.. that **enthusiasm**	Inscription	Inscribe +ve Judge self
		4	只是你不好接受	It's just that you **don't accept** it	Denial	Invoke -ve Judge antagonist
		5	不想接受..我没办法	If you **don't want to accept** it.. I can't do anything about it	Denial	Invoke -ve Judge antagonist; invoke +ve Judge self

(continued)

Excerpt 6.3 (continued)

Turn	Speaker	Move	Utterance (Chinese)	Utterance (English translation)	Attitude signal	Attitudinal complex
220	Wife_ H03_AW	1	我慢慢地接受..只能	I will **accept** it gradually.. only	Evoke	Invoke +ve Judge self; invoke +ve Judge antagonist
		2	我相信他	I **believe** him	Attitudinal instance of inscribed Affect (potential invocation of Judgement)	Inscribe +ve Affect self; invoke +ve Judge antagonist; invoke +ve Judge self
		3	以后...他会..他会变得好的	In the future…he will.. he **will be good**	Inscription	Inscribe +ve Judge antagonist

[a]The wife used a Chinese proverb in this utterance: '天上掉馅饼', which literally translates 'pies falling from the sky'. Prior to this excerpt, the husband had given her a gold necklace, explicitly apologised for neglecting her emotions, and attempted to hug her. The husband's behaviours assumingly were in sharp contrast to what he did before the couple entred the mediation. In this context, the wife used this proverb to describe her surprise and delight. She indicated that something unexpectedly fortunate (but seemingly impossible) had happened to her

3 Attitudinal Disposition Stability when Interacting with Different Addressees

While the attitudinal disposition shift across different mediation stages might be expected since different mediation stages mean different contexts of situation, I wanted to explore whether the disputants presented the same 'self' or the same aspect of the 'self' when speaking to different addressees. For instance, if all the disputants have the same primary communicative concern of condemning the antagonist (see Chap. 4 for details), did they convey their negativity toward the antagonist regardless of who the addressee is—their spouse, the hostess, the mediators? Or did the disputants deploy different attitude-associated resources when speaking to different addressees to 'strategically' present different aspects of the 'self' in front of different people with whom they obviously had different relationships and statuses? The answers to these research questions provided insights into the stability or fluidity of attitudinal disposition under changes in the addressee.

The disputants had the opportunity to directly address three addressees across the episode in its entirety: the antagonist, hostess, and mediator(s). (As discussed in Chap. 3, in some stages, the disputants may choose whom they address at different points in the stage. For example, in the Problem Discussion, they may choose to address their spouse or the hostess, indicating this either by body position, gaze or by terms of address 'you' versus 'he/she/they'.) In this analysis, I used the same subset of seven attitudinal complexes as the previous section (concerned with

Excerpt 6.4 Husband_W01_AH's attitudinal profile in the Problem Discussion stage

Turn	Speaker	Move	Utterance (Chinese)	Utterance (English translation)	Attitude signal	Attitudinal complex
89	Wife_W01_WW	1	转身我老公回来怎么骂我	How did my husband **curse at** me when I came back	Inscription	Inscribe -ve Judge antagonist
		2	他说我没有见过你这么不要脸的女人	He said I have never seen a shameless woman like you	Quotation: Other	Invoke -ve Judge antagonist
		3	去这样的问账(2. 2)	You went to claim a debt like this (2.2)	Quotation: Other	Invoke -ve Judge antagonist
		4	他骂我不要脸	He scolded me for being shameless	Quotation: Other	Invoke -ve Judge antagonist
		5	我是为了这个家	I did this for this family	Evoke	Invoke +ve Judge self; invoke -ve Judge antagonist
90	Husband_W01_AH	1	当时就吵架	We quarrelled at that time		
		2	她具体说这句话的时候其实我..可能现在还有一点那个..对她吧..有一点愧疚哦	When she specifically said this I actually.. maybe even now I still have a little bit of that.. for her.. a little **guilty**	Inscription	Inscribe -ve Judge self
		3	可能是..当时说重了	It may be.. I said something **too harsh** at the time	Inscription	Inscribe -ve Judge self
		4	我也不知道自己怎么回事	I didn't know what's wrong with me	Denial	Invoke -ve Judge self
		5	会说出这么一句话	I would have said such a sentence	Evoke	Invoke -ve Judge self

attitudinal disposition shift across different mediation stages). The reasons for singling out these seven attitudinal complexes were the same as discussed previously (i.e., they comprise the attitudinal 'core' of these conflictual interactions). The findings indicate that the attitudinal disposition shifts did occur in conjunction with shifts in the addressee.

Excerpt 6.5 Husband_W01_AH's attitudinal profile in the Private Mediation stage

Turn	Speaker	Move	Utterance (Chinese)	Utterance (English translation)	Attitude signal	Attitudinal complex
114	Mediator_ Wu_W01	1	你一个人说了算. . 就是错的	If you alone had the final say.. That's wrong		
		2	你要还给人家公平	You have to give your wife an equal change		
		3	还给人家尊重	Give back your respect for her		
		4	还给人家理解	Give back your understanding to her		
115	Husband_ W01_AH	1	这些..错误..我也..意识到了	These.. **mistakes**.. I also..have realised	Inscription	Inscribe -ve Judge self; invoke +ve Judge self[a]
		2	其实我..内心..不是这样的	Actually I.. in my heart.. it's not like this	Denial	Invoke +ve Judge self
116	Mediator_ Wu_W01	1	嗯	Hmm		
117	Husband_ W01_AH	1	但是嘴巴里面偏偏去让她心里	But what I said made her feel	Contrast	Invoke -ve Judge self
118	M_Wu_ W01	1	对	Yes		

[a]This utterance involved two layers of attitudinal positioning. The first layer was that, by admitting his mistakes, the husband explicitly blamed the self for his wrong doings. Additionally, given that the husband was interacting with the mediator directly, his admission of mistake indicated his willingness to reconcile and readiness to salvage the relationship. Thus, the same utterance potentially activated a second layer of attitudinal positioning, which was a positive self-Judgement

3.1 General Patterns

Figure 6.3 visualises the disputants' attitudinal arrangements when addressing the antagonist, hostess, and mediator(s). The x-axis illustrates the three addressees in three columns. From left to right are 'antagonist', 'hostess', and 'mediators'. The y-axis presents the ratio of the attitudinal complex in the disputant's talk when speaking to a specific addressee. The coloured bars represent the seven attitudinal complexes, with the legend on the right side of the figure.

Figure 6.3 demonstrates a noticeable attitudinal disposition shift as a response to addressee change. For the seven attitudinal complexes pivotal to the disputant's authorial attitudinal positioning of the self and the antagonist, none of the 12 disputants deployed the same arrangement of the attitudinal complexes in front of

Excerpt 6.6 Husband_W01_AH's attitudinal profile in the Post-mediation stage

Turn	Speaker	Move#	Utterance (Chinese)	Utterance (English translation)	Attitude signal	Attitudinal complex
133	Hostess_W01	1	问一下. . 吴女士和胡先生. . 现在. . 什么想法	Let me ask.. Ms. Wu and Mr. Hu.. Now.. What do you think		
134	Husband_W01_AH	1	我(1. 3)以前是很多事. . 做得不好	I (1.3) there were a lot of things.. I **didn't do well**	Inscription	Inscribe -ve Judge self
		2	对她确实有一些意识不到的错误	I really **made some mistakes** that I was unaware of	Inscription	Inscribe -ve Judge self
		3	很多是..误解了她	Many mistakes were about.. **misunderstanding** her	Inscription	Inscribe -ve Judge self
		4	然后冤枉了她	And then I **wronged** her	Inscription	Inscribe -ve Judge self
		5	以后我保证我..信任她	From now on I promise I..will trust her	Irrealis affect	Invoke +ve Judge self
		6	也不给她..增加很多麻烦了	I won't bring her.. a lot of troubles either	Irrealis affect	Invoke +ve Judge self
		7	好吧. . 老婆	Ok.. my wife		
		8	今天我在这里哈. . 对你道歉了	I am here today.. I apologise to you	Evoke	Invoke -ve Judge self; invoke +ve Judge self[a]
		9	对不起	I am sorry	Evoke	Invoke -ve Judge self; invoke +ve Judge self
		10	以前都是我的错	It was **all my fault** in the past	Inscription	Inscribe -ve Judge self
		11	但是你从来不给我机会去沟通	But you never gave me a chance to communicate	Denial	Invoke -ve Judge antagonist
		12	很多时候我真的是. . 有话都没地方说了	Many times I really am.. I had no one to talk to	Denial	Invoke -ve Judge antagonist
		13	以后. . 我保证两个人共同. . 承担这些. . 担子	In the future.. I promise that the two of us will share these burdens together	Irrealis affect	Invoke +ve Judge self
		14	不要你去扛	I will not let you carry them by yourself	Irrealis affect	Invoke +ve Judge self
		15	不要你去承担	I will not let you shoulder them	Irrealis affect	Invoke +ve Judge self

[a]This and the following utterances are double coded because the husband's apology indicated his acknowledgement for having done something wrong in the past, hence, invoking negative self-Judgement. Meanwhile, the apology also signalled the husband's willingness to reconcile, thus invoking positive self-Judgement.

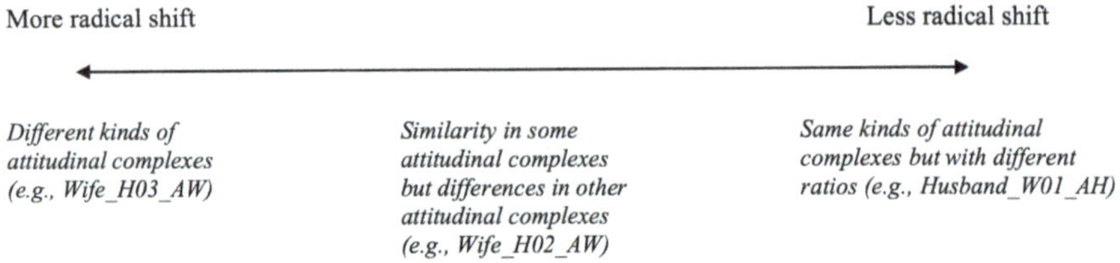

Fig. 6.2 A cline of radicality of the attitudinal disposition shifts.

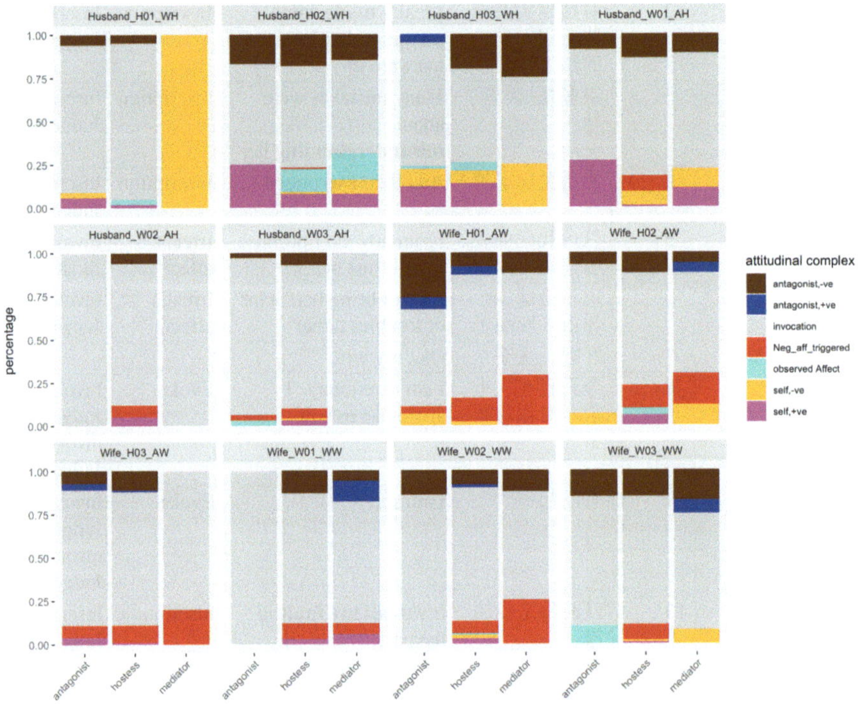

Fig. 6.3 Disputants' attitudinal orientations when interacting with different addressees

different addressees. The pattern by which all disputants adopted different attitudinal dispositions when interacting with different addressees indicates the performative and interactive nature of discursive self-presentation in this setting.

It is obviously not possible, given space limitations, to provide text extracts to illustrate what is happening in all the disputants' language when interacting with different addressees. Nevertheless, I offer the following to provide some qualitative sense of what is at stake communicatively. With this in mind, I have selected extracts from Wife_W01_WW's (second from the left on the bottom row in Fig. 6.3) utterances when speaking to different addressees. It is noticeable that there was a clear contrast in the wife's attitudinal orientation. The wife seldom directedly addressed the antagonist. When she did so (exemplified by Excerpt 6.7), she had minimal input and relied totally on invocations. When speaking to the hostess, she tended to perform a confrontational aspect of the 'self', confrontational against the antagonist, by being explicit with her complaints directed at the antagonist (exemplified by Excerpt 6.8). She also reported her negative emotions triggered by the husband and explicitly praised herself. When speaking to the mediators, the wife revealed both the confrontational and conciliatory aspects of the 'self', with instances of inscribed positive Judgement of her husband (indicating a more conciliatory orientation) and some negative Judgements of him (exemplified by Excerpt 6.9). (A full analysis of the wife's language can be found in the book's GitHub repository.)

There is also a pattern of variability regarding the degree of attitudinal disposition shift among the disputants in the dataset, similar to the cline of attitudinal disposition shift discussed in the previous section (about the disposition shift across the different mediation stages). It means that when addressing different people, the disputants had different degree of attitudinal disposition shift. Some disputants demonstrated relatively more radical shifts (e.g., Wife_W01_WW in Excerpts 6.7, 6.8, and 6.9, where different attitudinal complexes were used when addressing different people). In contrast, some disputants demonstrated relatively less radical shifts (e.g., Husband_H03_WH on the top right corner who deployed similar sets of attitudinal complexes but different ratios of use of these attitudinal complexes). The following excerpts—Excerpts 6.10, 6.11, and 6.12—exemplify a speaker with less

Excerpt 6.7 Wife_W01_WW's attitudinal profile when speaking to the antagonist

Turn	Speaker	Move	Utterance (Chinese)	Utterance (English translation)	Attitude signal	Attitudinal complex
83	Husband_ W01_AH	1	那个时候回来..她还没说离婚	Back then.. she didn't say divorce yet		
		2	我是看了你的..那个信息以后..她同学老婆..要过来	After I read your.. that message.. that her classmate's wife.. would come over		
		3	跟她吵架的时候我们才..发现她是..跟同学有..那个	To quarrel with her then we.. we realised that she was.. with that classmates.. **had something (wrong)**	Inscription	Inscribe -ve Judge antagonist
84	Wife_ W01_WW	1	如果有什么..我们没必要坦白这个东西	If there was something.. we didn't have to confess this thing[a]	Denial	Invoke +ve Judge self; retract -ve Judge wife[b]

[a]'This thing' referred to the trip to Beijing on which the wife went together with the alleged third party. After the trip, the wife 'confessed' to the husband

[b]This utterance is double coded. By 'confessing' what she had done, the wife attempted to invoke a positive self-Judgement for her veracity. Simultaneously, her 'confession' indicated her fidelity for the relationship, hence retracting the husband's accusation of her in the previous turn.

Excerpt 6.8 Wife_W01_WW's attitudinal profile when speaking to the hostess

Turn	Speaker	Move	Utterance (Chinese)	Utterance (English translation)	Attitude signal	Attitudinal complex
92	Hostess_ W01	1	这件事情会让你对这个男人有什么看法	What does this incident make you think of this man		
93	Wife_ W01_ WW	1	没有担当呀	**Not responsible**	Inscription	Inscribe -ve Judge antagonist
		2	当时我就不同意借啊	I didn't agree to lend him[a] the money at that time	Contrast	Invoke -ve Judge antagonist; invoke -ve Judge antagonist
		3	他对家里的所有事情都没有==担当==	He **doesn't have a responsibility** towards anything in the family ==at all==	Inscription	Inscribe -ve Judge antagonist
94	Hostess_ W01	1	==明白==了	==I see==		
		2	这件==事情==	For ==this matter==		
95	Wife_ W01_ WW	1	==我要离开==他的主要原因就是我在他的面前得不到自尊	==I want to leave== the main reason is that I don't get self-esteem in front of him	Denial	Invoke -ve Judge antagonist
		2	没有担当	**Not responsible**	Inscription	Inscribe -ve Judge antagonist
		3	再有就是怀疑	Then there is **suspicion**	Inscription	Inscribe -ve Judge antagonist

[a]'Him' refers to the husband's friend who borrowed money from the couple.

radical shifts. The speaker in these three excerpts is Husband_H03_WH, who used similar attitudinal complexes (inscribed negative self-Judgement) when interacting with different people. (A full analysis of the husband's language can be found in the book's GitHub repository.)

Thus far, the above two sections have outlined evidence of attitudinal disposition shifts across different mediation stages and vis-à-vis addressee change. The shifts were observed to occur across all the disputants in the dataset. The evidence demonstrates an observable degree of fluidity in the disputants' attitudinal disposition construction when the overall context of situation changes.

Excerpt 6.9 Wife_W01_WW's attitudinal profile when speaking to the mediators

Turn	Speaker	Move	Utterance (Chinese)	Utterance (English translation)	Attitude signal	Attitudinal complex
120	Mediator_Su_W01	1	在你的内心里面这个男人..除了你..看到的那么多缺点之外..你觉得他有好的地方吗	In your heart this man.. except all the shortcomings you have seen.. do you think he has something good		
121	Wife_W01_WW	1	勤奋这一块应该是说还是可以	In terms of **diligence** I would say he is so-so with diligence	Inscription	Inscribe +ve Judge antagonist
		2	但是就是说他赚不了活钱	But I mean he can't make clever money	Denial	Invoke -ve Judge antagonist
122	Mediator_Su_W01	1	很勤奋	Very hardworking		
		2	我们不说..不说但是	We don't say.. don't say but		
		3	我们来看看有多少	Let's see how many		
123	Wife_W01_WW	1	他就是做事..做事勤奋这一块	He as far as working is concerned.. he is **hardworking**	Inscription	Inscribe +ve Judge antagonist
124	Mediator_Su_W01	1	做事很勤奋	He is very hardworking		
125	Wife_W01_WW	1	勤奋这块..就是太拖拉	In terms of hardworking.. He is just **procrastinates too much**	Inscription	Inscribe -ve Judge antagonist

4 Chapter Summary

This chapter has reported findings relating to the second line of exploration of the attitudinal disposition—a dynamic view of attitudinal disposition. This line of inquiry examined the disputants' self-presentation by reference to their deployment of attitudinal complexes in an unfolding text. The analysis focused on the stability of the disputants' attitudinal orientation (1) across different mediation stages and (2) when interacting with different addressees.

The findings revealed multiple patterns in attitudinal disposition shifts. The general pattern suggested that all parties presented distinct attitudinal orientations, indicating they constructed various 'selves' or different aspects of the 'self' in response to changes in the situation. While some disputants exhibited more radical shifts in

Excerpt 6.10 Husband_H03_WH's attitudinal profile when speaking to the antagonist

Turn	Speaker	Move	Utterance (Chinese)	Utterance (English translation)	Attitude signal	Attitudinal complex
197	Husband_ H03_WH	1	老婆. . 对不起啊	Wife.. sorry	Evoke	Invoke -ve Judge self; invoke +ve Judge self[a]
		2	这几年你辛苦了	You have **worked hard** in recent years	Inscription	Inscribe +ve Judge antagonist
		3	几十年过来. . 我这个家打拼得是有点辛苦	In these years.. our family business has been **hard to build up**	Attitudinal token of appreciation	Invoke +ve Judge couple
		4	是我忽略了你	It's true that I **ignored** you	Inscription	Inscribe -ve Judge self
		5	忽略了你的感受	I **ignored** your feelings	Inscription	Inscribe -ve Judge self
		6	从今天开始. . 我要改变	Starting from today.. I **want to change**	Irrealis affect	Invoke +ve Judge self
		7	改变你高兴吗	Are you happy that I **will change**	Irrealis affect	Invoke +ve Judge self
198	Wife_H03_ AW	1	只要你改变了就好	As long as you change **it's ok**	Irrealis affect	Invoke +ve Judge antagonist

[a]Similar to the justifications provided in Excerpt 6.6, this instance of apology is double coded.

Excerpt 6.11 Husband_H03_WH's attitudinal profile when speaking to the hostess

Turn	Speaker	Move	Utterance (Chinese)	Utterance (English translation)	Attitude signal	Attitudinal complex
42	Hostess_ H03	1	她就觉得跟别人说说笑笑. . 对她很冷淡	She felt that you talked and laughed with others.. but were very cold to her		
		2	很平淡	Very cold		
43	Husband_ H03_WH	1	我可能在这个夫妻感情方面. . 沟通方面. . 是有点欠缺	I may be **not good** enough.. in terms of couple relationship.. in term of communication	Inscription	Inscribe -ve Judge self
		2	欠一点	**Not good** enough	Inscription	Inscribe -ve Judge self

their attitudes, others demonstrated fewer pronounced changes. This study proposes a cline of radicalness regarding attitudinal disposition shifting.

Excerpt 6.12 Husband_H03_WH's attitudinal profile when speaking to the mediators

Turn	Speaker	Move	Utterance (Chinese)	Utterance (English translation)	Attitude signal	Attitudinal complex
169	Husband_ H03_WH	1	两个小孩跟我们两个大人根本无法沟通	The two children could not communicate with the two of us	Denial	Invoke -ve Judge couple
170	Mediator_ Wu_H03	1	为什么	Why		
171	Husband_ H03_WH	1	沟通不了.. 不是	We can't communicate.. right	Denial	Invoke -ve Judge couple
		2	可能我没有方法吧	Maybe I **don't have a method**	Inscription	Inscribe -ve Judge self

The findings resonate with the proposal that conflict are strategies (Knapp et al., 1988; Pruitt, 1983) or intentions (Thomas, 1992), which disputants choose to align with the circumstances or the relationship at hand. As a result, conflict styles should not be treated as stable traits, but as adaptive choices that depend on context. This study provides solid linguistic evidence for the adaptability of attitudinal-based conflict style in response to the changes in context.

Although it might be anticipated that disputants would exhibit diverse attitudinal dispositions during different mediation stages and when addressing different parties, there is uncertainty about whether their attitudinal self-presentation will remain consistent throughout a single mediation stage when the context remains unaltered. The subsequent chapter extends this dynamic examination by focusing on the consistency of the disputants' preferences within a specific segment of discourse—specifically, the Problem Discussion stage.

References

Halliday, M. A. K., & Matthiessen, C. M. I. M. (2014). *Halliday's introduction to functional grammar* (4th ed.). Routledge.

Knapp, M. L., Putnam, L. L., & Davis, L. J. (1988). Measuring interpersonal conflict in organizations: Where do we go from here? *Management Communication Quarterly, 1*(3), 414–429. https://doi.org/10.1177/0893318988001003008

Martin, J. R. (1992). *English text: System and structure*. John Benjamins Publishing Company.

Pruitt, D. G. (1983). Strategic choice in negotiation. *American Behavioral Scientist, 27*(2), 167–194. https://doi.org/10.1177/000276483027002005

Thomas, K. W. (1992). Conflict and conflict management: Reflections and update. *Journal of Organizational Behavior, 13*(3), 265–274.

Chapter 7
Micro-Shifts: Attitudinal Dynamics within the Problem Discussion Stage

Contents

1 Introduction

Building upon the dynamic exploration introduced in the previous chapter, this chapter investigates potential observable shifts in disputants' preferred attitude-associated resource during the 20–30-min Problem Discussion stage, when the context of situation remained consistent. During this mediation stage, the disputing spouses and hostess engaged in dialogue about relationship problems within an unchanged situational environment. The guiding analytical question was: To what extent and in what patterns do disputants' attitudinal arrangements transform within a stable context of situation?

As noted in Chap. 1, the scholarly investigation of a speaker's discursive self-presentation stability during extended interactions represents a relatively unexplored research terrain, motivating this comprehensive exploration. In conflict management studies, some scholars argue that situational circumstances are

Q. Xu, *Appraisal Approach to Conflict Styles*, The M.A.K. Halliday Library Functional Linguistics Series, https://doi.org/10.1007/978-981-95-6256-5_7

antecedents of conflict styles, which include factors such as conflict type (e.g., inter-personal vs inter-organisational), the identities of the parties involved (e.g., a subordinate vs. a spouse), and disputants' status within an organisation (Brewer et al., 2002; Friedman et al., 2000; Rahim, 2023; Zarankin, 2008). Nonetheless, it remains to be investigated whether a disputant's conflict style is subject to change when the contextual factors remain constant.

This exploration builds upon the findings reported in Chaps. 4 and 5, which examined two complementary dimensions of attitudinal disposition construction. The first line of inquiry (Chap. 4) investigated disputants' attitudinal disposition through their deployment of key attitudinal expressions—conceptualised as 'attitudinal complexes'. The second line of inquiry (Chap. 5) focused on the framing strategies employed when articulating these attitudinal assessments. Correspondingly, the current exploration of attitudinal disposition stability in the Problem Discussion stage pursued two parallel investigation tracks: (1) examining the unfolding patterns of attitudinal complexes potentially signalling shifts in attitudinal disposition, and (2) identifying the unfolding patterns of the framing of these attitudinal complexes (including scaling and dialogistic positioning options) that might also indicate shifts in attitudinal disposition.

The subsequent sections present findings from these two lines of inquiry. Each line of inquiry begins by delineating general patterns of attitudinal disposition shifts, revealing shared tendencies among disputants. Following this, the analysis contextualises these shifts by exploring the contextual factors potentially motivating or influencing attitudinal reconfigurations.

2 Attitudinal Disposition Stability Vis-à-Vis Attitudinal Complex

2.1 General Patterns

Regarding the disputants' attitudinal disposition vis-à-vis the disputants' preference in attitudinal complexes, the analysis revealed a notable degree of fluidity in their attitudinal orientations. The disputants in the dataset demonstrated the capacity to 'favour' different attitudinal complexes across various interaction phases. For instance, a disputant might initially exhibit inscribed positive self-Judgement, subsequently transitioning to a preference for inscribed negative self-Judgement. Two distinctive patterns of attitudinal disposition shift emerged from the dataset: permanent shifts and temporary shifts.

2.1.1 Permanent Shift

A permanent shift represents a fundamental reconfiguration of a disputant's attitudinal profile within a single interaction. This pattern manifests when a speaker adopts distinctly different attitudinal orientations across two interaction phases. Specifically, the disputant initially favours one set of attitudinal complexes in phase 1, then transitions to a markedly different attitudinal profile in phase 2, maintaining this new orientation until the interaction's conclusion. From a discursive identity perspective, this shift reveals the multifaceted nature of self-presentation, where two equally significant 'aspects of self' are dynamically negotiated and performed.

Husband_H01_WH exemplifies a prototypical permanent attitudinal disposition shift. As noted in Chap. 4, his synoptic attitudinal disposition was characterised as 'narrow range', primarily deploying three attitudinal complexes: inscribed negative Judgement of the antagonist, inscribed positive Judgement of self, and invocations. He also had low explicitness in terms of the linguistic construal of the attitudinal complexes, with less than 10% of attitudinal complexes being inscriptions.

The Problem Discussion stage revealed two distinct locally actualised aspects of his stage-global attitudinal disposition. The first phase (Turns 1–89) featured exclusively attitudinal complexes of positive self-Judgement and invocations, with minimal attitudinal inscription (only three instances across 90 turns). The second phase (Turn 90 to stage conclusion) pivoted dramatically, focusing solely on negative Judgements of the antagonist and invocations, with increased explicitness (four inscription instances across 40 turns). This transformation unveiled two contrasting attitudinal profiles: an initial self-praising and highly implicit, followed by a more hostile and explicit approach. Critically, once initiated, this attitudinal shift remained consistent until the interaction's conclusion. Therefore, his shift was permanent.

The following excerpts illustrate the husband's attitudinal profiles before and after the shift. Excerpt 7.1 demonstrates that prior to the shift, the husband opted for invocations. He employed a diverse range of attitude signals—including attitudinal tokens, upscaling or downscaling, counter-expectancy, and rhetorical questions—to signal his attitudinal positioning and prompt specific attitudinal assessments from the audience. Because he never used inscriptions, his attitudinal disposition remained highly implicit with an extremely low degree of expressivity. In Turns 31–32, even when confronted with the wife's explicit accusation of lying, he deliberately avoided a tit-for-tat game. Instead of directly refuting accusation with statements like 'I did not lie' or 'You are lying', he used a rhetorical question—'Do I NEED to lie?'—as a defence.

Excerpt 7.2 captures the husband's attitudinal disposition shift in Turn 95. Here, he finally articulated a negative attitudinal inscription targeting the wife. He explicitly criticised her for using language intended to irritate him. Subsequently, he clarified his attitudinal positioning: the wife's irritating language and behaviour were responsible for their disputes. From Turn 95 onward, the husband transitioned to a more expressive and confrontational attitudinal disposition.

To more comprehensively illustrate the husband's attitudinal disposition shift and its permanence, Fig. 7.1 provides a visual representation. The horizontal axis

Excerpt 7.1 Husband_H01_WH's attitudinal profile before the shift

Turn	Speaker	Move	Utterance (Chinese)	Utterance (English translation)	Attitude signal	Attitudinal complex
28	Husband_H01_WH	1	当时对我来说.. 才开始玩这个微信	At that time for me.. I was a new user of WeChat	Evoke	Counteract wife's -ve Judge husband[a]
		2	很多都不懂	There were many things I didn't know	Denial	Counteract wife's -ve Judge husband[b]
29	Hostess_H01	1	嗯	Mhm		
30	Husband_H01_WH	1	感觉好奇嘛	I simply felt **curious**	Attitudinal token of Affect	Counteract wife's -ve Judge husband[c]
		2	然后无聊的情况下... 就加她微信	Then when I **felt bored**... I added her to my WeChat	Attitudinal token of Affect	Counteract wife's -ve Judge husband[d]
		3	然后就这样聊下天	Then we chatted briefly	Downscaling	Counteract wife's -ve Judge husband[e]
		4	实际上这个女人都不在重庆	In fact this woman was not even in Chongqing	Counter-expectancy	Counteract wife's -ve Judge husband[f]
		5	外面做生意	She did business elsewhere	Contrast	Counteract wife's -ve Judge husband[g]
		6	我怎么解释她都不相信	No matter how hard I explained that to her she still would not believe it	Counter-expectancy	Invoke +ve Judge self; invoke -ve Judge antagonist[h]

[a]We need to reference co-textual cues to understand the attitudinal work in this excerpt. In previous turns, the wife reported that the husband befriended the female neighbour on WeChat and initiated some chats. Subsequently, the wife positioned the audience to negatively assess the husband for his having a flirtatious relationship with the opposite sex. In this turn, the husband explained that he was a 'new user of WeChat'. For an audience holding the position that 'It is common for a new user to try all the functions on an APP' or 'It is okay for a new user to make some mistakes', the husband's explanation counteracted the wife's negative positioning directed at him

[b]In this turn, the husband explains that he did not know the functions or practices for using WeChat. For an audience holding the position that 'It is common for a person to make mistakes if they did not know about the rules', the husband's negative Judgement of capacity directed at the self could function as an attitudinal token to counteract the wife's negative positioning directed at him

[c]Curiosity as 'a feeling of deprivation reflects feelings of uncertainty and tension' (Litman & Jimerson, 2004, p. 147). In this utterance, the husband argued that he added the female neighbour as a friend and chatted with her because of curiosity, rather than intentionality. In Appraisal terms, the husband used curiosity as an Affectual token to counteract the wife's negative positioning directed at him

(continued)

Excerpt 7.1 (continued)

[d]In this utterance, feeling 'boring' can be interpreted as an Affect of dissatisfaction, with the trigger unknown. For an audience holding the position that 'If you feel boring, it's natural for you to initiate a chat with someone', the husband's Affect of boring served as an attitudinal token to counteract the wife's negative positioning directed at him

[e]By the downscaling device—'briefly', the husband rejected the underlying message in the wife's account that there was an abnormal relationship between him and the female neighbour. For an audience holding a position that 'It is normal for one to have a brief chat with an opposite-sex' or 'Nothing can happen in a brief chat', the downscaling counteracted the wife's negative positioning directed at the husband

[f]By this utterance, the husband reported that he and the female neighbour were not in the same city. This information countered the expectation of the audience who might assume that neighbours lived in the same neighbourhood. By the counter-expectancy formulation—'not even', the husband indicated that an intimate relationship between him and the female neighbour was physically impossible. Therefore, the wife's accusation of him was groundless

[g]In this utterance, a contrast was made between Chongqing—the husband's city of residence, and 'elsewhere'—the city where the female neighbour resides. By this contrast, the husband positioned the audience to infer that nothing intimate was possible between the husband and the female neighbour

[h]This utterance could potentially invoke two attitudinal positionings. One was directed at the husband. For an audience holding that 'It is a good personal trait to patiently explain what has happened to your partner if there is a misunderstanding', the husband's behaviour of explaining could invoke a positive assessment of the self. The other attitudinal positioning was directed at the wife. By the counter-expectancy formulation—'no matter how..., she would not...', the husband positioned the audience to negatively assess the wife for her lack of understanding

represents the text's temporal progression, spanning from Turn zero to Turn 140 (the final turn in the Problem Discussion stage). The vertical axis indicates the number of attitudinal instances per turn, with bar heights corresponding to the frequency of specific attitudinal complex instances. The graph uses color-coding to differentiate attitudinal complexes: brown bars represent inscribed negative Judgement of the antagonist, pink bars show inscribed positive self-Judgement, and grey bars indicate invocations. Drawing on Martin and White's (2005) observation that inscriptions tend to 'colour more of a text than their local grammatical environment circumscribes' (p. 63), the inscriptions serve as signposts for the speaker's overall attitudinal positioning. The dashed line divides the phases, with a colour legend provided on the graph's right side. This graphical approach will be consistently used in subsequent analyses unless otherwise specified.

Husband_H01_WH was not alone in having a permanent shift. In fact, seven out of 12 disputants in the dataset demonstrated a similar permanent shift in their attitudinal disposition, as summarised in Table 7.1.

2.1.2 Temporary Shift

The second pattern observed in the disputant's speech involved repeated shifts in attitudinal profile. This dynamic manifested as a cyclical process where the speaker would: (1) begin with an initial attitudinal profile (phase 1—favouring a specific

Excerpt 7.2 Husband_H01_WH's attitudinal disposition shift in Turn 95

Turn	Speaker	Move	Utterance (Chinese)	Utterance (English translation)	Attitude signal	Attitudinal complex
91	Husband_H01_WH	1	唉…为什么会吵架吵得这么厉害哦	Aww… Why do we quarrel so fiercely		
		2	今天我上班	(For example) I go to work[a] today		
		3	晚上三点钟回家	I come back home at three o'clock in the morning	Upscaling	Invoke +ve Judge self
		4	吵到天亮	(We will) quarrel until dawn	Upscaling	Invoke -ve Judge antagonist
		5	然后下午接着又开车	Then I continue to drive in the afternoon	Upscaling	Invoke +ve Judge self
		6	并且跟她说了.. 我这个开车安全第一啊.. 对吧	Moreover I have told her.. My safety in driving should be the priority.. right	Quotation: self	Invoke +ve Judge self; invoke -ve Judge antagonist
		7	你不让我睡觉	If you don't allow me to sleep		
92	Hostess_H01	1	嗯	Mhm		
93	Husband_H01_WH	1	我下午怎么开车呀	How can I drive in the afternoon	Rhetorical question	Invoke -ve Judge antagonist
94	Wife_H01_AW	1	那你在家休息的时候… 我和你聊天	Then when you are at home... I chat with you		
		2	我找你说话的时候.. 你为什么视我不存在	When I want to talk to you.. Why do you **treat me as something invisible**	Inscription	Inscribe -ve Judge antagonist
95	Husband_H01_WH	1	在家里面聊天.. 你就是拿语言来刺激我	When we chat at home.. you simply use language to **irritate me**	Inscription[b]	Inscribe -ve Judge antagonist
		2	你说这个咋聊啊	You tell how we can chat	Rhetorical question	Invoke -ve Judge antagonist

[a]The husband worked as a commercial driver. By saying 'I go to work', he meant that he went out to drive. According to the context, it seems that he usually drove on the night shift

[b]According to the MLC and BCC corpora (see Chap. 3 for details), the Chinese formulation '刺激我 irritate me' is always used in a negative context, such as '不要刺激我don't irritate me' and '刺激我、伤害我 irritate me and hurt me'. The action of '刺激irritate', regardless of the intention of the actor, can trigger several negative feelings from the recipient of the irritating action, such as discomfort, shame, annoyance, or anger. Therefore, '刺激我 irritate me' was annotated as a negative attitudinal inscription directed at the wife

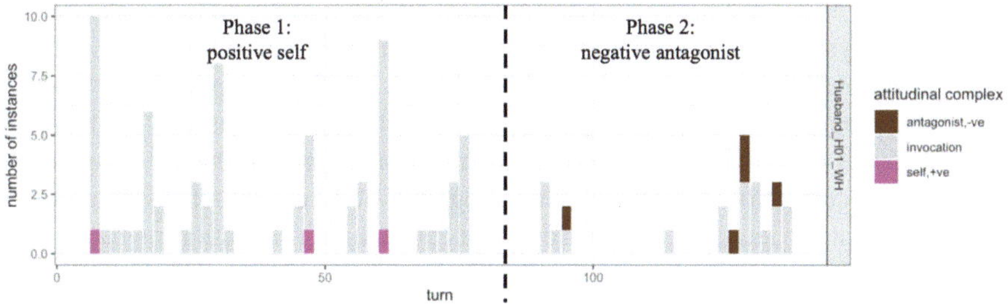

Fig. 7.1 Husband_H01_WH's attitudinal disposition shift

Table 7.1 Attitudinal complex preferences for the disputants having a permanent shift

Speaker	Phase 1	Phase 2
Husband_H01_WH	inscribe +ve Judge self, invocations (Turn 1–89)	inscribe -ve Judge antagonist, invocations (Turn 90–end)
Wife_H01_AW	inscribe -ve/+ve Judge antagonist, -ve Affect triggered by the antagonist, invocations (Turn 1–119)	inscribe -ve Judge antagonist, inscribe +ve Judge self (Turn 120–end)
Wife_H02_AW	inscribe -ve Judge antagonist, -ve Affect triggered by the antagonist, observed Affect, invocations (Turn 1–123)	inscribe +ve Judge self, -ve Affect triggered by the antagonist (Turn 124–end)
Husband_H03_WH	inscribe -ve/+ve Judge antagonist, -ve/+ve Judge self, observed Affect, invocations (Turn 1–63)	inscribe -ve Judge antagonist, inscribe +ve Judge self, observed Affect, invocations (Turn 64–end)
Husband_W01_AH	inscribe -ve Judge antagonist, inscribe +ve Judge self, invocations (Turn 1–11)	inscribe -ve Judge antagonist/self, -ve Affect triggered by the antagonist, invocations (Turn 12–end)
Husband_W02_AH	inscribe -ve Judge antagonist, invocations (Turn 1–28)	-ve Affect triggered by the antagonist, invocations (Turn 29–end)
Wife_W02_WW	inscribe -ve/+ve Judge antagonist, -ve Affect triggered by the antagonist, observed Affect, invocations (Turn 1–92)	inscribe -ve/+ve Judge antagonist, inscribe +ve Judge self, -ve Affect triggered by the antagonist, invocations (Turn 94–end)

subset of attitudinal complexes), (2) shift to a different profile (phase 2—favouring an alternative subset), and then (3) return to the original profile (phase 3). In some cases, this initiate-shift-resume pattern occurred multiple times, creating a recursive attitudinal dynamic. Notably, despite these fluctuations, one attitudinal profile consistently dominated the disputant's speech. This means that, while multiple profile shifts occurred, one attitudinal orientation remained relatively stable and prominent. The temporary nature of these shifts was characterised by the speaker's consistent return to their original attitudinal preference. From a discursive self-presentation perspective, speakers with temporary shifts revealed different 'aspects of self' throughout the conversation, with one aspect maintaining primary significance.

Husband_W03_AH provides a prototypical example of this pattern. (A comprehensive analysis of his attitudinal arrangements can be found in the book's GitHub repository.) As previously noted in Chap. 4, this disputant deployed a relatively extensive range of attitudinal complexes and was characterised as the 'least expressive' in terms of attitudinal overtness. His inscriptions predominantly consisted of negative Judgement of the antagonist and negative Affectual responses triggered by the antagonist. A detailed examination of his attitudinal orientation revealed three distinct phases:

(1) Phase 1 (Turns 1–121): The husband employed four primary attitudinal complexes:

  - Inscribed negative Judgement of antagonist
  - Inscribed positive Judgement of self
  - Inscribed negative Affectual responses triggered by the antagonist
  - Invocations

This phase was predominantly combative in nature.

(2) Phase 2 (Turns 122–124): The husband's attitudinal complex narrowed to a single type: inscribed negative Judgement of self. This marked a significant shift from combativeness to a more conciliatory approach.
(3) Phase 3 (Turn 125 to stage conclusion): The husband reverted to the same attitudinal complexes observed in phase 1. Because Phases 1 and 3 were nearly identical and constituted the majority of his speech, the phase 2 shift can be characterised as temporary.

Some background knowledge might be needed to understand the attitudinal positionings in the following excerpts. Husband_W03_AH, an aggrieved husband, resided in his hometown while his wife ran business in another city. The dispute resolution episode centred on his accusation of her maintaining a close relationship with her first love.

In Excerpt 7.3, the husband used a past event to substantiate his allegation of the wife's potential infidelity. He recounts a birthday visit to his wife during which he discovered her secretly communicating with her first love. To construct his attitudinal positioning, he deploys multiple attitudinal complexes: inscribed negative Judgement of the antagonist, inscribed positive Judgement of self, and invocations.

In Excerpt 7.4, the wife levels accusations against the husband, alleging years of stringent financial control. Her narrative strategically positioned the audience to evaluate the husband negatively, portraying him as excessively miserly. In response to these accusations, the husband exhibited a singular instance of inscribed negative self-Judgement—a rare departure from his typical discursive pattern within the Problem Discussion stage.

Excerpt 7.5 demonstrates the husband's attitudinal arrangement following the temporary shift presented in the above excerpt. Here, he reverted to his characteristic attitudinal orientation, advancing an instance of inscribed positive self-Judgement—a return to his default discursive stance.

Excerpt 7.3 Husband_W03_AH's attitudinal profile before the shift

Turn	Speaker	Move	Utterance (Chinese)	Utterance (English translation)	Attitude signal	Attitudinal complex
24	Husband_W03_AH	1	二月初一过生日我是提前到她那个做生意的那个地方去	When she had her birthday on the first day of the second lunar month I went to her place in advance where she did business		
		2	陪她过生日	I went to stay with her to celebrate her birthday	Evoke	Invoke +ve Judge self
		3	过生日的第二天. . . 对方打电话来	The day after her birthday... the other party called		
		4	她就拒绝	She just refused to answer	Counter--expectancy	Invoke -ve Judge antagonist
		5	当时问她. . 为什么不接	I asked her at the time.. why didn't you answer		
		6	她就. . 什么也没给你解释	She just..she didn't give me any explanation	Denial	Invoke -ve Judge antagonist
		7	**找个**借口..去其它地方..去做什么	Later she **found an excuse**.. saying she needed to go somewhere.. to do whatsoever	Inscription	Inscribe -ve Judge antagonist
		8	去联系他了	She went to contact him	Evoke	Invoke -ve Judge antagonist
25	Hostess_W03	1	你怎么知道	How did you know		
26	Husband_W03_AH	1	我的猜测**没错啊**	My guess was **correct**	Inscription	Inscribe +ve Judge self; invoke -ve Judge antagonist
		2	你问她吧	You can ask her		

Excerpt 7.4 Husband_W03_AH's attitudinal disposition shift in Turn 124

Turn	Speaker	Move	Utterance (Chinese)	Utterance (English translation)	Attitude signal	Attitudinal complex
122	Hostess_W03	1	那日常生活怎么办	Then how about daily expenses		
123	Wife_W03_WW	1	给你十块钱你去买菜	He would give you [me] ten yuan to buy groceries		
		2	买菜剩下几毛钱也要退给他啊	If there were a few cents left after the grocery shopping I needed to return the change to him	Evoke	Invoke -ve Judge antagonist
		3	他还怎么说我	And even guess what he said about me	Counter--expectancy	Invoke -ve Judge antagonist
		4	他说. . . 不花钱的不是好货	He said… a woman who didn't know how to spend money is not a good bitch	Quotation: other	Invoke -ve Judge antagonist
		5	他是这样**侮辱**我	He **humiliated** me just like this	Inscription	Inscribe -ve Judge antagonist
124	Husband_W03_AH	1	以前...也许...年轻..**不懂事**说出来的话	In the past… maybe… when I was young.. I said such things because I was **not mature**	Inscription	Inscribe -ve Judge self

Figure 7.2 visualises Husband_W03_AH's attitudinal profile vis-à-vis attitudinal complex preference, representing five attitudinal complexes through colour-coded bars:

(1) Inscribed negative Judgement of the antagonist (brown),
(2) Invocations (grey),
(3) Inscribed negative Affectual responses triggered by the antagonist (red),
(4) Inscribed negative Judgement of the self (orange), and
(5) inscribed positive Judgement of the self (pink).

Excerpt 7.5 Husband_W03_AH's attitudinal profile after the shift

Turn	Speaker	Move	Utterance (Chinese)	Utterance (English translation)	Attitude signal	Attitudinal complex
167	Hostess_W03	1	你觉得自己在这方面做得怎么样	How do you evaluate your behaviour in this aspect		
168	Husband_W03_AH	1	我还是..比较...公认的一个..比较好的人	I am nevertheless.. more or less... everyone agrees.. more or less a **good** person	Inscription	Inscribe +ve Judge self

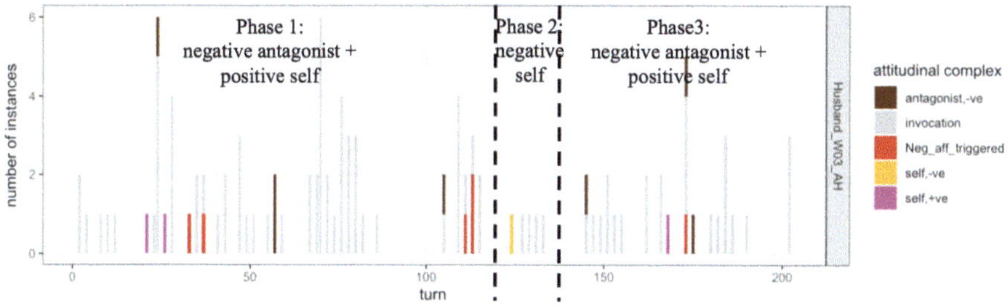

Fig. 7.2 Husband_W03_AH's attitudinal disposition shift

Besides Husband_W03_AH, four additional disputants demonstrated a comparable temporary shift pattern. Table 7.2 summarises the attitudinal complex preferences across these five disputants' speeches. Phases 1, 3, and 5 feature more stable and permanent attitudinal dispositions. Phases 2 and 4 constitute temporary attitudinal shifts.

The observed patterns of permanent and temporary shifts reveal a consistent characteristic among disputants: a remarkable adaptability in attitudinal complex preferences throughout interaction progression. This linguistic flexibility emerged as a universal feature, with disputants demonstrating notable variations in preferred attitudinal complexes as conversational dynamics unfolded.

Upon microscopic examination of these shift moments, I identified potential motivational patterns. While absolute causation remains challenging to definitively establish, the findings offer plausible insights into the contextual and interactional factors potentially triggering mid-interaction attitudinal shifts. The subsequent analysis will explore these nuanced shift mechanisms, acknowledging the inherent complexity of discursive adaptability while presenting empirically grounded observations about linguistic self-presentation strategies.

Table 7.2 Attitudinal complex preferences for disputants having a temporary shift

Speaker	Phase 1	Phase 2	Phase 3	Phase 4	Phase 5
Husband_H02_WH	inscribe -ve Judge antagonist, inscribe +ve Judge self, observed Affect, invocations (Turn 1–30)	inscribe -ve Judge self, observed Affect, invocations (Turn 31–32)	inscribe -ve Judge antagonist, inscribe +ve Judge self, observed Affect, invocations (Turn 33–106)	-ve Affect triggered by the antagonist, inscribe -ve Judge antagonist, invocations (Turn 107–108)	inscribe -ve Judge antagonist, inscribe +ve Judge self, invocations (Turn 109–end)
Wife_H03_AW	inscribe -ve Judge antagonist, -ve Affect triggered by the antagonist, invocations (Turn 1–108)	inscribe +ve Judge self, -ve Affect triggered by the antagonist, invocations (Turn 108–110)	inscribe -ve Judge antagonist, -ve Affect triggered by the antagonist, invocations (Turn 111–end)		
Wife_W01_WW	inscribe -ve Judge antagonist, -ve Affect triggered by the antagonist, invocations (Turn 1–28)	inscribe +ve Judge self, -ve Affect triggered by the antagonist, invocations (Turn 29–75)	inscribe -ve Judge antagonist, -ve Affect triggered by the antagonist, invocations (Turn 76–end)		
Husband_W03_AH	inscribe -ve Judge antagonist, inscribe +ve Judge self, -ve Affect triggered by the antagonist, invocations (Turn 1–121)	inscribe -ve Judge self (Turn 122–124)	inscribe -ve Judge antagonist, inscribe +ve Judge self, -ve Affect triggered by the antagonist, invocations (Turn 125–end)		

(continued)

Table 7.2 (continued)

Speaker	Phase 1	Phase 2	Phase 3	Phase 4	Phase 5
Wife_W03_WW	inscribe -ve Judge antagonist, -ve Affect triggered by the antagonist, invocations (Turn 1–89)	inscribe -ve Judge self (Turn 90–91)	inscribe -ve Judge antagonist, -ve Affect triggered by the antagonist, invocations (Turn 92–140)	inscribe +ve Judge self (Turn 141–142)	inscribe -ve Judge antagonist, -ve Affect triggered by the antagonist, observed Affect, invocations (Turn 143–end)

2.2 *Contextual Factors and Shifts*

Two distinctive patterns of co-occurrence between a contextual factor and a shift were identified. In other words, there were two situations when the disputants could be seen to shift their attitudinal complex preference. The first pattern involves one spouse beginning to deploy attitudinal complexes typically used by the other spouse. This pattern is interpreted as a shift motivated by peer influence. The second patten occurs when the mediation facilitator intervenes, prompting the disputant to use atypical attitudinal complexes. This pattern is interpreted as a shift motivated by the mediation facilitator's elicitation.

2.2.1 Shift Motivated by Peer Influence

Peer influence-motivated shifts occur through accumulated antagonist interaction. Consider a hypothetical disputant X who typically employs the attitudinal complex of negative Judgement of the antagonist and positive self-Judgement, thus demonstrating a confrontational attitudinal positioning. If the antagonist consistently deploys positive Judgement towards disputant X, an interesting psychological dynamic emerges. Disputant X might experience social discomfort continuing explicit condemnation, potentially leading to occasional positive assessments of the antagonist or a temporary modification of their attitudinal positioning.

These shifts emerge when the antagonist's habitual attitudinal disposition distinctly differs from that of the disputant, and the antagonist has consistently maintained this disposition over an extended period. As a result, the disputant's transition from their typical attitudinal stance to the antagonist's perspective is interpreted as a consequence of accumulated interpersonal influence.

Peer influences were observed to coincide with both permanent and temporary attitudinal disposition shifts. However, it is crucial to recognise that not all disputants modify their attitudinal orientation to align with the antagonist's perspective.

Therefore, peer influence is conceptualised as a potential contextual catalyst for attitudinal disposition shifts, rather than a guaranteed mechanism. Notably, shifts motivated by peer influence invariably occurred during the later stages of the Problem Discussion phase, suggesting a gradual and cumulative process of interpersonal persuasion and adaptation.

Husband_H01_WH's case exemplifies a classic peer influence-motivated shift. He was a wayward husband being accused of maintaining an allegedly flirtatious WeChat conversation with a female neighbour. As noted in Sect. 2.1.1, his attitudinal disposition moved from an invocative and self-praising approach in Phase 1 to a more explicit and combative disposition in Phase 2, with the turning point occurring at Turn 95—his first negative inscription targeting his wife. The husband's attitudinal profiles before the shift and after the shift were exemplified in Excerpts 7.1 and 7.2 in the above section (the discussion about permanent shift).

The husband's attitudinal disposition profile can be compared with that of the wife, who demonstrated significantly more expressive communication, characterised by a wide range of attitudinal meaning-making resources, explicit negative Judgement of the antagonist, and consistent negative Affectual reactions.

Based on the contrast between the husband's and the wife's regular attitudinal dispositions in the unfolding text and the contrast between the husband's disposition in phase 1 and phase 2, it is reasonable to argue that Husband_H01_WH's attitudinal disposition shift can be interpreted as a response to accumulated peer influence. The wife had explicitly criticised her husband for 94 consecutive turns, and his initial self-praising approach seemed inadequate in the dispute resolution context.

As Atkinson and Drew (1979) suggest, in situations like court settings or dispute resolutions, disagreement or contradictions are the preferred activities, especially after accusations. 'If the accused person does not defend her- or himself, the inference is often drawn that she or he accepts the negative attributions' (Kotthoff, 1993, p. 195). Therefore, the husband's attitudinal shift can be plausibly seen as representing a strategic adaptation to persistent spousal criticism, demonstrating the complex interplay between individual communication styles and interpersonal dynamics. This analysis reveals how attitudinal dispositions are not static but dynamically negotiated through interaction, with peer influence serving as a significant motivational factor.

2.2.2 Shift Motivated by Mediation Facilitator's Elicitation

The second type of attitudinal disposition shift was found to co-occur with elicitations from mediation facilitators. In this dataset, these facilitators were typically the hostess, who attempted to elicit specific responses from disputants. These elicitations could involve seeking clarification about past events that the speaker had been avoiding or denying, requesting an assessment of someone, or probing areas where the speaker's position remained unarticulated. Under such elicitation, speakers demonstrated a tendency to deviate from their regular attitudinal disposition, resulting in a temporary attitudinal disposition shift. This phenomenon highlights the dynamic nature of communication during mediation processes.

Wife_W03_WW's speech provides an example of this shift. As noted in Sect. 2.1.2 and Table 7.2, her speech could be divided into five phases regarding her preference in attitudinal complexes. In Phases 1, 3, and 5, she maintained a consistent attitudinal orientation: negative Judgement of the antagonist, negative Affectual responses triggered by the antagonist, and invocations.

However, two notable temporary shifts occurred in Phases 2 and 4. In Phase 2, she shifted from her regular negative Judgement of the antagonist to negative self-Judgement. Similarly, in Phase 4, she transitioned from negative Judgement of the antagonist to positive self-assessments. These shifts represented significant departures from her typical antagonistic communication style. The wife's attitudinal profile was characterised by a progression from half-explicit and antagonistic communication to momentary periods of explicit self-blame and self-praise, before returning to her default antagonistic approach. Her regular attitudinal disposition remained fundamentally half-explicit and antagonistic throughout the interaction.

Notably, these two temporary shifts were realised through two specific inscriptions—the only two negative inscriptions in her utterances that were not directed at her husband. Both instances emerged when the hostess persistently attempted to elicit a particular response from the wife. The attitudinal profiles of these two instances distinctly differed from the wife's regular disposition during the exchanges. Consequently, these changes in attitudinal orientation were interpreted as disposition shifts directly responding to the hostess's elicitation. Detailed analyses of these shifts are presented in.

Excerpts 7.6 and 7.7, which provide deeper insights into the nuanced communication dynamics. Figure 7.3 visually represents the wife's attitudinal profile throughout the unfolding exchange, illustrating the two temporary shifts in her speech.

The co-text of shift 1 is illustrated in Excerpt 7.6. This excerpt reveals a nuanced interaction involving the wife, husband, and hostess, centred on an alleged flirtatious communication between the wife and her high school sweetheart. Initially (Turns 77–82), the husband presented WeChat messages between the wife and the high school sweetheart as evidence, which the wife did not contest. Instead, she strategically highlighted her subsequent corrective actions (Turns 83–87), positioning the audience to positively evaluate her corrective actions as a genuine gesture to repair the relationship. These corrective actions might also potentially activate negative evaluation of the husband, especially for an audience that held that the husband had overreacted given the wife's corrective actions.

In Turns 88 and 90, the hostess brought the wife back to the veracity of the messages. In two consecutive turns, the hostess probed the wife to confirm and assess the quoted WeChat messages. Upon the hostess elicitations, the wife responded with a rare negative self-Judgement (Turn 91), acknowledging she had 'gone too far' in her communication with the high school sweetheart. This unexpected self-reflection represented a significant departure from her typical defensive stance.

The co-text of shift 2 is illustrated in Excerpt 7.7, which involved a discussion about the financial management issue between the couple. Prior to this excerpt, the

Excerpt 7.6 Wife_W03_WW's attitudinal disposition shift in Turn 91

Turn	Speaker	Move	Utterance (Chinese)	Utterance (English translation)	Attitude signal	Attitudinal complex
77	Hostess_W03	1	不仅仅是简单的联系	More than simple greetings	contrast	invoke -ve Judge wife
78	Husband_W03_AH	1	对对对	yes yes yes	agreement	invoke -ve Judge antagonist
		2	都是她自己主动的	It's all that she started the conversation	upscaling	invoke -ve Judge antagonist
		3	说. . 是. . 想他啊干嘛的	She said.. said…that she missed him something like that	quotation: other	invoke -ve Judge antagonist
79	Hostess_W03	1	这次你看到了有一些**暧昧**内容了	This time you saw some **flirtatious** content	attitudinal token of Appreciation	invoke -ve Judge wife
80	Husband_W03_AH	1	对	Correct	agreement	invoke -ve Judge antagonist
		2	我就是说. . 她的这个微信号码电话号码必须换掉	I mean... She must change her WeChat ID her phone number	directive	invoke -ve Judge antagonist
		3	不不能让她再用	I can't let her use this number again	directive	invoke -ve Judge antagonist
81	Hostess_W03	1	停止	Stop them		
82	Husband_W03_AH	1	对对对	yes yes yes		
		2	她不肯==啊	She refu==sed	denial	invoke -ve Judge antagonist
83	Wife_W03_WW	1	==电==话也给==你..在==	==I gave== you the ==phone..when==	evoke	invoke +ve Judge self
84	Husband_W03_AH	1	==我==知道啊==	==I== know==		

85	Wife_W03_WW	1	==该注销的都注销了==	==I cancelled the numbers which should be cancelled==	upscaling	invoke +ve Judge self
86	Husband_W03_AH	1	==都是你..都是你**不**==**乐意**的..你知道吗	== It's all that you..all that you did it== **unwillingly**.. you know	attitudinal token of Affect	observed Affect of the antagonist; invoke -ve Judge antagonist
87	Wife_W03_WW	1	该没用的都没用了	I didn't use the numbers whichever shouldn't be used	upscaling	invoke +ve Judge self; invoke -ve Judge antagonist[a]
		2	乐不乐意. . 反正做了	Willingly or not.. I did it anyway	contrast	invoke +ve Judge self; invoke -ve Judge antagonist[b]
88	Hostess_W03	1	是如他所讲的吗	Is what he said true		
89	Wife_W03_WW	1	聊天是有	We did chat	evoke	invoke -ve Judge self
		2	我当时没有什么你干嘛要做得那么**过分**	I had done nothing wrong at the first place why did you **overreact** in such a way	inscription	inscribe -ve Judge antagonist; invoke +ve Judge self

(continued)

Excerpt 7.6 (continued)

Turn	Speaker	Move	Utterance (Chinese)	Utterance (English translation)	Attitude signal	Attitudinal complex
90	Hostess_W03	1	如果你第二次你仍然让他看到的是没什么	If for the second time when he saw nothing wrong in your messages		
		2	正常的联系... 我想他也不会这样	if it were normal messages... I think he would not have done this		
		3	可是他看到了不好的内容	but he saw some content that was not good		
91	Wife_W03_WW	1	那就是..**过了**呗	Then that was.. I **went too far**	inscription	inscribe -ve Judge self

[a]The utterance in Turn 87 used an upscaling device—'该…都… (whichever…)'—to activate attitudinal assessments from the audience. It could potentially activate two attitudes, one directed at the wife herself and the other at the antagonist. The attitude targeting herself was a positive evaluation of her behaviour of cancelling all the phone numbers. Because the cancelation of the numbers was demanded by the husband (Turn 80), the wife's cancelation of the numbers could be viewed as a corrective action for mending the relationship. For an audience holding a position that 'Taking corrective action to repair relationship damage deserves praise', the wife's upscaling emphasised her cooperativeness and sincerity in mending the relationship. Hence, the wife's behaviour could be positively assessed. This utterance could also potentially trigger a negative assessment of the husband. Because the husband criticised the wife for lacking willingness when cancelling the phone numbers (Turn 86), For an audience holding a position that 'The wife has done enough to show her sincerity in mending the relationship', the husband's criticism could be viewed unreasonable as lacking forgiveness.

[b]In this utterance, a contrast was made between the husband's accusation that 'you did it unwillingly' (Turn 86) and the wife's real action that 'I did it anyway' (Turn 87). By this contrast, the wife highlighted her sincerity in mending the relationship via corrective actions, hence having the potential to activate a positive assessment of the wife and a negative assessment of her husband.

Excerpt 7.7 Wife_W03_WW's attitudinal disposition shifts in Turn 142

Turn	Speaker	Move	Utterance (Chinese)	Utterance (English translation)	Attitude signal	Attitudinal complex
137	Hostess_W03	1	后来呢	What happened next		
138	Wife_W03_WW	1	我在贵州做生意了嘛	I went to do business in Guizhou		
		2	我那个.. 平安金管家里面有三千块钱	I had..in that Ping'an Gold Manager[a] three thousand Yuan		
		3	后面他就说要我... 放在存在他的那个卡上	Then he said he asked me.. to transfer the money to his account	quotation: other	invoke -ve Judge antagonist[b]
		4	我当时我没存	I didn't transfer the money to him		
139	Hostess_W03	1	你以前... 做生意挣的钱	In the past...the money you earned from business		
140	Wife_W03_WW	1	都是给他啊	All was given to him	evoke	invoke +ve Judge self[c]
141	Hostess_W03	1	全部	All the money		
142	Wife_W03_WW	1	全部啊	ALL the money	upscaling	invoke +ve Judge self
		2	其实我也没的什么事情	In fact I had nothing (with other men)	denial	invoke +ve Judge self
		3	但是他要我给的时候我就偏偏不给	But when he asked me to give him the money I would deliberately not give it to him		
		4	我就觉得我在外面这样..**起早贪黑**的	I just felt that I worked outside like this.. **worked from dawn to dusk**	inscription	inscribe +ve Judge self
		5	我身上连三千块钱都不能放吗	Can't I have even three thousand Yuan at my disposal	rhetorical question	invoke -ve Judge antagonist; invoke +ve Judge self

(continued)

Excerpt 7.7 (continued)

[a]Ping'an Gold Manager is a personal financial management product by Ping'an Insurance Group.
[b]The background of this utterance was that the wife had a small business in another city and earned some money there. She saved the earnings to her personal Ping'an account. In this turn, the wife quoted the husband asking her to submit her money to him. This quotation could trigger a negative assessment of the husband from contemporary Chinese audiences even if they hold different positions. For the audience holding that 'One has the right to control the money they have earned', the husband's requirement was an affront to the wife's financial independence. For the audience holding that 'There should be equality and financial independence in a relationship', the husband's requirement was at odds with equality in the relationship. Moreover, it is a common practice in China that a husband submits his salary to the wife and the wife controls the family finance. For people following this practice, the husband's asking the wife to submit her money would be judged as a violation of normality. Therefore, no matter what the audience's reading position is, the wife's utterance had the potential to invoke a negative Judgement of the husband.
[c]In most Chinese households, one spouse controls the family finance. This utterance indicated that the husband controlled the family finance in the past and the wife was very cooperative in handing over her earnings. Therefore, this utterance could potentially trigger a positive assessment directed at the wife for her financial contribution to the family and her obedience in submitting her earnings to the husband.

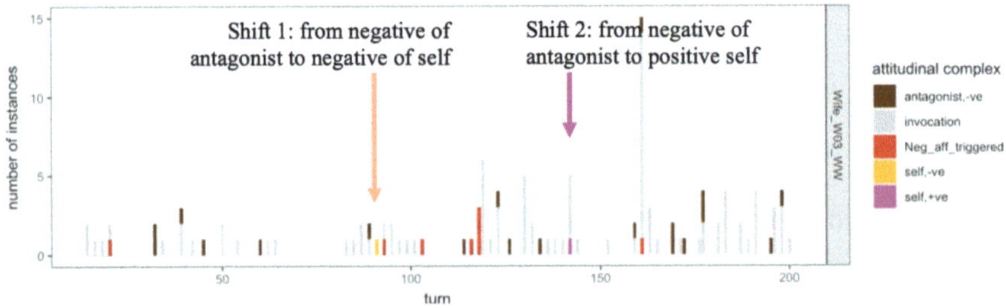

Fig. 7.3 Wife_W03_WW's attitudinal disposition shifts

wife had consistently criticised her husband's financial control, describing a restrictive environment where she received only a few Yuan[1] daily grocery funds and endured humiliating comments. Her narrative positioned the husband as oppressive and controlling.

From Turn 137 in Excerpt 7.7, the hostess strategically redirected the conversation, systematically exploring the wife's financial contributions and historical money management. In three consecutive turns (Turns 137, 139, and 141), the hostess tried to clarify how the wife had handled the money she earned from her own business in the past. This elicitation prompted a transformative moment in Turn 142, where the wife positively evaluated her own efforts, describing herself as working '起早贪黑 (work from dawn to dusk)[2]'—the only self-praising inscription in her entire interaction.

---

[1]Yuan is the basic unit of the Chinese currency. As to the average exchange rate in 2026, one Yuan equals 0.20 Australian dollars. Hence, a few Yuan is around one dollar, which is very little money.
[2]The phrase '起早贪黑 work from dawn to dusk' is a Chinese idiom. It is used to praise someone's diligence and hardworking.

These disposition shifts demonstrate the nuanced dynamics of mediation facilitation. While the hostess maintained a seemingly neutral position, her institutional role enabled subtle yet significant interventions that could momentarily alter participants' communicative strategies. The wife's attitudinal shifts were temporary, quickly returning to her default antagonistic positioning. However, these moments of deviation reveal the potential depth of mediation facilitators' influence. Unlike traditional assumptions about mediation, this analysis suggests facilitators can subtly reshape interaction trajectories without explicitly providing advice.

Previous research has documented various mediation facilitator interventions, such as reframing or refocusing discussions in an effort to stop the disputants arguing (Greatbatch & Dingwall, 1997) and reminding the disputants of the ground rules of the session (Garcia, 2019). This study extends those insights by illustrating that the mediation facilitators' intervention can be as significant as changing the disputant's attitudinal positioning, albeit temporary. The disposition shifts underscore the complex, dynamic nature of conflict resolution communication. They highlight how institutional contexts and skilled facilitation can create spaces for momentary self-reflection and narrative reconstruction.

The preceding analysis has explored one dimension of attitudinal disposition stability: examining how disputants' preferences for attitudinal complexes evolve during interaction. Our findings reveal a dynamic communicative landscape where participants experienced both permanent and temporary shifts in their attitudinal positioning throughout the mediation process. Moreover, these shifts were not random but appeared to be influenced by specific contextual factors that emerged consistently across different interactions. Building upon these insights, the subsequent section will delve into an alternative line of inquiry, investigating attitudinal disposition stability through the lens of attitudinal complex framing, thus providing a comprehensive understanding of communicative transformations in mediation contexts.

3 Attitudinal Disposition Stability Vis-à-Vis the Framing of Attitudinal Complex

Building upon the analytical approach established in Chap. 5, this section explores attitudinal disposition stability through the framing of attitudinal complexes. The analysis focuses on how speakers modulate their attitudinal expressions using two primary evaluative meaning-making resources: the resources of scaling (upscaling, downscaling, or not scaling—drawing on the GRADUATION system in Appraisal) and/or resources for dialogistic positioning (monoglossing, contracting, or entertaining—drawing on the ENGAGEMENT system in Appraisal. This section reports findings regarding whether the disputants favoured the same set of framing resources as the interaction unfolded.

In this section, again in the interest of manageability, the analysis of framing was streamlined to provide for a binary division—between attitudinal expressions which I termed 'mitigated' and those I termed 'unmitigated'. To achieve this binary division, I classified the attitudinal expressions (1) as 'mitigated attitude' if they were downscaled, entertained, or both and (2) as 'unmitigated attitude' if they were not downscaled (i.e., upscaled or unscaled), not entertained (i.e., monoglossed or dialogistically contractive—proclaimed or disclaimed), or both. This classification was based on the proposition that the resources of downscaling and entertaining function to make an attitudinal assertion less interpersonally challenging. When one or both resources are deployed, less is put at stake in terms of speaker-addressee rapport than when attitudes are upscaled and/or monoglossed, proclaimed or disclaimed. The unmitigated attitudes are relatively more forceful and involve more authorial investment into the warrantability of the attitudinal proposition. (In the 'hedging' literature (Hyland, 2004; Hyland & Sancho Guinda, 2012; Myers, 1989; White, 2003), it is common to treat instances of downscaling and instances of entertain as members of the single category of 'hedge'.) Based on the discussion in Chap. 5, the 'mitigated attitudes' reveal a lower degree of attitudinality, and the 'unmitigated attitudes' indicate a higher degree of attitudinality.

Also, following the methods used for the synoptic view analysis reported in Chap. 5, the analysis concentrated exclusively on framing patterns within seven attitudinal complexes: six inscribed attitudinal complexes and an attitudinal complex of invocations. This focused approach ensures that the most transparent and direct insights into a speaker's attitudinal orientation are captured.

3.1 General Patterns

The research revealed a compelling pattern in how disputants deployed mitigated and unmitigated attitudinal complexes. Participants demonstrated a consistent tendency towards either mitigation or non-mitigation across their interactions. In other words, those who chose to mitigate their attitudinal expressions did so repeatedly and across various attitudinal complexes, while others maintained minimal or no mitigation throughout the interaction. For instance, speakers who mitigated negative inscribed Judgements of antagonists typically extended this mitigation strategy to other attitudinal complexes, such as positive assessments and Judgements. This consistent approach suggests that mitigation is more of an individual linguistic preference than a contextually driven choice, indicating a deeply ingrained communicative strategy.

Two examples can illustrate this relative stability in the disputant's deployment of mitigated and unmitigated attitude. One example is the speech of Wife_W01_WW, who exhibited a consistent pattern of avoiding mitigation across all her attitudinal inscriptions, irrespective of the attitudinal orientation of the inscriptions. Her attitudinal preference remained uniformly unmoderated, with unmitigated inscriptions characterising her entire discursive performance. Wife_W01_WW's framing of the attitudinal complexes in an unfolding text is illustrated in Fig. 7.4, where invocations appear in grey bars and unmitigated inscriptions are represented by mint green bars. (A comprehensive Appraisal analysis of her speech can be found on the book's GitHub repository.)

The second illustrative example is Wife_H02_AW, who was previously noted in Chap. 5 for her distinctively high frequency of downscaling and entertaining

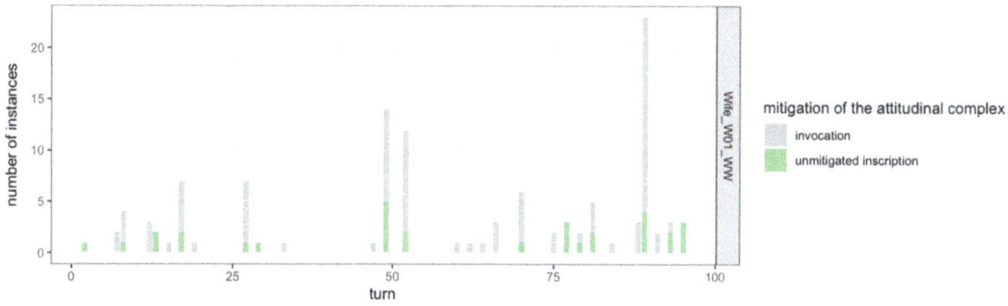

Fig. 7.4 Wife_W01_WW's mitigation of the attitudinal complexes

attitudinal complexes compared to other disputants in the dataset. She demonstrated a marked preference for mitigating her attitudinal expressions, with a particular emphasis on softening negative inscribed Judgements of the antagonist and positive inscribed Judgements of herself. A detailed examination of her speech revealed a remarkably consistent pattern in attitudinal framing. Figure 7.5 provides visual evidence of this linguistic stability, displaying her mitigated instances of negative inscribed Judgement towards the antagonist (represented by brown bars) and positive inscribed Judgement of herself (in pink bars). These mitigated expressions exhibited a distinct rhythmic pattern, consistently appearing throughout the interaction. Concurrently, her unmitigated inscriptions (shown in mint green bars) were equally persistent, spanning from the interaction's beginning to its conclusion. This consistent pattern underscores the wife's stable preference for framing attitudinal complexes, demonstrating a clear and persistent style to linguistic moderation that remained largely unchanged throughout the communicative exchange.

These examples—Wife_W01_WW's unchanged avoidance and Wife_H02_AW's unchanged preference for using mitigation to frame some attitudinal complexes, along with observations of other disputants, point to a significant degree of stability in framing preferences. Speakers tended to maintain their chosen approach to attitudinal expression, whether through mitigation or direct assertion.

However, the research also acknowledged a nuanced complexity. While the overall preference for framing remained relatively stable, disputants exhibited some flexibility in their use of the framing resources. Such shifts can be interpreted as an attitudinal disposition shift which will be discussed in the following section.

3.2 *Contextual Factors and Shifts*

The disputants sometimes changed which attitudinal complexes were to be mitigated or unmitigated. For example, while some disputants predominantly maintained unmitigated attitudinal positionings, they were observed to occasionally use some mitigation devices to frame some attitudinal complexes at specific interaction points. In other words, these speakers, who typically presented their attitudinal assessments via assertion or with additional uplifting force, would unexpectedly shift to using downscaling or entertaining formulations to present the attitudinal.

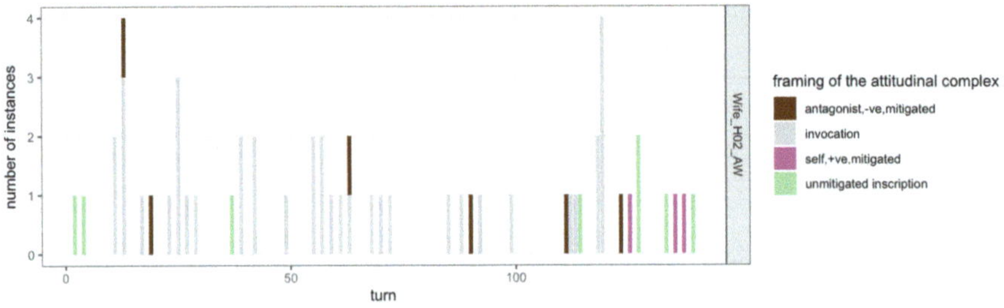

Fig. 7.5 Wife_H02_AW's framing of the attitudinal complexes

Such shifts transformed their attitudinal expressions from definitive statements to more negotiable and softened positionings. Critically, these shifts were not arbitrary but tended to co-occur with changes in the target with whom the speaker was communicating, which for convenience is labelled as 'communication target'.

To comprehensively analyse these communicative nuances, the research drew upon Berry's multi-layered exchange analysis framework (Berry, 1981a, 1981b), developing a two-dimensional classification of communication targets.[3] This classification distinguished between two fundamental dimensions:

(1) Communication Target of Addressing: Focusing on the immediate recipient of the speaker's turn, identifying the direct addressee within the interaction's immediate conversational space.
(2) Communication Target of Responding: Centring on the underlying informational or contextual resources that prompted the speaker's response, identifying the source of the resources for exchange or to whose information/demand the speaker responded.

Both dimensions were analysed retrospectively, that is, by relating the current utterance to the utterance(s) in the previous turn.

[3] It is worth mentioning the classification of interlocutor roles in the existing literature. With respect to the SFL literature on exchange structure, two sets of interlocutor roles have been proposed: 'primary knower' versus 'secondary knower' in knowledge exchange (Berry, 1981a) and 'primary actor' versus 'secondary actor' in action exchange (Berry, 1981b). However, these classifications of interlocutor roles are not applicable to the current analysis. This is because the distinction of these speech roles presupposes a 'degree of hierarchy' (Berry, 2016) with respect to the interlocutor's possession of knowledge or the obligatoriness of carrying out an action. In my data, there was no such degree of hierarchy between the two disputants. The disputants had equal power and access to what happened in the past and what to be proposed in the dispute exchanges. Meanwhile, with respect to the more general literature, there is the classification of interlocutor roles as 'speaker' or 'addressee'. This classification cannot cover the complicated speaker-addressee relationship in adversarial multi-party interaction, either. This is because it was commonly seen in my data, for example, when one disputant talked to the hostess, the speaker actually was responding to what was said by the antagonist in the prior turn. In such situations, it was difficult to determine definitely who the addressee was—the hostess, or the other disputant, or both. Therefore, in my dataset, it was useful to track the participant-relationship not only in terms of who spoke, but also in terms of who provided the resource for exchange and who was directly addressed.

Excerpt 7.8 illustrates this two-dimensional communication target classification, unfolding within a three-party interaction involving a hostess, a wayward husband, and his aggrieved wife. Right before this excerpt, the husband gave his wife the sole available bottle of mineral water. Intrigued by this seemingly deliberate gesture, the hostess prompted the wife to interpret the husband's behaviour. The wife characterised her husband's action as a performative display in a TV studio. Her response implied that the mineral water distribution was less an act of genuine consideration and more a calculated public performance—a deliberate attempt to craft a specific social image or narrative when in public.

Excerpt 7.8 demonstrates that a speaker might have different communication targets within a single conversational turn or move. In Turns 59 and 61, the husband's use of the personal pronoun 'you' indicates that he directly addressed the wife. Simultaneously, the substantive content of his utterances was responsive to the wife's prior claims—her assertion of his pretence ('he is pretending' in Turn 58) and inquiry ('what is the reason' in Turn 60). Consequently, during these turns, both the communication targets of addressing and responding were directed towards the wife.

In contrast, Turn 63 has two different communication targets. The husband switched the personal pronoun from 'you' to 'she', signalling a deliberate transition in his communication target of addressing—moving from the wife to the hostess. Meanwhile, the utterance's substantive content remained a response to the wife's previous inquiry in Turn 62, which questioned whether she had performed something shameful.

This linguistic manoeuvre creates a sophisticated communicative scenario: in Turn 63, the husband simultaneously maintains the wife as his communication target of responding while redirecting his immediate addressing to the hostess. The progression from Turns 59/61 to Turn 63 thus reveals a strategic shift in the communication target of addressing, while preserving a consistent communication target of responding.

Interestingly, the change in communication target converged with an attitudinal disposition shift in the husband's speech. Figure 7.6 provides a nuanced visualisation of the husband's preference of framing.

Briefly speaking, the husband's attitudinal positioning demonstrated a sophisticated asymmetry: positive self-oriented attitudes were consistently presented as

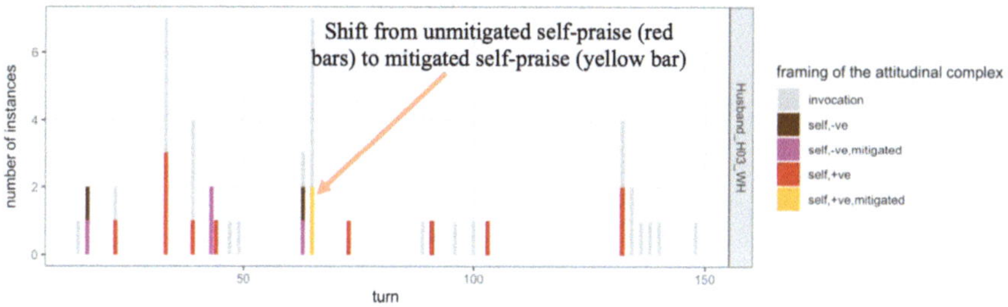

Fig. 7.6 Husband_H03_WH's mitigation framing for self-oriented attitudinal complexes

Excerpt 7.8 Communication target in a three-party interaction

					Communication target	
Turn	Speaker	Move	Utterance (Chinese)	Utterance (English translation)	Addressing	Responding
58	Wife_H03_AW	1	做样子	He is pretending	Hostess	Hostess
59	Husband_H03_WH	1	什么叫做做样子	How come is pre- pretending	Wife	Wife
		2	我本来到. . 我跟你说了	I came here.. I have told you		
		3	对所有人好	I am good to everyone		
		4	为什么对你不好	Why am I not good to you		
		5	就是这个==原因	This is just ==the reason		
60	Wife_H03_AW	1	==那是什么原因==	==Then what is the reason==	Husband	Husband
61	Husband_H03_WH	1	你要找==清楚	You should ==find out	Wife	Wife
62	Wife_H03_AW	1	哦	Oh	Husband	Husband
		2	我是做了对. . 见不得人. . 见你. . 做了. . ==让你不光彩的事==	Have I done something for.. shameful.. seeing you.. done something.. ==making you feel disgraceful==		
63	Husband_H03_WH	1	==她..她来..她来到这里..她是辛苦了==一生中	==She.. she came.. she came here.. she has been working hard== for a lifetime	Hostess	Wife
		2	是辛苦了一生	Has been working hard for a lifetime		
		3	这点我是惭愧是理亏的	I am regretful.. for this		
		4	那是有点不错	That is quite true		
		5	==没有伺候到她==	==I didn't take care of her==		

(continued)

Excerpt 7.8 (continued)

					Communication target	
64	Hostess_H03	1	==所以你那瓶水送给==她是	==So you gave her the == water to	Husband	Husband
65	Husband_H03_WH	1	表达一点心意吧	To express a little bit of caring	Hostess	Hostess
		2	安慰她一下嘛	To comfort her a little bit		

[a]At an earlier phase of the interaction, both the husband and the wife mentioned a shared cultural norm: 'A woman deserves to be treated well because she has been hardworking in her lifetime.' At that time, the wife challenged the husband by asking why he did not treat her well even though she was a woman. The husband did not respond to the challenge directly. In this excerpt, the wife referred to this cultural norm again, by challenging the husband as to whether she had done anything shameful so that she did not deserve to be treated well despite her being a woman

unmitigated and absolute (represented by red bars), while negative self-directed attitudes exhibited a more nuanced approach, oscillating between mitigated (pink bars) and unmitigated (brown bars) framings. Hence, the husband's regular attitudinal disposition was to present the positive 'self' as incontestable and the negative 'self' as something negotiable.

However, concerning the positive attitudinal assessment of the self, which was regularly unmitigated (red bars), there was a shift in the middle of the interaction. There were two instances where he used mitigation resources to soften his positive assessments towards the self (yellow bars). These two instances can be found in Turn 65 in Excerpt 7.8 and are represented in Excerpt 7.9 with Appraisal annotations. The linguistic formulations realising the mitigation are highlighted in bold.

Excerpt 7.9 shows that when both the communication targets of addressing and responding converged on the hostess, the husband deployed mitigation devices to soften his positive self-assessments. In stark contrast, Excerpt 7.10 exemplifies the husband's conventional communicative pattern—his default mode of authorial self-representation. Here, the unmitigated, assertive framing of self-praise emerges as the predominant linguistic strategy, presenting personal achievements and qualities as incontestable and absolute.

In Excerpt 7.10, there were two inscriptions of self-praise (in Turn 33). Both were framed with the ENGAGEMENT resource of proclamation, with one instance further enhanced by the GRADUATION resource of upscaling. The communication target of addressing and the target of responding were different. The husband directly addressed the hostess, but the content of his utterance was fundamentally a response to the wife's prior discourse.

A comparative analysis of Excerpts 7.9 and 7.10 regarding the communication targets and the attitudinal disposition choices reveals a pattern in the husband's attitudinal disposition shift vis-à-vis the framing of the attitudinal complex. When confronted with an assertion from an antagonistic interlocutor (in this case, the

Excerpt 7.9 Husband_H03_WH's mitigated inscription of self-praise in Turn 65

					Communication target		Appraisal	
Turn	Speaker	Move	Utterance (Chinese)	Utterance (English translation)	Addressing	Responding	Attitudinal complex	Mitigation device
64	Hostess_H03	1	所以你那瓶水送给她是	So you gave her the water to	Husband	Husband		
65	Husband_H03_WH	1	表达一点心意**吧**	To express **a little bit of** caring [+ particle **ba**[a]]	Hostess	Hostess	inscribe +ve Judge self	downscaling; entertain
		2	安慰她一下嘛	To comfort her **a little bit** [+ particle ma[b]]			inscribe +ve Judge self	downscaling

[a]According to Ding et al. (1999, p. 213), when the clausal particle吧 (*ba*) is used at the end of declaratives, it expresses the speaker's uncertainty about the proposition. Through an Appraisal lens, the particle turns a statement from a bare assertion into to heteroglossic entertaining

[b]According to Chao (1965, p. 801) and Halliday and McDonald (2004, p. 342), when the clausal particle嘛 (*ma*) is used at the end of declaratives, it indicates the speaker's position of considering the proposition as self-evident and unproblematic. Through an Appraisal lens, the particle proclaims the proposition

Excerpt 7.10 Husband_H03_WH's unmitigated inscription of self-praise in Turn 33

					Communication target		Appraisal	
Turn	Speaker	Move	Utterance (Chinese)	Utterance (English translation)	Addressing	Responding	Attitudinal complex	framing devices
31	Hostess_H03	1	有没有什么确凿一点的事情能够说明他们确实有不正常的关系	Is there any concrete evidence proving that they did have an abnormal relationship				
32	Wife_H03_AW	1	她经常就是在我们门口过. . 路过	She often passed by in front of our doorstep.. passing by	Hostess	Hostess		
		2	她到那个方向去他就跟	When she went in that direction he would quickly follow				
		3	一会儿就跟她一起走了	Later he went away with her				
		4	你问他	You ask him				

(continued)

Excerpt 7.10 (continued)

					Communication target		Appraisal	
33	Husband_H03_WH	1	正常的	(It's) Normal [+particle de][a]	Hostess[b]	Wife	inscribe +ve Judge self	Contract: proclaim
		2	就是她住在我家旁边嘛.. 偶尔上碰上了	It is just that she lived next to my/our house [+particle ma].. occasionally I ran into her				
		3	像那个江边啊..洗衣服钓鱼啊..那都是就是平常一样的	Things like by the riverside.. washing clothes and fishing.. it is **all** it's **just** normal **[+particle de]**			inscribe +ve Judge self	Upscaling; Contract: proclaim
		4	就是碰上了	Just ran into each other..				
		5	就是没有什么事情	It's just there was nothing				
		6	就青天白日的	It's in broad daylight				
		7	那有什么关系的	Is there anything serious				
		8	又不是我一个人	It's not me alone				

[a]When 的 (de) is used as a 'situation *de*', it 'refers to the whole situation with the meaning of 'such is the case', 'this is the kind of situation'' (Chao, 1965, pp. 314–315). Lü (1999, p. 162) proposes that this usage of *de* does not change the meaning of the proposition but adds a layer of confirmation to the proposition. Through an Appraisal lens, the particle proclaims the proposition

[b]The addressee in this turn is indicated by the husband's use of possession pronoun when he referred to his house. He used 我家 (*wǒjiā*, my/our house) instead of 咱家(*zán jiā*, our house). 我 (*wǒ*, I/my/our) includes the speaker and a person or persons spoken of, but not the person spoken to (Chao, 1965, p. 648), whereas 咱 (*zán*, us/our) 'automatically includes the addressee' (Zhao, 1987, p. 156). Because the husband's house was the same the wife's house, if he was directly addressing the wife, he would have used 咱家(*zán jiā*, our house)

wife), the husband consistently adopted a categorical and unmitigated attitudinal framing. This attitudinal preference remained consistent irrespective of the immediate addressee. In other words, the husband's attitudinal disposition shift tends to be more strongly correlated with the source of the preceding discourse than with the immediate recipient of his communication.

The attitudinal disposition shift as a response to communication target change is a more nuanced and covert type of attitudinal disposition shift. It suggests that in a multiparty interaction, a speaker's discursive self-presentation may be dependent not only on the coparticipant that they directly address. It may also be contingent on whose material they are responding to. Our observation reveals that the speaker's framing choice is fundamentally reactive, calibrated more precisely to the relational and discursive context of the interaction rather than to surface-level communicative targeting. The communicative response becomes a strategic negotiation of interpersonal dynamics, where the underlying conversational antagonism triggers specific linguistic defensive mechanisms. In short, the above analysis illuminates the complex interplay between communication targets, interpersonal tensions, and linguistic self-presentation strategies, revealing attitudinal disposition construction as a dynamic, strategically negotiated performance.

4 A Multifacetedness of Attitudinal Disposition from a Dynamic View

Chapters 6 and 7 have systematically explored the stability or fluidity of disputants' attitudinal disposition from a dynamic perspective. The findings reveal that the disputants had different attitudinal orientation patterns at different points in the dispute resolution exchanges. The findings reveal the multifacetedness of attitudinal disposition, similar to the findings in the previous two chapters, but from a dynamic perspective. Specifically, the multifacetedness of a dynamic view can be argued from the following line of reasoning: attitudinal disposition is not a static, monolithic construct but a fluid, context-responsive mechanism of self-presentation.

The findings provide compelling linguistic evidence for Goffman's dramaturgical accounts of social interaction in everyday life (see Chap. 2 for details). Goffman holds that it is in an individual's interest to control 'the definition of the situation [...] by expressing himself in such a way as to give the kind of impression that will lead (the others) to act voluntarily in accordance with his own plan' (Goffman, 1959, p. 4). The fluidity of the disputants' attitudinal dispositions reflects this performative aspect of discursive self-presentation. By having control over their attitudinal arrangements and responding to contextual change with attitudinal disposition shifts, the disputants crafted specific performances at different points in the dispute resolution exchange, consciously or unconsciously, to position the audience in a certain way and potentially influence the mediation outcome. The result of this 'impression management' (Goffman, 1959, 1967) was the observed multifacetedness of attitudinal disposition.

The observed fluidity reveals a profound insight into identity construction. The universal tendency of disputants to present different 'selves' or different aspects of the 'self' across multiple mediation stages and to different addressees challenges the notion of a permanent, unchanging identity. This was evident not only in shifts across different contexts but also within extended interactions like the Problem Discussion stage, where contextual factors triggered attitudinal disposition shifts even when the immediate situation remained unchanged.

Interestingly, the research also uncovered a nuanced pattern of stability-in-fluidity. Some aspects of attitudinal disposition—such as the tendency to mitigate or un-mitigate attitudinal complexes—proved relatively more stable than other aspects (e.g., attitudinal orientation towards the self). Moreover, individual speakers demonstrated varying degrees of attitudinal shifts, suggesting a complex interplay between personal preference and contextual constraints. This observation partially echoes Johnstone's (2009) proposal about the enactment of 'ideologies of identity' in discourse. She argues that a speaker for whom identity is fundamentally social could be found to adopt different styles in different situations. In contrast, a speaker for whom identity is fundamentally personal could be expected to be more consistent in different situations. What my findings suggest is not, however, a relationship between the speaker's ideology and their discursively constructed identity.

The entanglement of fluidity and stability reflects a fundamental tension in discursive self-presentation. A speaker's choice of evaluative meaning-making resources is simultaneously a personal preference and a response to local interactional conditions. This dynamic suggests that identity is not a fixed construct but a continually negotiated performance, responsive to contextual nuances while maintaining certain underlying patterns of linguistic behaviour.

5 Chapter Summary

This chapter and the previous chapter have reported findings relating to the second line of exploration of the attitudinal disposition—a dynamic view of attitudinal disposition by exploring the stability of disputants' deployment of attitude-associated resources within an unfolding text. Attention in this chapter was paid in particular to attitudinal disposition stability within the Problem Discussion stage, a communicative situation with an unchanged context.

The analysis pursued two lines of inquiry. The first explored attitudinal disposition in relation to attitudinal complexes, revealing that all the disputants deployed different sets of attitudinal complexes as the interaction unfolded. Seven disputants demonstrated permanent shifts in their attitudinal disposition, while five exhibited a more consistent attitudinal preference with temporary orientation changes. Two contextual factors were identified as co-occurring with these attitudinal disposition shifts: peer influence and mediation facilitator's elicitation.

The second line of inquiry investigated the stability of disputants' preference for mitigating or un-mitigating an attitudinal complex. Findings suggested that a speaker's preference for mitigation or non-mitigation remained relatively stable throughout the interaction. This pattern indicates that mitigation resource deployment is largely an idiosyncratic preference, less susceptible to contextual influences. However, a notable exception emerged when the 'communication target' changed, prompting disputants to alter their mitigation preferences.

It is worth noting that the interpretation of these shifts as 'responses' does not imply conscious management by speakers. Instead, the repeated co-occurring patterns between disposition shifts and contextual factors suggest a more nuanced, potentially unconscious linguistic adaptation. Hopefully, what has been presented so far has provided evidence for the patterned changes in a disputant's speech which were interpreted as their attitudinal disposition shifts and the co-variational or converging relationship between the shifts and the contextual factors. Drawing on Halliday and Matthiessen's conceptualisation, these emerging patterns in the unfolding text 'acquire added value through resonating with other patterns in the text or in the context of situation' situation' (Halliday & Matthiessen, 2014, p. 63). Hence, the fluidity of the attitudinal disposition converges with the progress of the text, and its resonance with the contextual factors gives the attitudinal disposition a new layer of meaning: fluidity.

So far, Chaps. 4–7 have explored and discussed the disputants' discursive self-presentation via their use of attitude-associated resources: their enactment of attitudinal disposition. The exploration attended to two complementary perspectives: the disputants' attitudes and their framing of the attitudes. Both perspectives were attended to through synoptic and dynamic lenses, respectively. The subsequent chapter will synthesise the book's findings and conclude the book with some additional proposals around what I have been terming the multifacetedness of discursive self-presentation.

References

Atkinson, J. M., & Drew, P. (1979). *Order in Court: The organisation of verbal interaction in judicial settings*. Humanities.

Berry, M. (1981a). Systemic linguistics and discourse analysis: A multi-layered approach to exchange structure. In M. Coulthard & M. Montgomery (Eds.), *Studies in discourse analysis* (pp. 120–145). Routledge & Kegan Paul.

Berry, M. (1981b). Towards layers of exchange structure for directive exchanges. *Network, 2*, 23–31.

Berry, M. (2016). On describing contexts of situation. In W. L. Bowcher & J. Y. Liang (Eds.), *Society in language, language in society: Essays in honour of Ruqaiya Hasan* (pp. 184–205). Palgrave Macmillan.

Brewer, N., Mitchell, P., & Weber, N. (2002). Gender role, organizational status, and conflict management styles. *International Journal of Conflict Management, 13*(1), 78–94. https://doi.org/10.1108/eb022868

Chao, Y. R. (1965). *A grammar of spoken Chinese*. University of California Press.

Ding, S., et al. (1999). 现代汉语语法讲话 *Xiandai Hanyu Yufa Jianghua [Talks on modern Chinese grammar]*. Commercial Press.

Friedman, R. A., et al. (2000). What goes around comes around: The impact of personal conflict style on work conflict and stress. *International Journal of Conflict Management, 11*(1), 32–55. https://doi.org/10.1108/eb022834

Garcia, A. C. (2019). *How mediation works: Resolving conflict through talk* (Studies in interactional sociolinguistics). Cambridge University Press.

Goffman, E. (1959). *The presentation of self in everyday life*. Doubleday Anchor Books.

Goffman, E. (1967). *Interaction ritual: Essays in face to face behavior*. Patheon Books.

Greatbatch, D., & Dingwall, R. (1997). Argumentative talk in divorce mediation sessions. *American Sociological Review, 62*(1), 151–170. https://doi.org/10.2307/2657457

Halliday, M. A. K., & Matthiessen, C. M. I. M. (2014). *Halliday's introduction to functional grammar* (4th ed.). Routledge.

Halliday, M. A. K., & McDonald, E. (2004). Metafunctional profile of the grammar of Chinese. In A. Caffarel, J. R. Martin, & C. M. I. M. Matthiessen (Eds.), *Language typology: A functional perspective* (Current issues in linguistic theory) (pp. 305–396). John Benjamins Publishing Company. https://doi.org/10.1075/cilt.253.08hal

Hyland, K. (2004). *Disciplinary discourses: Social interactions in academic writing*. University of Michigan Press.

Hyland, K., & Sancho Guinda, C. (Eds.). (2012). *Stance and voice in written academic genres*. Palgrave Macmillan Limited.

Johnstone, B. (2009). Stance, style, and the linguistic individual. In A. Jaffe (Ed.), *Stance: Sociolinguistic perspectives* (pp. 29–52). Oxford University Press.

Kotthoff, H. (1993). Disagreement and concession in disputes: On the context sensitivity of preference structures. *Language in Society, 22*(2), 193–216.

Litman, J. A., & Jimerson, T. L. (2004). The measurement of curiosity as a feeling of deprivation. *Journal of Personality Assessment, 82*(2), 147–157. https://doi.org/10.1207/s15327752jpa8202_3

Lü, S. (1999). 现代汉语八百词 *Xiandai Hanyu Babaici [800 Words of Modern Chinese]*. Commercial Press.

Martin, J. R., & White, P. R. R. (2005). *The language of evaluation: appraisal in English*. Palgrave Macmillan.

Myers, G. (1989). The pragmatics of politeness in scientific articles. *Applied Linguistics, 10*(1), 1–35. https://doi.org/10.1093/applin/10.1.1

Rahim, M. A. (2023). *Managing conflict in organizations* (5th ed.). Routledge. https://doi.org/10.4324/9781003285861

White, P. R. R. (2003). Beyond modality and hedging: A dialogic view of the language of intersubjective stance. *Text, 23*(2), 259–284. https://doi.org/10.1515/text.2003.011

Zarankin, T. G. (2008). A new look at conflict styles: Goal orientation and outcome preferences. *International Journal of Conflict Management, 19*(2), 167–184. https://doi.org/10.1108/10444060810856094

Zhao, H. (1987). The Chinese pronoun zan and its personal and social deictic / 汉语代词"咱"及其人称与社会指示特征. *Journal of Chinese Linguistics, 15*(1), 152–176.

Chapter 8
Beyond Conflict Styles: Toward Multifaceted Semiotic Identities

Contents

1 Introduction

This chapter concludes the monograph with a summary of key findings in response to the research questions initially posed in Chap. 1. Additionally, it assesses the contributions made by the current study to the SFL and Appraisal-based discursive identity scholarship, examining both theoretical and methodological advancements. The chapter concludes with suggestions for future research.

2 Review of Key Findings

The purpose of this research has been to investigate how participants in family dispute resolution exchanges discursively present themselves via the use of attitude-associated resources (resources for conveying or activating positive or negative assessments). This investigation originated from my personal encounter with family

Q. Xu, *Appraisal Approach to Conflict Styles*, The M.A.K. Halliday Library Functional Linguistics Series, https://doi.org/10.1007/978-981-95-6256-5_8

dispute exchanges and observations of online comments on the discursive behaviour exhibited by disputants in Chinese reality TV mediation programmes. The study's goal contrasts with existing research on interpersonal conflict, which has identified various 'conflict styles' to describe how individuals behave during dispute interactions. However, none of these previous studies have explored self-presentation strategies via principled linguistic analysis.

This study is grounded in Goffman's dramaturgical perspective on personal identity, which conceptualises the 'self' as an entity constructed through its actual performance within social interactions. The disputants' self-presentation can be identified and characterised by examining their deployment of semiotic resources during these interactions. Building upon SFL and Appraisal-based studies of textual identity, particularly SFL/Appraisal's insights into the interpersonal functionality of evaluative language, this research examined the disputants' self-presentation through their use of attitude-associated resources. The data consisted of recordings from six couples contemplating divorce who participated in a reality TV mediation program broadcast in China. The analysis centred on identifying recurrent patterns in the evaluative language used by these individuals, drawing upon existing Appraisal framework. These patterns were characterised as a distinct aspect of the disputants' discursive self-presentation, with variations across speakers reflecting differences in their attitudinal dispositions.

This study examined disputants' attitudinal dispositions from two complementary perspectives: the attitudes they expressed and how these attitudes were framed. The first perspective looked at variations in how disputants utilised ATTITUDE resources as schematised in the Appraisal framework to position themselves, their antagonists, and others. It analysed the disputants' attitudinal self-representations and those of others. The second perspective focused on how disputants framed attitudes by examining the co-occurrence of evaluative meaning-making resources such as ATTITUDE, GRADUATION, and ENGAGEMENT within the Appraisal framework. This analysis sought to understand which attitude-associated resources were favoured, in what combinations, and at what frequencies. By identifying recurring patterns across multiple disputants, this study interpreted these patterns as reflecting their attitudinal dispositions.

To best capture the interactive nature of family dispute resolution exchanges, which involve immediate responses among multiple parties, the study was organised into three lines of inquiry: (1) a synoptic view examining the attitudes expressed or activated; (2) a synoptic view investigating the framing of these attitudes; and (3) a dynamic view considering both the attitudes conveyed and how they are framed in an unfolding mediation episode. Each line of inquiry attended to a specific aspect of the disputants' attitudinal disposition and conducted multivariable analyses by deploying computational tools. Findings of each line of inquiry are reviewed as follows.

2.1 Findings from the Synoptic View Focusing on Attitudes

The first line of inquiry involved a synoptic view focusing on attitudes. This analysis examined the recurrent patterns in the disputants' attitudinal positionings of themselves, their antagonists, and others within the Problem Discussion stage.

This analysis explored aspects of the disputants' attitudinal disposition by tracking the tendencies and patterns among multiple disputants regarding which attitudinal options (positive/negative assessments of a particular set of attitudinal targets) they used and at what ratios. It took a holistic view of attitudinal assessment (via what I term 'attitudinal complex') and consisted of two stages. First, it investigated the 'occurrence' of these attitudinal complexes, examining the range of attitudinal orientations available in the dataset and identifying which orientations were adopted by the disputants at least once. The second stage focused on the 'ratio' of attitudinal complexes, revealing the disputants' degree of preference for specific attitudinal configurations.

In the first stage of analysis—which was referred to as the 'occurrence' analysis—I examined nine distinct attitudinal complexes (comprising both inscriptions and invocations) by considering variations in attitude types (Judgement, Appreciation or Affect), polarity (positive or negative), explicitness (inscribed or invoked), and a taxonomy of attitudinal target/type (self, antagonist, other persons, or the marital situation). When each attitudinal complex was considered as an independent parameter for variation, it became clear that disputants exhibited differences in their deployment of attitudinal complexes and in the types they employed. A common pattern across the dataset emerged, with disputants frequently criticising their spouses and individuals outside the marriage relationship, portraying their spouses as responsible for causing emotional pain, and praising their own behaviour or character. When all the nine attitudinal complexes were used collectively as one parameter combination, three clusters were identified among the disputants: those with a 'narrow range', those with a 'middle range', and those with a 'wide range' of deploying attitudinal complexes. Notably, the disputants within each group tended to favour similar subsets of attitudinal complexes, revealing variability in their use of these resources across the dataset. Additionally, there was an observed covariation between the deployment of particular sets of attitudinal complexes and wayward behaviour. In general, spouses who exhibited more wayward behaviours were found to engage in a broader range of attitudes, whereas those aggrieved spouses tended to emotional victimise the self and employ a more limited set of attitudinal resources.

In the second stage of analysis—referred to as the 'ratio' analysis—my focus was on the degree to which disputants preferred certain types of attitudinal complexes. The analysis identified ten attitudinal complexes present in the dataset, indicating a reservoir of resources at the disputants' disposal in family resolution settings. Four attitudinal complexes were found to be consistently used across all or most disputants at similar frequencies. This suggests that there was a common inclination among the disputants to construe a 'like-minded' putative audience (White,

2021, 2025) that shared their attitudes (as they frequently relied on addressees to infer particular attitudes based on materials which invoked rather than inscribed attitudinal assessments) and to foreground a confrontational stance towards their spouse (via strongly negative assessments of their counterpart). When each attitudinal complex or pair of complexes was examined as parameters for analysis, variations among in-group disputants emerged. When considering all ten attitudinal complexes collectively, the clustering analysis indicated varying levels in the disputants' 'expressiveness' in articulating their overall attitudinal positioning. Some spouses were relatively 'more expressive' in advancing their attitudes, while others were 'less' or 'least expressive'. Interestingly, a common pattern observed was that wayward spouses tended to be more explicit and direct in expressing their attitudes compared to those who felt aggrieved.

2.2 *Findings from the Synoptic View Focusing on the Framing of the Attitudes*

In the second line of inquiry—synoptic view focusing on the framing of the attitudes, I explored the variability in how speakers presented their attitudes via the deployment of scaling or dialogistic positioning resources. In Appraisal terms, this line of inquiry dealt with variation in the disputants' self-presentation arising from their making different use of certain co-selections of ATTITUDE, GRADUATION and ENGAGEMENT resources. The analysis was divided into three stages with distinct focuses: (1) the scaling of attitudinal complexes, (2) the dialogistic framing of these complexes, and (3) the co-occurrence of scaling and dialogistic framing in the presentation of attitudinal complexes. It is important to note that this investigation did not concern itself with disputants' preferences for specific framing tools (e.g., upscaling versus downscaling), but rather aimed at understanding their preferences for presenting particular attitudinal complexes in a certain way, such as upscaled positive self-Judgement versus downscaled positive self-Judgement, or upscaled negative self-Judgement and so on.

The first stage centred on the tendencies in the scaling of attitudinal complexes—that is, whether the disputants preferred to (1) intensify attitudinal assessments through upscaling, (2) moderate or soften them via downscaling, or (3) maintain their attitudinal stance without altering the intensity of the attitude. The exploration identified 16 'scaling + attitudinal complex' options in the dataset, reflecting the range of choices available for the disputants. Notably, a frequent pattern emerged in which disputants tended to prefer not scaling or upscaling negative self-Judgement towards their antagonist, as well as avoiding any change (no-scaling) when presenting negative Affect triggered by their antagonist. These commonalities indicate that all participants predominantly foregrounded 'hostile' and 'victimised' aspects of the self. The examination of each 'scaling + attitudinal complex' option, along with pairs of these options, as parameters for variation revealed observable variations within subgroups among disputants. This classification demonstrated multiple groupings based on their degree of preferences towards specific combinations, showcasing the diversity in how attitudes were framed by different individuals.

In the second stage, I drew on the ENGAGEMENT system in the existing Appraisal framework and focused on tendencies in dialogic framing of attitudinal complexes. This analysis focused on whether the disputants preferred to (1) straightforwardly expressing attitudes without acknowledging alternatives, as in monogloss, or (2) considering alternative perspectives by entertaining other possibilities, or (3) explicitly aligning themselves with their addressee's views or distancing themselves from alternative opinions through contractions. The exploration found 17 'dialogistic framing + attitudinal complex' options. The analysis revealed that disputants tended to favour four combinations: monoglossed/contracted negative Judgement of the antagonist and monoglossed/contracted negative Affect triggered by the antagonist. These common patterns indicate that all participants in the dataset preferred to present their hostility against the antagonist and the emotional victimisation caused by the antagonist's behaviour as categorically unproblematic or with additional authorial investment. The analysis also examined each combination of dialogic framing device and attitudinal complex – 'dialogistic framing + attitudinal complex' option, along with pairs of these combinations, as parameters for variation. This revealed observable variations within subgroups among disputants. The disputants could be classified into multiple groups regarding their degree of preference for a specific option.

In the third stage of this investigation, I tracked how the attitudinal expressions were simultaneously scaled and dialogistically positioned. The analysis first identified 40 'scaling + dialogistic framing + attitudinal complex' options, then explored the variability among disputants in their co-selection of these options. The clustering revealed a cline of 'attitudinality'—the strength of an attitudinal complex. The concept of 'attitudinality' encompasses at least two dimensions of strength—assertiveness (related to patterns of use of options from the ENGAGEMENT system) and forcefulness (connected to patterns of use of options from the GRADUATION system). The disputants in this dataset were classified into three groups based on their variations in attitudinality: 'weak attitudinality', 'middle attitudinality', and 'strong attitudinality'. Notably, the wayward spouses tended to exhibit stronger attitudinality, whereas the aggrieved spouses showed weaker attitudinality.

The conclusion of my synoptic analysis on attitudinal disposition reveals that a speaker's attitudinal disposition can vary significantly across various dimensions (the multitude of options available for expressing attitudes) and, accordingly, discursive performances of the self must be viewed as multifaceted. Notably, two or more disputants might exhibit similarities in certain aspects of their self-presentation but differences in others. This observation is rooted in the analyses that demonstrated when a single parameter (such as an attitudinal axis, attitudinal complex, or framing option) was used for variation analysis, it showed observable similarities and variations among the disputants. The selection and combination of these features define the disputants' attitudinal dispositions, suggesting the existence of multiple attitudinal dispositions. This perspective suggests that a speaker's deployment of attitudinal meaning-making resources can be examined and interpreted from diverse angles, revealing different aspects of their attitudinal disposition. There is no single or absolute standard for determining which disposition or aspect of the attitudinal self is more authentic or legitimate. Instead, these distinct attitudinal dispositions represent different dimensions of a speaker's discursive identity and language use, reflecting the complexity of interpersonal communication.

2.3 Findings from the Dynamic View of Attitudinal Disposition and Self-Presentation

The third line of inquiry of the whole research—a dynamic view on attitudinal disposition—aimed to investigate how the disputants' attitudinal disposition evolved as their interactions progressed over time. I placed the disputants' attitudinal meaning-making arrangements into an unfolding timeframe, focusing on the consistency of their attitudinal positionings. There were three sub-lines of inquiry. Firstly, I explored whether the disputants maintained a consistent attitudinal disposition across different mediation stages, examining if they presented the same aspects of themselves in different communicative contexts. Secondly, I examined whether there were any shifts in the disputants' attitudes when interacting with different addressees (the antagonist, mediators, or hostess). This involved analysing if the disputants maintained a consistent self-presentation when communicating with different people. The last sub-line of inquiry concerned the stability of the disputants' attitudinal disposition within the Problem Discussion stage, where I examined whether the 'self' they presented, as indicated by their attitudinal orientation, was stable when the context situation remained stable.

When comparing the disputants' attitudinal arrangements across different mediation stages, I found that all the disputants exhibited shifts in their attitudinal disposition. Similarly, when examining the disputants' attitudinal arrangements as they interacted with different addressees, my analysis showed that all participants adjusted their attitudinal disposition. A notable pattern emerged where the disputants tended to favour a specific set of attitudinal complexes in one mediation phase or before addressing one individual, only to opt for a different set in another phase or when interacting with someone else. Additionally, the disputants also varied in terms of what I termed the 'radicality' of the attitudinal disposition shifts. Given that different mediation phases and interactions with diverse individuals entail unique contexts of situation, it is reasonable to expect these attitudinal disposition shifts.

In the third sub-line of inquiry, which focused on the development of disputants' attitudinal disposition within the Problem Discussion stage, I examined the stability and fluidity of their attitudinal arrangements when interacting within a constant context of situation. This investigation was approached from two angles: analysing the stability of attitudinal disposition in relation to preferred attitudinal complexes and examining the stability of attitudinal disposition concerning the framing of these complexes. Regarding the disputants' preferences for attitudinal complexes, all participants demonstrated some degree of flexibility in their attitudinal arrangements. This means they favoured different attitudinal complexes at various phases of the interaction. Two patterns of shifts were identified: 'permanent shift' and 'temporary shift'. Additionally, two contextual factors that frequently coincided with attitudinal disposition shifts were discussed. These included peer influence and facilitator elicitation. In terms of the framing of attitudinal complexes, the disputants' preference for presenting them through mitigation remained relatively stable throughout the interaction. This suggests that a speaker's deployment of mitigation resources tends to be an idiosyncratic choice rather than being vulnerable to contextual influence. One contextual factor was found to be associated with attitudinal disposition shifts in this regard: changes in the addressee with whom the speaker interacted.

The dynamic view of attitudinal disposition offered fresh insights into the fluidity of disputants' discursive self-presentation vis-à-vis their attitudinal arrangements. The observed general tendencies in attitudinal disposition shifts, regardless of whether the disputants interacted within similar or different contexts, indicated that presenting different 'selves' or foregrounding different aspects of the same 'self' was a characteristic common to all these disputants' discursive self-presentation. At the same time, this observed variability in each disputant's attitudinal disposition also underscore the necessity for acknowledging the discursively constructed 'self' as multifaceted, with certain facets visible in one situation and different facets prominent in another communicative setting.

In the analysing data from both synoptic and dynamic views, complexities arose in drawing conclusions about 'what kind of attitudinal disposition did the disputants enact' or 'what subtypes of attitudinal dispositions were identified in the dataset'. The disputants' use of attitude-related resources could be interpreted as revealing different personas or aspects of their persona when examined through distinct analytical lenses. Moreover, the similarities and differences among the disputants were not absolute or definitive. The multivariate analyses enabled by computational tools facilitated a comprehensive investigation into possible variations, yielding insights into the disputants' patterns of using these resources from multiple dimensions. A disputant's pattern of use of these resources could align with another disputant's use along one or several axes of variation, across some or many axes, or even theoretically span all axes. While the multivariate analysis did not straightforwardly result in clear taxonomies or sub-classifications, it offered valuable insights into the multifaceted nature of attitudinal disposition—highlighting the complex and varied aspects of the discursively constructed 'self'.

3 A Multifacetedness of Attitudinal Disposition and the Presentation of the Self

By way of concluding the discussion, I would like to return to this notion of 'multifacetedness', which has been touched upon at various points throughout this monograph, though without in-depth exploration until now. This multifacetedness encompasses several key aspects. Firstly, my analyses suggest that when characterising and identifying similarities/differences in speakers' attitudinal dispositions—and consequently their discursive performance of self—it is beneficial to consider a wide array of potential lines of variation. As illustrated through my examples, insights emerge not only by focusing on the nature of the attitudes expressed but also by examining their polarity, explicitness, and who/what is being appraised in these contexts. This multifaceted nature of attitudinal disposition reveals that how a speaker's disposition might be characterised can also depend on preferences for certain aspects of polarity, explicitness, types of attitude targets, or specific combinations of these aspects of attitudinal orientation. Furthermore, my research demonstrates that attitudinal disposition can be even more finely nuanced when the analysis is expanded to include the tracking of tendencies regarding up/downscaling and dialogistic positioning of attitudinal expressions. These findings underscore the complexity and diversity inherent in discursive identity construction.

Of course, it needs to be noted that prior related literature on patterns of evaluative meaning and the discursive performance of 'the self' has also treated what I term 'attitudinal disposition' as multifaceted. For example, in White's (2008) analysis of evaluative dispositions in an 'amateur' and a 'professional' movie review, it is observed that these can be characterised and differentiated on two key counts: first, the amateur reviewer frequently reports his authorial Affectual responses to the movie, whereas the professional reviewer does not; secondly, the amateur reviewer frequently modalises ('entertains') his assessments, whereas the professional reviewer almost always categorically asserts ('monogloss') them. This highlights that the evaluative dispositions (and thereby the 'persona' being performed) involve multiple dimensions—one pertaining to preferences for attitude type (the professional avoiding making this a matter of his feelings about the movie), and another related to dialogistic positioning (the amateur presenting his views on the film as his personal opinion, leaving them open to question and negotiation). Regarding 'multifacetedness,' in light of these considerations, my work contributes by demonstrating the extent to which multifacetedness pervades attitudinal dispositions. Moreover, my findings suggest that a more nuanced understanding of attitudinal disposition can be achieved by attending to additional facets of attitudinal orientation.

The depth of my analysis, which encompasses a wide array of potential variations in attitudinal disposition, has led me to discover that an individual's attitudinal disposition (and consequently the way they present the self) can exhibit dynamic changes. This variability is not limited to differences between contexts but also extends to shifts within a single communicative context and textual stage—such as during the Problem Discussion stage. Therefore, we can argue that a speaker's attitudinal disposition demonstrates multifacetedness due to its propensity for change in this manner. Specifically, a speaker presents different 'facets' of their attitudinal self in different parts of the text, showcasing the fluid nature of discursive self-presentation.

It's also worth mentioning another dimension of 'multifacetedness' that emerges from my analysis. The classification of disputants, and thereby their characterisation, can change depending on the specific perspective or line of inquiry employed. For example, in Chap. 4, which focuses on attitudinal complexes, certain disputants might be grouped together based on their strong expressiveness; however, in Chap. 5, which examines the framing of those complexes, they could be categorised differently according to attitudinality levels. This highlights that different aspects or facets (such as 'attitudinality' versus 'expressiveness') can lead to different groupings or characterisations of disputants. This diversity in analysis and understanding underscores the multifaceted nature of speaker self-presentation, where different facets are emphasized depending on the focus of interest.

Moreover, it's important to acknowledge another critical aspect. As discussed in Chap. 2, the dramaturgical view of 'self' and 'self-presentation' recognises that an individual's self is constructed semiotically. This study has exclusively examined the discursive dimension of self-presentation through the lens of attitude-associated resources deployed by speakers. Undoubtedly, other meaning-making dimensions are functional in the construction of discursive self, such as how disputants negotiate attitudes in conflict talks (as outlined in Chap. 1), their preference for experiential meaning-making resources, and logical meaning-making resources, to name a few. Furthermore, there are various non-linguistic semiotic dimensions that contribute to understanding an individual's self-presentation beyond linguistic resources alone. It is crucial to recognise that there can never be an exhaustive list of the dimensions, or semiotic resources, that can be deployed in the construal of a person's self-presentation and the perception of a person's self-presentation. The discursive self, as a multifaceted semiotic construct, entails heterogeneity and situatedness.

My conclusions as to the multifaceted nature of discursive self-presentation provide support for the notion that selfhood is multiple and fluid. Each individual appears as a continuous, unified semiotic singularity when observed from one dimension, yet, once observed from multiple dimensions, they emerge as a cluster of discontinuous and diverse semiotic multiplicities. All the dimensions are complementarily related, and yet, each provides a unique insight into the discursive identity construction. In a sense, this duality resonates with Goffman's understanding of 'the multidimensional nature of reality and his realisation of the complexity of the individual's obligation to maintain order' (Misztal, 2001, p. 322). By moving beyond simplistic notions of 'situational determinism' (Plotz, 2019, p. 443), Goffman argued that interactions are multidimensional and that the individual has multiple obligations and interests in maintaining order (Diehl & McFarland, 2012; Goffman, 1983). Goffman's multidimensional sociology and this project's linguistic evidence for multifaceted discursive identity echo with the Deleuzian conceptualisation of reality as a 'rhizome': 'the rhizome connects any point to any other point, and its traits are not necessarily linked to traits of the same nature; it brings into play very different regimes of signs, and even nonsign states. [...] It is composed not of units but of dimensions, or rather directions in motion' (Deleuze & Guattari, 1987, p. 21). Rather than seeking to categorise the disputants' discursive self-presentation based on a single trait or dimension, my research advocates for embracing multidimensional heterogeneity and continuity in understanding selfhood construction in social interactions.

4 Contributions of this Study

Via these key findings, this book has demonstrated that attitudinal disposition (and the performances of the self thereby enacted) can be seen as multifaceted and heterogeneous. Therefore, it can be said that this study has enhanced the understanding of discursive self-presentation as an emergent identity construction process, with both theoretical and methodological insights. The theoretical insights lie in its development and extension, in various ways, to the existing SFL/Appraisal-based textual identity studies. The methodological contribution is to conduct a meaning-oriented discourse analysis in a computing environment with data mining methods.

As foreshadowed in Chap. 1, this research makes original theoretical contributions to the existing SFL/Appraisal-based discursive identity scholarship in the following five areas. Firstly, this research explored discursive self-presentation in immediately interactive, multiparty, adversarial interactions, a text type that has been rarely touched in the current literature. By systematically tracking the disputants' use of attitude-associated resources, I provided a comprehensive characterisation of how disputing spouses attitudinally position themselves and each other in family dispute resolutions. I also identified a certain degree of covariation between the disputants' language choice and their waywardness/aggrievedness. Although it is a somewhat complex question as to whether ethe findings provided a basis for taxonomies of attitudinal disposition subtypes and hence for attitude-related presentations of the self, my findings nevertheless offered fresh insights into people's discursive behaviour in emergent situated interactions through an Appraisal lens. This research thus adds to the existing SFL/Appraisal-based identity studies by attending to data featuring non-English, immediately interactive, adversarial, and multiparty texts.

Secondly, I characterised the disputants' discursive self-presentation by identifying tendencies and patterns in two aspects of the disputants' use of attitude-associated resources: the attitudes conveyed by the speakers and how they frame the attitudes. The exploration of the tendencies in the disputants' framing of the attitudes constitutes a significant development or extension of the prior Appraisal-based identity literature. The variability in the co-occurrence of multiple Appraisal resources (the simultaneous presence of options from the ATTITUDE, GRADUATION, and ENGAGEMENT systems) provided advanced in our understanding of the interplay among multiple evaluative meaning-making resources. Thirdly, this research also provided a comprehensive exploration of the disputants' discursive identity construction by examining the disputants' language use from both synoptic and dynamic perspectives. The dynamic exploration of the disputants' construal of attitudinal disposition revealed stability/fluidity in a person's discursive self-presentation. The multiple lines of exploration revealed a multifacetedness of discursive identity construction. Fourthly, when exploring the stability/fluidity of attitudinal disposition construction, I examined speakers' use of attitude-associated resources within an extended chunk of exchange, where the context of situation largely remained unchanged. The stability/fluidity in an unfolding interaction in the same context of situation suggested a tension or a balance between the contextual conditioning and idiosyncratic preference in an individual's language use. The findings extended our understanding of the unfolding of a speaker/writer's discursive performance. Last but not least, I conducted multivariate analyses in search of repeated patterns among multiple disputants. The multivariate analyses allowed me to adopt a holistic view towards attitudinal meaning-making and conduct a comprehensive exploration into the disputants' use of attitude-associated resources. The repeated patterns observed among multiple disputants brought to light what may be the tendencies in how people more broadly might interact verbally in similar conflictual situations. The findings have important implications for understanding the enactment of interpersonal relations and the distribution of meaning-making resources among the individual users in functionally comparable texts. In summary, from a theoretical point of view, this research makes a significant original contribution to SFL/Appraisal-based identity studies.

Alongside the implications of the development of theorisation around these issues, this research also has a methodological significance: the method of carrying out a meaning-oriented discourse analysis with computational tools. In each analysis, I identified the similarities and differences among multiple disputants by examining multiple variables in a computing environment and with data mining methods. For example, I examined the disputants' co-selection of nine attitudinal complexes in identifying and characterising the attitudinal disposition according to the occurrence of particular attitudinal complexes. Likewise, I simultaneously considered 40 'scaling + dialogistic framing + attitudinal complex' options when exploring the disputants' attitudinal disposition vis-à-vis the framing of attitudinal complexes. From the perspective of Data Science, these were multiple variables or multidimensional data. While it is easy to compare speakers by reference to any two variables manually, it is highly challenging to identify and characterise variations among multiple speakers with multiple variables. In this sense, the human-computer integrated research method adopted by this research provided advances towards solving a methodological problem long-recognised as a limitation for the field of semantics-oriented discourse analysis, particularly the 'two-culture' phenomenon discussed in Chap. 3. This research processed data via, firstly, 'human annotation' and then via 'computerised pattern recognition', then via 'human review and interpretation'. The data processing and data analysis were based on manual and nuanced linguistic annotations, hence transforming the meaning-making choices into structured, computer-readable data so that pattern recognition could be operated on an infinite dataset. This data processing process optimised both the human and the computer potential in discourse analysis at a semantics level, arguably providing a solution to the standoff between patterns in meaning-making and the multidimensionality of data. This research hence incorporated a multitude of approaches, including Appraisal-based text analysis, interactional linguistics, computational data mining methods, and sociological interpretation of findings. It is, in a sense, a 'research-assemblage' (Fox & Alldred, 2017). The method(s) deployed in this research aligns with the new materialist view towards humanities and social sciences research methodology. According to Lupton (2019, p. 2000), the critical question 'is not what a method "is" but what it can "do": What does the research assemblage offer to answer a particular research question'. It is no longer meaningful to classify the current research as a qualitative and descriptive exploration or quantitative and analytical reasoning. What matters is that by deploying this research method, I arrived at a deeper understanding of the disputants' discursive self-presentation regarding their use of evaluative language.

In short, this research adds to the growing body of SFL/Appraisal-based literature that is interested in the role language plays in discursive identity construction. The theoretical contributions, the methodological insights, and the findings open up many critical new possibilities towards a better knowledge of the relationship between language, language user, and social interaction.

5 Limitations and Future Directions

Given the complexity of human behaviour and dispute interaction, this research project inevitably has limitations in the following three areas: analytical focus, interpretation of the meaning of the findings, and relating the finding to a broader socio-cultural context.

Firstly, as already noted, this research has limited its scope of analysis on the attitude-associated resources deployed by the disputants in their construal of discursive identity. It has attended to two aspects of attitudinal meaning-making: attitudes and the framing of attitudes, respectively. It has not managed to attend, however, to other meaning-making resources that are arguably equally crucial in construing a person's discursive self-presentation in adversarial interactions. For example, this research does not consider tendencies and patterns in the disputants' preference for types of ideational meanings. No transitivity analysis (which might well provide insights into the nature of the 'self' being enacted) was possible, given space limitations. As well, the analysis of attitudinal disposition generalised all the assessments directed at the antagonist and the antagonist's behaviours into one category: the attitudinal target of 'antagonist'. The analysis did not go into further details as to the specific qualities of the antagonist and the particulars of the antagonist's behaviours which were attitudinally assessed. As shown by previous studies (e.g., Martin, 2008; White, 2008; Zappavigna & Martin, 2018), the ideational content of a speech can also reveal an essential aspect of the speaker's discursive identity. Future research, therefore, might go even further into the disputants' talk and explore the recurrent patterns in other aspects of meaning-making.

The second limitation is concerned with the interpretation of the meaning of the findings. Because this research adopted a dramaturgical view of self and self-presentation, I, as the analyst, positioned myself as an observer of the disputants' discursive performance. All the patterns identified in the analysis were characterised and interpreted from my personal perspective. Other analysts or observers might well characterise and interpret the disputants' performances in other ways, given the potentially different values, background and reading positions they would bring to the interpretation of these texts. While admitting the inevitable personal bias in interpreting the meaning of the findings as a limitation of the research, it is also essential to accept that there is no absolute objectivity, and all interpretations are subjective and relative. Similar to what has happened to the disputants in our dataset (i.e., the spouses disputed because of their opposing positions when facing the same reality), the meaning of the findings resides in the interpretation of the analysts and the observers. In Charles Sanders Peirce's words, the meaning is in the 'interpretant' (Peirce, 1998; Short, 1996).

The third limitation of the present research is about relating its findings to a broader socio-cultural context. The research topic of the current book—family dispute resolution—is a topic with great social significance. One aspect of social significance is the relationship between the disputants' discursive behaviour and the development of dispute or dispute resolution. As noted by the dramaturgical view of 'self' and self-presentation, the disputants' use of attitude-associated resources potentially will leave particular impressions on each spouse's partner and the dispute mediators, which eventually impact the dispute resolution outcome. This research, however, did not correlate the disputants' attitudinal disposition with the mediators' comments and the outcome of the dispute resolution. It only sought to analyse what was in the disputants' speech. Future research, therefore, might attend to the relationship between the disputants' construal of attitudinal disposition and mediation outcomes. Another aspect of social significance that might have been dealt with in this research (but was not) would be a more topic-based analysis of the disputants' speech. Several intriguing topics emerged from the dataset, such as the disputants' representations and understandings of domestic violence and the disputants' stereotypical view of gender roles in a relationship. Detailed analysis on these topics will presumably reveal more aspects of the disputants' discursive self-presentation, as well as the social-cultural meaning of their discursive identity. Furthermore, the mediators' and the online viewers' comments on the disputants' behaviours also deserve attention. By observing and analysing their comments in response to the disputants' self-presentations, we might derive interesting insights into the value positions and cultural norms held by the so-called family relationship experts and the public at large. The comments of these other participants might also provide further insights into 'impression' (Goffman, 1959) that the disputants aim to win over the audience through their particular discursive self-presentations or the specific aspect of the 'self' they t presented. Finally, it might be valuable to explore the cultural influence on the disputants' attitudinal disposition, such as whether disputants from a Chinese cultural background tend to enact the same or different attitudinal dispositions as the disputants from a western European cultural background. A cross-cultural comparison regarding the disputants' attitudinal disposition in functionally comparable settings would generate new knowledge on the cultural meaning of a person's discursively construed 'self'.

In summary, this research has suggested many fruitful areas for further investigation. More research is needed, across a much more comprehensive dataset, to examine the disputants' speech and the relationship between the disputants' discursive self-presentation and the broader social-cultural context.

6 Concluding Remarks

Despite its limitations in various aspects, this research offered fresh insights into the disputants' discursive behaviour in dispute resolution interactions. It argued for the multifacetedness of discursive self-presentation. By conducting a multidimensional and principled linguistic analysis, this research identified and characterised several attitudinal disposition types regarding the attitude the disputants favoured and how the disputants framed the attitudes. The findings of the analysis revealed the multiplicity and fluidity of disputants' discursive self-presentation. The findings have relevance for different disciplines ranging from linguistics to interpersonal conflict communication studies, identity studies, and meaning-oriented discourse analysis.

References

Deleuze, G., & Guattari, F. (1987) *A thousand plateaus* (Translated by B. Massumi). University of Minnesota Press.

Diehl, D., & McFarland, D. A. (2012). Classroom ordering and the situational imperatives of routine and ritual. *Sociology of Education, 85*(4), 326–349. https://doi.org/10.1177/0038040712452093

Fox, N. J., & Alldred, P. (2017). *Sociology and the new materialism: Theory, research, action*. SAGE Publications. https://doi.org/10.4135/9781526401915

Goffman, E. (1959). *The presentation of self in everyday life*. Doubleday Anchor Books.

Goffman, E. (1983). The interaction order: American Sociological Association, 1982 Presidential address. *American Sociological Review, 48*(1), 1–17. https://doi.org/10.2307/2095141

Lupton, D. (2019). Toward a more-than-human analysis of digital health: Inspirations from feminist new materialism. *Qualitative Health Research, 29*(14), 1998–2009. https://doi.org/10.1177/1049732319833368

Martin, J. R. (2008). Innocence: Realisation, instantiation and individuation in a Botswanan town. In A. Mahboob & N. K. Knight (Eds.), *Questioning linguistics* (pp. 32–76). Cambridge Scholars Publishing.

Misztal, B. A. (2001). Normality and trust in Goffman's theory of interaction order. *Sociological Theory, 19*(3), 312–324. https://doi.org/10.1111/0735-2751.00143

Peirce, C. S. (1998). Nomenclature and divisions of triadic relations, as far as they are determined (1903). In The Peirce Edition Project (Ed.), *The essential peirce: Selected philosophical writings. Volume 2 (1893–1913)* (pp. 289–299). Indiana University Press. https://

www.scribd.com/book/148937417/The-Essential-Peirce-Volume-2-Selected-Philosophical-Writings-1893-1913. Accessed 13 April 2020
Plotz, J. (2019). Having it both ways with Erving Goffman. *Victorian Literature and Culture, 47*(2), 439–448. https://doi.org/10.1017/S1060150319000068
Short, T. L. (1996). Interpreting peirce's interpretant: A response to Lalor, Liszka, and Meyers. *Transactions of the Charles S. Peirce Society, 32*(4), 488–541.
White, P. R. R. (2008). Praising and blaming, applauding and disparaging - Solidarity, audience positioning and the linguistic of evaluative disposition. In G. Antos, E. Ventola, & T. Weber (Eds.), *Handbook of interpersonal communication* (Handbooks of applied linguistics) (pp. 567–594). Mouton de Gruyter.
White, P. R. R. (2021). Alignment, persuasiveness and the putative reader in opinion writing. *Language, Context and Text, 3*(2), 247–273. https://doi.org/10.1075/langct.21001.whi
White, P. R. R. (2025). Appraisal theory and the analysis of point of view in news and views journalism – Unpacking journalistic "persuasiveness". *Language & Communication, 100*, 95–107. https://doi.org/10.1016/j.langcom.2024.11.005
Zappavigna, M., & Martin, J. R. (2018). *Discourse and diversionary justice*. Palgrave Macmillan.

MIX
Papier aus verantwortungsvollen Quellen
Paper from responsible sources
FSC® C105338

If you have any concerns about our products,
you can contact us on
ProductSafety@springernature.com

In case Publisher is established outside the EU,
the EU authorized representative is:
Springer Nature Customer Service Center GmbH
Europaplatz 3, 69115 Heidelberg, Germany

Printed by Libri Plureos GmbH
in Hamburg, Germany